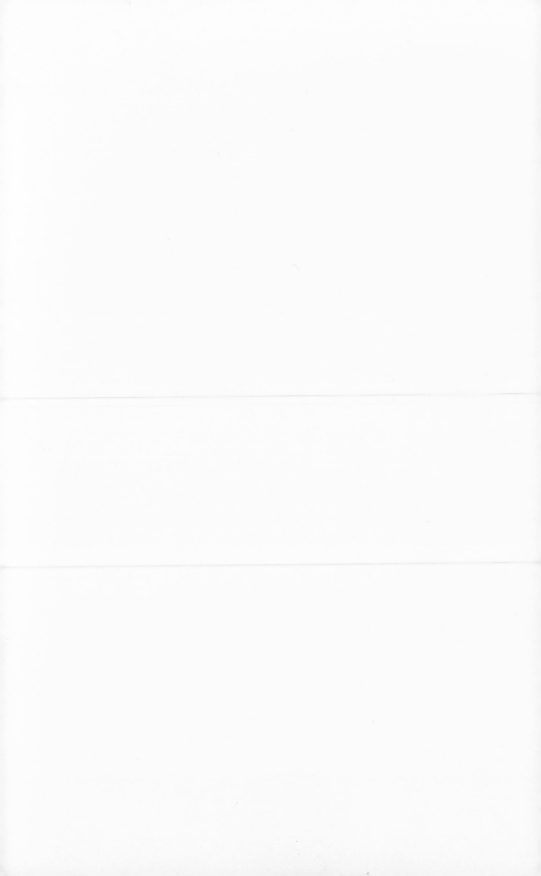

Choral Masterworks

CHORAL
MASTERWORKS
A Listener's Guide

MICHAEL STEINBERG

OXFORD
UNIVERSITY PRESS

2005

OXFORD
UNIVERSITY PRESS

Oxford University Press, Inc., publishes works that further
Oxford University's objective of excellence in research,
scholarship, and education.

Oxford   New York
Auckland   Cape Town   Dar es Salaam   Hong Kong   Karachi
Kuala Lumpur   Madrid   Melbourne   Mexico City   Nairobi
New Delhi   Shanghai   Taipei   Toronto

With offices in
Argentina   Austria   Brazil   Chile   Czech Republic   France   Greece
Guatemala   Hungary   Italy   Japan   Poland   Portugal   Singapore
South Korea   Switzerland   Thailand   Turkey   Ukraine   Vietnam

Published by Oxford University Press, Inc.
198 Madison Avenue, New York, NY 10016
www.oup.com

Oxford is a registered trademark of Oxford University Press

Library of Congress Cataloging-in-Publication Data
Steinberg, Michael, 1928–
Choral masterworks : a listener's guide / Michael Steinberg.
p. cm.
ISBN-13: 978-0-19-512644-0
ISBN-10: 0-19-512644-0
1. Choral music—Analysis, appreciation. I. Title.
MT110.S74   2005   782.5—dc22
2004013619

9 8 7 6 5 4 3 2 1

Printed in the United States of America
on acid-free paper

To Robert Shaw,
in loving memory

Introduction

Many of these essays began life as program notes for concerts. All have been revised and rewritten, some just slightly and with primarily cosmetic intent, many of them quite thoroughly. The following notes originally appeared in the program book of the Boston Symphony, whose annotator I was from 1976 to 1979: Bach's *Magnificat*, Berlioz's *Requiem*, Brahms's *A German Requiem*, Janáček's *Glagolitic Mass*, Mozart's *Mass in C Minor*, Sessions's *When Lilacs Last in the Dooryard Bloom'd*, Stravinsky's *Persephone* and *Symphony of Psalms*.

The following notes first appeared in the program book of the San Francisco Symphony, where I was the program annotator from 1979 to 2000: Adams's *Harmonium*; Bach's *Saint John Passion* and *Saint Matthew Passion*; Beethoven's *Missa solemnis*; Brahms's *Schicksalslied*, *Nänie*, and *Gesang der Parzen*; Elgar's *The Dream of Gerontius*; the Handel-Mozart *Messiah*; Haydn's *The Creation* and *The Seasons*; Kodály's *Psalmus hungaricus*; Mendelssohn's *Elijah*; Mozart's *Requiem*; Orff's *Carmina burana*; Rachmaninoff's *The Bells*; Stravinsky's *Canticum sacrum* and *The Wedding*; Walton's *Belshazzar's Feast*; and Wuorinen's *Genesis*.

The essay on Tippett's *A Child of Our Time* was originally written for the Kansas City Symphony; the one on the Verdi Requiem had its origins in an article for *The Dial*. A few notes were commissioned by organizations that no longer exist: Bach's *Mass in B Minor* and Handel's *Messiah* by the Festival Chorus and Orchestra (New York), and Britten's *War Requiem* by the Festival of Masses (San Francisco). I am grateful to all these organizations for the opportunity to write about these wonderful works and, where applicable, for their gracious permission to reuse this material.

I did all the listening and studying and typing, but behind these pages lie mountains of generosity and support. Often this help came in responses to specific questions or pleas; hardly less often it came from people unaware of how helpful they were being when they innocently mentioned a name or offered some stimulating remark. Quite a few of these debts go back many years.

In the earliest stages of preparing this book, I asked several friends and colleagues for advice on what works to include. Vance George,

Michael Kennedy, Paul Meecham, Sir Roger Norrington, and Bruce Phillips all responded quickly and thoughtfully, and I hope they will not be too chagrined when they discover that I did not always follow their suggestions. My final choices are bound to puzzle, irritate, or enrage some readers and browsers. I don't blame them: probably, by the time these words are in print, some of those decisions will annoy me as well. The choices are entirely personal. The omissions of many works I love pain me, but they were not made thoughtlessly. I hope that some day I can write some words on behalf of Berlioz's *Te Deum*, Delius's *Mass of Life*, Roberto Gerhard's *The Plague*, Martinů's *Field Mass*, and Pfitzner's *Von deutscher Seele*, to name a few. I do not, however, intend to apologize for anything I did include.

Anne Montague, friend and champion editor, read almost all of the book in typescript, bringing her passion for clarity to bear on sometimes–unruly material as well as being generously helpful in a hundred ways. I am very grateful to Philip Brunelle and to Dean Streit at Frank Music (New York) for making some hard-to-get-hold-of scores available to me. As always, I hugely valued the help of John Van Winkle, John Campbell, and Margo Kieser in the library of the San Francisco Symphony, and of Paul Gunther and Eric Sjostrom in that of the Minnesota Orchestra. I also want once again to acknowledge the wonderful collaborators with whom I have been blessed in my work with orchestras: Marc Mandel and Jean Miller Mackenzie at the Boston Symphony, and, in San Francisco, Susan Feder, David Bowman, and Larry Rothe as program editors, and Katherine Cummins, now publications managing editor, in many roles.

Then, begging the forgiveness of those I have inadvertently omitted, I also want to thank these friends and colleagues for a wide assortment of generosities: Brent Assink, David Cairns, Peter Caleb, Virginia Danielson, Robert Dennis, Sister Carlota Duarte, Tim Eickholt, Linda Fairtile, Laurel Fay, Nola Frink, Roger Frisch, Paul Gunther, Bob Guter, Tom Hall, D. Kern Holoman, Maria Jette, James Keller, Margo Kieser, Hugh Macdonald, Kevork Mardirossian, the late Sister Margaret William McCarthy, Judith Anna Nitchie, Garrick Ohlsson, Dennis Pajot, Peter Pastreich, Brother Robert Hugh, S.S.F., Norman Ryan, and Leo Schneider. I am most appreciative of Paul Gerike's elegant work in preparing the musical examples.

At Oxford University Press, I extend warm and loving thanks to Sheldon Meyer, for many years the czar of music books at that house, and I am happy also to be able to extend my thanks to his excellent and worthy successor, Kimberly Robinson. Both have been helpful and encouraging at every step, to say nothing of having been amazingly patient with this dilatory author. I am most grateful to Joellyn Ausanka, Eve Bachrach, Paul Schlotthauer, and Matthew Sollars for everything they did to turn pages of typescript into a book. I also thank my friends for each time they refrained from asking me how the book was coming along.

Writing about this ever-amazing music, I often found myself remembering performances that revealed it to me in some special way. In that spirit I want, in gratitude and with special pleasure, to set down the names of the conductors who gave my life these wonderful jolts: Sir John Barbirolli, Thomas Dunn, Claus Peter Flor, Erich Leinsdorf, James Levine, Alfred Mann, Sir Roger Norrington, Helmuth Rilling, Robert Shaw, Arturo Toscanini, Bruno Walter, and Carl Weinrich.

I have dedicated this book to the memory of Robert Shaw. It saddens me that he did not live to see it, and I feel a greater grief at the thought that he could not realize a long-cherished plan to write a book of his own about some of the choral masterworks he so deeply understood. It would have been a work of extraordinary insight and originality.

I first saw Robert in Carnegie Hall in September 1945, when he bounded on stage to take a bow at the end of a Toscanini performance with his chorus of the Beethoven Ninth. The last time was in Minneapolis in 1999, bent and exhausted after giving us a Brahms Requiem at once radiant and deeply meditative. I first met him in Cleveland in 1966, when he led a *Messiah* whose swiftness, lightness, and exhilaration made it thrillingly revolutionary at a time when darkness and weight were still the norms for that much-battered masterpiece. After that, there were many concerts, many conversations, many meals, even a few arguments. (I know he would not have been happy with my omission of Hindemith's setting of Whitman's Lincoln ode, *When Lilacs Last in the Dooryard Bloom'd*, a work he loved and whose dedication to him he treasured as perhaps the most significant honor of his professional life.)

We program annotators loved Robert because he always read what we wrote and enjoyed engaging us in discussions about it. His generous compliments meant a lot to me, and I won't deny that I always delighted in his little notes or CD inscriptions addressed to Saint Michael and, once, to the Archangel Michael. But what I most loved Robert for was the depth of his commitment to music. Once over lunch—at which I learned from him how to order an omelet runny in French (*baveuse*), he told my wife and me that the reason he so revered Toscanini was that "he never felt sorry for himself, he only felt sorry for the composer." It was clear both that this was a story he had told often and that Toscanini's feeling was a life principle he had made his own.

I am particularly grateful to Thomas Shaw and Alexander Hitz for their kind permission to dedicate this book to their father and stepfather, and I also thank Robert's devoted assistant, Nola Frink, for putting me in touch with his son and stepson—and also, of course, for the pleasures of her warm-hearted company.

Once again, the most deeply felt and ardent thanks go to my wife, Jorja Fleezanis, for being another living example of a musical life well lived, and for her unwavering support, encouragement, and love.

Edina, Minnesota   Michael Steinberg
August 2004

Contents

Choral Masterworks

Sacred Texts in a Secular World: A Word to Nonbelievers—and Believers

Many of the works discussed in these pages are settings of sacred Christian texts. The commentary on them is by a writer of Jewish birth who happily accepts for himself the description the Israeli historian Yehuda Bauer came up with to define his own stance: "a religion-loving atheist."

I think I am safe in assuming that many, perhaps even most, readers of this book will have at least a nominal connection with some branch of the Christian church, and that for those listeners such works as the Bach Passions have a significance and carry a meaning beyond the musical and the aesthetic.

Which raises a multitude of questions. Ought we to transport these towering musical achievements from the liturgical setting for which Bach imagined and composed them into the concert hall at all, or, thanks to recordings, into our living rooms? If we do take them into the concert hall, how should we respond? Or, to bring it more down to earth, how should we behave? Do we applaud? Is it right to have Chardonnay or a cappuccino between Parts I and II of the *Saint Matthew Passion* rather than a sermon? Also—and this is something I have been asked in all seriousness—do atheists, agnostics, Jews, Muslims, Buddhists, or Hindus even have a right to listen to this music, let alone claim that they can make meaningful contact with it? And for that matter, what about compositions intended for the concert hall but involving biblical or liturgical texts—Handel's *Messiah*, for example, or the Verdi Requiem?

But let us return to the Bach Passions and consider some of the differences between hearing one of them in Saint Thomas's or Saint Nicholas's Church in Leipzig on a Good Friday in the 1720s, and hearing it in Carnegie Hall in the twenty-first century—leaving aside here all the vexatious issues of "authentic" performance practice (the number of singers and players, boy sopranos versus women, pitch, wooden flutes, gut strings, and so on).

We can begin by looking at the calendar. The chances are good that when you have an opportunity to hear one of the Passions in concert—even more so when you put on a CD at home—it will not be on Palm Sunday, Good Friday, or any other liturgically relevant occasion.

More important, we can look at ourselves and think about our eighteenth-century counterparts in Leipzig. They were at a church service, involved in an act of divine worship—and I allow for the presence of a few unwilling children or, for that matter, the burgher who was there to be a good example to his family and to assert his respectability to his neighbors. We may be at a concert or perhaps at home, absorbing—with more or less concentration and devotion—an entertainment. It is, to be sure, a special sort of entertainment, one with high spiritual potential, but it is an entertainment nonetheless. For those Leipzigers the music was part of something greater, a religious service on the darkest day of the church calendar. For us, the music is the main reason for being where we are, and if we are talking about a concert performance, we may well have bought our tickets as part of a package that brings us some distinctly secular music by Tchaikovsky or Richard Strauss as well. And probably there will be applause.[1]

Ready to observe an especially solemn occasion, the Leipzig worshippers were seated in uncomfortable pews in what might, at that time of year, still have been a disagreeably cold building. They got up early to be there and most of them walked. In addition to listening to two or three hours of Bach's music, they participated in prayers and, at half-time, they got a sermon—a long one—followed by the celebration of Holy Communion. In any case, Bach's music for them was not a hallowed classic; indeed, many of them found it needlessly complicated and thus irritating.

On the other hand, they had compensations. The most important was that the singers sang in German, in the listeners' own language. And, by the way, just as you get the German text and English translation at a concert or in a CD box, so did the churches provide librettos: it was considered essential for everything to be understood, but the two main churches in Leipzig were huge, their cubic volume hardly less than that of a hall like Carnegie, and words could escape.

The congregational hymns or chorales provided another anchor. The congregation did not sing along with these at Passion performances, but still, the appearance of these familiar tunes and mostly familiar words

---

[1]Here I must resist the temptation to go on at length about applause. But in brief, asking an audience to refrain from applause at a concert is never comfortable and hardly ever feels genuine. (I mean an entire concert: a single piece played in memoriam is another matter.) And the opera-house custom of no applause after the first and third acts of Parsifal, though it goes back to the earliest performances at Bayreuth, feels thoroughly phony and pretentious. Wagner himself violated this taboo by applauding the Flower Maidens in the middle of Act II and was angrily shushed by audience members who did not know the identity of the offender.

meant solid ground, home, reassurance amid Bach's thickets of counter-point with their snaking melodies and arcane harmonies.[2]

We can also be confident that there would have been more general knowledge of the Bible in a Lutheran congregation in the 1720s than in a concert audience today.[3] Moreover, those Leipzigers would have been more untroubled readers of Scripture than their twenty-first-century counterparts, many of whom, even if they have not actually read such books as Raymond Brown's *The Death of the Messiah* and John Dominic Crossan's *Who Killed Jesus?*, are at least aware of the trend and tone of re-cent Biblical studies and criticism, and who read the Gospels, if they read and reflect on them at all, not as Revealed Word, but as culturally impor-tant documents that are a mixture of history remembered and "prophecy historicized" (Professor Crossan's phrase): hearsay, legend, love, wisdom, and propagandistic interpolations.

We can be sure, too, that virtually no one in that Leipzig congrega-tion would have noticed, let alone been troubled by, something that bothers a growing number of musicians today about the *Saint John Pas-sion*, namely, the anti-Judaic tone of the account of Passion Week in the Fourth Gospel. (I touch on this in my essay on that work.) The assump-tion that the Jews were responsible for the death of Jesus is still lodged in the minds of some people; it was much more generally in the air in 1720s Leipzig. Probably not many worshippers in those churches had actually read Martin Luther's *The Jews and Their Lies*, but the senti-ments and arguments in that book were common intellectual and emo-tional property. That most Leipzigers had never had contact with Jews, who were not allowed in the city except for the few days of the trade fair, would have made no difference: anti-Semitism flourishes equally in the presence or absence of Jews. The often-subtle question of how the anti-Judaic element of John's Gospel is or is not reflected in Bach's music is searchingly discussed by Michael Marissen, who pronounces a resound-ing Not Guilty, in an interesting book, *Lutheranism, Anti-Judaism, and Bach's St. John Passion*.

My own first meaningful encounter with the Bach Passions occurred when I was eighteen or so and heard a recording of the *Saint Matthew*

---

[2]Recognition happens on different levels of immediacy. I recognize the chorales in Bach's Pas-sions and cantatas because I have heard and sung them in those works, because I studied a lot of them in harmony class, and because some of them survive in American hymnals and so I sang them in my college's chapel choir (in which I participated as a music-loving tourist). I also un-derstand their function in Bach's sacred works and thus am cued to respond to them in a special way. But I am aware as well that my response, which is by no means devoid of emotion, is not the same as that of someone in Bach's Leipzig congregation.

[3]For Bible texts throughout this book, I have mostly used the King James Version because it is the one I know best and because I love its language.

Passion made in Leipzig in 1941. It was important because it was the only alternative to a really dreadful recording by Koussevitzky, and that it came from Leipzig and involved the Saint Thomas Choir and its then-director, Günter Ramin, Bach's successor at I-don't-know-how-many removes, gave it a certain aura as well. I recognized its faults—huge cuts, spineless conducting, muddy playing by the Gewandhaus Orchestra—but the good things overwhelmed me. Chiefly, that meant the committed, searingly communicative singing of the soloists: Karl Erb, thought the greatest Evangelist of his time, and still unsurpassed; the honey-voiced Gerhard Hüsch, from whose recordings I had first learned the Schubert song cycles, as Jesus; the soprano Tiana Lemnitz, with her miraculously pure yet expressive singing; and a motherly contralto with the homespun name of Friedel Beckmann. It was enough to take me right to the heart of the work, or so it seemed to me at the time; certainly it took me closer to Bach than any previous experience I had had with his music.

The second time I had toted that huge and heavy stack of 78s from the library to my room something happened. I no longer remember just what it was, but I think it must have been some extraneous noise like that of a page being turned or a bow hitting a music stand. Whatever it was, it suddenly awakened me to the fact that this was not just Bach coming from the speaker, but that these were sounds made by particular human beings. And these human beings were Germans in Leipzig in March 1941, a year and a half into the war, with battles raging in North Africa, U-boat attacks in the Atlantic, London bombed nightly, concentration camps in operation.

Even then I was not so naive as to think that the singer of Jesus in the *Saint Matthew Passion* had to be Christlike, or that the personal lives of the soprano and alto would be perfectly in tune with the messages of love, compassion, and consolation Bach had given them to deliver. Nonetheless, questions nagged. Were some of those singers and players members of the Nazi party? Did they wear swastika lapel pins? Had they used the so-called German greeting "Heil Hitler" when they arrived at the recording session, or did they still say "Guten Tag"? Did they sign their letters with that same "German greeting"? Did they look at the street-corner displays of the anti-Semitic newspaper *Der Stürmer*, and, if so, what did they think? Had they enjoyed Werner Krauss's magnificent acting in that winter's hit movie, the anti-Semitic *Jud Süss*?

Contact with the *Saint Matthew Passion* and with Bach had suddenly become complicated. To be sure, my questions were the special preoccupations of a Jewish refugee from Hitler's Germany, but I soon saw that larger issues were involved. Works of art and the work of artists did not exist in a protected vacuum; they were part of the fabric of life, and life is a mixed-up mess that gives us incredible richness and beauty and lovingkindness but also Dachau and Golgotha. And having been pulled so powerfully, even violently, into the world of the *Saint Matthew Passion*, I suddenly felt pushed out again: an outsider, a non-Christian, a person who had been expelled from German life, culture, and language, face to face with a work that had been composed solely "to incite listeners to devotion" (in the words of Bach's contract with the city of Leipzig).

Around the same time, I had the wonderful experience of learning the *Saint John Passion* by singing in the chorus—and there is no better way of possessing a piece of music than singing or playing it. Then I knew again that Bach's Passions were addressed to me as well as to the parishioners of Saint Nicholas's and Saint Thomas's. I hear them differently, no doubt. I readily believe that there are dimensions I miss, but I also maintain that a musical person gets more from the *Saint John* or *Saint Matthew Passion* than the most devout imaginable Christian with a tin ear.

The critic Andrew Porter has written: "A great opera composer can make us believe anything." Even if we omit the word "opera," Porter's claim is still true. Just think of what Beethoven puts over on us in the Ninth Symphony, how he can make us believe in the power of joy as no lecture or dissertation on joy could and, more important, as Schiller's ode cannot do by itself. And I have never met a musical person—of whatever faith or lack of it—who is not moved, not stirred and awed, by those few seconds of music in the *Saint Matthew Passion* when the earthquake after the Crucifixion has subsided and the chorus sings, "Truly, this was the Son of God."[4]

Moreover, Bach's sacred compositions—the cantatas as much as the Passions—deal with issues that go beyond matters of faith and dogma. To take just one obvious and dramatic example in the Passion story: betrayal. There is the sad figure of Judas, of course, but just now I am thinking of Peter. To Bach, Peter's denial of Jesus and his pain at what he has done are so important that when the composer wrote the *Saint John Passion* he lifted words from the Gospel according to Saint Matthew and moved them into the text so as to intensify the narrative and to heighten this moment. And he set those words to the most agonized bars of music he penned in his whole life. I don't believe there is a single person

---

[4]Great painters can make us believe anything, too. Think of the overwhelming power of Piero della Francesca's *Resurrection* at Sansepolcro, the earthly/unearthly tenderness of Filippo Lippi's *Adoring Madonna* in the Uffizi in Florence, or the sense of awe evoked by Caravaggio's *Calling of Saint Matthew* in San Luigi dei Francesi in Rome. The fingers of God and Adam on Michelangelo's Sistine Ceiling could do more for creationism than all the fulminations of the anti-Darwinists. And reading a poem such as George Herbert's *Love Bade Me Welcome* reminds us of the similar persuasive power of words.

who has ever heard one of the Bach Passions who has not at some time committed some act of betrayal, great or small, and felt remorse for it, even lifelong remorse. This is music addressed to all of us. And have we not all known love, sacrifice, compassion, awe, transcendence, and the other facets of experience we encounter in the Passion story?

The great works of sacred art are not exclusive. In that sense, too, they are transcendent. And if we have had creative musicians who were deeply religious, as Bach and Stravinsky were, I have always derived a certain pleasure from remembering that some of the most transfiguring of sacred compositions were created by composers who never darkened the doors of a church unless to perform or listen to music, who subscribed to no orthodoxy, whose faith was shaky or outright nonexistent, who were engaged in an unceasing struggle to reinvent God, who were angry with him. I offer, in evidence, Handel's *Messiah*, the Beethoven *Missa solemnis*, the Berlioz Requiem, Brahms's *German Requiem*, the Verdi Requiem, Elgar's *Dream of Gerontius*, Janácek's *Glagolitic Mass*, Schmidt's *The Book with Seven Seals*, and *Sancta Civitas* by Vaughan Williams. "Religion-loving atheist," which we might expand to include "religion-loving agnostic," fits some of these great composers also.

I love William Bronk's poem "The Conclusion" (in his collection *Silence and Metaphor*):

> I thought
> we stood at the door
> of another world
> and it might open and we go in.
> Well,
> there is that door
> and such a world.[5]

Indeed, the door is there. It is not locked. When the Bach Passions and the *Missa solemnis*, *Sancta Civitas*, and *The Book with Seven Seals* are sung and played, we are all invited.

---

[5]William Bronk, *Life Supports: New and Collected Poems* (Talisman House, 1997). "The Conclusion" is printed here by kind permission of Columbia University Libraries, Columbia University in the City of New York.

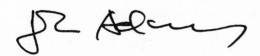

John Adams

John Coolidge Adams was born in Worcester, Massachusetts, on 15 February 1947 and now lives in Berkeley, California.

Harmonium for Chorus and Orchestra

A dams began *Harmonium* in February 1980 and finished the composition on 25 October that year, completing the orchestration in
March 1981. *Harmonium* was commissioned by the San Francisco
Symphony to celebrate its first season in Louise M. Davies Hall. The score
is dedicated to Edo de Waart, who conducted the first performance with
the San Francisco Symphony Orchestra and Chorus on 15 April 1981.

**Mixed chorus *divisi*. Four flutes (three doubling piccolo), three oboes, three
clarinets (third doubling bass clarinet), three bassoons (third doubling contrabassoon), four horns, four trumpets, three trombones, tuba, glockenspiel,
crotales, two marimbas, metallophone, bass drum, tubular bells, suspended
cymbal, sizzle cymbal, crash cymbals, xylophone, triangle, medium and large
tom-toms, anvil, cowbells, tambourine, harp, celesta, piano (synthesizer), and
strings (all parts *divisi*).**

Harmonium is the work that put John Adams on the map. Professionals
knew about him, especially in the Bay Area, where he had lived the past

nine years, but the wildly successful *Harmonium* premiere was his first performance by a major, mainstream organization.

Born and raised in New England and a Harvard graduate, he decided in 1971, the year he turned twenty-four, to pack his possessions into his VW Beetle and head west. Not that the East had not been good to him: it had given him contact with his Vermont neighbor, Walter Piston, a kind, informative, and encouraging friend to the gifted and inquisitive boy; put Leon Kirchner into his life as an imaginative and intellectually vigorous teacher of composition; allowed him to get to know Kirchner's own teacher, Roger Sessions, a humane and compassionate presence at a time when Adams, like so many of us, was depressed by what was going on in Vietnam; brought him the practical experience of exercising his clarinet skills as a substitute player in the Boston Symphony; and afforded him his first adventures in conducting as director of Harvard's Bach Society Orchestra. But his parents had unwittingly planted the seeds of unrest by giving him a copy of *Silence*, John Cage's collection of lectures and writings, as a graduation present. Of *Silence*, the *Village Voice* critic Jill Johnston said when it appeared in 1962 that "those who read [it] should find it impossible to curl up inside any comfortable box made before picking up the book." Sure enough, for John Adams it called into question everything that "Cambridge, Mass. 02138" stood for. Packing up the Beetle was the inevitable next step.

Adams first found a job as a forklift operator in an Oakland warehouse, but only a year later he had joined the faculty of the San Francisco Conservatory and had become part of the Bay Area's music community. He got involved with the work of Cage and other figures of the avant-garde, he organized concerts of electronic and chance music, and he built his own synthesizer.

Paradoxically, it was what he called his "electronic immersion" and his involvement with technical points of tuning and the harmonic series that led to his "diatonic conversion. It made me realize the resonant power of consonance." In 1980, the examples he cited were Beethoven, Sibelius, the orchestral Wagner, and early Stravinsky. That would still be his core list, though on the whole his sympathies are larger now than they were then.

In the mid-1970s, Adams encountered the new minimalist music of Steve Reich and others, and saw how its rediscovery of what he calls "the primordial elements of music—pulse, repetition, tonality—might hold the key to creating something closer to my own musical genotype. . . . Minimalism was a profound breath of fresh air." But even in 1980, in the first conversation I had with him about *Harmonium*, he voiced reservations, describing himself as "a minimalist bored with minimalism. It can really be a bore—you get those Great Prairies of non-event—but that highly polished, perfectly resonant sound is wonderful."

In that same conversation, the future composer of *Harmonielehre*, named for Arnold Schoenberg's great, far-reaching, imaginative treatise, pulled Charles Rosen's book on Schoenberg from a shelf and read: "Originality requires the exploration of a self-created universe coherent and rich enough to offer possibilities beyond the development of an individual manner." His hope, Adams said then, was "to build forms more impacted" than those of Reich and Philip Glass, "forms that grow," and the big works he has written since—notably *Harmonielehre*, his operas *Nixon in China* and *The Death of Klinghoffer*, the Violin Concerto, and *Naïve and Sentimental Music*—attest to how confidently and successfully he has realized the program he had assigned himself. Actually, as we can hear in *Shaker Loops*, whose original version dates from 1978, and in *Phrygian Gates* (1977), he had already set out on that path by 1980.

When Edo de Waart became the San Francisco Symphony's music director in 1977, he said he would value the assistance of someone who could bring him up to speed on the subject of recent American music and who could keep him informed. Milton Salkind, then president of the San Francisco Conservatory of Music, suggested that Adams, who was teaching theory and running a new-music ensemble at the Conservatory, would be ideal for the task, and what began as an informal arrangement grew into a real position as the orchestra's composer-in-residence, an appointment that came to serve as a model for many such relationships between composers and orchestras in the United States. At de Waart's urging, the San Francisco Symphony commissioned *Harmonium* for the orchestra's first season in its new home, Davies Symphony Hall, and over the years, going far beyond the end of Adams's composer-in-residence tenure, this was followed by commissions to which Adams responded with *Harmonielehre* (1984), *El Dorado* (1991), the Nativity oratorio *El Niño* (2000, commissioned jointly with several other organizations in America and Europe), *My Father Knew Charles Ives* (2003), and another work to follow in about 2007.

In 1981 I was in my second season as the San Francisco Symphony's Artistic Adviser. Given Adams's references to Beethoven as his ideal consonant composer (I vividly remember how moved he was by the simplicity of the soft G-major chords and their lingering resonance in the little Goethe cantata, *Meeresstille und glückliche Fahrt* [Becalmed at Sea and Prosperous Voyage], which he had just heard), I wish I could claim that putting *Harmonium* and the "Emperor" Concerto on the same concert was an inspired programming idea of mine; it was only happy chance.

Particularly in its magnificent first movement, the "Emperor" is one of those amazing pieces in which Beethoven makes drastically basic and seemingly neutral material—scales and arpeggios and clichés such as "horn fifths"—yield a triumphantly personal music. No less than that great concerto, *Harmonium* is a celebration of the "primordial," most especially a celebration of major and minor chords. That is, in fact, one of the sources of its provocative title. Another was the thought, abandoned almost immediately, that he might set poems from Wallace Stevens's debut collection by that name.

A question I always like to ask a composer is: "What was the first thing you knew about this piece?" The answer for *Harmonium*, as Adams formulated it in a 1984 essay, was that the work

> began with a simple, totally formed mental image: that of a single tone coming out of a vast, empty space and, by means of a gentle unfolding, evolving into a rich, pulsating fabric of sound. This wordless "preverbal" creation scene describes the opening of the piece, and it was fixed in my mind's eye long before I had even made the decision whether or not to use a text. Some time passed before I was able to get beyond this initial image. I had an intuition of what the work would *feel* like, but I could not locate the poetic voice to give it shape.

At one stage, Adams considered writing a choral piece with no text, just syllables and sounds. Then, having rejected Wallace Stevens as a voice alien to his own, Adams almost at once and almost simultaneously came across the poems by John Donne and Emily Dickinson that he went on to set in *Harmonium* and which give it its distinctive texture and shape.

Harmonium begins with quietly insistent repetitions of one note (D) and one syllable ("no"). (Something else Adams loves about Beethoven is his "rhetorical repetitions.") The Donne poem he had found was *Negative Love*. Its title, which Adams found "irresistible," also suggested to him the repetitions—two minutes of them—of "no no no no no no no no no no no no no no no,"—"and I wanted a syllable that I could use as a kind of sonorous building block." "No" becomes "ne," which is repeated equally urgently with the pulsing of what Adams once called "Beethoven quarter-notes," until syllables become words, and the music suddenly opens onto the broad declamation, on simple chords, of Donne's first lines: "I never stoop'd so low, as they / Which on an eye, cheek, lip, can prey."

Donne, that tough-minded, early-seventeenth-century cleric, can be a difficult poet, and that was in fact one of the qualities that drew Adams to *Negative Love*: "Each time I read it, it seemed to mean something different." In a brilliant essay on Donne in Louis Kronenberger's *Atlantic Brief Lives*, Denis Donoghue summarizes the poet's intellectual temper thus:

> Donne's mind delights in conflict, challenge, interrogation. "I would not that death should take me asleep," he wrote to Sir Henry Goodyer. . . . Far from evading paradoxes and problems, he conspired with them, lest he should miss the pleasures of casuistry. He preferred the possible to the probable, because it provided more scope for energy and force.

In dense, characteristically argumentative terms, Donne compares—in order to reject—physical and intellectual love with the love of God. Adams proclaims the first stanza in grandly sonorous block chords. His harmonies are diatonic with an occasional touch of something modal, heading, as the poet rejoices in the braveness of his love, for the "Emperor" Concerto's E-flat major. But while the harmonies for the most part move and change slowly, the surface of the music is a continuous rippling, an exhilarating surge in relentless crescendo, and—shades of Beethoven again—possessed of a powerfully determined sense of harmonic and rhetorical goal. After an interlude comes Donne's second stanza, with more friction between the chords than before, and with more clash between conflicting rhythms as well. And when Donne finally sets the word "no" as an end-rhyme (with "know")—catching up, as it were, with what Adams has been doing since measure 1—the music returns to and expands the iterations of the opening pages. Slowly, tempo and temperature subside, and a few sopranos sing the last line: "Though I speed not, I cannot miss."

The only well-known musical setting of Donne before *Harmonium* was Benjamin Britten's *Holy Sonnets of John Donne* (1945); several American composers, on the other hand, have been drawn to Emily Dickinson, most famously Aaron Copland, but also Ernst Bacon, Elliott Carter, John Harbison, George Perle, and Michael Tilson Thomas. It is hard to imagine lives of poets more different than those of the eloquent dean of Saint Paul's Cathedral in London, so much the public figure, and the maiden lady in white who passed almost every day of her fifty-six years in her parents' house in Amherst, Massachusetts.

Emily Dickinson was known to have written a few poems as a girl, and in 1862—she was then thirty-two—she hesitantly showed some more recent ones to the essayist Thomas Wentworth Higginson, asking, Did they breathe? No one was prepared to find that on her death she had left 1,175 poems, most of them on sheets of five-by-eight-inch letter paper stitched in fascicles of five or six, but many, the unrevised or unfinished ones, in the margins of letters, on brown paper bags, on bills, programs, invitations, leaves torn from old notebooks, subscription blanks, drugstore bargain flyers, recipes, shopping lists, cut-off margins of newspapers, a Chocolat Meunier wrapper, the insides of used envelopes, and detached envelope flaps—a catalogue I take from Millicent Todd Bingham's introduction to *Bolts of Melody*, a 1945 gathering of hitherto unpublished Dickinson poems.

She used common words as though they were new, as, with what the poet Jean Garrigue called "her astigmatic gaze," she saw all substances as rare. Lungs and ears, not the grammar book, determined her wondrous, breathing—yes, breathing—punctuation. Copland, in his preface to his *Twelve Poems of Emily Dickinson*, lists the "subject matter particularly close to Miss Dickinson: nature, death, life, eternity." Like Donne, she wrote about transcendental love, and her words, also aimed at God, are rich with erotic imagery.

Adams begins his setting of *Because I could not stop for Death* virtually without preamble (in contrast to the long one that prepares *Negative Love*), and he proceeds through the poem swiftly and simply. (Adams sets the poem in the version he first read it in, the one generally in circulation before the appearance of Thomas H. Johnson's scholarly 1970 edition that undid Higginson's taming of Dickinson's punctuation and vocabulary.) Notable here, and in striking contrast to *Negative Love*, is the series of sudden and bold shifts of harmonic center. In his 1984 essay on *Harmonium*, Adams wrote that "the 'placing' of the speaker—in a slowly moving carriage while the sights and sounds of her life gradually pass her by—created an irresistible opportunity for a slow, disembodied rhythmic continuum."

Mounting sonority and gathering speed create an overwhelming surge. This makes a bridge to *Wild Nights*, words that in this impassioned projection often turn into "wi-hild" or "oho-wild" nights. These are not words we are apt to associate with Emily Dickinson, but this ecstasy is also part of her ever-mysterious essence. Propelled by obsessive repetitions of rapid broken chords, the music moves with enflaming energy. The phrase "Rowing in Eden" becomes a series of canons, set over a return of the Beethoven quarter-notes and under a broad and powerful declamation of the final lines: "Might I but moor—Tonight— / In Thee!"

Again I quote the composer:

If *Negative Love* is a meditation on love and *Because I could not stop for Death* a sequence of tableau-like images about the arrest of time, *Wild Nights* embraces both . . . themes with a poetic intensity that is at once violent and sexual and full of that longing for forgetfulness which is at the core of all Dickinson's works. Her goal is far from being some kind of Apollonian serenity of self-realization, her Eden is the sea, the universal archetype of the Unconscious, an immense, nocturnal ocean of feeling where the slow, creaking funeral carriage of the earlier poem now yields to the gentle, unimpeded "rowing" of the final image.

Yields, I want to add, after a passage through tempests, winds, and waves that lift us up and bring us crashing down. At the end, Emily Dickinson's and John Adams's great *Liebestod*—or at least *Liebesnacht*—rises to one last luminous chord of A major (with an F-sharp sounding softly in the bass), and from that height the orchestra, leaving the chorus behind, makes the descent alone to recede into silence.

Johann Sebastian Bach

Johann Sebastian Bach was born in Eisenach, Thuringia, on 21 March 1685 and died in Leipzig, Saxony, on 28 July 1750. The BWV numbers refer to Wolfgang Schmieder's catalogue of Bach's works, published in 1950. Schmieder was as retiring as one imagines librarians and archivists to be, and he did not want the items in the catalogue he spent years making referred to by S-numbers, comparable to the K-numbers associated with Ludwig Köchel's Mozart catalogue; he recommended instead the use of BWV for *Bach Werke Verzeichnis* (Catalogue of Bach's Works). Schmieder's catalogue is arranged by categories rather than chronologically; thus his numbers tell us nothing about when a given work was composed. This is just as well, given the extensive revisions in Bach chronology that were made not long after the publication of the catalogue.

The Passions

The *Oxford English Dictionary* gives the primary meaning of the word *passion* as the suffering of pain, specifically "the sufferings of Jesus Christ on the Cross (also often including the Agony in Gethsemane)," citing as a medieval source the Latin *passio* as used by the third-century Christian theologian and moralist Tertullian. By Passion story we mean the account of Jesus' last days as found in the four Gospels of the New Testament, from the planning of the Last Supper to the events immediately following his burial.

When Bach moved to Leipzig in 1723 to assume his taxing and exasperating bundle of offices there—cantor at Saint Thomas's School, music director at the city's four principal Lutheran churches (Saints Thomas, Nicholas, Peter, and Matthew, the last also called the New Church), making him in effect music director of the City of Leipzig—elaborate Passion music for Good Friday services was new to that community, although elsewhere the practice of singing the Passion story had been going on for centuries.

In the Middle Ages it was done in plainsong, with different singers, each with a distinctive style and speed of declamation, taking the roles of the narrating Evangelist, Jesus, and the other *dramatis personae* such as Peter, Judas, Pilate, and so on. Both text and music changed over the centuries. Gradually, and specifically in the Protestant tradition, commentary came to be added to the story, and in the eighteenth century new and often quite awful verse sometimes supplanted the biblical text entirely.

As for the music, in the fifteenth century composers began to set some of the text polyphonically, and in the seventeenth, they borrowed recitative and aria, and for that matter the orchestra, from opera as a way of enriching the language of the Passion. The *Saint John Passion* composed in 1643 by Thomas Selle was the first really complex setting, and it was widely imitated. But Selle was working in progressive and opera-loving Hamburg; Leipzig was stuffier, and not until 1721 did Johann Kuhnau, Bach's predecessor, give that town its first taste of a concerted Passion setting. Historically, the way was well prepared for Bach. As Arthur Mendel, the great American Bach scholar, put it: "Bach's Passions contained no new element—except Bach's music."

The purpose of performing a Passion on Good Friday was not just to tell the familiar story as vividly and affectingly as possible, but also to teach its meaning. It is worth remembering that as part of his "audition" for Leipzig, Bach underwent an exceedingly thorough examination in theology administered by professors in that field at the University of Leipzig: he was, after all, to be a kind of preacher in music.

Teaching the meaning is one function of the interpolated commentary of the arias and congregational hymns (often called chorales) that were added to the biblical narrative. The other function is artistic, in that the arias and hymns are music very different from that used for the narrative, and the sustained melodies, stable rhythms, and more complex harmonic and polyphonic language all provide a welcome contrast to the less-densely-composed reciting styles of the Evangelist and the other characters.

The two layers of commentary—the arias with their recitatives and the choruses on one hand, the hymns on the other, and the differences between them—create the rich and telling verbal, spiritual, musical, and psychological counterpoint that makes the Bach Passions so powerfully expressive.[1] In the imagery of their poetry and the elaborateness of their music, the arias represent the highest level of complexity. The hymns are a plainer sort of verse, and they are also the most popular sort of music in the Passions. Even to a modern concert audience it is clear that the hymns stand for something simple and familiar in style; to the congregations in the Leipzig churches they would, of course, have been completely familiar.

After Bach's two great surviving Passions the genre all but disappears. Later Passion settings do exist, and one of them, *Der Tod Jesu* (The Death of Jesus), by the Berlin composer Carl Heinrich Graun, was considered a masterwork when it was new in 1755, but not even Beethoven's *Christus am Ölberge* (Christ on the Mount of Olives), really more of an oratorio than a straight Passion setting, has been consistently able to engage the imagination of listeners.

Some life returned in the twentieth century when Krzysztof Penderecki's *Saint Luke Passion* was sung in Münster Cathedral in 1966, garnering much attention and admiration. And at the very end of that century, in honor of the 250th anniversary of Bach's death, the conductor Helmuth Rilling took the imaginative step of commissioning four Passions, one on each Gospel, from four extraordinarily individual composers: Tan Dun (Matthew), Osvaldo Golijov (Mark), Wolfgang Rihm (Luke), and Sofia Gubaidulina (John). As I write in 2004, the two works that have made a strong impact are Golijov's, which involves Latino folk elements and performers, and Gubaidulina's, a composition that in its dark complexity is characteristic of this profound composer.

The Passion of Our Lord Jesus Christ According to the Evangelist John, BWV 245

Some of the music in the *Saint John Passion* goes back to Bach's years at Weimar (1708–1717), but the bulk of the work was probably written at the beginning of 1724. It was first performed on Good Friday of that year, 7 April, at Saint Nicholas's Church, Leipzig. Bach made revisions on three subsequent occasions: more on that below.

---

[1] A good performance of one of the Passion settings by Heinrich Schütz, the greatest composer of Protestant church music before Bach, shows what wonders can be achieved without any of that operatic frou-frou.

Tenor and bass soloists (Evangelist and Jesus) and a solo quartet of soprano, alto, tenor, and bass (for arias and the roles of Pilate, Peter, servant, and maid); four-part chorus. Two flutes, two oboes (doubling oboes d'amore and oboes da caccia), two solo viole d'amore, viola da gamba, lute, strings, and organ.

Most of us probably come to the *Saint John Passion* knowing the *Saint Matthew Passion* first. The bigger and more elaborate *Saint Matthew,* which was written three or possibly five years later (there is some uncertainty about the date), has tended to cast a shadow in which the earlier work is swallowed up. This has been so ever since Mendelssohn's 1829 performance of *Saint Matthew* marked the beginning of the public rediscovery of J. S. Bach. (The professionals had never forgotten.) But if the *Saint John* is smaller in scale than the *Saint Matthew,* it is hardly the lesser work in quality, though it would of course be silly to imagine that the master of the *Saint Matthew Passion* had not learned from the experience of setting *Saint John.*

The most interesting differences between these two towering attestations of faith are differences in intention. Read Matthew 26–27, Mark 14–15, Luke 22–23, and John 18–19, and you get four tellings of the last days in the life of Jesus that diverge amazingly in tone, emphasis, and detail. Much of what gives Bach's *Saint John Passion* its special character and those qualities that make it so deeply cherished by those who know it well can be traced to the character of the Fourth Gospel itself, with its highly personal tone of pathos.

For us, the *Saint John* is the first of two Passion settings by Bach, but the long obituary of Bach written in 1754 by his son Carl Philipp Emanuel, with the help of Johann Friedrich Agricola, one of his father's pupils, mentions five such works. A complete picture of Bach's activity as a composer of Passion settings will probably never be produced, but our best guess is this:

1. At some point while he was in Weimar, where he was appointed organist in 1708 and Concertmeister in 1714, Bach perhaps wrote a Passion, now lost. A few movements in the *Saint John* and *Saint Matthew* Passions do seem to go back to that period, and they may be the only surviving portions of that putative Weimar Passion.
2. In 1724, Bach composed the *Saint John Passion,* which he revised several times in later years.
3. In 1729 (or 1727) he composed the *Saint Matthew Passion.*
4. In or about 1730, Bach copied the score of a *Saint Luke Passion.* This survives in a manuscript that is partly in Bach's hand, though the

music is certainly not his own. Presumably Bach performed it in Leipzig, or intended to do so. C.P.E. Bach and Agricola may have mistaken it for a work of Bach's and thus included it in their census. Of course, given his delight in exhaustive cycles, Bach *should* have composed a *Saint Luke Passion*.

5. In 1731, Bach composed a *Saint Mark Passion*, all of whose text and some of whose music survive. The complete score was last seen in 1764.

As part of the process of applying for a multiheaded position as music director of several Leipzig churches, Bach had presented a cantata, *Jesus nahm zu sich die Zwölfe* (Jesus took unto him the Twelve), BWV 22, as an audition piece to be performed on Sunday, 7 February 1723, but there is no foundation for the supposition that he was given the opportunity to present the *Saint John Passion* for the same purpose seven weeks later, on Good Friday, 26 March. That score was for the most part written in Leipzig and performed on Bach's first Good Friday in office there, 7 April 1724.

Bach changed the work considerably when he brought it back for Good Friday in 1725, altered it again for a performance about 1730, and finally, some time in the 1740s, restored it to something very close to its original shape.

The work consists of words and music from many sources. The core of the libretto is chapters 18 and 19 of Saint John's Gospel (in Martin Luther's German translation). Upon this, Bach superimposes an elaborate body of commentary, consisting of hymns—or chorales, as they are often called—and arias.

The chorales in the *Saint John Passion* come from several sixteenth- and seventeenth-century hymnals. For the other "editorial" interpolations, Bach went chiefly to *Der für die Sünden der Welt gemarterte und sterbende Jesus* (Jesus Tortured and Dying for the Sins of the World) by Barthold Heinrich Brockes, a Hamburg senator and polymath, who published this poem, which quickly became immensely famous and popular, in 1712. (The three most important Hamburg composers of that period, Reinhard Keiser, Telemann, and Handel, all set it to music.) Bach's second source was a Passion based on Saint John by another writer from Hamburg, the poet and librettist Christian Heinrich Postel. For the soprano aria "Ich folge dir gleichfalls" (I, too, follow thee), the American Bach scholar Arthur Mendel, who knew more about the *Saint John Passion* than anybody since Bach himself, cites as source *Der Grünenden Jugend Nothwendige Gedancken* (Thoughts Necessary to Growing Youth) by the Saxon poet and playwright Christian Weise. None of these texts is taken over verbatim. We do not know who adapted them for this libretto; it could well have been Bach himself.

I don't think it would be useful to give a detailed, movement-by-movement account of the *Saint John Passion*. I do, however, want to point out some special features here and there.

Bach begins with a grand chorus, "Herr, unser Herrscher" (Lord, our master), a song of praise and at the same time a reminder to the congregation of the fundamental theme of the Passion. This is one of the movements that Bach first replaced but ultimately restored. What he temporarily replaced it with you can now hear in the *Saint Matthew Passion*, for it is the immense setting of the chorale *O Mensch bewein' dein' Sünde gross* (O Man, Bewail Thy Grievous Sins) that now closes Part I of that work.

Bach reverted to his original design after *O Mensch bewein'* had found a permanent place in the *Saint Matthew Passion*. *O Mensch bewein'* and "Herr unser Herrscher" are strikingly different in character, and not only because the former is anchored to a familiar hymn. *O Mensch bewein'*, for all the torment in its text, is a serenely majestic piece of music; "Herr, unser Herrscher," with its chains of unrelenting dissonance between the two oboes and the turmoil of the roiling sixteenth-notes in the strings, especially when they invade the bass, is full of anguish, and thus more characteristically *Saint John*. Bach's ultimate disposition of the two choruses between the two Passions was clearly the right one.

Part I, which makes up about one-third of the score, takes us through Peter's betrayal of Jesus. It includes three commenting arias, the alto's "Von den Stricken meiner Sünden" (From the tangle of my transgressions), whose intertwined oboe lines hark back to that most characteristic sound of the opening chorus; the enchanting flute-and-soprano duet (actually for both flutes in unison), "Ich folge dir gleichfalls," where the verbs "ziehen" (to draw) and "schieben" (to push) stimulate Bach's delight in musical illustration; and the impassioned and tormented tenor solo, accompanied by *tutti gli stromenti* (all the instruments), "Ach, mein Sinn" (O my soul). (This last number Bach replaced for awhile with an even more wildly emotional piece, the bass aria "Zerschmettert mich" [Shatter me], to which a soprano adds a chorale.)

These soprano and tenor arias show especially clearly how such commentary works. The Evangelist has just sung the words "And Simon Peter followed Jesus, and so did another disciple," whereupon the soprano, speaking for the Christian congregation, declares her intention also to follow Jesus "with joyous footsteps." This is the more poignant because we know that Simon Peter will follow Jesus only as far as the door of the palace of the high priest, and that just outside that door he will betray his master. Those in the congregation who knew their Bible would at this point have recalled a passage from an earlier chapter of Saint John's Gospel:

> Simon Peter said unto him, "Lord, whither goest thou?" Jesus answered him, "Whither I go, thou canst not follow me now; but thou shalt follow me afterwards." Peter said unto him, "Lord, why cannot I follow thee now? I will lay down my life for thy sake." Jesus answered him, "Wilt thou lay down thy life for my sake? Verily, verily, I say unto thee, The cock shall not crow, till thou hast denied me thrice."

We hear Peter deny Jesus three times, and at the third time, John tells us, "immediately the cock crew." Here Bach borrows two sentences from Saint Matthew: "And Peter remembered the word of Jesus, which said unto him, Before the cock crow, thou shalt deny me thrice. And he went out, and wept bitterly." (Bach was counting on his listeners' memories, since in the *Saint John Passion* there is no explicit reference before this to Jesus' prophecy of Peter's betrayal and the crowing of the cock.) In the difference between Bach's setting of these words here and in the *Saint Matthew Passion* we can sense, in microcosm, the difference between these two great works: "weinete bitterlich" in the *Saint John Passion* is by far the more extreme in tortured expression, more extravagant in line and harmony. It is raw and unbridled. The later work is more "finished" and "classical."[1]

As soon as the "weeping" melisma has come to rest, the full orchestra bursts out in the same key, F-sharp minor, a long way indeed from the G minor of "Herr, unser Herrscher," to begin the tenor's self-flagellating "Ach, mein Sinn." Here Bach adds a second commentary from another perspective, a simple hymn in the major key closest to F-sharp minor, expressing the wish that Peter's example may sharpen the believer's conscience in the wake of evil. Bach returns to this hymn twice more, once when the crucified Jesus has said to John, "Behold thy mother!" and again immediately following Jesus' death.

Bach begins Part II with another simple hymn, seeming thus to reduce the intermission to a technical convenience rather than treating it as a great structural divide. (In the Leipzig churches a sermon would have

---

[1] A comparison might be made with Beethoven's second and third *Leonore Overtures*.

been preached between the two parts.) This chorale also returns, immediately before the deposition of Jesus' body from the cross.

Now the work begins to move forward with extraordinary swiftness, and as the dialogue between Jesus and Pilate unfolds, Bach imposes a powerful symmetrical design on the music. (This was first pointed out in the study of the *Saint John Passion* published in 1924 by the German Bach scholar, Friedrich Smend.) The chorales *Ach, grosser König* (Ah, Great King) and *In meines Herzens Grunde* (At the Bottom of My Heart) are the outer brackets of this design. Just after the former and again just before the latter, Bach places a triptych, consisting of a pair of crowd choruses each separated by an aria: the arias are, respectively, the tenor's "Erwäge" (Behold then), preceded by the bass recitative, "Betrachte, meine Seel'" (Consider, my soul) and the bass aria with chorus, "Eilt, ihr angefocht'nen Seelen" (Make haste, you beleaguered souls). As we move further inside this design, we find the two choruses, two different treatments of the same musical idea, in which the crowd calls for Jesus' crucifixion. These enclose another pair of musically similar choruses, "Wir haben ein Gesetz" (We have a law) and "Lässest du diesen los" (If you let this one go). These in turn occur on either side of the centerpiece of this grand structure, the chorale *Durch dein Gefängnis, Gottes Sohn* (Through your imprisonment, O Son of God).

The crowd choruses, whose chromatic lines thrust their way through the texture, are ferocious. The arioso/aria pair "Betrachte, meine Seel'"/ "Erwäge" is Bach's most expansive interpolation, and it is also the most difficult aria he ever wrote. Bach replaced this pair for a time with another tenor aria, but one imagines that he was finally glad to experience again his original sonorities of lute and two viole d'amore, so fragrant and special. There is nothing else quite so exotic in either of the Passions, and the rainbow in the aria elicits one of Bach's loveliest pictures in music. The Evangelist's recitatives are so beautifully efficient as vivid text-carriers that one hardly stops to consider them as music, but for a wonderful example of the inspired strokes in which they abound, take the powerful harmonic wrench when Pilate points to the crowned and robed Jesus and says to the crowd, "Sehet, welch ein Mensch!" (Behold the man).

Nothing challenges a composer of a Passion more than setting the words that recount the moment of Jesus' death upon the cross. Here the narration is simple, even as John's account is simple, lacking, for example, the "ELI, ELI, LAMA SABACHTHANI?" of Matthew and Mark, or the conversation with the thieves, "Today thou shalt be with me in paradise," in Luke. But the commentary is rich. Jesus' last words, "Es ist vollbracht!" (It is accomplished) are set as a descending scale.[2] Immediately a solo viola da gamba echoes that musical gesture, very slightly elaborated and in another key, to begin one of Bach's most expansive and rapturous melodies. Then a human voice, a contralto, picks up that same descending line, once again slightly altered and on yet another set of pitches, in fact picking up not only the melody but the very words "Es ist vollbracht," to begin a deep and wondrous meditation. Suddenly the music turns to a vigorous allegro as the picture of "victorious Judah's hero" is evoked. It is central to Lutheran theology that triumph and victory coincide precisely with the moment of deepest abasement, death on the cross between two thieves. This "victory *allegro*" is torn off in mid-phrase. The alto sings "Es ist vollbracht" once more, this time at the pitch at which the viola da gamba had suggested it in the first place, and that instrument brings the aria to a close, the voice joining it for the end of the last measure.

Bach never wrote an aria more original and unconventional in form—consider just the allegro interruption, the nonconclusion of that allegro, and the daring stroke of ending with the voice rather than an instrumental ritornello—nor one more powerfully apposite in its pacing and immediate in impact. It is a miracle of unexpected extensions, and the miracle continues, for seamlessly there grows from this final "Es ist vollbracht" the next simple sentence of John's account: "And he bowed his head and departed."[3] Bach reflects on this in one of his most inspired arias, "Mein teurer Heiland" (My dearest Saviour), subtly related to "Es ist vollbracht!" in that it, too, features a low voice and a low stringed instrument (now bass rather than contralto and cello instead of viola da gamba). It is, however, very different in character and texture. Most concerted Passions offer a hymn immediately after the death of Jesus; here, Bach combines both modes of commentary by setting into this place an aria with a lovely and subtle intertwining of voice and cello, upon which he superimposes a chorale intoned *piano sempre* by the chorus.

[2]In his important study *Lutheranism, Anti-Judaism, and Bach's St. John Passion* (Oxford University Press, 1998), Michael Marissen points out that "the word for 'es ist vollbracht' [Luther's translation] in the original Greek was *tetelestai*, a cry of triumph, something that is obscured in the common English rendering [in the King James version] 'it is finished.'" Marissen also cites the Bible commentary of the seventeenth-century theologian Johann Olearius, whose *Principal Key to the Entire Holy Scriptures* Bach owned: "Olearius mentions that the Greek here reads *tetelestai*, and he goes on to say that this involves 'triumph . . . and the joyous resurrection of our redeemer . . . so it is expressed, accordingly: "the battle is accomplished [vollbracht], the victory is secured." ' " The Latin Vulgate has "Consummatum est," and the Douay-Rheims version translates this exactly as "It is consummated." In his recent translation of *The Four Gospels and the Revelation*, Richmond Lattimore perpetuates the English tradition, rendering the sentence as "It is ended."

[3]The King James version says "and gave up the ghost," but "departed" comes nearer to the German "und verschied" that Bach had before him.

Something we do not find in John's account of the crucifixion is the earthquake of which Matthew, Mark, and Luke speak. Bach the drama-tist obviously hated to do without it, for he interpolates here the two rel-evant verses from Matthew. The tenor arioso "Mein Herz!" (My heart) comments on the earthquake and continues its musical mood; in turn, the soprano aria with flutes and oboes da caccia, "Zerfliesse, mein Herze" (Dissolve, my heart) continues the thought of the arioso. In the third ver-sion of the *Saint John Passion* Bach omitted this entire sequence, substi-tuting a now-lost orchestral sinfonia, but restored it in his final revision.

We have had rich and expansive commentary, but now Bach moves swiftly to the close of the work. The last great set piece is a lullaby, "Ruht wohl" (Rest well), in musical language Bach would replicate very closely when he came to the corresponding place in the *Saint Matthew Passion*. In the *Saint Matthew* the lullaby is the last music we hear. In the *Saint John* Bach adds a wonderful postscript; in fact, he had trouble deciding which of two wonderful postscripts to use. In his second and third versions, he used one of the greatest of his chorale settings in an elaborate style, cor-responding to the *O Mensch bewein'* with which the work then began. This is the setting of *Christe, du Lamm Gottes* (Christ, Thou Lamb of God) that we now know as the final movement of the cantata No. 23, *Du wahrer Gott und Davids Sohn* (Thou Very God and David's Son). Its loss from a work that gets many more performances than that beautiful and neg-lected cantata is sad; however, Bach was right in thinking that something simpler was needed after the spacious "Ruht wohl," and what he put here, a simple four-part setting of another hymn, *Ach Herr, lass dein lieb' Engelein* (O Lord, thy little angel send), is a miracle in its own right. And so the *Saint John Passion* ends with that sense of expressive immediacy that is one of its most lovable characteristics.

Something that has dogged the *Saint John Passion* at least since the middle of the twentieth century is the problem of the pronounced anti-Judaism of the author (or authors) of the Fourth Gospel, one of the many fea-tures that set it apart from the three Synoptic Gospels attributed to Matthew, Mark, and Luke. It is a problem no one seems to have noticed before Auschwitz. This is a complex issue, and it is carefully and thor-oughly dealt with in a book I cite in footnote 2, Michael Marissen's *Lutheranism, Anti-Judaism, and Bach's St. John Passion.*

That there is a strong tradition of anti-Judaism in Protestant theol-ogy is not in question, and Bach, who was well grounded in theology, was aware of it. Its *fons et origo* is one of the more excessive of Martin Luther's screeds, *On the Jews and Their Lies* (1543), in which (and I quote a *New York Times* article of Marissen's) Luther proposes "sanctions for

Jews who would not embrace his Christianity: burn their places of worship, destroy their homes, seize their prayer books and Talmudic writings, and finally expel them from areas of Europe. (Lutheran church bodies have officially repudiated Luther's anti-Jewish writings.)"

The question here is: Does the *Saint John Passion* reflect this anti-Judaism? Yes, insofar as Bach sets all of John's Passion narrative, in which the Jews are consistently placed in the worst possible light. No, insofar as the commenting arias and hymns shift blame for the death of Jesus to the congregation of Christians—and, of course, Bach could choose arias and hymns as he could not very well choose to edit or censor the text of the Gospel. The hymn we hear just after the telling of the story of Peter's betrayal is exemplary of this: "I, I, and my sins, / Which are as numberless / As the grains of sand by the sea, / They have caused you / The misery that assails you." The "Crucify him" crowd choruses and the utterances of the contemporary congregation are a way of making a powerful statement that all bear the responsibility for Jesus' death. A conductor could make a really nasty thing of the *Saint John Passion* by assigning the hostile crowd choruses and the chorales to two different groups of singers, stationing them in different parts of the hall or church, perhaps even giving them distinctive dress.

Performances of the *Saint John Passion* have sometimes aroused protest, and I have mentioned elsewhere that Lukas Foss, who came to America in 1937 as a Jewish refugee from Nazi Germany, has done what Bach could not have done: namely, palliate the Gospel text by changing the "Juden" to "Leute" (people). Coming from a background similar to Foss's, I can understand anyone's dismay with John's Gospel and the concomitant preference for having nothing to do with it or any musical setting of it (though I am not persuaded by Foss's solution). I also believe that Bach must be held blameless here. The conductor Tom Hall has put it clearly: "It is [the commentaries, i.e., the hymns and arias] which serve to enlighten us as to Bach's take on this fundamental theological issue. . . . Ultimately I am convinced by Michael Marissen's argument that the commentary texts . . . 'take the focus away from the perfidy of "the Jews" and onto the sins of Christian believers.'"

The Passion of Our Lord Jesus Christ According to the Evangelist Matthew, BWV 244

The *Saint Matthew Passion* was first performed at Saint Thomas's Church, Leipzig, on Good Friday, 15 April 1729, but possibly as early as

Good Friday, 11 April 1727. Bach expanded the work considerably for a performance on Good Friday, 30 March 1736, making further slight changes on into the 1740s, and it is in that final form that the work is known today.

The score calls for tenor and bass soloists for the parts of the Evangelist and Jesus, and a solo quartet of soprano, alto, tenor, and bass for the arias and the roles of Pontius Pilate, Judas, Peter, the High Priest and two other priests, two maids, Pilate's wife, and two witnesses. In addition, there are two choruses and two orchestras. Each chorus has the usual four sections of sopranos, altos, tenors, and basses, but the opening and closing choruses of Part I call for an additional group of sopranos. Orchestra I consists of two flutes, oboe, oboe d'amore, two oboes da caccia, viola da gamba, a normal string section of violins, violas, cellos, and basses, and organ. Orchestra II has two flutes, oboe, two oboes d'amore, viola da gamba, strings, and organ.

The core of the libretto of this work is chapters 26 and 27 of the Gospel according to Saint Matthew in Martin Luther's German translation. That itself is a lot of words: it takes about twenty minutes to read the two chapters aloud. Upon this, Bach superimposes an elaborate body of commentary. Some of this material comes from sixteenth- and seventeenth-century hymnals. In addition, Bach had a living collaborator in Christian Friedrich Henrici (1700–1764), a civil servant who rose to positions of high authority in the Saxon postal and tax departments and who, under the nom de plume of Picander, was a fluent, musically expert, versatile, and well-paid poet. Bach set about thirty of his cantata texts, and the lost *Saint Mark Passion* was also Picander's work.

    The *Saint Matthew Passion* has fifteen arias, ten of which are preceded by contemplative recitatives. I count as one of the arias "So ist mein Jesus nun gefangen" (So my Jesus is now taken) near the end of Part I, though it is in fact a duet with choral interjections. Several of the arias have such interjections—in effect, commentary on the commentary. When Bach does not put a recitative before an aria it is for a special reason. "Ach, nun ist mein Jesus hin" (Ah, now my Jesus is gone) has none because it is the first number in Part II, and an aria-plus-chorus is a stronger architectonic pillar than a recitative. The other arias without recitatives all occur at moments of particular intensity: after Judas' decision to betray Jesus, the arrest of Jesus, Peter's remorseful weeping, and Judas' suicide. The opening and closing choruses are also part of this layer of freely invented commentary.

The other layer is embodied in the interpolated hymns. Of these hymns or chorales there are also fifteen, although only eight different tunes are involved. Twelve of these hymns appear in simple four-part settings; however, *O Mensch, bewein' dein' Sünde gross* (O Man, Bewail Thy Grievous Sins), which closes Part I, is presented in richly elaborated form, and two other chorales are embedded in the opening chorus and in the tenor recitative "O Schmerz!" (O pain), which is the response to Jesus' suffering and sorrow in Gethsemane.

Immediately, Bach establishes his intention to present—and fill—a vast canvas. Never before had he, or anyone else, written a single movement on such a scale as this opening chorus, and only once more would he undertake such a thing, in the first "Kyrie" of the Mass in B Minor. To the complex orchestral texture Bach adds a vocal polyphony that becomes more and more involved as the dialogue unfolds between the Faithful and the Daughter of Zion, who is the personification of the city of Jerusalem. To all that, at a different tempo and in a different key, Bach adds the chorale *O Lamm Gottes unschuldig* (O Innocent Lamb of God). To emphasize the differentness of that element, conductors often assign it to boy sopranos, sometimes placing them in some special location in the hall. So, within one piece, Bach gathers the principal themes of the Passion: lament, the mystical union of Christ and his church, his innocence, his bearing of the cross even as he bore for others their sins, his patience, his free acceptance of death to effect redemption and reconciliation with God. Bach also conveys an extraordinary sense of motion, of tension, of gathering throngs; he combines both his chosen modes of commentary; and he erects a pillar that effortlessly holds the weight of his immense design. Not surprisingly, he sensed the need for something monumental at the close of Part I to balance this opening chorus.

Both these great choral movements, the opening chorus, "Kommt, ihr Töchter" (Come, ye daughters) and *O Mensch, bewein'*, are in the key of E (to be precise, the first is in E minor with a final cadence in major; the other is in E major); the Passion as a whole, however, will end in a darker place, C minor. This casting of a harmonic shadow appears throughout the Passion as a microcosm of the large structure. At the Last Supper, for example, when Jesus says to the Twelve, "One of you shall betray me," the harmony moves suddenly to C minor, and the word "verraten" (betray) is underlined by a poignant dissonance between Jesus' voice and the accompanying strings. And as in response the disciples become "exceedingly sorrowful," the harmony moves still further toward the dark side.

Very soon it happens again, and more dramatically still. Jesus has reminded his disciples of the prophecy of Zechariah, who is himself citing the words of the Lord: "I will smite the shepherd, and the sheep of the flock shall be scattered abroad." After this, the chorus, which is the symbolic congregation, for the first time sings the so-called Passion Chorale to the words "Erkenne mich, mein Hüter" (Remember me, my guardian). Less than a minute later we hear the same chorale again, identically harmonized, but a half-step lower in pitch in E-flat (the relative major of C minor) instead of E. In that brief interval Jesus has said to Peter, "This night, before the cock crow, thou shalt deny me thrice" and Peter has replied, "Though I should die with Thee, yet will I will not deny Thee." This falling of the shadow is unmistakable.

The original tonality of E is asserted for the last time when the chief priests and scribes and elders mock the crucified Jesus. Their derisive unison—landing hard on E—as they fling into his face the words "Ich bin Gottes Sohn" (I am the Son of God) is the most shocking musical detail in the Passion. The Evangelist's next few words—"And the thieves who also were crucified with him"—violently wrench the harmony into C minor, and except for the moment of transfigured serenity of the chorale immediately after Jesus' death, it remains in darker regions until the end of the work. The darkest moment of all comes when Jesus cries out "with a loud voice" the beginning of the Twenty-Second Psalm, "ELI, ELI, LAMA SABACHTHANI?" (My God, my God, why hast Thou forsaken me?), and it is there that Bach withdraws the halo of string tone that has, up to then, shed its radiance on every one of Jesus' words, thus setting them apart from everyone else's.

Some comment, now, on a few details and special features:

Bach was an inveterate illustrator in music. When, after Jesus has prophesied betrayal by one of the Twelve, they respond with "Herr, bin ich's?" (Lord, is it I?), "Herr" is pronounced eleven times. Judas does not join in because he needs to ask his own "Master, is it I?" And in the very first aria, Bach makes two flutes draw a clear picture of the sinning alto's teardrops. Likewise, there is no missing the snake in the soprano aria that follows upon Judas' covenant with the chief priests.

The first two pieces for solo tenor, the recitative "O Schmerz!" and the aria "Ich will bei meinem Jesu wachen" (I will keep watch with Jesus), are among the most remarkable in the score. The harmonies and orchestral colors, the trembling of the anguished heart, take hold of our imagination. What is still more extraordinary—and subtle—is the role of the chorus in this pair of pieces: its interventions, first in a recapitulation of the Passion's first chorale, then in freely invented music of immense evocative power, grow increasingly bold, to the point where they cease to be commentary but become the heart of the matter.

The duet "So ist mein Jesus nun gefangen" shows Bach as a master both of unexpected conclusions and of powerful dramatic contrast. Nothing could set off the outraged exclamations of "Lasst ihn!" (Release him!)

and the ferocious thunder-and-lightning chorus more strikingly than the despondent beginning, full of pathos, almost directionless, with no instrument lower than a viola.

Bach's feeling for dramatic pacing is evident as well in his decision of where to put the division between the two parts of the Passion. Of course Henrici-Picander gets credit here as well, for presumably the two discussed such questions together. Chapter 26 of the Gospel ends with Peter's weeping; Bach prefers to stop with Jesus' arrest. The mob, guided by Judas and absurdly armed for the taking of an itinerant teacher, arrives in the garden. There is violence and confusion, and all the disciples abandon Jesus and flee into the darkness. Then: "O Man, bewail thy grievous sins."

As the drama of Jesus' trial and death moves toward its terrible climax, the musical contrasts become more and more drastic. The commentary grows richer and more elaborate even as the narrative itself becomes ever more terse and, in the crowd choruses, ever more brutal. The cry for the release of Barabbas is an astonishing stroke of economy and power. The very placement of the commentary plays a role in this development. What could be bolder than to interrupt the proceedings at the height of furor by giving a softly ironic, infinitely touching answer to Pilate's question to the mob, "Why, what evil hath he done?" When the story is resumed after the "interrupting" recitative and aria—"Er hat uns allen wohl getan"/"Aus Liebe will mein Heiland sterben" (He has done good to us all/It is out of love that my Savior wants to die)—the force of "Let him be crucified" is the more shattering for the musical and verbal sweetness of what has intervened.

When the famous and beloved Passion Chorale is sung after Jesus' giving up the ghost, and sung in a particularly fragrant harmonization, it is the fifth time we hear it. Four of the five occurrences were late additions by Bach, and they all symbolize Jesus' progress toward his end by being so arranged that each comes in a lower key than the preceding one.

After the eclipse, the earthquake; and with the earthquake, physical turmoil reaches its highest point. From that violence Bach moves directly to one of the most wondrous phrases in all music, the two measures in which the awed centurion and his soldiers suddenly understand that "truly, this was the Son of God" ("erschraken sie sehr" [they were filled with awe] brings the last of those shuddery shifts to the darker harmony I mentioned earlier). "Truly, this was the Son of God" sounds like nothing else in the Passion. It is in a remote key hardly touched before (A-flat major), and it suggests the simplicity of a hymn, although the writing, for the few seconds it lasts, is far more elaborate. This, of course, had to be a special moment, for to find in the experience of the crucifixion the meaning of Jesus' life is to understand the essence and the purpose of the Passion.

From here on, the music is at peace. Picander's beautiful apostrophe to eventide evokes a quietly ecstatic response from Bach, and the aria that follows—"Mache dich, mein Herze, rein" (Purify yourself, my heart)—is a masterpiece of serene euphony.

At the end, the Daughter of Zion and the Faithful are again brought together in dialogue. Each soloist in turn speaks a line of love, of remorse, of thanks. The chorus responds with its refrain of "Good night." It is a farewell gently touching in its combination of naïveté and solemnity, and the whole vast contemplation ends in a lullaby that is at once grand and gravely tender.

Magnificat, BWV 243(243a)

Bach originally composed his *Magnificat* in E-flat major for performance at Saint Thomas's Church, Leipzig, on Christmas Day 1723. The cantata *Christen, ätzet diesen Tag* (Christians, Engrave This Day), BWV 63, and probably the D-major Sanctus, BWV 238, were also sung at this service for the first time. On this occasion Bach interpolated settings of four Christmas texts, two in German and two in Latin, into the *Magnificat*. At some point between 1728 and 1731, he adapted the work for use on any feast day by dropping the Christmas interpolations. At the same time, he transposed the music from its original key to D major, and this has become the standard version of the score. The special advantage of this version, besides the release from the Christmas connection, is that D major allows for a far greater brilliance of sound both from the strings and the trumpets. Conductors sometimes adopt what is in effect a third, synthetic edition by using the movements of the first version but in the key of the second. The BWV number for the D-major version is 243; 243a is the E-flat version with the Christmas interpolations.

Five soloists: two sopranos, contralto, tenor, and bass. Two recorders, two oboes (both doubling oboes d'amore), three trumpets, timpani, and strings, plus organ for the continuo.

The text of the *Magnificat* comes from the Gospel according to Saint Luke (1:46–55), to which the Doxology is added. The Annunciation has just taken place—"Behold, thou shalt conceive in thy womb, and bring forth a son, and shalt call his name Jesus"—and the angel has told Mary that her cousin Elisabeth has also conceived (the boy to whom she will give birth is John the Baptist). Mary sets out to visit Elisabeth at her house in Judea and, after the salutation to her cousin, she speaks the words of praise and thanksgiving that begin, "My soul doth magnify the Lord." Part of the Office of Vespers, in Bach's day the Magnificat was usually sung in German and in plainchant, but on high feast days it was sung in Latin and in fully composed form. Bach's *Magnificat* is extraordinary in its concision, and he wrote no work in which he realized his principles— or habits—of text-setting more tellingly.

"*Magnificat anima mea Dominum.*" The full choir and orchestra are on hand to make the most brilliant effect. The movement is short, but because its mere forty-five measures of singing are enclosed between orchestral ritornelli, it comes across as spacious and grand. Bach's decision to begin the setting of Mary's words with sopranos only is surely symbolic.

"*Et exsultavit spiritus meus.*" An aria for soprano II, accompanied by strings and continuo. In the Christmas version, this is where we hear the first of the four interpolations. It is a hymn still current in Germany in the Christmas season, *Vom Himmel hoch, da komm ich her* (I Come from Heaven Above). Sopranos sing the tune in long notes, while the rest of the chorus adds polyphonic elaborations of it. There is no instrumental accompaniment.[1]

"*Quia respexit humilitatem*" and "*Omnes generationes.*" This begins as a contemplative duet for soprano I and oboe d'amore. First they share material, but at the words "ecce enim ex hoc beatam," the singer changes to a simpler, slightly more declamatory style. If you look at the full text, you see that in Latin the subject of the sentence, "omnes generationes," comes at the end. Like many of his predecessors among *Magnificat* composers, Bach seizes the advantage of this syntactic quirk, and he does it with a splendid and exciting sense of drama: When the words "omnes generations" (all generations) arrive, they do so in the voices of the full chorus. Bach gives them tidal force with his tightly piled up entrances, often bringing in the next voice on a higher scale degree than the one before, creating tense dissonances by doing so. He also creates a sense of irresistible momentum through his tremendous march across key after key in scarcely more than a minute of music, with his dramatic pause near the end followed by the sound, so rare in Bach, of unaccompanied voices, and indeed by insisting that these generations declaring the Virgin blessed are not just "omnes generationes" but "omnes, omnes generationes."

---

[1]Near the end of his life Bach composed a virtuosic set of canonic variations for organ on *Vom Himmel hoch*, the occasion being his election to the select Society for Musical Science. The most famous portrait of Bach, by Elias Gottlieb Haussmann, was painted for the same occasion and shows him holding a sheet of the music. In *his* old age, Stravinsky made a no-less-brilliant and distinctly interventionist transcription of these variations for chorus and orchestra.

"*Quia fecit mihi magna.*" After the drama and the polyphonic swirl of "Omnes generationes" comes the *Magnificat*'s simplest aria, the bass voice accompanied only by bass instruments and keyboard. This is where the second Christmas interpolation fits in, *Freut euch und jubiliert* (Rejoice and Be Glad), presented in lively four-part texture with much canonic imitation and accompanied by figured bass.

"*Et misericordia.*" The music sways in a gentle 12/8 meter and the accompanying strings are muted. Near the end, the tenor graphically evokes the fear and (literally) trembling in "timentibus."

"*Fecit potentiam.*" Bach gives us an astounding collision of declamatory choral style and dazzling coloratura: it's the tenors against everyone else at first, but sooner or later each section of the chorus gets its turn at the driving sixteenth-notes. The proud whom God scatters are disposed of in one contemptuous shout of "superbos." In the Christmas version, Bach now inserts a setting for five-part chorus, violins, and figured bass of the words familiar, in slightly different form, from the beginning of the Gloria in the liturgy of the Mass.

"*Deposuit potentes.*" Here is another duet, quite militant, for all the violins in unison and the solo tenor.

"*Esurientes implevit bonis.*" In this contralto aria, it is not only the rich who are "sent empty away," but also the two flutes, who, in Bach's most playful bit of musical symbolism, are deprived of their final cadence. The fourth and last of the Christmas interpolations, *Virga Jesse floruit* (Let the House of Jesse Flourish), is a duet for soprano and bass with figured-bass accompaniment. Both singers are given brilliant coloratura. The movement breaks off in measure 30; luckily, Bach recycled it (with a different text) in his 1725 Christmas cantata, *Unser Mund sei voll Lachens* (Let Our Mouths Be Full of Laughter), and one can easily reconstruct the missing conclusion from that source.

"*Suscepit Israel.*" The three high solo voices weave a lovely and gentle imitative texture. The melody sounded by the oboes across their serene singing is one that members of Bach's Leipzig generation would have recognized as part of the German *Magnificat*—*Meine Seel' erhebt den Herrn.* You might recognize it from Mozart's Requiem, where the sopranos sing it near the beginning to the words "Te decet hymnus." In the familiar later version of Bach's *Magnificat*, this Gregorian tune is played by the oboes in unison, but in the original version he gave it to a trumpet.

"*Sicut locutus est.*" A choral fugue, deliberately and satisfyingly prosaic and foursquare in contrast to the "Suscepit Israel" just finished and the flamboyant "Gloria" to come.

"*Gloria Patri.*" The shouts of "Gloria" rise like flames—and how canny Bach is about just when to bring in the trumpets and drums, which we have not heard since the end of "Fecit potentiam." To conclude, he gives us the literalness, both grand and witty, of his reading of "as it was in the beginning."

Mass in B Minor, BWV 232

Bach's labors on the composition we usually call the B-Minor Mass were spread over many years. The title is a nineteenth-century invention; Bach never gave the work a single collective designation. The earliest music in the Mass is the "Crucifixus," which is a reworking of a chorus from Cantata No. 12, *Weinen, Klagen, Sorgen, Zagen*, composed in Weimar for Easter Sunday 1714. Except for the Sanctus, written in 1724 for performance on Christmas Day, the music from the Credo to the end was composed or reworked from earlier compositions between August 1748 and October 1749. Now that *The Art of Fugue* has been redated to the early 1740s, it would appear that these later movements of the Mass are Bach's last compositions. Aside from Bach's own performance of the Sanctus in 1724, the only eighteenth-century performance of music from the B-Minor Mass that we know of for certain is of the Credo, or "Symbolum Nicenum" (as Bach called it), in Hamburg by Carl Philipp Emanuel Bach in March 1786. Beginning in 1811 and continuing over several years, Carl Friedrich Zelter rehearsed and performed various movements with his Berlin Singakademie (Mendelssohn joined as a boy soprano in 1819), and other conductors followed suit during the subsequent decades; for example, the composer Gaspare Spontini presented the Credo as far as the "Et resurrexit" in Berlin in 1828, and Mendelssohn led the Kyrie, Gloria, and Credo there some years later. Finally, the first complete performance of the Mass was given in Leipzig in 1859 under the direction of Carl Riedel.

Five voices (solo and chorus): soprano I and II, alto, tenor, and bass, but in the "Osanna" the chorus expands to eight voices.[1] Two flutes, three oboes (sometimes two oboes d'amore), two bassoons, horn, three trumpets, timpani, and strings, plus organ for the continuo.

---

[1]In the early 1980s, the American musicologist Joshua Rifkin proposed that Bach intended the Mass to be performed with just one singer on each part. A summary of his provocative thesis can be found in his Elektra/Nonesuch CD box of what some skeptics have called the "B-Minor Madrigal." Since the 1960s, many conductors have used solo voices to good effect for at least parts of some of the choruses, in other words, applying *concertino-ripieno* contrasts analogous to those in Bach's concertos.

The Mass is the commemoration and the symbolic-mystical reenactment of the Last Supper. As such, it is the most solemn service in the Catholic liturgy, and in the eighteenth century the Kyrie and Gloria were still in regular use in many Lutheran services as well. Some parts of the text of the Mass, known as the Proper, change from occasion to occasion; others—the Kyrie, Gloria, Credo, Sanctus and Benedictus, and Agnus Dei—are always the same, and are called the Ordinary of the Mass. Among thousands of settings of the Ordinary, two stand out as creations whose performance is always a special event: Bach's, and Beethoven's *Missa solemnis* of 1819–1823, the result of the composer's second wrestling with the text. Both works are larger than life and occupied their composers for exceptional spans of time. Both are compendia of everything their composers knew about the musical traditions in which they worked and of the history of those traditions, Bach and Beethoven alike being in sovereign command of the tools for integrating the most diverse styles and manners, and achieving an exquisite balance between what comes from the past and what is most modern. These two works are late-in-life summations of musical technique and spiritual experience. For Bach as for Beethoven, different though their approaches are, the one grandly hieratic, the other desperately subjective, the Mass was *the* journey to the summit of Sinai, the ultimate confrontation.

The history of Bach's Mass is complicated, and even now our knowledge is full of gaps. We know that Bach began in 1733 by setting the text from "Kyrie eleison" through "Cum Sancto Spiritu in Gloria Dei Patris, Amen," the parts familiarly known as the Kyrie and Gloria. At this point the Sanctus already lay to hand, but when Bach composed it in 1724 he presumably had no thought of its eventually becoming part of a complete Mass. The Kyrie and Gloria were also used in the Lutheran liturgy, in Latin, and were known simply as "Missa" or Mass; accordingly, Bach gave the title of *Missa a 5 Voci* to these movements. (Later in the 1730s, Bach wrote four more of these relatively short Lutheran Kyrie-and-Gloria Masses.)

On 27 July 1733, Bach sent a set of performance parts (but no score) of the Kyrie and Gloria to Frederick Augustus II, the new elector of Saxony, as part of the apparatus designed to win him an appointment as court composer in Dresden. In Leipzig, where Bach had worked since 1723, he was unhappy, frustrated, and angry, the target of political intrigues meant to drive him out. He had already made inquiries about other job possibilities and he hoped that some sort of title from the elector would, if not actually win him a position in Dresden, at least strengthen his hand in Leipzig. All this he explained candidly in the cover letter to what he called "this trifling token of what science I have achieved in music."

The letter is dated from Dresden because Bach had gone there with his eldest and favorite son, Wilhelm Friedemann, in support of the young man's application for the post of organist at Saint Sophie's Church. That aspect of the trip was successful, and Friedemann entered his new position on 1 August 1733. The father had to wait rather longer, for it was not until 19 November 1736 that a certificate was issued appointing him "Compositeur to the Royal Court Capelle . . . with his Royal Majesty's Most August Signature." Moreover, the certificate is all Bach really got from the affair. His discontent with working conditions at home continued and grew, and the title from Dresden turned out to give him no clout with his employers, the Noble and Most Wise Council of the City of Leipzig. And Leipzig is where Bach remained until his death in 1750.

The rest of the Mass after the Kyrie and Gloria survives in an autograph score divided by its title pages into three sections. First comes the "Symbolum Nicenum a 5 Voci," the part generally known as the Credo. ("Symbolum Nicenum" is Lutheran terminology and refers to the Nicene Creed, long thought, but probably mistakenly, to have been promulgated at the Council of Nicaea in 325.) Then comes the "Sanctus a 6 Vocibus," and the final section comprises the "Osanna," Benedictus, and "Agnus Dei et Dona nobis pacem."

Of all that, the Sanctus has the clearest history, for, as I mentioned earlier, it was performed in slightly different form as part of the Christmas music in 1724 and again either at Christmas 1726, Easter 1727, or both. "Credo in unum Deum," "Et in unum Dominum," "Et incarnatus est," "Et in Spiritum Sanctum," and "Confiteor unum baptisma" were composed and the other movements adapted in 1748–1749, and thus belong with those profound late works, *The Art of Fugue*, the Canonic Variations on *Von Himmel hoch*, and *The Musical Offering*. This late music is of an astonishing adventurousness and reminds us that Bach is one of those glorious old-age radicals of the stamp of Haydn, Beethoven, Verdi, Schoenberg, Stravinsky, and Carter.

What about those "adapted" movements? Several sections of the B-Minor Mass, including two in the 1733 *Missa*, are borrowed from earlier compositions. Borrowing can mean the straight transfer of a piece from one context to another, but it may also involve far-reaching revisions and changes in design. Why the later sections of the Mass contain so many borrowed or adapted pieces—"parodies" is the technical term—is one of the puzzles surrounding the B-Minor Mass. The Bach scholar Georg von Dadelsen attributed the presence of so many parodies to Bach's awareness of the decline of his melodic inspiration as he grew older. I am unconvinced, not only in light of melodies such as those in "Et in Spiritum Sanctum" and the Agnus Dei, but also because the *Christmas Oratorio* of 1734, for example, includes an even higher proportion of borrowed material. It has also been suggested that Bach used so many adaptations because the Mass was needed in a hurry; however, aside from the fact that there is no trace of a performance, no one has been able to suggest an occasion for which so outsized a piece of liturgical music might have been used in Leipzig. In sum, we have no idea why Bach borrowed so much, and we could indeed go on to say that the most fundamental question about the B-Minor Mass is that of its very existence.

One trouble is that there are still so many gaps in our picture of Bach's later years. Bach scholarship in the 1950s was very much concerned with questions of chronology, and we can now assign a definite date to many a composition about which guesswork had to suffice in the past. But the revised chronology established primarily by Georg von Dadelsen and Alfred Dürr raised many new questions in the act of answering old ones. It turned out that most of the surviving church cantatas were written much earlier than previously supposed and that, except for the few special pieces that belong in the 1740s, the bulk of Bach's work was achieved by 1726. The gap of more than two decades between that point and the completion of the Mass is by no means devoid of major works: the *Saint Matthew Passion*, the lost *Saint Mark Passion*, the *Christmas Oratorio*, the large collection of harpsichord and organ works known as the *Clavier-Übung* (Keyboard Exercise), and some cantatas belong to this period. Nonetheless, whether because of unhappiness with his professional life, the pressures of teaching, his obligations as director of the University's Collegium Musicum, or his gradually failing eyesight, Bach's work tempo was slowing down.

As Bach grew older, he moved away more and more from the eighteenth-century pattern according to which a composer generally produced music only as the nature of his office or other contracts demanded it, when there was a special commission or occasion, or when he wished to make an impression on a prospective patron or employer. Bach's church music, and also, if we think of his home as part of his "office," his teaching pieces for keyboard, are examples of the first category; cantatas for birthdays, weddings, funerals, public occasions, and professional promotions of the second; and the 1733 *Missa* of the third. Rather, as Bach grew older, he became increasingly interested in musical challenges for their own sake. Also his lifelong passion for collecting and compiling was channeled into a process of setting his musical house in order. Perhaps there we can find what is behind the impulse that led him to complete what he had begun with the 1733 *Missa*: the aging master wished to go on record as having composed an entire Ordinary of the Mass, thus becoming one link in a three-centuries-long chain of composers seeking to fulfill what many of them—certainly his fifteenth- and sixteenth-century precursors—would have regarded as the most ambitious as well as the most solemn of all musical obligations.

Kyrie and Gloria

The Kyrie is symmetrical textually and musically in that it consists of two choruses bracketing a duet for solo voices. Bach does not, however, present the Kyrie as a freestanding structure in closed form, for the key sequence of the three movements takes us from B minor to D major to F-sharp minor. Rather, he thinks of the Kyrie and Gloria as belonging together, and in a church service there is no break between them. Thus the key cycle is closed only with the end of the Gloria, whose destination is D, the major-key partner to B minor. Harmonic unity in fact goes further than that: the Kyrie-Gloria group begins with a movement in B minor and continues with one in D major; it concludes with a pair of movements in B minor ("Qui tollis" and "Qui sedes") leading to a pair in D major ("Quoniam tu solus Sanctus" and "Cum Sancto Spiritu"). The work gets its common title of "B-Minor Mass" from its opening movement, but to the extent that there is one central tonality it would really be D major, the key in which the Credo ends as well as that of the Sanctus and the final "Dona nobis pacem" of the Agnus Dei.

Bach begins the first "Kyrie" with a four-bar invocation that is as massive as it is brief. The score gives no tempo, but the parts say *Adagio*. It is grand enough to support the weight of everything that follows. It was also an afterthought, as though even at this early stage Bach began to have a vision of an entire Mass, which, given the dimensions of the first "Kyrie," would need to be a vast structure requiring an exordium of uncommon gravitas and strength. This is an awe-inspiring half-minute of music, this threefold cry of "Kyrie," massive, firmly rooted, but at the same time possessed of an immensely powerful forward thrust, as it presses toward a Phrygian half-cadence that opens the portals to this mighty and inexhaustible work.

These magnificent opening bars introduce a chorus of extraordinary breadth and force. Only once before had Bach written a single movement on such a grand scale, namely the opening chorus of the *Saint Matthew Passion*, and there certainly is nothing comparable by anyone else. Not least, the ratio of music to words, of which there are, after all, only two, is remarkable, and the effect of the saturation with the sound of "Kyrie eleison" is compelling. Consider the three-movement Kyrie-Christe-Kyrie sequence together: it is astonishing to think of two phrases composed of just three different words yielding something like eighteen to twenty minutes of music. But of course, to the believer this primal plea for mercy is an idea of infinite dimensions.[2]

There is something concertolike in the design of the opening ritornello for orchestra, whose music, reappearing in the middle of the movement and at its conclusion, both times with voices added to the instruments, functions as a structural anchor. The first vocal entrance is fugal, though Bach has no intention of writing a strict fugue. The tenors lead off with the gravely poignant, intensely chromatic subject. One of my favorite details is the single brief touch of major the second time the orchestra plays alone.

If the first "Kyrie" is, among other things, a wonderful blend of ancient and modern (fugue and concerto), the "Christe," with its sweet parallel thirds and sixths for two sopranos and the entrancing grace of the melodies for the singers and the strings, is altogether and deliciously modern. That Dresden, unlike Leipzig, was an opera town had a lot to do with this.

The second "Kyrie," by contrast, is entirely committed to the *stile antico*: this is a real four-part fugue, though with an independent instrumental bass, severe and chromatic, as gripping in its concentration as the first "Kyrie" is in its grandeur. After the first two movements Bach commands *segue*; now he writes a fermata to signal that he has arrived at the first major point of arrival in his design. In the three movements we have heard thus far, Bach has given us a sense of the range of the musical language he intends to use in his Mass.

"Gloria in excelsis Deo" has its own symmetry in that it starts with Bach's most exuberant trumpets-and-drums D-major brilliance, turns to something more lyric for "Et in terra pax," also changing the meter from swift 3/8 to a more spacious 4/4, to return finally to the jubilant sonorities of the opening while retaining the slower pace. The quiet reappearance of the trumpets in the "Et in terra pax" is one of Bach's great coloristic inspirations in the Mass. Here we have an example of borrowing in the other direction: at some unknown date after 1735, Bach used this chorus along with two other movements from the Mass, "Domine Deus" and "Cum Sancto Spiritu," to make a Christmas cantata, *Gloria in excelsis Deo*, BWV 191.

The "Laudamus te" is a duet for soprano II and violin. The American Bach scholar Arthur Mendel suggested that Bach may well have written it specifically for two celebrated Dresden musicians, the mezzo-soprano

---

[2]Another view: Asked why so many vocal pieces had so much word repetition, the Argentine composer Mauricio Kagel replied: "So that you will start listening to the music."

Faustina Bordoni, one of the great divas of her day and married to the Dresden Capellmeister Johann Adolf Hasse, and Johann Georg Pisendel, the violinist for whom Bach very possibly composed his solo sonatas and partitas.[3]

With "Gratias agimus tibi" we come to the first of the borrowed movements, this music having first served in 1731 as the opening chorus of a cantata to celebrate the election of Leipzig's Municipal Council, *Wir danken dir, Gott*, BWV 29.[4] This is a fugal movement of exceptional splendor. Once again, Bach's cunning economy with trumpets and drums is telling.

"Domine Deus" is a trio for soprano I, tenor, and flute, with an accompaniment for muted strings. It goes without break into the "Qui tollis," another borrowed movement, this one taken from the 1733 cantata *Schauet doch und sehet*, BWV 46, where the music carries the words "Behold, and see if there be any sorrow like unto my sorrow." The scoring in the new version is quieter, omitting the doubling of the voices by trumpet and oboe da caccia, and the rhythm is made more fluid by changing the upbeat from two quarter-notes to a swifter two eighths. Bach ends on a half-cadence and commands that "Qui sedes," a duet for alto and oboe d'amore, follow without a break.

"Qui tollis" and "Qui sedes" are the two movements in B minor I referred to earlier. Now Bach is ready to go on to his D-major finale. "Quoniam tu solus Sanctus" is a bass aria with a virtuosic horn obbligato and busy parts for a pair of bassoons, plus of course a bass line—a bold and colorful study in low-register sonorities. Late in life, Haydn acquired a score of the B-Minor Mass, and I have often thought that this is where he got the idea for the amusing bassoon obbligato in the delightful Hound-Dog Aria in *The Seasons*.

The sounds of the "Quoniam" perfectly set off the ones that follow. The aria's final cadence is elided with the first downbeat of the "Cum

[3]That keen observer of singers, Dr. Charles Burney, notes in *A General History of Music* that "E was a remarkably powerful note in [Bordoni's] voice, and we find most of her capital songs in sharp keys." The Handel scholar Winton Dean points out that most of the arias Handel wrote for her are in A or E, and Bach's "Laudamus te" is also in A major. Burney quotes Johann Joachim Quantz as saying that Bordoni's "execution was articulate and brilliant. She had a fluent tongue for pronouncing words rapidly and distinctly, and a flexible throat for divisions. . . . The passages might be smooth, or by leaps, or consist of iterations of the same tone, their execution was equally easy to her." Pisendel, said to be an especially expressive player of slow movements, was also an outstanding director of orchestral music as well as a violinist and a good composer. Vivaldi, Albinoni, and Telemann all wrote pieces especially for him.

[4]BWV 29 begins with one of Bach's most amazing self-borrowings, the Prelude to the E-major Partita for solo violin being turned into a concerto movement for solo organ with a brilliant orchestra including three oboes, trumpets, and drums.

Sancto Spiritu" chorus. Here, too, Bach had luxurious Dresden performance conditions in mind: none of his Leipzig works has parts for two obbligato bassoons, nor would you find a horn solo followed without break by a trumpet part, since in Leipzig one musician played both instruments. The chorus makes for a jubilant close, and its bravura fugal interlude—nothing in Bach is more fun to sing—provides an extra infusion of fiery energy.[5]

Credo

In Renaissance and early Baroque Masses it was traditional for composers to begin their Gloria settings with the words "Et in terra pax" and their Credos with "Patrem omnipotentem," letting the celebrant sing the opening in plainsong. (Bruckner, Vaughan Williams, and Stravinsky are later composers who observed this convention.) Bach ignored this tradition in the Gloria, but in the Credo he flings forth a magnificent variation on it, using the ancient Gregorian melody as the subject of a seven-voice fugue (five-part chorus plus two sections of violins) over a "walking" bass striding along in steady quarter-notes.

Numerology buffs, among them several Bach scholars, have noted that in alphabetical numerology, where A is 1, B 2, and so on (I and J counting as the same letter), the word "credo" adds up to 43, and that in this chorus "credo" is pronounced forty-three times. There is more such symbolism in the next chorus, "Credo in unum Deum/Patrem omnipotentem," borrowed from the cantata, *Gott, wie dein Name*, BWV 171, probably from 1729. Here the key numbers are 7 and 12 with their many Christian associations: "credo" is sung twelve times and the number of measures is eighty-four.

The soprano-alto duet "Et in unum Dominum" is built around one of Bach's most famous musical symbols. The instruments are in free canon, but the leading voice (oboe d'amore I and first violins) has detached notes while the following voice (oboe d'amore II and second violins) gives us the same music with slurred ones. Thus the unity of Father and Son is illustrated, but the Persons are not confounded and the Substance is not divided.

The chorus "Et incarnatus est," with its haunting downward-curving violin figure, was an afterthought. Originally these words were incorporated in the preceding "Et in unum Dominum" duet, which explains the

---

[5]Here is another instance of Bach's drive to elaborate. In the Mass, the fugal passage is accompanied only by figured bass, but in the later version, in Cantata No. 191, it is accompanied by full orchestra (except trumpets and drums).

otherwise-inexplicable sense of darkness and wonder of its closing measures, an atmosphere perfectly suited to the mystery of the Incarnation but hard to understand in connection with "qui propter nos homines et propter nostram salutam descendit de coelis" (who for us men and for our salvation came down from heaven).

Bach moves from musical marvel to musical marvel. For his "Crucifixus," a set of variations on a reiterated descending bass that is itself a real Baroque cliché, Bach reached back thirty-five years to the opening chorus of one of his earliest cantatas, *Weinen, Klagen, Sorgen, Zagen*, BWV 12. The most miraculous touches, however, all belong to the revisions Bach made when he incorporated this chorus into the Mass: the sighing flutes, the throbbing quarter-notes in the bass (half-notes in the original), and above all the thirteenth appearance of the ground bass when the music moves from dark E minor into G major. It is a close of unearthly peace, with the orchestra, all save the bass group, fallen silent.

Emerging from deepest darkness into a blaze of light, the brilliant and extended chorus on "Et resurrexit" bursts forth in glory and returns us to the world of trumpets and drums and D major. Normally, musical propriety would dictate a big orchestral ritornello as the opening of such a chorus, but here propriety gives way to drama, and the words "Et resurrexit" explode without break after "et sepultus est." As in the "Cum Sancto Spiritu," Bach makes captivatingly energetic use of a virtuosic fugal episode, here on the words "cujus regni non erit finis." The movement begins with voices but, so as to avoid a false impression of finality, Bach ends the chorus with a big wrap-up for orchestra alone.

Next comes "Et in Spiritum Sanctum," an aria for baritone with a double obbligato for two oboes d'amore. Here Bach provides a lovely, lyrical setting for all those doctrinal clauses that composers have never found inspiring. (Beethoven drowns them in shouts of "Credo, Credo"; Schubert leaves them out altogether.) This aria lives in a much higher register than the "Quoniam"; few singers find it comfortable to undertake both, and many conductors therefore use a bass or bass-baritone for the first and a real baritone for the second.[6] It is essential that "Et in Spiritum Sanctum" be a continuation of "Et resurrexit," not just a pretty interlude.

With the addition of the "Et incarnatus est" chorus, the Credo as a whole becomes a beautiful chiastic design, dominated by threes for the Trinity. At the center you have a succession of three choruses, "Et

[6]Richard Zeller, one of the soloists at a performance by the Saint Paul Chamber Orchestra in 1999, made this aria sound like the most important part of the whole Mass text. When I remarked on this to him afterward, he replied: "First of all, I believe it."

incarnatus est," Crucifixus, and "Et resurrexit." This choral triptych, whose textures are of five, four, and five voices respectively, is flanked by solo numbers, the duet "Et in unum Dominum" before and the aria "Et in Spiritum Sanctum" after. The outside pillars at each end are pairs of choruses, separate but linked, "Credo in unum Deum" with "Patrem omnipotentem" at the beginning, "Confiteor unum baptisma" with "Et exspecto resurrectionem mortuorum" at the end.

And it is at this last pair that we have now arrived. The first "Credo" chorus quotes plainsong, and so does the "Confiteor"; both at their climaxes use augmentations of the Gregorian melody, that is, presentations in longer note values that hugely bestride the texture. "Et exspecto" is a version, much transformed, of a chorus from another election cantata, *Gott, man lobet dich in der Stille,* BWV 120, probably from 1728. Aside from the way the overall harmonic design fits, another feature suggests that Bach was taking pains to make the Credo match the *Missa.* Each contains the following sequence: a four-part D-major chorus with trumpets and drums ("Gratias agimus tibi" and "Patrem omnipotentem"), a G-major duet in 4/4 in free canonic style ("Domine Deus" and "Et in unum Dominum"), and a solemn B-minor chorus in triple meter ("Qui tollis" and "Et incarnatus est"). The text that ends the Creed inspires some of Bach's most intense religious and dramatic response. "Confiteor" is a sturdy, energized expression of faith. Then, with the last singing of "peccatorum" (sins), the music suddenly slows drastically. What hits us even more is what happens to the harmony. At the first declaration of hope for the resurrection of the dead, the music becomes utterly obscure, both in the literal sense of dark as well as in the sense of difficult to fathom and follow. For a minute or more, Bach gives us the strangest harmonic progressions he ever invented, moving in awe from mystery to deeper mystery, disconcerting us ever more, until the orchestral bass leads us into the clarity and safety of D major. And there the Credo comes to its exuberant conclusion.

From the *Sanctus* to the End

Bach now gives us a series of big D-major choruses, alternating with solo arias in minor keys. The Sanctus is for six-part chorus (S-S-A-A-T-B) to suggest the six-winged seraphim, and the "Osanna" expands the sound to eight voices (two S-A-T-B choruses). The Sanctus, as I noted earlier, started life as an independent Christmas piece; the "Osanna" is Bach's third use of this music, both earlier versions sounding the praises of the king of Saxony. We know very little about the lovely Benedictus, not even the intended obbligato instrument that plays a duet with the tenor.

So far as I know, Donald Tovey was the first to question the decision of the Bach-Gesellschaft editors in the 1850s that "such beautiful music must be for violin." Observing that the part never goes below D, Tovey proposed flute as more plausible, and gradually, after the publication of his essay on the Mass in 1937, the performing practice for the Benedictus began to shift from violin to flute.

The Agnus Dei starts like the aria "Ach, bleibe doch" in the *Ascension Oratorio* of 1735, but the relationship of the two pieces is far from simple; indeed, this relationship is much the most complex of any of the parody numbers in the Mass with its source. The two arias are alike in instrumentation, and they share a ritornello and a thematic point of departure. All in all, though, their differences are more striking than their similarities, the "Agnus Dei" being a far more searching exploration of the theme's possibilities. "Agnus Dei" is the last solo in the B-Minor Mass and, characteristically enough, Bach makes its instrumental obbligato of unison violins the same as that for the first solo in the score, the "Christe eleison."

For the "Dona nobis pacem," Bach exactly recapitulates the "Gratias agimus tibi" in the Gloria, returning to four-part choral writing. And here is an oddity. For this movement, which requires fourteen staves for its notation, Bach rules his paper with eighteen staves, leaving four of them blank. Arthur Mendel thought that this perhaps indicates that Bach originally envisioned a completely different setting for this text. Or had Bach simply forgotten how many staves his "Dona nobis pacem" would need? But there is one thing that Bach surely saw at this point when it came to concluding this masterpiece, at once so miscellaneous and so integral: setting "Gratias agimus tibi" and "Dona nobis pacem" to the same music, he reminds us that the prayer and the thanks are one.

Ludwig van Beethoven

Ludwig van Beethoven was born in Bonn, then an independent electorate, probably on 16 December 1770 (he was baptized on 17 December), and died in Vienna on 26 March 1827.

Missa solemnis, op. 123

Beethoven composed the *Missa solemnis* between 1819 and 1823 (a detailed chronology appears below). It was first performed in Saint Petersburg on 6 April (Old Style)/18 April (New Style) 1824.[1]

Soprano, alto, tenor, and bass soloists; four-part chorus. Two flutes, two oboes, two clarinets, two bassoons and contrabassoon, four horns, two trumpets, three trombones, timpani, organ, and strings (including a major violin solo).

[1]Until the 1917 Revolution, Russia used the Julian (Old Style) calendar, which in the nineteenth century was twelve days behind the Gregorian (New Style) calendar used by the West.

This is the ultimate story of a missed deadline. So, first a calendar, amazing and fascinating:

- *Late summer of 1818*: Beethoven, stone deaf and soon to turn forty-eight, finishes his "Hammerklavier" Sonata, op. 106. The completion of this, his greatest work so far, begins the process that Maynard Solomon in his Beethoven biography describes as the composer's "reconstructing his life and completing his life's work." In his remaining eight and a half years he will compose his most rhetorical music and his most inward, his most public works and his most esoteric, his biggest pieces and his most compressed, compositions that celebrate the inexhaustible possibilities of the sonata style and others that propose utterly new approaches, works that are totally centered alongside a few that approach the bizarre. At no previous stage in Beethoven's life would the sheer comprehensiveness and multiplicity of the *Missa solemnis* have been possible.
- *Winter of 1818–1819*: Word gets around in Vienna that the Archduke Rudolph, son of Emperor Leopold II, is to be made a cardinal and archbishop of Olmütz (Olomouc) in Moravia. Rudolph, who had started to study composition, theory, and piano with Beethoven in 1803, had also become an understanding friend and a patron, one of the group of noblemen who banded together in 1808 to provide the composer with a lifetime stipend so as to keep him in Vienna. Rudolph was the one member of that group who was unfailingly punctual in his payments. No one else was the dedicatee of so extraordinary a list of Beethoven scores: the Fourth and Fifth Piano Concertos, three piano sonatas (the "Farewell," the "Hammerklavier," and Opus 111), the Opus 96 Violin Sonata, the "Archduke" Trio, and the *Great Fugue*. Of course, no relationship with Beethoven was uncomplicated, and this one was not exempt, either.
- *Early 1819*: Beethoven is one of about fifty composers to receive an invitation from Anton Diabelli, newly set up in the music-publishing business in Vienna, to contribute to a "patriotic anthology" by writing a variation on a little waltz by the ambitious publisher. Schubert, whose first publisher Diabelli was, and Liszt, still a young boy, are among those invited. Beethoven dislikes Diabelli's waltz, but before long, as the musicologist Ludwig Finscher put it, "his displeasure became productive," and he begins to work not on a variation, but on a whole series of them. In February or March, he also begins to sketch a Kyrie.
- *4 June 1819*: Rudolph, made a cardinal two months before, is appointed archbishop of Olmütz, and 9 March 1820 is set as the date

of his installation. Beethoven writes to him: "The day on which a High Mass composed by me is performed during the ceremonies solemnized for Your Imperial Highness will be the most glorious day of my life, and God will enlighten me so that my poor talents may contribute to the glorification of that solemn day." There is no evidence that Rudolph asked Beethoven for a Mass; it seems to be an offering made of the composer's free will.

- *July 1819*: Beethoven begins the Gloria.
- *August 1819*: Anton Schindler, later Beethoven's factotum and sometimes-mendacious biographer, visits the composer: "As soon as we entered . . . we heard the Master singing part of the fugue in the Credo—singing, howling, and stamping." For reasons both of chronology and of musical character, this must have been the "In gloria Dei patris" fugue from the Gloria rather than the "Et vitam venturi" from the Credo.
- *December 1819*: Beethoven completes the Gloria.
- *January–March 1820*: Beethoven drafts the Credo and begins to sketch the Sanctus. He also continues with the "Diabelli" Variations.
- *10 February 1820*: Offering the Mass to Simrock in Bonn, Beethoven begins a long series of questionable negotiations with publishers.
- *20 March 1820*: Rudolph is installed as archbishop of Olmütz. The music is by Haydn and Hummel.
- *April 1820*: Beethoven begins a set of three piano sonatas, opp. 109–11.
- *October 1820–March 1821*: Beethoven completes Opus 109. In persistently poor health, he works on the Credo and Sanctus, and begins the Benedictus. By New Year's Day 1821, he has also completed five bagatelles of what will be Opus 119.
- *March–August 1821*: Beethoven works on the Agnus Dei. Although miserable with jaundice, he begins Opus 110.
- *December 1821*: Beethoven begins Opus 111 and completes Opus 110.
- *Spring 1822*: Beethoven completes Opus 111. The Mass is complete in outline.
- *May–Early winter 1822*: Beethoven begins to sketch the String Quartet, Opus 127, returns to the "Diabelli" Variations, starts to give serious thought to the Ninth Symphony, writes the overture and chorus *For the Consecration of the House*, and completes the Opus 119 Bagatelles. He keeps adding to the "Diabelli" Variations and continues to tinker with the Mass, about which his biographer Alexander Wheelock Thayer would remark that it was "several times completed but never complete so long as it was within reach." He promises one

publisher the Mass by Easter and tells another that he has written two and is trying to decide which one to send him.

- *January–February 1823*: Beethoven writes to various courts offering manuscript copies of the Mass for fifty ducats, with a promise not to publish the score for the time being. He gets several acceptances and asks Goethe and Cherubini, among others, to put pressure on prospective buyers.

- *March 1823*: Beethoven sends a bound manuscript copy of the Mass to Archduke Rudolph.

- *April 1823*: Beethoven completes the "Diabelli" Variations, thirty-three in all. In comprehensiveness and sense of adventure they are a good match for the *Missa solemnis*.

- *Summer 1823*: Beethoven finally lets go of the Mass, about forty months after his self-imposed due date.

- *18 April 1824*: The Mass is performed in Saint Petersburg under the auspices of Prince Nikolai Galitzin, who has also commissioned three of Beethoven's last quartets.

- *7 May 1824*: The Ninth Symphony is performed in Vienna, preceded by the *Consecration of the House* overture and the Kyrie, Credo, and Agnus Dei of the *Missa solemnis*. Because concert performances of liturgical music are forbidden, the movements from the Mass are billed as "Three Grand Hymns" and sung to minimally relevant German texts.

- *26 March 1827*: Beethoven dies. Around the same time, and in accordance with a contract worked out three years before, the publisher Schott in Mainz issues full and piano-vocal scores of the *Missa solemnis*. This wraps up negotiations that had lasted seven years and had frustrated and enraged at least eight publishers.

To no other composition had Beethoven given so much time—time for sketching, composing, scoring, and polishing, and before that for historical, intellectual, and spiritual preparation. He had already set the Ordinary of the Mass once. That was in 1807 on commission from Prince Nikolaus Esterházy, who wanted the work for his wife's name day. (The six great Masses of Haydn's old age were composed for the same occasion in previous years.) "I believe I have treated the text as it has seldom been treated before," Beethoven said then. Esterházy's response to the music presented the reverse of that coin, a puzzled and somewhat insulting, "My dear Beethoven, what have you done this time?" (That, we might add, is puzzling to us: the C-major Mass is not radically different from Haydn's late Masses.) Beethoven left in anger, and when he published the C-major Mass in 1812, it bore a dedication to neither of the Esterházys but to Prince Ferdinand Kinsky, one of the guarantors of Beethoven's annuity.

Although brought up Roman Catholic, Beethoven had probably not entered a church since childhood unless to play music or listen to it. He therefore prepared for his Esterházy assignment by having the text newly translated and explained, line by line. Never an orthodox church-man, though glad to receive extreme unction on his deathbed, he was profoundly religious, especially in his later years. His diaries and note-books are full of prayers and invocations. Nature was the most nourish-ing of forces for him: he saw it, as did the theologian Christoph Christian Sturm in this passage that Beethoven copied out, as

> a glorious school for the heart. . . . Here I shall learn wisdom, the only wis-
> dom free from disillusionment. Here I shall learn to know God and enjoy
> a foretaste of heaven in that knowledge. Among such occupations, my
> earthly days will flow peacefully by until I am taken up into that world
> where I shall no longer be a student but a possessor of wisdom.

Another passage from Sturm that he cherished reads: "I will humbly sub-mit to all of life's chances and changes, and put my sole trust in Thy im-mutable goodness, O God!"

From Schiller's essay *The Mission of Moses* he copied and kept framed on his desk these words: "I am that which is. I am all that is, that was, and that will be. No mortal man has raised my veil. He is solely from Himself, and all things owe their being to Him alone." To Rudolph he wrote soon after completing the *Missa solemnis:* "There is no loftier mis-sion than to come nearer than other humans to the Godhead and to dis-seminate the divine rays among humankind."

Beethoven drew his sense of religion from many sources. He owned devotional books by Johann Michael Sailer, an influential if controver-sial figure who propagated a faith as subjective as the bounds of Catholic orthodoxy would allow. Beethoven was aware of the conflict between, on one side, the rather desiccated form of Catholicism sponsored by that Enlightenment hero, Emperor Joseph II, whose death he had mourned in a remarkable cantata written at age nineteen, and, on the other side, the distinctly moist revivalist currents stirred up by Matthias Werner and Clemens Maria Hofbauer, the latter canonized by Pope Pius X in 1909. One of Beethoven's close friends was August Friedrich Kanne, described by Warren Kirkendale in a singularly stimulating study of the *Missa solemnis* as the most talented, original, and alcoholic of Beethoven's intimate companions, a human encyclopedia, a former student of theology, and the composer of a Mass. He had become Vienna's most perceptive music critic and protagonist of Beethoven's music, and finally was to serve him as a torchbearer at his funeral and as necrologist.[2]

Kanne also wrote a history of the Mass sufficiently heterodox never to have made it out of the censor's office. He must have been a mine of information on history, tradition, and interpretation during the composing of the Missa solemnis.

In Beethoven: His Spiritual Development, J.W.N. Sullivan writes: "Beethoven's Missa solemnis shows that some of his most important experiences could be contained within the shell of words provided by the Mass." Martin Cooper, whose book Beethoven: The Last Decade offers the best brief account of the composer's religious attitudes and beliefs, is thinking along the same lines when he writes that Beethoven was

> a deeply religious man who was brought up formally as a Catholic and never formally renounced his Church membership, but only came at the end of his life, through misfortune and illness, to understand the close connection between the religious sentiments and often unformulated convictions of a lifetime and the fundamental teachings of the Church, to which he had been for the most part indifferent or hostile.

In contrasting the Missa solemnis with Bach's B-Minor Mass, Robert Shaw, who must have conducted more performances of it than anyone else in the work's history, always referred to Beethoven as someone who, unlike Bach, was forever on the quest of reinventing God. That is deeply true, but the greatness of the Missa solemnis derives in a very special way from the tension between that self-imposed quest and the powerful structure—the text of the Ordinary—within which Beethoven chose to work, however much he subjectified it in detail.

What begins to be clear is that in 1818–1819 Beethoven was profoundly ready—indeed, eager—to compose a Mass, and that the news of the Archduke's impending installation provided the probably unconsciously awaited occasion. Once that occasion had presented itself, the issue was how to give musical utterance to a broad, rich, intensely lived-with welter of thoughts and feelings.

When Beethoven began work on the Missa solemnis, he had been composing for something like thirty-seven years, for more than twenty-five

---

[2]"New Roads to Old Ideas in Beethoven's Missa solemnis," in The Creative World of Beethoven, ed. Paul Henry Lang (Norton, 1971). Later citations of Kirkendale are from the same source.

of them on the highest plane. That in itself is no mean preparation. His most recently completed piece, the stupendous "Hammerklavier" Sonata, established him as the most advanced composer alive, but Beethoven was also the man who, in the summer of 1818, wrote himself a note on how to find the key to the writing of "true church music": "Look through all the church chorales of the monks and also the strophes in the most correct translations and perfect prosody in Christian-Catholic psalms and hymns generally." Ten years earlier he had written: "In the old church modes the devotion is divine. . . . May God permit me to express it some day."

As long ago as 1810, Beethoven had tried to get hold of Bach's still unpublished B-Minor Mass, a work he knew by reputation—and evidently more, since by way of identification in his request he quoted the ground bass of the "Crucifixus." Now he drew as well on the rich collections of his old friend and patron Prince Franz Joseph von Lobkowitz (the prince himself had died in 1816), and he added to his curriculum the sacred music of Carl Philipp Emanuel Bach. From the notebooks in which visitors carried on conversations with the deaf composer, we learn that Beethoven was looking for and evidently found the *Dodecachordon*, a treatise on the church modes and counterpoint published in 1547 by Heinrich Glarean, a Swiss theorist, and the *Istitutioni harmoniche*, a wide-ranging book of theory, history, speculation, and criticism, a sort of *Harmonielehre* of its day, put out in 1558 by Gioseffo Zarlino, whom Dragan Plamenac describes in Oliver Strunk's *Source Readings in Music History* as "easily the most influential personality in the history of musical theory from Aristoxenus to Rameau."

In sum, as Maynard Solomon puts it, feeling "the Classic tradition to be insufficient for the composition of a major [Mass] or for the expression of highly sublimated spirituality . . . [Beethoven] systematically and painstakingly set about mastering the musical vocabularies of religious music of earlier periods." Even "ordinary" sacred music of Beethoven's day tended to make certain obeisances to the past—for example, through the use of fugue, which was less a contemporary technique than one in quotation marks, as it were. From writings such as E.T.A. Hoffmann's review of his C-Major Mass and Hoffmann's essay *Old and New Church Music*, Beethoven would have been aware of current discussions on the appropriateness of maintaining separate styles for sacred and secular music. But Beethoven was ready to go much further. Martin Cooper likens his studies of early music to Milton's study of Virgil while writing *Paradise Lost* and to Virgil's study of Homer while working on the *Aeneid*. As Kirkendale notes: "We see that [Beethoven] not only retained traditional thought to an unexpected degree, but even uncovered much older, buried traditions."

Kyrie

Beethoven begins with a D-major chord, *forte*, for woodwinds, horns, strings, and organ. D major, the trumpets-and-drums key of Classical and Baroque music, is itself a quotation, a *topos* or traditional formulation. At the same time, Beethoven took pride in making "ordinary" things like chords extraordinary and individual, and this D-major chord, rich and luminous, firm but neither brilliant nor aggressive, is a vivid instance: one could not mistake it for any other in his music. The tempo direction—actually it is a direction for both tempo and character—of *Assai sostenuto* (very sustained) is supplemented by something further for the conductor, the singers, and the players to reflect on: *Mit Andacht* (devoutly, or with devotion). This is something new in Beethoven, though we shall meet it again in the *Missa*, and a few years later he would use *Adagio ma non troppo, ma divoto* for the awed "Ihr stürzt nieder" (You fall headlong) in the finale of the Ninth Symphony. And across the top of the first page of his *Missa* manuscript, Beethoven has written "Von Herzen—möge es wieder—zu Herzen gehen!" (From the heart—may it go again—to the heart!).

But to return for a moment to that D-major chord: the most remarkable thing about it is its rhythmic placement. As a sonority it has enough weight for a downbeat, but in fact it begins in the middle of a measure. Now if you are not watching the conductor you cannot tell that the music starts on "two," but the entrance of the trumpets and drums a second later clearly marks the "one" and thus retroactively places the opening chord for us. The chord is twice repeated, articulating the rhythm of the word "Kyrie." Once again, Kirkendale is provocative. He identifies this as a Kyrie topos that has "opened countless orchestral Masses," Beethoven's own earlier Mass among them, and continues:

> Recent research has demonstrated that slow tempo and avoidance of melodic and harmonic movement belonged since the early Baroque to the musical decorum of the King of Heaven. The *topos* reflects the ancient conception of God as the one who possesses *apatheia*, is free from all passions, and, as the first cause of being, is himself immovable. . . . Beethoven's formulation, unlike those of his predecessors, begins on a weak beat, thus removed still further from the dynamics of human passion.

One needs also to put Beethoven's arresting rhythmic gesture into the context of his lifelong delight in surprising rhythms and accents, most often manifested in his habit of arriving at a new harmony that you expect, but just a hair before you expect it. No work of his so often confounds one's ordinary rhythmic expectations as the *Missa solemnis*, and this is a characteristic Beethoven wants to give notice of with the very first sound. But then he quickly orients us as to scale, mood, key, and pace, and the clarinets, followed by bassoon and oboe, enter with what is unmistakably the word "Kyrie." There are few works in which instruments are so intimately drawn into the task of pronouncing and interpreting a text. When at last the singers enter, they simply make more explicit what we already know. The orchestral chords become great choral invocations; solo voices take on the lines of the solo winds.

Beethoven had once written to Rudolph: "On Him alone I place my reliance and hope that in all my manifold miseries the All-Highest will not let me perish utterly." His "Kyrie eleison" setting, with those solo voices so small and lonely yet so fervent and confident (their "Kyries" are on downbeats), is a beautiful translation of that thought into music. "Christe eleison," the more personal prayer, moves with new energy and vigor. Then, by way of a harmonic pun, stunning and bold in its simplicity, Beethoven returns to his "Kyrie," which sinks to a serene close. The choir's final "-son" together with its accompanying chord is, like the opening chord, on "two."

Gloria

The Kyrie text consists of only three different words; that of the Gloria is broad, varied, and immensely rhetorical. The movement begins with a mighty uprush symbolic of the celebrant's raising his arms in joy. Here, too, the voices, pronouncing the words, have but to echo what the orchestra has already sung. "Et in terra pax" and "adoramus te" bring the hush that is traditional in the setting of those words. Through "glorificamus te," the singers and players exult ever more, with both rhythm and harmony reinforcing the brilliance of the sound. A sudden change to a newly pliant and lyrical music heralds the "Gratias agimus tibi." At "Domine Deus," this yields to a return of the opening music, but now in the vastly distant key of E-flat. For the word "omnipotens" Beethoven reserves his first *fff* and the first blast of trombones. It is also on that word that he suddenly swings back into D major with one of those shifts of his that are not modulations but a ruthless picking up of the harmony and putting it down somewhere else: The potential for drastic harmonic change includes the ability here to move in a single beat from the dominant seventh of E-flat to the doorstep of D.

Traditionally the "Qui tollis" is sung to slower music, and here Beethoven sets the words in a *larghetto* whose beats are sufficiently slow to allow for much internal rhythmic elaboration for the pleas of "miserere nobis." The music waxes intense, the orchestra emits great shudders, and, the tenor showing the way, the soloists preface their "misereres" with entirely unliturgical and poignantly human "O's." "Quoniam tu solus sanctus" traditionally reintroduces faster music, and Beethoven sets this text to a hugely striding *Allegro maestoso*. The tenors lead off, and what a striking thing it is how often in the *Missa solemnis* Beethoven entrusts the task of introducing new ideas to that voice.[3]

At last Beethoven arrives at the ferociously emphatic fugue on "in gloria Dei patris," the one Schindler presumably heard him sing and howl and stamp that August day in 1819. It unfolds at great breadth, more so than anything in the Mass so far. The soloists add their voices to the assertion of God's glory, the harmonies move with sometimes-bewildering speed, the tempo increases, voices and instruments join in most unfugal unisons. The "Amen" has sounded, and Beethoven makes as though to wind up with some of his characteristically vehement dominant-and-tonic cadences, when suddenly the tumult of the "Gloria in excelsis Deo" bursts out once more, and with wilder rhythmic dislocations than ever. The final shout of "Gloria" explodes into the spaces of the cathedral *after* the orchestra has finished—an amazing inspiration that came to Beethoven in the course of his very last revisions to the score.

Credo

The first chord of the Credo is mighty indeed, although, poised on the verge of B-flat and lacking trumpets and drums, it seems muted in color and harmony after the Gloria's final D-major conflagration. Once again the orchestra speaks the text before the voices do, and for Beethoven this text is not so much "Credo" as "Credo, credo." There is, as Stravinsky remarked about his own Mass, much to believe, and there is also much to illustrate. "Omnipotentem" is again the occasion for a *fortissimo* of special weight and glory, and Beethoven observes the traditional hush that distinguishes the invisible from the visible.

Soon we hear what touches Beethoven most deeply. In the first moment of real let-up to the singing, a few instruments play a rising scale to introduce, in a wondrously soft D-flat major, words of awe and gratitude: "qui propter nos homines et propter nostram salutem" (who for us men and for our salvation). The conclusion of the clause "descendit de coelis"

[3]Kirkendale suggests that this can be related to the traditional role of tenor as narrator in Passion settings.

is grandly enunciated, the better to set off the marvel now to come. Beethoven gives us a sudden shift of harmony and pace, and slowly, with all the distance and mystery lent by the old church modes, the tenor tells of the Incarnation.[4] The other solo singers continue the thought, and on the words "de spiritu sancto" a single flute illuminates the texture with its weightless flutter, an image long identified as depicting the Holy Spirit as heavenly messenger in the form of a dove. The chorus reenters on an almost toneless murmur. But instantly we are returned to earth, that is, to D major and *fortissimo* and to the tenor's triumphant proclamation, "et homo factus est." Beethoven made a note to himself at this spot, "hier menschlich" (here human), and we can hear that "Menschlichkeit" not only in the bright solidity of D major but also in the repetition of "et" and the cantabile glow of the beautiful cello line.

Swiftly Beethoven moves to the "Crucifixus," with strange before-the-beat attacks borrowed from the Representation of Chaos in Haydn's *Creation*. Most of Beethoven's attention goes to "sub Pontio Pilato passus et sepultus est." If the "Crucifixus" is brief, "et resurrexit tertiam die, secundum scripturas," announced by the tenors in a single, wild shout of reckless excitement, goes by even more swiftly. Returning to modal harmony and set *a cappella*—and in that respect, all but unique in the Missa—it jumps out in extraordinarily vivid relief. Beethoven makes magnificent announcement of Christ's coming again in glory to judge both the quick and the dead. Clearly to be heard here, as it was at the "Incarnatus," the "homo factus est," and the "resurrexit," is that most personal device of isolating and repeating the word "et" for suspense and emphasis. The "judicium" itself is announced by the trombone because, to German-speaking people, what we call the Last Trumpet is "die letzte Posaune," the Last Trombone.

Then comes the third section of the Creed, the series of doctrinal clauses that begins with "Et in spiritum sanctum." These have not usually stimulated composers the way the sections concerning the first two persons of the Trinity have: Haydn hurries over them in his most amiable *allegro* manner; Schubert leaves them out altogether. Beethoven's setting has been much commented upon, puzzled over, and criticized. In his musical design this is the recapitulation, and he begins by reintroducing the "Credo, credo" phrase he proclaimed so powerfully at the beginning. What is remarkable, though, is that "Credo, credo" will not go away: someone is always singing it right across the clauses about the genealogy of the Holy Spirit, the one catholic and apostolic church, and baptism.

---

[4]In the autograph, the line is given to the chorus tenors; in all subsequent copies overseen by Beethoven it is assigned to the soloist.

And because it is a melodic phrase both sharply profiled and familiar, it commands our attention much more than do the repeated-note chantings of "Dominum et vivificantem," "unam sanctam catholicam et apostolicam ecclesiam," and the other clauses.

The traditional interpretation has been that, to the fideistic Beethoven, the general necessity of belief and faith outweighed the importance of these technical-political clauses. Theodor W. Adorno quotes with approval Eduard Steuermann's observation that the stubborn insistence on "Credo, credo" is the frenzy of a nonbeliever desperately trying to talk himself into believing, a reading I find preposterous.[5] Once again, Warren Kirkendale has something interesting and helpful to contribute. Citing many examples in support of his thesis, he suggests that

> we may relate Beethoven's treatment of dogma to his well-known statement that religion and figured bass are "closed subjects on which there should be no further dispute." Declamation on a quasi-monotone often serves for affirmative statements which reject contradiction. . . . Here in the *Missa solemnis* the monotone declamation of dogma combines simultaneously with the determined *Credo* motif to form a most forceful expression of faith.

"Et exspecto resurrectionem mortuorum" unites the voices in a splendid and climactic unison, after which Beethoven begins, quietly and with no urgency to be assertive, the words about the life of the world to come. As tradition dictates, "et vitam venturi" is a fugue, its subject here an expansion of the "credo" motif. With its repeated high notes and its long garlands of quarter-notes, it is probably the most difficult fugue ever written for voices. Beethoven spins it out with a wondrous sense of timelessness. Like the fugue at the end of the Gloria, it moves into a quicker tempo. This time, though, the close is sublime and mysterious peace— and once again some strangely dislocated rhythms. Brahms studied these pages carefully when he was writing his *German Requiem*.

Sanctus and Benedictus

The Sanctus is an *Adagio*, and here we again encounter the direction *Mit Andacht*. It is music very different from the only previous *Adagio*, which was the "Crucifixus"—different in meter (2/4 now versus 3/4 then), but different also in character, the "Crucifixus" being a craggily defined, active piece, whereas the Sanctus is still. It also brings a new kind of

[5]See also Adrienne Rich's *The Ninth Symphony of Beethoven Understood at Last as a Sexual Message*, from *Diving into the Wreck* (Norton, 1973)—a punchy poem, though I have not yet been persuaded by the point Rich makes so powerfully.

sonority: the rich, dark sound—a bridge from Mozart to Brahms—of an orchestra in which violas and cellos are divided into two sections each and trumpets stay with their lowest notes, and from which flutes, oboes, and violins are absent. Again we hear choral murmuring. Then the "Pleni sunt coeli" bursts forth in a quick fugue, actually not more than a fugal exposition plus another eight bars. The accompaniment is weighty, leading to much speculation as to whether Beethoven had written the vocal parts into the solo staves by mistake; however, all copies seen and supervised by him are consistent on this point. "Osanna" is a similar movement, quicker still, and more brilliant.

Now comes the central moment of the Mass. The celebrant elevates the Host, and the Missal calls for the singing to cease so that the choir may join the congregation in adoration. Tradition has the organist play—perhaps improvise—an interlude before the Benedictus. Beethoven actually composes such a bridge, but for orchestra. Calling it "Praeludium," he means that it is a prelude to the Benedictus, but also remembers that "präludieren" means to improvise, thus referring to the traditional practice at this moment in the Mass. For the Praeludium—to me, the most miraculous page in the *Missa solemnis*—Beethoven reduces the orchestra to flutes, bassoon and contrabassoon, violas and cellos (both divided), basses, and organ, a sound at once glowing and covered. This sonority suggests a sublime translation of organ music.

The harmonic changes become slower. A beam of brightest light penetrates the soft penumbra, as though from the cupola. It is the Real Presence, Christ upon the altar and in the Host. In earthly terms, it is a chord, more than an octave higher than any we have heard since the end of the "Osanna," sounded by just two flutes and a single violin. Step by step these gleaming sounds descend, and the basses in the chorus intone the words "Benedictus qui venit in nomine Domini" (Blessed is he who cometh in the name of the Lord). As the brass and drums softly repeat the "Benedictus" rhythm—it is one of the few moments in the *Missa* where the singers pronounce a text ahead of the instruments—the violin, *dolce cantabile*, soars in what Martin Cooper has so aptly called "a celestial 'Romance.'" We can find music something like this in the sublime *Molto adagio* of the E-minor Quartet, op. 59, no. 2, and again in the slow movement of Opus 127, the quartet that followed the *Missa solemnis*. No Mass has anything remotely resembling it. Except for a few beautifully placed blossomings, the singing is held to chantlike, repeated-note iterations of the words, while the violin, growing ever more ecstatic, carries the burden of the spacious discourse. So powerful is the impression of this passage that it embraces even the return of the "Osanna." To Adorno, this intensely personal music suggests the occasional practice of "late medieval artists placing their own likenesses somewhere on their tabernacle so that they might not be forgotten."

Agnus Dei and "Dona nobis pacem"

After that radiant Benedictus, the Agnus Dei begins in B minor (a key Beethoven thought of as black), *adagio,* and in the dark sounds of bassoons, horns, and low-register strings. Except where explicit recapitulations are involved, the Agnus Dei and the "Incarnatus" are the only two movements (out of thirty-two) to use the same combination of key and meter, though their harmonic and rhythmic physiognomies could hardly be more different. The first invocation of the Lamb of God resonates in the voice of the solo bass, introduced by bassoon and accompanied by the chorus. Alto and tenor sing the second; and the third, the music having grown ever more forceful, is given to the entire solo quartet, with the chorus joining in.

Gently, Beethoven slips into a lilting 6/8, a meter not heard before in the *Missa,* and begins the "Dona nobis pacem." Here he attaches another of his glosses in German, marking this page *Bitte um innern und äussern Frieden* (Plea for inner and outer peace). It is the prayer of a man who had lived most of his adult life in war: he was just into his twenties when the Napoleonic wars began, and there was nowhere you could live in Europe without being affected by those. He was forty-four the year of Waterloo, and he remembered well the terrifying bombardment of Vienna in 1809 when, with pillows around his head to protect the remaining shreds of his hearing from the roar of the cannon, he sat in a friend's basement struggling over the sketches of the "Emperor" Concerto. Kirkendale—to go to him one last time—points out that Beethoven's plea and the astonishing musical form it takes are not merely subjective excursions, but that

> the reference to inner and outer peace . . . is deeply rooted in ancient theological concepts. Prayers for inner and outer peace had formed an essential part of the liturgy from the earliest Christian era. Beethoven's dual concept is fully developed in twelfth- and thirteenth-century commentaries on the *Dona nobis pacem.* . . . That Beethoven attached particular importance to the peace of mind is revealed by the note in his sketches for the Agnus Dei: "Strength of the sentiments of inner peace above all . . . Victory!" Does the word "victory" in this context allude to the familiar image of the Lamb of God carrying the flag of victory?

For a few moments the music proceeds in a polyphony only slightly restless. Then comes one of those interruptions so characteristic of the

Missa solemnis: four bars for chorus *a cappella* (the first since the six-measure shout of "et resurrexit") and an unmistakable allusion to "And he shall reign for ever and ever" from the "Hallelujah Chorus" in Handel's *Messiah.* Later the allusion becomes more explicit still, virtually a quotation. The flow returns to its previous course. The pleas of "pacem, pacem" become more urgent. Suddenly the music ceases altogether. Silence, distant drumming, unrest in the strings, far-off trumpet calls, and appeals to the Lamb: *timidamente* and *ängstlich* (fearful) for the alto, who begins them; a full *fortissimo* outcry for the soprano. The sounds of war have come very near. Once again, the music seems to get back on track with an extensive and developed presentation of the 6/8 "Dona nobis pacem" material. From there, Beethoven moves into an orchestral fugato, quick, intense, and incorporating his most rapid harmonic changes since the "In gloria Dei patris" fugue. But without warning, the trumpeting and the drumming are upon us again, fiercer, the words of the chorus compressed into anguished, terrified repetitions of "dona, dona" and "dona pacem."

Nothing in the *Missa solemnis* has been more discussed and disputed than this war music. Schindler was so offended by it that he recommended cutting it. The immediate model to hand would have been Haydn's *Missa in tempore belli* (Mass in Time of War) of 1797, although the violence of Beethoven's music, his Goyaesque picture of sheer bloody terror drawn without reservation, has in its effect nothing in common with his teacher's stylized and "classical" representation.[6]

At last something like peace envelops the music. There is one final reminder, a drum on a strangely foreign note and coming as though from a great distance. The chorus responds to this with its softest pleas of "pacem, pacem." Into the stillness there falls a gentle rain of scales, *pianissimo* and staccato. The chorus sings one last "dona pacem" to the Handelian phrase: Hallelujah and thanksgiving for peace and victory— inner and outer—by the man who was for Beethoven the monarch of composers and before whom alone he "bent the knee." Perhaps it is not by chance that this is also music associated with England's victory in the Napoleonic wars. And upon this mosaic, this often-so-private utterance in a public genre, this most-intensely-worked composition of his whole life, Beethoven sets the seal of an orchestral "Ite, missa est"—six bars of radiant simplicity.

The *Missa solemnis* is an offering to God and a declaration of love for God. I have given many words to that point but not, I think, too many.

---

[6]We do not know whether the fanfares here were actual military signals of the Austrian (or French?) armies: such signals were military secrets and not written down.

The *Missa* is also, I believe, a declaration of human love, of the composer's feelings for the friend and patron whom protocol made, in a sense, inaccessible. And Beethoven, I feel sure, also meant us to perceive that love as a reflection of human love for God and God's love for humankind. It is that intersection of the deeply personal and the hieratic that makes the *Missa solemnis* so moving—for many of us, so uniquely and penetratingly moving.

Of all the inscriptions that composers have written on their scores, two have always touched and stirred me beyond all others. One is what Beethoven wrote on the first page of the *Missa solemnis*: "From the heart—may it go again—to the heart." The other I have quoted elsewhere in this book—in its proper place, as it were. It is a sentence of John Ruskin's that Edward Elgar placed as a postscript to the score of his oratorio *The Dream of Gerontius*. The tone is not Beethoven's, but for what they say, these words could stand after the last bar of the *Missa* as well: "This is the best of me; for the rest, I ate, and drank, and slept, loved and hated, like another; my life was as the vapour, and is not; but this I saw and knew: this, if anything of mine, is worth your memory."

Hector Berlioz [signature]

Hector Berlioz

Hector-Louis Berlioz was born at Côte-Saint-André, department of Isère, France, on 11 December 1803 and died in Paris on 8 March 1869.

Requiem (*Grande Messe des Morts*), op. 8

The Requiem was commissioned in March 1837 by Comte Adrien de Gasparin, Minister of the Interior, for a ceremony honoring the 1830 Revolution and those who lost their lives in that cause. Berlioz completed the score on 29 June 1837, but it incorporates ideas that go back as far as 1824. The first performance, with François-Antoine Habeneck conducting a massive ensemble of 210 singers and 190 players, took place in the Chapel of Saint Louis at the Invalides, Paris, on 5 December 1837. The tenor soloist was Gilbert-Louis Duprez.

Solo tenor; chorus. Four flutes, two oboes, two English horns, two clarinets, four bassoons, eight horns, six trumpets, four cornets, eight trombones, four tubas, timpani and percussion (requiring fourteen players), and a string section of fifty violins, twenty each of violas and cellos, and eighteen basses. For the chorus, Berlioz asks for eighty women (altos have extended independent parts only in the "Quaerens me," the Sanctus, and the Agnus Dei), sixty tenors, and seventy basses, but adds that these numbers "are only relative, and one can, space permitting, double or triple the vocal forces and increase the orchestra proportionally. If one had an immense chorus of 700 or 800 voices, the entire group should sing only in the *Dies irae*, the *Tuba mirum*, and the *Lacrimosa*, using no more than 400 voices in the rest of the score."

Charles X of France was the younger brother of Louis XVI, guillotined in 1793, and of Louis XVIII, who had become titular monarch in 1795 and had been installed as puppet king by the Allies both times they had sent Napoleon into exile.[1] Even in the 1820s, more than thirty years after the revolution that cost his eldest brother his head, Charles clung firmly to his belief in the divine right of kings. Constitutional monarchy held no charms for him: he would rather hew wood, he declared, than reign under the conditions his colleague in England had to put up with.

Three days of violent protest in July 1830 put an end to his six years on the throne. Under his successor, Louis-Philippe (not counting the four-day tenure of Charles's ten-year-old grandson, the Duc de Bordeaux), an annual commemorative service honored those who had lost their lives in the revolution of 1830, and it was for one of those services that Comte de Gasparin bade Berlioz to compose a Requiem.

The text of the Requiem, Berlioz wrote in his *Memoirs*, was a "prey I had long lain in wait for. Now at last it was mine, and I fell upon it with a kind of fury. My brain felt as though it would explode with the pressure of ideas. The outline of one piece was barely sketched before the next formed itself in my mind. I could not write fast enough." Gratefully, Berlioz dedicated the score to de Gasparin, an act that gave him the greater satisfaction because by the time the score was completed, that cultivated minister, "part of that small minority of French politicians interested in music, and of the still more select company who have a feeling for it," was no longer in power.

But if writing the Requiem was easy and a pleasure, almost nothing else connected with its early history was. The government Director of Fine Arts tried to abort the commission. The obvious candidate for this commission would have been Luigi Cherubini; offended to see it go instead to an unruly anti-Establishment composer, that powerful figure in the musical life of Paris was therefore in active opposition. The commission could not be rescinded, but it was decreed that the

[1]Louis XVII, son of Louis XVI and Marie Antoinette, briefly succeeded his father on the throne and died in prison at age ten.

commemorative service in July 1837 would have no music. Purchase orders and invoices and memoranda made their sluggish way from one government bureau to another, and it took five months for the copyists, the choristers (who had already been in rehearsal), and Berlioz himself to get paid.

Then, just at the point when there seemed to be no hope for a performance, the news came that Field Marshal Damrémont had been shot through the heart in the assault on the Algerian town of Constantine.[2] A service was to be held in the Invalides for Damrémont and the others who had lost their lives in the siege of Constantine. This came under the jurisdiction of the Minister of War, General Bernard, who was friendly to Berlioz—or at least, not against him—and suddenly the Requiem was on again.

Bernard, however, had a nasty surprise to spring on the composer, which was that the performance would have to be conducted by François-Antoine Habeneck, *premier chef* at the Opéra, which made him the most powerful figure among Parisian performers. Habeneck was one of the old-style leaders who conducted with a bow, and not from a score, but from a first-violin part with the other instrumental lines cued in; nevertheless, he was an able musician and a doggedly thorough workman, and during his years at the Opéra performance standards were high. Wagner, far from easy to please (and particularly by a Frenchman), praised his performances of the Beethoven symphonies, most of which Habeneck introduced to Paris, as the best he had ever heard, and indeed those concerts were life-changing experiences for Berlioz as well.

Berlioz and Habeneck were on generally poor terms, a situation not improved when, at the first performance of the Requiem, Habeneck laid down his bow and took a pinch of snuff at the first measure—with its tricky tempo change—of the "Tuba mirum." "With my habitual distrust I had stayed just behind Habeneck," Berlioz reported.

> I had been keeping my eye on him. In a flash I turned on my heel, sprang forward in front of him and, stretching out my arm, marked out the four great beats of the new tempo. The bands followed me, and everything went off in order. I conducted the piece to the end. . . . When at the final words of the chorus, Habeneck saw that the *Tuba mirum* was saved, he said, "God, I was in a cold sweat. Without you we would have been lost." "I know," I replied, looking him straight in the eye.

[2]In 1827 in the Kasbah of Algiers, a Turkish official had struck the French consul with a fly swatter, setting off a series of incidents and reprisals that led to the French conquest and colonization of Algeria.

What was this about? That Habeneck took snuff at that point is certain. The question is, was this negligence or malice? In his edition of the Berlioz *Memoirs*, David Cairns, after summing up the evidence calmly and at length, concludes:

> As for Habeneck's motive, this is pure conjecture. [The pianist and conductor Charles] Hallé was sure it was thoughtlessness; yet, even allowing for the vast difference between modern and early nineteenth-century notions, the opening of the *Tuba mirum* is of all places in the Requiem the most unlikely for snuff-taking if the conductor is merely negligent, the most likely if he is actuated by malice.

Elsewhere, Cairns writes: "The account of [Berlioz and Habeneck's] relations given in the *Memoirs*, though heightened here and there for effect . . . will seem improbable only to those who have no experience of musical politics and no inkling of the peculiar venomousness of the French variety." But Berlioz acknowledged that ultimately "the success of the Requiem was complete, despite all the intrigues and stratagems, blatant or underhand, official and unofficial, which had been resorted to to stop it."

Berlioz is one of those seemingly paradoxical figures, the agnostics or atheists who composed great works of sacred music. (In the case of Berlioz one must add to the Requiem the 1849 *Te Deum* and *L'Enfance du Christ*, completed in 1854.) The nearest he came in his adult years to having a god was in his passion for and faith in Shakespeare. "It is you that are our father, our father in heaven, if there is a heaven," he exclaimed when his wife, Harriet Smithson, a Shakespearean actor, died in 1854, an alcoholic, paralyzed, and ravaged by years of illness. The other members of Berlioz's quasi-divine literary trinity were Virgil, whom he was taught as a boy to love by his father and whom he celebrated in his opera *Les Troyens*, and Goethe, to whom he set a grand monument in *La Damnation de Faust*.

Berlioz had been a fervent believer when he was very young—"For seven whole years, [religion] was the joy of my life"—but, as he writes in his *Memoirs*, "we have long since fallen out." As a twenty-year-old student he wrote a Mass and in 1831 he sketched an opera-oratorio whose subject was "The Last Day of the World," and parts of both those works found homes in the Requiem. But his falling-away did not keep him from composing the three sacred masterpieces just mentioned, the two later ones written without commissions and entirely out of his own desire. Moreover, as David Cairns has pointed out, Berlioz's secular works abound in religious imagery:

> Think of the haunting Funeral Procession in the *Romeo and Juliet* Symphony, the Pilgrims' March in *Harold in Italy* . . . the chanting monks in the last act of *Benvenuto Cellini*, the peasants praying at their wayside cross as Faust rides to the abyss, and the Amen chords on which the tormented *idée fixe* comes momentarily to rest at the end of the first movement of the *Symphonie fantastique*.

As it would be for Verdi later on, religion was for Berlioz the stuff of drama, and he treats the text as a libretto, feeling free to reorder and to omit. One difference between the two masters is that in Berlioz—perhaps it is a difference between Berlioz and all the other nonbelieving composers—you feel that the apostasy did not happen without pain. It is as though he can admit in his music—or cannot help admitting—what he could not permit himself to acknowledge in the *Memoirs*. Again I quote Cairns: "[The music] conveys an intense regret that he finds it impossible to be [a believer], and a profound awareness of the need, the desperate need to believe and to worship. His own lack of faith is used . . . to evoke the eternal hopes and fears of the human race . . . Berlioz's imagination believes, even if his intellect does not."

Berlioz begins with the chorus and modest orchestral forces of woodwinds, horns, and strings. (All through the Requiem he is sparing—and precise—with the heavy brass.) He uses an expressive *cantabile*, for instance, in the "Requiem aeternam" and "Te decet hymnus," contrasted with a quiet rhythmic declamation for "Et lux perpetua" and "Kyrie eleison." In fact, when the voices first enter he suggests both manners, the basses' melody being accompanied by the detached syllables of the tenors, who in turn are doubled by the bassoons playing the same melody legato.

The "Dies irae" begins with the same vocal and orchestral forces, and with striking contrast between the stern phrase of the cellos and basses (quite obsessive, this will turn out to be) and the plaintive line of the sopranos and woodwinds.

At the "Tuba mirum," the evocation of the Last Trumpet, Berlioz in a dramatic stroke adds four brass groups, stationed north, east, south, and west, at the corners of the grand mass of singers and instrumentalists. Let Berlioz describe it:

> First all four groups break in simultaneously . . . then successively, challenging and answering one another from a distance, the entries piling up, each a third higher than the one before. It is . . . of the utmost importance to indicate the four beats of the new, slower tempo very clearly the moment it is reached; otherwise the great cataclysm, a musical representation of the Last Judgment, prepared for with such deliberation and employing

an exceptional combination of forces in a manner at that time unprecedented and not attempted since—a passage which will, I hope, endure as a
landmark in music—is mere noise and pandemonium, a monstrosity.[3]

(It was just there that "our hero of the snuffbox," as Berlioz calls Habeneck, committed his indiscretion.)

Given a highly resonant acoustic such as the Invalides afforded, the
effect of this passage is stunning, provided also that the listener does not
mind a certain amount of imprecision; at least I have never heard a performance in which the ensemble was not a bit frayed. Part of the problem
is the inability of conductors to resist the temptation of placing the four
brass groups at the corners of the hall rather than the corners of the performing group as Berlioz asks.[4]

As the "Tuba mirum" proceeds, Berlioz also unleashes a tremendous barrage of percussion produced by four pairs of timpani, two bass
drums, four tam-tams, and ten pairs of cymbals. As Death and Nature
stand astounded—"Mors stupebit et natura"—the music falls into silence. Here is where Berlioz recycled some music from his 1824 Mass.

The obsessive bass phrase from the beginning of the "Dies irae"
continues to sound through the "Quid sum miser," a movement both
brief and quiet in which the words are assigned almost entirely to the
tenors, who are particularly asked to express humility and fear in their
singing. English horns, bassoons, cellos, and basses accompany.

The "Rex tremendae majestatis" is another conception on a huge
scale, and on the words "ne cadam in obscurum!" (lest I fall into darkness!) the Day of Judgment brass and percussion intervene once more. But
thought of the Fount of Mercy, "Salva me, fons pietatis," brings quiet.

"Quaerens me sedisti lassus" (Seeking me, Thou didst sit weary)—
words that, according to Donald Tovey, "Dr. Johnson sometimes tried to

---

[3]Berlioz must have known the *Symphonic Ode* by his teacher Jean-François Le Sueur, a work
written in 1801 to celebrate the anniversary of the 1789 Revolution, and which calls for four
orchestras, each stationed at one of the corners of the Invalides, where the Berlioz Requiem
would be performed thirty-six years later. Berlioz's claim of originality—"a manner at that
time unprecedented"—is surely an instance, and far from the only one, of memory edged out
by invention. This does not make the *Memoirs* less than a wonderful book and a delight to read.
[4]The challenge of where to place the four groups is more complicated than at first it appears.
The Berlioz scholar Hugh Macdonald notes that "Berlioz's instructions almost prevent the
bands from being heard separately" and adds, "Pragmatism should overrule authenticity,
shouldn't it?" Another leading Berlioz scholar, D. Kern Holoman, who has also conducted the
Requiem several times, observes that while "the back two [groups] are easy to place, to the left
and right of the choir, the front two, practically speaking, have to go where they will fit," and
that is not always easy to figure out, either in concert halls or in churches. Holoman notes,
too, that "it's also important to get N E S W correct, else the antiphony goes wrong in the
Lacrimosa."

quote, but never without bursting into tears"—is sung by unaccompanied voices and very softly throughout.

Sheer terror whips through the "lamentable day" called up by the "Lacrimosa." After the gentle interlude of "Pie Jesu," the brass choirs and percussion join to tie this movement to the earlier parts of the "Dies irae."

The Offertory, "Domine, Jesu Christe," is another movement of touching musical delicacy. At the same time, here is Berlioz's text-setting at its boldest as the chorus stammers out the words with great spaces between them. Almost to the end, the voices sing on just two notes, and only the word "promisisti"—in the phrase "quam olim Abrahae promisisti" (which Thou didst once promise unto Abraham)"—releases them.

The "Hostias" is for male voices with instrumental punctuation. But what punctuation it is, that series of chords for four high flutes with eight trombones swelling and receding on their deepest pedal notes!

High solo violins, flute, and violas divided into four sections and playing "a very dense tremolo" accompany the solo tenor and the choral responses in the Sanctus. The "Hosanna" is fugued, and Berlioz implores the chorus to sing "without violence, sustaining the notes well instead of accenting them one by one." He makes the return of the Sanctus into something extraordinary by adding the sounds of cymbals and bass drum in ghostly *pianissimo*. At the first performance the tenor solo was taken by Gilbert-Louis Duprez, the first Edgardo in Donizetti's *Lucia di Lammermoor* and also Berlioz's first Benvenuto Cellini, in which opera he got lost at the premiere when his wife's physician arrived in mid-performance to signal in pantomime the birth of a baby boy.

The Agnus Dei, like the "Dies irae" and the Offertory, is a movement in which Berlioz somewhat reorders the text. This is a movement of summation and of recapitulation of words, musical themes, and textures. Woodwinds, trombones, and voices sing repeated Amens across the *pianissimo* arpeggios of strings and the softly thudding punctuation of eight kettledrums.

Johannes Brahms

Johannes Brahms was born in the Free City of Hamburg on 7 May 1833 and died in Vienna on 3 April 1897.

A German Requiem on Words from Holy Scripture, op. 45

Using an idea from 1854 for its second movement, Brahms began work on his *German Requiem* early in 1865 and completed all but what is now the fifth movement in August 1866. Johannes Herbeck conducted the first three movements in Vienna on 1 December 1867. The first performance of the six movements then extant was given in the Bremen cathedral on Good Friday 1868, with the composer conducting and Julius Stockhausen as baritone soloist. Brahms added the fifth movement, "Ihr habt nun Traurigkeit," in May 1868; that was first sung in Zurich on 17 September that same year by Ida Suter-Weber, with Friedrich Hegar conducting the Zurich Tonhalle Orchestra. The work was first given in its final seven-movement version in Leipzig on 18 February 1869 with Carl Reinecke, conducting the Gewandhaus Orchestra and Chorus, and soloists Emilie Bellingrath-Wagner and Franz Krückl.

Soprano and baritone soloists, four-part mixed chorus. Two flutes and piccolo, two oboes, two clarinets, two bassoons and contrabassoon, four horns, two

trumpets, three trombones, bass tuba, harp (only one part, but preferably doubled), timpani, organ, and strings.

Surely, the death of Brahms's mother in February 1865 played a crucial part in calling *A German Requiem* into being, and so, hardly less likely, did his lingering—indeed, life-long—feelings about Robert Schumann's passing in July 1856. Brahms, however, was always reticent about such matters, and we cannot be absolutely certain. He wrote the last notes of the work in 1868, but its beginnings, at least its musical beginnings, go back as far as 1854. That was the year of Schumann's mental collapse and attempted suicide, and of Brahms's move to Düsseldorf to be near Clara Schumann and help her and her seven children. At that time he wrote the first version of his B-major Trio, op. 8, and the *Variations on a Theme by Schumann*, op. 9. He also started a D-Minor Sonata for Two Pianos, a work that was to trouble him for years. He perhaps considered turning it into a symphony—here, too, the history is not clear—but in 1856, salvaging and using parts of the first movement of the abandoned piece, he began work on the first movement of his Piano Concerto No. 1. Another movement of the abandoned sonata/symphony, a section Brahms imagined as a scherzo in the manner of a sarabande, became the starting point for the *German Requiem*'s second movement.

His mother's death, which grieved Brahms painfully, seems to have provided the immediate impulse for beginning the work. By the end of April 1865, two months after that event, he had finished the first, second, and fourth movements. Sending the last of these to Clara Schumann, he wrote that the piece was meant to be "a sort of German requiem." (Brahms was much moved when he learned many years later that Schumann had at one time planned a composition with that title.) Only an exceptionally heavy concert schedule kept Brahms from completing the score as swiftly as he had begun it. The partial premiere in Vienna in 1867 went badly, and the first performance in Leipzig fourteen months later turned out to be another of Brahms's bruising failures in that city (the most brutal had been the rejection of the D-Minor Piano Concerto in 1859), although it no longer mattered. The Bremen performance in 1868 had been a great success and indeed marked a turning point in Brahms's career. Now, at thirty-five, he was acknowledged a master.

About the time Brahms began concentrated work on his *German Requiem*, a poet far away in America was writing an exalted meditation on death. He had visited battlefields and seen "the debris of all the slain soldiers of the war." He saw—and it surprised and moved him—that

> They themselves were fully at rest, they suffer'd not,
> The living remain'd and suffer'd, the mother suffer'd,
> And the wife and the child and the music comrade suffer'd,
> And the armies that remain'd suffer'd.

Had Brahms read those lines—he did not, because he could not read poetry in English, and German translations of Whitman began to come out only in the 1880s—he surely would have done so with emotion and sympathy, for the pity and the understanding in them is nourished by the same source that fed the Requiem he planned.

Brahms himself put the libretto together. As a sacred, nonliturgical text for music, *A German Requiem* has but one peer, and that is the Jennens-Handel *Messiah*. Like Handel, Brahms knew his Bible well. In an essay entitled *The Cultural World of Brahms*, Michael Musgrave points out that although Brahms was

> not a conventional believer and resisted dogmas . . . he was deeply absorbed in the ideas from which formal religious thought is derived. The centre of his interest was the Lutheran Bible, of which he possessed two copies, one from 1833 and one a collector's item from 1545, as well as three New Testaments, one in Italian and one a seventeenth-century edition bound with the Marot-Beze Psalms. The newer of the Bibles is marked extensively and confirms the intimate knowledge that enabled him to select texts which ideally suited his purpose.[1]

The title gave Brahms some unease. "German" refers simply to the language, but he told Karl Reinthaler, director of music at the Bremen cathedral, that he would gladly have dispensed with that adjective and called his work *A Human Requiem*.

The words that begin the Mass for the Dead in the Catholic liturgy are "Requiem aeternam dona eis, Domine" (Grant them eternal rest, O Lord), but that is not the concern on Brahms's mind. The dead are not mentioned in *A German Requiem* until the penultimate section, and then it is in the phrase "denn die Toten werden auferstehen unverweslich" (the dead shall be raised incorruptible). And when the last movement begins with the words from Revelation, "Selig sind die Toten, die in dem Herrn sterben, von nun an" (Blessed are the dead which die in the Lord from henceforth), we hear not anxious or ardent prayer, but the voice of assured faith. Brahms's address is to us, the living, who remain to mourn and suffer. The verse from Revelation which ends *A German Requiem*

---

[1]*Brahms: Biographical, Documentary and Analytical Studies*, ed. Robert Pascall (Cambridge University Press, 1983).

closes the circle that begins with the Beatitude "Selig sind, die da Leid tragen, denn sie sollen getröstet werden" (Blessed are they that mourn, for they shall be comforted)."

That first movement is somber in color. Brahms was always a chaste and sparing orchestrator, whose treatment of, for example, trombones and contrabassoon in the four symphonies is a miracle of economy and effectiveness. In *A German Requiem*, he uses his full orchestral complement only in the second movement. In the dark first movement, he dispenses with piccolo, clarinets, one pair of horns, the trumpets and tuba, timpani, and—most strikingly—violins.[2] The use of the harp—such an atypical sound for Brahms—is wonderful in the first discreet entrance at "Die mit Tränen säen" (They that sow in tears), the bright accompaniment to the promise of reaping joy, and, just before the close, the glorious upsurge of the F-major chord as the sopranos reach their high A.[3]

The cellos' first phrase alludes to a seventeenth-century Lutheran hymn, *Wer nur den lieben Gott lässt walten* (They Who Leave All to God), about which Brahms said later, "Oh well, if nobody notices I suppose that's all right too." The first choral entry, "Selig sind" (Blessed are), spells out the melody F/A/B-flat, a small leap followed by a step in the same direction. Brahms isolates and dramatizes this shape here because he will use it to bind the entire work together (see Example 1). The poignant "mit Tränen" (in tears) brings the same pattern, but in reverse order.

The second movement opens with it as well but in reverse order: G-flat/F/D-flat. Now that Brahms introduces the violins (playing the music that survived from that early attempt at a sonata or symphony), he does so in a very high register—as violinistically as possible. The drums are heard for the first time as they beat their ominous triplets across that strange blend of march and dance. The accompaniment to the passage about "the early rain and the latter rain" (den Morgenregen und Abendregen) is so pictorial it might be by Bach. Twice the death march rises to its great climax, finally to open out into the magnificent chorus about the joy of those "redeemed of the Lord" ("Die Erlöseten des Herrn"), a movement astounding in its rhythmic freedom and energy. Not the least of its surprises, though, is the quiet close with its throbbing drums and

[2]I imagine that this orchestral coloration without violins in this particular place was inspired by the similarly scored first two movements of Cherubini's Requiem in C minor, a work Brahms admired enormously and which he conducted several times. In 1858–1859, Brahms had also written his A-major Serenade totally without violins.
[3]Brahms explained that he deliberately masked the first entrance of this dangerously ostentatious instrument so that it should "for God's sake not go make an effect."

Some instances of the *German Requiem's* unifying motive:

the first choral entrance

Se - lig sind,

Die— mit— Trä - nen,

Die— mit— Trä - nen,
also from the first movement

pp legato ma un poco marcato
the opening of the second movement

Bariton Solo

Herr, leh-re doch mich, daß ein En - de mit mir ha - ben muß

Kontrabaß. *pizz.*

p

the opening of the third movement

Der Ge-rech-ten See-len sind— in— Got-tes Hand, und kei-ne Qual rüh - ret sie an,
the fugue subject at the
end of the third movement

p dolce
p

Wie lieb-lich sind dei-ne Woh-nun - gen,

the opening of the fourth movement: the first phrase in
the flutes and the answer in the sopranos.

the oboe solo that accompanies
the soprano's first phrase
in the fifth movement

f
f

Herr, du bist wür - dig zu neh-men Preis und Eh - re und Kraft,

the two fugue themes at the end of the sixth movement, violins in the upper line, altos in the lower garlands of scales: here Brahms remembered the way Beethoven had ended the Adagio of the Ninth Symphony and the Credo in the *Missa solemnis*.

Now the baritone begins a somber recitative in dialogue with the chorus, set against orchestral scoring that tastes of *Don Giovanni*. Agitation grows over the question "Nun, Herr, wes soll ich mich trösten?" (Now, Lord, with what shall I console myself?). The pulsating triplets in the woodwinds cease—they are yet another daring and loving tribute to the Beethoven Ninth (the passage about him "who lives beyond the stars" [Über Sternen muss er wohnen])—and the answer, "Ich hoffe auf dich" (My hope is in thee), rises from the depths in a single sentence of transcendent radiance. As the chorus tells us that "the souls of the righteous are in the hands of God" ("Der Gerechten Seelen sind in Gottes Hand"), their fugue is accompanied by another in the orchestra. The sure faith that "no torment shall touch them" ("und keine Qual rühret sie an") is firmly established in the D-pedal of low brasses, strings, drums, and organ, sustained without break through thirty-six spacious measures.

What happens next is in complete contrast to the drama of the previous movement. The key of the chorus "Wie lieblich sind deine Wohnungen" (How lovely is thy dwelling place), E-flat major, is infinities away from the preceding D major, and the orchestral sound is reduced almost to the scale of chamber music. Near the end, Brahms produces a lovely choral texture by making octave couplings of sopranos with tenors and altos with basses.

Then comes the late insert into the *German Requiem*, the insert that truly completed it. Here is music delicate in sound and deeply inspired in the way the solo soprano and chorus create their touching counterpoint of Saint John, Isaiah, and Ecclesiastes. In its quiet and intimacy, this movement inhabits a world apart from the rest of the work. Even the choice of key marks it as something special: the key centers in the Requiem tend generally toward the flat side—F, B-flat minor, D minor, E-flat thus far—and G major comes in now with lovely freshness, sweetness, and luminosity.

This sixth movement is the one that most clearly defines the difference between Brahms and his contemporaries. Brahms is no less exciting than Berlioz or Verdi in his contemplation of "the last trump," yet there is no hint of theatrical effect here. Brahms does it all on sheer harmonic energy, an energy that reaches overwhelming proportions in the hugely swinging sequences of "Der Tod ist verschlungen in den Sieg. Tod, wo ist dein Stachel? Hölle, wo ist dein Sieg?" (Death is swallowed up in victory. Death, where is thy sting? Hell, where is thy victory?). But Brahms reserves his most blazing climax for the triumphant entry into C major for the fugue on "Herr, du bist würdig" (Thou art worthy, O Lord). This is Handelian not just in its vigor but also in the grand and easy euphony of the choral writing. The contrast of polyphonic textures against chordal ones is especially effective. But the most impressive moments are the quietest, those strange modal cadences where Brahms remembers Heinrich Schütz. Four times the music reaches *fortissimo*, but it is characteristic of that Brahmsian trait Erich Leinsdorf liked to call "antiemphasis" that both here and in the third movement the ending is on simple *forte*.[4]

The sixth-movement fugue grows from the work's basic three-note motif, and this immediately begins again in the first notes of the final movement—at the original pitch, too, with the F of the basses followed by the A and B-flat of the cellos. Donald Tovey's inspired interpretation of the "surging accompaniment" is that Brahms had in mind the phrase in Revelation that precedes the one he actually set to music. Thus the text really begins: "I heard a voice from heaven, saying unto me, 'Write, Blessed are the dead which die in the Lord from henceforth.'"

Then the end and the beginning become one, a device Brahms would use again, so variously, so subtly, in the G-major Violin Sonata, the Third Symphony, and the Clarinet Quintet.[5] Remotely, in the key of E-flat (the key associated with the Lord's "lovely dwelling place") and to the melody of "Selig sind, die da Leid tragen," the chorus intones "Selig sind die Toten" (Blessed are the dead). Across wide harmonic voyagings the music returns at last to F major. The glorious climax with the sopranos on high A is attained once more on the word "Herrn" (Lord), and just at that moment the harps, which we have not heard since halfway through the second movement, begin their heavenward climb. They enter on their lowest note as the singers touch their highest, and when the harps reach, in the last measure, their own summit, the chorus is heard in the depths with distant echoes of "selig" (blessed)."

---

[4]The *fortissimos* in the sixth movement occur when the chorus first sings the word "Posaune" (trombone) in the extended "Death, where is thy sting?" passage, and at the top of the "Jacob's ladder" ascents to the word "Kraft" (power) in the fugue. Brahms the classicist knows that a climax is one thing and a conclusion another. It would be nice if more conductors were aware of this distinction.

[5]Brahms cherished a sentence by the eighteenth-century dramatist and critic Gotthold Ephraim Lessing: "Without coherence, without the most intimate connection among all its parts, music is a vain heap of sand, incapable of making any lasting impression; only coherence can make it into that solid marble in which the hand of the artist can immortalize itself."

The Shorter Choral Works: *Schicksalslied* (*Song of Destiny*), *Nänie* (*Lament*), and *Gesang der Parzen* (*Song of the Fates*)

In these three works we meet Brahms in complex readings of poetry that expresses a tragic view of the world. We also meet a Brahms little known to most listeners. For most of us, knowledge of Brahms's choral music begins and ends with *A German Requiem*, includes perhaps the *Alto Rhapsody* (insofar as one can even count that as a choral work), possibly the *Schicksalslied* but hardly *Nänie*, and almost certainly not the *Gesang der Parzen*. With *Rinaldo*, *Triumphlied*, and the large body of *a cappella* motets and part songs, we penetrate ever further into *terra incognita*.

Intensely personal, *Schicksalslied*, *Nänie*, and *Gesang der Parzen* are extraordinary settings of extraordinary texts, bringing us sonorities, harmonies, and expressive gestures we shall not find elsewhere in Brahms's music. The subject of these three compositions, saturated in the atmosphere and imagery of classical antiquity, is divine indifference to the human condition, but in spite of that common ground, and though they all fall into the category of short settings of dark texts for chorus and orchestra, they embody personalities as distinct as Brahms's three violin sonatas, piano trios, or string quartets, or any three of the symphonies. Even the tempos—*Langsam und sehnsuchtsvoll* (slow and yearning), 4/4, in *Schicksalslied*; *Andante*, 6/4, in *Nänie*; *Maestoso*, 4/4, in *Gesang der Parzen*—represent three wholly different aspects of "not fast."

Brahms the songwriter has been accused of having no literary taste, especially when compared with his mentor Schumann and his younger and hostile contemporary Hugo Wolf. It is true that in casting around for lieder texts he was not looking for the exquisite lyric as much as for the stimulus of atmosphere or the telling phrase, and he often found what he wanted in the verse of minor writers whom, but for him, we would not know. In fact, though, Brahms was a reader of sharp discernment and huge appetite, who gathered a library including the complete available works of Boccaccio, Byron, Cervantes, Goethe, Keller, Lessing, Lichtenberg, Schiller, Shakespeare, and Tieck (the foreigners in German translation), as well as many anthologies of poetry and folk songs. In his choral works, which he regarded as "large statements," as distinct from the genre paintings and lyric contemplations of his lieder and part-songs, he turned to the books he cherished most and knew best—in the first place the Bible, then Goethe, and also Schiller and Hölderlin.

I wish space permitted an essay on one of the most powerful and interesting of Brahms's works for chorus and orchestra, the *Triumphlied* for baritone solo, double chorus, and orchestra. Using verses from the

Bible, specifically the book of Revelation, he wrote it in 1870–1871 in celebration of the German victory in the Franco-Prussian War and dedicated it to William I, the first emperor of the newly founded German Empire. And there is the problem: many people have chosen to get on their high horse in the matter of morality, disapproving of the piece because of the occasion of its origin. The German defeat in 1918 also contributed to its virtual disappearance from the repertory.

The Hohenzollern emperors and Chancellor Bismarck are not high on my list of cultural heroes, and crowing nationalism is a dangerous attitude responsible for many of the world's miseries, past and present; nonetheless, I think it a pity that we are turning our backs on a splendid piece by a great composer—especially when I think of the complacency with which we play and listen to the *1812 Overture*.[1]

Handel was not the hero for Brahms that he had been for Beethoven; this, however, is Brahms's Handel tribute. Specifically it is a salute to the Handel of works such as the *Dettingen Te Deum*, and Brahms brings it off with splendid panache. No piece by him is so formidably extroverted. The structure is powerful, pacing is sure, rhetoric and text declamation are gripping, and the D-major trumpet-and-drums sonority is ablaze (very eighteenth-century, that). As of the summer of 2004, I have never heard a concert performance of the *Triumphlied*.

Schicksalslied (*Song of Destiny*), by Friedrich Hölderlin, for Chorus and Orchestra, op. 54

Brahms made the first sketches for his *Schicksalslied* in the summer of 1868, probably completing a preliminary version by May 1870, but putting the work into its final form only a year later. He conducted the first performance at Karlsruhe on 18 October 1871.

Four-part mixed chorus. Two flutes, two oboes, two clarinets, two bassoons, two horns, two trumpets, three trombones, timpani, and strings.

Brahms first read Hölderlin in the middle 1860s when that writer was as good as unknown. Stefan George and Rainer Maria Rilke discovered him

---

[1] I recall the amused fantasy of the French composer Betsy Jolas, upon hearing *1812* played at Tanglewood at a Fourth of July celebration, that some day she might recompose the piece so that the French would win.

early in the twentieth century, and he has drawn sympathetic musical response from Hans Werner Henze, Benjamin Britten, and John Harbison. Now he is an imposing figure on the landscape of German literature, mentioned in the same breath as Goethe and Schiller, and probably more read than the latter.

Hölderlin's is a fate, and indeed a voice, not unlike that of William Blake. He was born in 1770, the same year as Beethoven. The philosophers Hegel and Schelling—the former an exact contemporary, the latter four years younger—were his companions at the University of Tübingen. Schiller befriended him, published him, and helped him find posts as a tutor. His poetry first appeared in print in 1791. For a little over a decade Hölderlin wrote odes, elegies, and other verse forms that are complex in thought and language, of vast breadth in their rhythm, a fascinating and unique fusion of Hellenism and Christianity, expressed in an idiom that joins an elevated classical style with startling and touching colloquialisms of his native Swabian speech. He wrote a novel, *Hyperion*; worked for years on a play, *The Death of Empedocles*; and translated Sophocles and Pindar (his version of Sophocles' *Antigone* was set as an opera by Carl Orff). Possessed always by a poignant awareness of his essential solitude and of the threat of impending mental darkness, racked by a tragic love affair with a woman whose children he taught, Hölderlin began to suffer spells of insanity. For a few years there were lucid passages, but from 1806 until his death in 1843, he lived in totally absented condition in Tübingen, first and briefly in hospital; then, overlooking the lovely Neckar River, in a tower room of the house of a kindly cabinetmaker who had a certain literary bent.

Hyperion, or The Hermit in Greece, the source of the *Schicksalslied*, is an epistolary novel that appeared in two installments in 1797 and 1799. Its topic is the contemporary struggle of the Greeks to liberate themselves from three and a half centuries of Turkish oppression. Hyperion himself, named for the Titan who was the father of Helios, the sun god, is a figure who reflects Hölderlin's own intellectual and spiritual development. He is a young idealist despondent at the gap between the drab present and the image of ancient Greece that he bears in his mind, and he is possessed by the wish to bring about a new Golden Age in which divinity, nature, and humanity are in perfect harmony. *Hyperion's Song of Destiny* is a lyric rendering of the contrast between Then and Now, transposed, in the words of the historian Peter Gay, into the "painful and yearning contrast between clear-eyed, unchanging Greek gods and restless, ever-suffering humanity." It is a theme we find often in Hölderlin's poetry.

The conductor and composer Albert Dietrich, best remembered as one of the authors, with Schumann and Brahms, of the composite F-A-E Sonata for Joseph Joachim, has left us an account of an excursion taken by the Dietrichs, the composer and conductor Karl Reinthaler and his wife, and Brahms to view the North Sea naval base at Wilhelmshaven in the summer of 1868.

> Our friend, usually so cheery, was silent and serious on the journey. He told us how, early that morning (he . . . got up extremely early), he had found Hölderlin's poems in the bookcase and been profoundly stirred by *Hyperion's Song of Destiny*. Later, as we rested by the sea after much walking about and looking at interesting sights, we discovered Brahms far removed from us, sitting on the beach and writing. It was the first sketch for the *Schicksalslied*.[1]

Brahms was happy and moved that the artist Max Klinger, in his *Brahms Fantasies*, used the seashore motif for his engravings on the *Schicksalslied*, the first of which shows a beach littered with the bodies of the shipwrecked while an old man seeks to draw from the shards of his lyre a song to those "who walk above in the light." "I see the music," Brahms wrote to Klinger,

> I see the beautiful words—and now your glorious drawings carry me yet further. Looking at them, it is as though the music were sounding on into the Infinite and were saying everything I might have said, more clearly than music can say it, yet just as replete with mystery and presentiment. Some-times I come close to envying you for being able to be so lucid with your pencil, sometimes I am happy that I don't have to be. Finally it seems to me that all art is one and speaks one language.

Brahms begins by setting the scene, putting before us in music that radiant cloudscape where the blessed genii "walk above in the light, / Weightless tread a soft floor." Here is a glorious melody, one of Brahms's most inspired, sung by muted violins against an accompaniment at once rich and soft. Only the relentless beat of kettledrums darkens the air. Max Kalbeck, Brahms's first biographer, points out that nowhere else does the composer use a direction like the *Langsam und sehnsuchtsvoll* (Slow and yearning) we find here, normally confining himself to tempo indications with an occasional *dolce* or *espressivo*.

After this spacious introduction, altos alone set forth the first two lines of Hölderlin's poem. The full chorus takes up their melody, another of Brahms's most beautiful, repeating the opening lines, and so the first two stanzas are sung in warm four-part harmony, sumptuously accompa-nied. The music fades into the distance, and the idyll is disturbed by a

---

[1]Albert Dietrich and J. V. Widmann, *Recollections of Johannes Brahms*, trans. Dora Hecht (Scribner, 1899).

wind chord of quietly penetrating dissonance. Strings turn this chord into a tempest, and a powerful quick movement, buffeted by edgy harmonies and syncopations, projects the image of

> suffering mortals . . .
> Hurled like water
> From ledge to ledge
> Downward for years to the vague abyss.

The "divine" slow movement was in E-flat major; the "human" *Allegro* is in its relative minor, C minor, and as the mortals are hurled into the vague abyss, the harmony freezes on C, that note reiterated through fifty-four measures in the cellos or the drums. In a characteristic touch of economy, Brahms withholds the basses here.

For a long time Brahms did not know how to end the *Schicksalslied*, and the solution he finally arrived at has given critics more food for thought than any other passage in his music. What happens is simple: the opening music returns, unchanged in shape and harmony, but set now in C major and orchestrated with more air in the texture, with a brighter radiance, and with the part of the drums greatly reduced. Also—and surely not insignificantly—the *Langsam und sehnsuchtsvoll* of the introduction has been replaced by plain (and Italian) *Adagio*.

When Brahms had completed the score—with this ending—he changed his mind and reverted to an earlier plan of having the chorus sing the first two lines of the poem during this postlude—not, however, with the original melody, but in the plainest possible chords, as though this were nothing more than an absolutely neutral filling-out of inner voices. It would sound well, he thought, and he did not even care much about the words: "Actually, I'd really like to have the chorus just sing 'ah' something like a drone." He also worried whether the audience would have the patience to sit through a long instrumental coda, and when, in response to the firm urging of the conductor Hermann Levi and with the encouragement of Clara Schumann, he had once again struck out these eleven measures for the chorus, he did insist that at the premiere the words "orchestral postlude" appear in the printed program at the conclusion of Hölderlin's text.[2]

---

[2]Levi made a copy of the postlude in the version with chorus, and it is reproduced in the second volume of Max Kalbeck's *Johannes Brahms*. Brahms usually took pains to destroy sketches and otherwise to keep people from seeing anything other than what he considered properly finished; this is therefore an extremely rare instance of the survival of a rejected alternative. Brahms also accepted some suggestions from Levi about the orchestration of the *Schicksalslied*. For a penetrating account of the fascinating and complex figure of Levi, whose friendship with Brahms dried up in the 1870s as he became more of a Wagnerian (he was the first conductor of *Parsifal*), see Peter Gay's *Freud, Jews, and Other Germans: Masters and Victims in a Modernist Culture* (Oxford University Press, 1978).

After all was done, Brahms wrote to Reinthaler:

> The Schicksalslied is being printed and the chorus is silent in the final Adagio. Well, it's . . . a stupid idea or what you will, but there's nothing to be done about it. I had gotten to the point where I actually wrote something in for the chorus, but it just isn't right. It may be a failed experiment. But pasting something on would merely produce something nonsensical. As we've discussed sufficiently, I simply say something the poet doesn't say, and to be sure it would be better if what's missing were in fact his main concern—but now, etc., etc. . . . But if you perform it, above all work on this postlude. The flutist must play very passionately, and you must have a large section of violins playing very beautifully.[3]

In a subsequent letter to Reinthaler, Brahms returned to the point that "the poet had not said the most important thing." As for what this "Hauptsache" was that Brahms thought Hölderlin had not said, we can only guess. Brahms's hard-won and ineffably lovely postlude has, in any event, elicited the most varied reactions. No one disputes the beauty of the music and the pleasure—perhaps the self-indulgent pleasure—of hearing that great melody one more time, especially in its new, luminous scoring. But clearly, Brahms has said something Hölderlin did not say: the poem's destination is not the depiction of clear-eyed and unchanging gods but the harshness of the fate of suffering mortals "hurled like water / From ledge to ledge / Downward for years to the vague abyss."

Does Brahms not trespass beyond a composer's—or any interpreter's—rights? That he was merely satisfying his classical (and quite un-Hölderlinian) lust for symmetry is a simple-minded notion, undone by his letters to Reinthaler. It has been proposed that Brahms was quarreling with Hölderlin to assert that, after all, "God's in his heaven, all's right with the world," to which another Brahms biographer, Peter Latham, remarks, "If you can believe that of the composer of the Requiem and the Four Serious Songs, you can believe anything." The Requiem is not in fact a good example, but the songs are, and the Gesang der Parzen (Song of the Fates) is a devastating one. Donald Tovey offers a provocative but tortured argument that musical time and musical chronology are not the same as ordinary time and chronology,

---

[3]Here is an example of Brahms's unconventional view of the flute, not as the frivolous and airy member of the woodwind group, but as a powerful vocalist capable of immense pathos and intensity. The two most famous examples of this occur in the finales of the First and Fourth Symphonies, in the former where the flute radiantly continues the mountain-horn–call of the introduction, in the latter in that "speaking" twelfth variation, which Erich Leinsdorf likened to the "dramatic flight of some hunted soul that tries laboriously to ascend, only to collapse at the end."

and that therefore a musical postlude need not be construed as coming literally after the poem it follows. A more powerful reading suggests that the reappearance of the "divine" opening music, especially with the "Sehnsucht" removed, the new sonority, and what Erich Leinsdorf called the "alabaster whiteness" of C major, is a way of dispassionately confronting us with the indifference to mortal suffering of those who "walk above in the light, / Weightless tread a soft floor"; that therefore Brahms's conclusion—and, in his view, the "Hauptsache" that Hölderlin omitted to stage specifically—is bitter pessimism.

A persuasive—and moving—interpretation of the *Schicksalslied* came my way in 1983 in the form of a generously argumentative response from the conductor Jonathan Khuner to an earlier version of this program note. Khuner proposes that at the root of human suffering is the combination of our "restless, homeless, buffeted" condition and our ability to imagine and to yearn for a "state of perfect, unconscious bliss" akin to that in which the gods live.[4]

In a letter, Khuner wrote:

> And the answer to this torment? Brahms's creative life is in its entirety a struggle to answer it, hence his strong attraction to the poem. . . . One need only look to the finale of the Haydn Variations or the finale of the Symphony No. 4 to see what he meant by the close of his *Schicksalslied*. The solution is to recreate that lost illusion of perfection, even in the expression of human imperfection and suffering, and by doing so to transcend, even deny it. . . . The finale of the Fourth Symphony barely manages to give victory to pure art over the maelstrom. The *Schicksalslied* rounds the form . . . to show that the idea of pure vision will always haunt the artist and force him to its pursuit.

Whatever the interpretation, the tension, the dissonance, between the violent close of Hölderlin's *Song of Destiny* and the wondrous serenity of Brahms's is overwhelming.

Nänie (Lament), by Friedrich Schiller, for Chorus and Orchestra, op. 82

Brahms was drawn to Schiller's *Nänie* in 1875, but deferred setting it then out of consideration for Hermann Goetz, who had set this text the year before. The death in January 1880 of the painter Anselm Feuerbach moved

[4]Thomas Hardy speaks to this pain in a powerful poem, *Before Life and After*, powerfully set by Benjamin Britten in his song cycle *Winter Words*.

Brahms to return to the poem and, oddly, so perhaps did the experience of hearing Goetz's version in Vienna a month later. Brahms made sketches that summer at Bad Ischl, but he did his concentrated work on the composition at Pressbaum near Vienna in the summer of 1881, completing it by 22 August. He dedicated the score to Henriette Feuerbach in memory of her son. Brahms conducted the first performance at a special concert of the Zurich Tonhalle Orchestra on 6 December 1881.

Four-part mixed chorus. Two flutes, two oboes, two clarinets, two bassoons, two horns, three trombones, timpani, harp, and strings. Brahms marks the harp part ad libitum and indicates alternative violin parts in the event of the harp's absence; at the same time, he asks for the harp part to be doubled if possible.

Nänie did not set Brahms the perplexing interpretive problems of Hölderlin's *Schicksalslied* (*Song of Destiny*) or Goethe's *Gesang der Parzen* (*Song of the Fates*). Schiller's lament gained immediacy for him through the death of his friend Feuerbach, the artist whom, together with Max Klinger, he admired most among his contemporaries, and it evoked an inspired flow of lyric music. Brahms's music suggests a gathering of mourning friends. So intimate is the expression that Brahms's surgeon friend, Theodor Billroth, questioned in more than one letter its suitability for public performance: "When I think of the average audience in a Viennese concert hall I get quite upset. Of what importance to them is the tragedy of the death of the beautiful and perfect? . . . What's Hecuba to them? Even when beauty is buried they must have a grand funeral!"

As in the *Schicksalslied* and the *Gesang der Parzen*, the subject is divine indifference. As Schiller has it here: "That which subdues men and gods does not move the steely heart of Stygian Zeus"—meaning Minos or Pluto. In what Brahms's biographer Hans Gál calls a "[characteristic] hypertrophy of mythological allusions," the poet evokes the deaths of Eurydice, brought back from the dead, but with that gift of second life sternly recalled at the last moment; of Adonis, killed by a boar; and of Achilles, slain by Paris at the gates of Troy.

Schiller's fluidly alternating pentameters and hexameters draw from Brahms a similarly flexible and flowing music. The gentle *Andante* begins with one of the great oboe solos, twenty-five measures of sweetly elegiac song. It is embedded in wind sonorities, strings offering only the most reticent punctuation and commentary. Brahms saves a real string presence for the entrance of the chorus, but characteristically, he modulates from one sound to the other by having bassoons and horns do a gentle fadeout during the first three measures of singing.

The choral style in *Nänie* is predominantly polyphonic, and the four voices enter one at a time, almost as though in a fugue. The setting is rhythmically elastic—for example, Schiller's first line is given eighteen measures of music, but the second is sung in just four—and the constantly varied texture covers a range from *a cappella* to richly elaborate orchestral scoring.

The vision of Achilles' mother, Thetis, and the other daughters of the sea-god Nereus rising from the water to mourn the slain hero—"Aber sie steigt aus dem Meer" (But she rises from the sea)—inspired one of Brahms's most radiant melodies. Having all the voices begin it in unison is a canny touch, and the orchestration—a rich impasto of woodwinds, harps, and pseudo-harps (pizzicato strings)—is gorgeous. The four measures that precede this great moment have the lone *fortissimo* in *Nänie* (what a master economizer Brahms always was!), and the great melody itself is "only" an effortless rich *forte*. The Thetis melody marks the first of just two major points of articulation in the work, with Brahms, moving with powerful stride, changing meter (from 6/4 to 4/4) and key (from D major to F-sharp major).[1]

For the beginning of the second-last line, "Auch ein Klaglied zu sein" (Even to be a lament), Brahms returns to 6/4, to D major, to the oboe melody, and gives us a compressed version of the first choral entrance. Here, as in the *Song of Destiny* and *Song of the Fates*, he takes a liberty with the text. Schiller's closing distich brings light: "Auch ein Klaglied zu sein im Mund der Geliebten ist herrlich" (Even to be a lament in the mouth of the loved one is glorious), followed by dark: "Denn das Gemeine geht klanglos zum Orkus hinab" (For what is common sinks in silence to the Kingdom of the Dead). Brahms softens Schiller's close by following this contrasting couplet with a repetition of "Auch ein Klaglied," with its promise of consolation. As the strings ascend into the empyrean, *Nänie* closes with softly musing repetitions of the word "herrlich" (glorious).

Gesang der Parzen (*Song of the Fates*), by Johann Wolfgang von Goethe, for Chorus and Orchestra, op. 89

Brahms composed the *Gesang der Parzen*, his last major work for chorus and orchestra, in the summer of 1882, completing it by 31 July. Brahms conducted the first performance in Basel on 10 December that year. During the next two months, he conducted performances in Zurich, Strasbourg, Bonn, Krefeld, Oldenburg, Schwerin, and Vienna, using this experience to

---

[1]Karl Geiringer points out in his Brahms biography that Goetz had made the same changes at the same point in the poem.

effect a few revisions. The work is dedicated to Duke George II of Saxe-Meiningen, under whose aegis the Meiningen Orchestra became one of the great European ensembles.

Six-part mixed chorus (SAATBB). Two flutes and piccolo, two oboes, two clarinets, two bassoons and contrabassoon, four horns, two trumpets, three trombones, tuba, timpani, and strings.

Iphigenia was the eldest daughter of Agamemnon, king of Argos. Eager to take part in the war against Troy, Agamemnon was kept by adverse weather from sailing to the besieged city, and so he made a bargain with the moon goddess Artemis: if she would bring about a change of wind, he in turn would sacrifice Iphigenia. Artemis, however, took pity on Iphigenia and sent her to Tauris (now the Crimea) to serve as a priestess. Years later, with Agamemnon murdered by his wife, Clytemnestra, upon his return from the Trojan War, Orestes, Iphigenia's younger brother, avenged his father's death by killing his mother. (In Aeschylus' *Agamemnon*, the king's ruthless treatment of Iphigenia is a central reason for Clytemnestra's decision to kill him.) Relentlessly pursued by the Furies, Orestes at last learned from the Oracle that the curse would be lifted as soon as he brought Iphigenia back to Greece. This is the substance of Goethe's play *Iphigenie auf Tauris*, and it was seeing the great Charlotte Wolter in the title role at the Vienna Burgtheater that moved Brahms to set the stanzas from Act 4 known as the *Song of the Fates* to music.[1]

Agamemnon, Clytemnestra, and the other members of the accursed house of Atreus were descendants of Tantalus, a mortal befriended by Zeus but who betrayed the friendship by giving away Olympian secrets and stealing the gods' food. In some versions of the legend, he invited the gods to a banquet and, running short of meat, served them his own son Pelops in a stew.

Zeus punished Tantalus mercilessly, first by condemning him to languish through eternity in a torment of hunger and thirst, with food and water always just out of reach, then by visiting upon his descendants a fearful heritage of violence. This is the background of the *Song of the Fates*, the Fates being the three goddesses who controlled human destiny.[2] For Iphigenia, this is something that her nurse had sung to her and Orestes and their sister Electra when they were children, and now long

[1]Another connection, and one of long standing, would be Brahms's love for the many and dark paintings of *Iphigenie* by Anselm Feuerbach, the artist and friend whose death he mourned in *Nänie*.
[2]The Romans gave them the name "Parcae," hence the German "Parzen."

and gladly forgotten, a "Song that the Fates sang amid shudders / When Tantalus fell from his golden seat."

Goethe's *Gesang der Parzen* is as terrifying a poem as I know, and I am sure that encountering it first in this musical setting has everything to do with that feeling. Brahms instantly embroils us in a maelstrom of dissonance whose effect is still in our ears—and hearts and brains—when, to relentlessly beating drums, the chorus begins its repressed but fiercely urgent march through the text. Brahms's friend Theodor Billroth remarked of these harmonies, "so peculiar to you," that "they certainly produce the effect of passionate desperation." Gleefully he added that the opening would give the famous and feared critic Eduard Hanslick a shock.[3] The scoring, with its contrabassoon, bass tuba, and six-part chorus with double sections of altos and basses, is calculated to yield a darkness remarkable even for this master of grays and browns.

Brahms sets Goethe's poem with unrelenting concentration, responsive to each detail and image. The picture of the gods endlessly feasting at their golden tables momentarily brings a softer, more lyric music, but this only sets into greater relief the turbulent dissonances which evoke the struggle for breath of the suffocating Titans, those unfortunate children of heaven and earth who went down to defeat in their revolt against Zeus.

Brahms brings back Goethe's first stanza before the final lines of the Fates' song, "Es wenden die Herrscher" (The rulers turn). His interpretation of these last lines is astonishing. The picture of the indifferent gods turning "their beneficent eyes away from entire races" is made into music completely different from any we have yet heard: minor becomes major, the marching quadruple meter turns into a flowing 3/4, fierce staccato gives way to lines more gently rounded and sustained. It is as though Brahms had suddenly shifted perspective. Rather than focusing on the tragic contrast between the gods and their victims, he wishes us to be suffused in pity for the accursed and abandoned descendants of Tantalus from whose sight the gods avert their eyes. He himself wrote of this passage: "Just the appearance of the major key alone should soften the heart and moisten the eye of the innocent listener. Only then does humanity's whole misery get to him."

For the epilogue, "So sangen die Parzen" (Thus sang the Fates) Brahms returns to the minor and to his opening music, but it is wholly transfigured—*pianissimo*, with a haunting sound of muted strings (and a luminous flute to brighten the violin melody) and quietly sustained oboe with high horn and trumpet. Against these strands of sound, the chorus stammers the last lines in dismay and dread.

---

[3]Billroth was a surgeon, no less important in his field than Brahms was in his. When Brahms sent Billroth a copy of the *Song of the Fates*, he remarked that it should interest him particularly in view of the shared professional interest in the matter of scissors and string.

Benjamin Britten

Edward Benjamin Britten was born at Lowestoft, Suffolk, England, on Saint Cecilia's Day, 22 November 1913, and died at Aldeburgh, Suffolk, on 4 December 1976. On 12 June 1976 he was made Lord Britten of Aldeburgh in the Queen's Birthday Honours, the first musician to be elevated to the peerage.

War Requiem, Words from the *Missa pro defunctis* and the Poems of Wilfred Owen, op. 66

The *War Requiem*, commissioned to celebrate the consecration of Saint Michael's Cathedral, Coventry, was composed in 1961, completed on 20 December that year, and first performed in that cathedral on 30 May 1962. The soloists were Heather Harper, Peter Pears, and Dietrich Fischer-Dieskau, who were joined by the Coventry Festival Chorus; the boys' choruses of Holy Trinity, Leamington, and Holy Trinity, Stratford; the City of Birmingham Symphony Orchestra; and the Melos Ensemble. The chorus and full orchestra were conducted by Meredith Davies; the composer conducted the chamber orchestra. That division of conductorial duties came about because Britten was in frail health just then, but it was obviously desirable to have him take part in the premiere in some way. Some performances still use two conductors, but most are handled by just one. The score is dedicated "in loving memory of Roger Burney, Sub-Lieutenant in the Royal Naval Volunteer Reserve; Piers Dunkerley, Captain, Royal Marines; David Gill, Ordinary Seaman, Royal Navy; and Michael Halliday, Lieutenant, Royal New Zealand Volunteer Reserve."

Soprano, tenor, and baritone solos; mixed chorus; boys' chorus. Three flutes (third doubling piccolo), two oboes and English horn, three clarinets (third doubling both E-flat and bass clarinet), two bassoons and contrabassoon, six horns, four trumpets, three trombones, tuba, piano, organ (or harmonium), timpani, two snare drums, tenor drum, bass drum, tambourine, triangle, cymbals, castanets, slapstick, Chinese blocks, gong, tubular bells, vibraphone, glockenspiel, antique cymbals, and strings, and a chamber orchestra of flute (doubling piccolo), oboe (doubling English horn), clarinet, bassoon, horn, timpani, snare drum, bass drum, cymbal, gong, harp, two violins, viola, cello, and bass.

> My subject is War, and the pity of War.
> The Poetry is in the pity.
> All a poet can do is warn.
> —Wilfred Owen

Britten had these words printed on the title page of his *War Requiem*. The music is the response of a lifelong pacifist to the words of the finest of the English poets whose subject was war. Owen's war was the catastrophe of 1914–1918, in numbers of casualties the worst we have yet unleashed. Owen himself was one of those thousands and thousands of victims, dying in battle a week before the Armistice, but his words have outlived the scoundrels and fools, those who started the fire and the ones who directed the fighting so ineptly.

As a schoolboy in England during the Second World War, the one that came after the War To End All Wars, I was fed the Romantic war poetry of Julian Grenfell and Rupert Brooke, both killed in 1915. I never heard the name of Wilfred Owen then, and my first knowledge of him came to me through Osbert Sitwell's ardent words about him and his poetry in *Noble Essences*, the postscript to his four-volume autobiography. Though Owen would never have said as much, poets like Grenfell and Brooke were his enemies, too: their sentimental glorification of war sickened him. He was clear-eyed when he looked at war, at what brought it about and its minute-by-minute realities. Neither World War II nor Vietnam nor anything else has diminished the immediacy of what he wrote, and the characters he wrote about are still on the scene; they have only acquired new names and dates and places of birth. It was an inspired stroke of Britten's to punctuate the Catholic Requiem's hieratic, supra-personal words in a dead tongue with the shocking directness of modern English.[1] He also brought Owen's poetry into the awareness of many who had not known it before.

Owen was born at Plas Wilmot, Oswestry, Shropshire, on 18 March 1893, attended schools in Birkenhead and Shrewsbury, contemplated the ministry, and was both pupil and lay assistant to a clergyman in Oxford-shire. In September 1915 he joined the army, a company called the Artists' Rifles. From December 1916 he served in France with the Lancashire Fusiliers, spent five months of 1917 recovering from shell shock at Craiglockhart War Hospital in Scotland, and, after several months of ser-vice in England, was again posted to France.[2]

Owen wrote verse fluently as a boy, mostly in emulation of Keats and Tennyson. Ironically, it was the war that felled him which also freed his poetic gift. Taking stock on the last day of 1917, he could write to his mother: "I go out of this year a poet, my dear mother, as which I did not enter it. I am held peer by the Georgians; I am a poet's poet. I am started."[3] In October 1918, Owen was awarded the Military Cross, and on 4 November he was machine-gunned to death as he was trying to get his company across the Sambre Canal. The war ended one week later, and the story goes that the church bells had just begun to ring in celebra-tion of the Armistice when Owen's parents received the telegram in-forming them of their son's death.

It had not taken Owen much of his ecclesiastical apprenticeship to realize that his future was not in holy orders. He distrusted the church as an institution and disliked most of its agents—particularly military chap-lains, whom he viewed as betraying the message of Christ. Owen speaks

---

[1]Britten was anticipated in this by Ralph Vaughan Williams, who, in his powerful 1936 cantata *Dona nobis pacem*, interspersed biblical texts with poetry by Walt Whitman and words from John Bright's "Angel of Death" speech against the Crimean War, delivered in the House of Commons in 1855. There is no mention of *Dona nobis pacem* in Britten's published letters or di-aries from the 1930s.

[2]Craiglockhart is the scene of Pat Barker's moving novel *Regeneration* (1991). The poet who fig-ures in that book is Owen's older contemporary, Siegfried Sassoon, who met Owen at Craiglockhart and was responsible for getting Owen's poetry published in 1920.

[3]The Georgians were a loosely affiliated group of poets, so named both because much of their work was pastoral (georgic, from the Latin "georgicus," means related to agricultural life) and because they had begun to make their mark in the reign of George V, who had ascended the throne in 1910. Some of them, including Sassoon, Robert Graves, and Edmund Blunden, did not even want to be identified as belonging to the group. Among the poets recognized as Geor-gians at various times were Brooke, John Masefield, D. H. Lawrence, Walter de la Mare, and an-other of the grippingly eloquent war poets, Isaac Rosenberg.

better than the chaplains. Here are words from a letter he wrote to his mother in May 1917 from the 13th Casualty Clearing Station at Gailly on the Somme:

> Already I have comprehended a light which will never filter into the dogma of any national church: namely, that one of Christ's essential commands was: passivity at any price! Suffer dishonor and disgrace, but never resort to arms. Be bullied, be outraged, be killed; but do not kill. It may be a chimerical and an ignominious principle, but there it is. It can only be ignored, and I think pulpit professionals are ignoring it very skillfully and successfully indeed. . . . And am I not myself a conscientious objector with a very seared conscience? . . . Christ is literally in "no man's land." There men often hear His voice: Greater love hath no man than this, that a man lay down his life for a friend. Is it spoken in English only and French? I do not believe so. Thus you see how pure Christianity will not fit in with pure patriotism.

In a gesture parallel to its mixing of modern English with Latin, the *War Requiem*, although composed for a great public occasion and in honor of a public edifice, also bears a private dedication "in loving memory" of four of Britten's friends. Three of them—Roger Burney, David Gill, and Michael Halliday—lost their lives in combat in World War II; the fourth, Piers Dunkerley, wounded during the Normandy invasion and taken prisoner by the Germans, continued in military service, but later became increasingly unstable and committed suicide in 1959, a year after returning to civilian life.[4]

The *War Requiem* was an important marker on Britten's road. Twice during his life, public awareness of his work advanced dramatically—even explosively. The first time was in 1945, when his opera *Peter Grimes* was produced for the postwar reopening of Sadler's Wells Theatre in London. The second was the premiere at Coventry and the subsequent series of performances all over Europe and North America of the *War Requiem*.

---

[4]Burney, an old friend of Peter Pears, served on a French submarine, the *Surcouf*, which was lost with all hands in February 1942. In *Letters from a Life: Selected Letters and Diaries of Benjamin Britten*, edited by Donald Mitchell and Philip Reed, a chilling illustration shows an envelope addressed to Burney and marked RETURN TO SENDER: SHIP OVERDUE. Gill, also from Lowestoft and a friend since Britten's adolescence (Gill himself was several years younger) was killed in the Mediterranean. Halliday also went back a long way in Britten's life, and Britten had been a kind of protector to the younger boy, who was a loner and given a hard time at school. The friendship with Dunkerley had also begun as one between an older boy serving as mentor to a much younger one; both that friendship and the one with Halliday were manifestations in an idealized form of Britten's lifelong attraction to adolescent boys.

The triumph of *Peter Grimes* served to confirm a prodigious talent. It also fulfilled the hope that, for the first time since the death of Henry Purcell in 1695, England had produced a composer of international stature. (At that time, Elgar and Vaughan Williams were still stamped NOT FOR EXPORT.) Dissenters of course there were—those who thought that milky pastoral was the only idiom appropriate for an Englishman, those who found the young Britten too clever by half, and, not least, those who were enraged by his pacifism, his ties to left-wing causes, his three-year residence in the United States at the beginning of the war, and his homosexuality.

The impact the *War Requiem* made seventeen years after *Peter Grimes* was wider and deeper by far. Britten, approaching fifty, had become an artist whose every new work was awaited with the most lively interest and the highest expectations. The *War Requiem*, moreover, was tied to a pair of events heavily freighted with history and emotion: the destruction of Coventry's fourteenth-century cathedral in an air raid during the night of 14–15 November 1940, and the consecration of a new building on that site twenty-one years later.[5] Very much in the spirit of Owen, the ruins of the original walls still stand as a reminder.

The *War Requiem* was a weighty and poignant statement on a subject of urgent concern, for 1961 was an anxious year, the year of the Bay of Pigs, the construction of the Berlin Wall, and the beginning of the dramatic escalation of the United States's involvement in Vietnam. The participants and the audience made the first performance an international event.[6] A significant symbol Britten built into that occasion was to provide roles for singers of three nationalities: the English tenor Peter Pears, the German baritone Dietrich Fischer-Dieskau, and the Russian soprano Galina Vishnevskaya. In the event, Ekaterina Furtseva, the Soviet Minister of Culture, would not permit Vishnevskaya to travel to England. As Britten wrote to E. M. Forster: "The combination of 'Cathedral'

---

[5]Two other works had their first performances at these consecration ceremonies: *The Beatitudes*, a cantata by Sir Arthur Bliss, Master of the Queen's Music, commissioned for the occasion, and Michael Tippett's *King Priam*, which Geraint Lewis has called "one of the most war-torn of all operas," produced at Coventry by the Royal Opera, Covent Garden.

[6]The concert was not without its share of hitches and anxieties. Britten and Davies made their way to the platform in something close to darkness because no one had remembered to switch on the floodlights. The BBC was there to broadcast the event, but the cathedral authorities had opened only one door, with the result that there was no hope of getting the audience inside and seated by the posted starting time. This brought another complication in that the transmitters were designed to turn off automatically after a certain amount of air silence. Moreover, the cathedral acoustics made such a muddle of the sound that listeners had to take musical excellence on faith; indeed, John Waterhouse, the critic at the *Birmingham Post*, declined to turn in a review until he could hear the work in an acoustically clearer space. At the end, when Meredith Davies congratulated Britten, he received a terse response: "Yes, the idea was good."

and Reconciliation with W. Germany . . . was too much for [the Soviets]." Vishnevskaya was later allowed to take part in the first recording of the *War Requiem*, and she sang many performances after that, often conducted by her husband and Britten's treasured friend Mstislav Rostropovich.

The *War Requiem* was not Britten's first peace manifesto in music: in 1937 he had composed a *Pacifist March* for a Peace Pledge Union concert. It was a combination of his pacifism and his despair at Stanley Baldwin's and later Neville Chamberlain's appeasement of Hitler that drove him to follow W. H. Auden and Christopher Isherwood to the United States in 1939. His companion on that journey—and for life, as it turned out— was Peter Pears, whom he had meet three years earlier when they had given a benefit concert for the Republican side in the Spanish Civil War. What drove Britten back to England was the chance discovery in a Los Angeles bookstore of a volume of poems by George Crabbe and, a few days later, of an article by E. M. Forster about Crabbe. "To think of Crabbe is to think of England," Forster began. That sentence changed Britten's life. It made inescapable his feeling that he must go home, and it was in fact in Crabbe's *The Borough* (1810) that he found the material for *Peter Grimes*.

Peter Grimes is one of many Britten works about the collision of innocence with wickedness and corruption, of innocence outraged, but in the *War Requiem* Britten for the first time presents this theme explicitly rather than as a parable or in symbolic form. Britten had twice planned projects, both aborted for external or technical reasons, that would serve as spiritual preparations for the *War Requiem*: an oratorio titled *Mea Culpa* after the dropping of the atomic bomb on Hiroshima and Nagasaki in 1945, and a work to commemorate the assassination of Gandhi in 1948. The commission from Coventry was what he was waiting for, what he needed.

For the *War Requiem*, Britten drew on forces larger and more complex than in any previous work of his. The basic division of the performers is into two groups, reflecting the dual source of the words: text (the Latin Mass for the Dead) and commentary (Owen's poems). The Latin text is essentially the province of the large chorus, but from this there is spillover in two opposite directions: the solo soprano represents a heightening of the choral singing at its most emotional, while the boys' choir represents liturgy at its most distanced. The mixed chorus and solo soprano are accompanied by the full orchestra; the boys' choir, whose voices should be distant, is supported by the organ. All this constitutes one group. The other group consists of the tenor and baritone soloists, who bring us the Owen songs, and they are accompanied by the chamber orchestra.

You feel the presence of three great classics behind the *War Requiem*: the two Passion settings of Johann Sebastian Bach, whose design of text-plus-commentary and the articulation of that design through distinctions of weight, color, and texture provided Britten with important models, and the Verdi Requiem, which Britten recognized as the most powerful setting of the words he himself was about to tackle.

"Requiem aeternam"

The orchestra represents stability, although the steady gait of four beats to the bar is broken from time to time by fives and threes, and the little bells on the dissonant interval of F-sharp and C add a certain restlessness. Against those solemn iambs (and occasional anapests) the chorus murmurs its prayer in rapid syllables. After the music rises to a climax and sinks again to *pianissimo*, the boys sing the "Te decet hymnus" calmly, dispassionately, in meters whose irregularity seems very much not of this earth, and with violins sounding a slow echo of the bells' F-sharp and C. The opening music returns, to be suddenly broken into by the quick and agitated notes of the harp, against which the tenor sings the first of the Owen tropes, that glorious series of songs that for many listeners constitutes the most deeply treasurable element of the *War Requiem*.

This first one is the sonnet *Anthem for Doomed Youth*: "What passing-bells for these who die as cattle?" At "Not in the hands of boys," the second line of the sestet, oboe and violin bring back the "Te decet hymnus" melody. Punctuated again by the strangely unsettling bells, the "Kyrie eleison" is sung by unaccompanied chorus on a harmonic path that carries the music from the unease of the F-sharp/C dissonance to a peaceful close in F major.

"Dies irae"

This is the longest text and thus also the longest musical movement. Distant fanfares bring the war scene before us; then chorus and orchestra in hushed staccato begin to paint the picture of the Day of Judgment. The key, G minor, is that of Verdi's "Dies irae," and the huge outburst of brass for "Tuba mirum" is another bow to that earlier Requiem. Britten incurs that debt not for want of originality, but out of a desire to establish a connection with the great tradition. Brass also introduces the next interpolation, "Bugles sang, saddening the evening air," an Owen draft for a poem tentatively titled *But I Was Looking at the Permanent Stars*. Britten uses only the first seven lines. These are given to the baritone, and they bring back the fanfares that began the "Dies irae."

The solo soprano is heard for the first time at "Liber scriptus." In contrast to the majesty of her phrases, the chorus timidly asks, "Quid sum miser tunc dicturus?" (What shall I, a wretch, say then?). A snare drum breaks into the quiet final cadence of "Rex tremendae majestatis," and tenor and baritone together sing the bitterly cheery *Next War*: "Out there, we've walked quite friendly up to Death." The rat-tat of that duet disappears into silence; then with great solemnity the altos begin the "Recordare." At "Confutatis maledictis" the music springs again into a fierce *allegro*, and that malediction is suddenly brought near as a brutal cannonade on the kettledrums introduces six lines from Owen's *Sonnet— On Seeing a Piece of Our Artillery Brought into Action*. "Be slowly lifted up, thou long black arm" is how it begins, and it ends: "May God curse thee, and cut thee from our soul!" Again the chorus invokes Judgment Day, this time in heavy *fortissimo*.

The music seems to move into the distance, and the soprano slowly intones the anguished, broken lines of the "Lacrimosa" (in Verdi's "Lacrimosa" key of B-flat minor). Flute, cymbal, and shuddering violins, all as quiet as possible, make a screen against which the tenor whispers "Move him into the sun," the first line of *Futility*, an elegy from the last spring of the war. The poet, seeing a dead young soldier, imagines how the sun's gentle touch awoke him once, but ends in a bitter cry: "O what made fatuous sunbeams toil / To break earth's sleep at all?" This time, to ineffably poignant effect, Britten intercuts two strains of music, brief phrases of the "Lacrimosa" punctuating the grief-laden song. Against the tenor's last word, the two bells again sound their dissonant notes, and the F-sharp-to-F chorale with which the "Requiem aeternam" ended also brings the "Dies irae" to a close as the choir softly intones "Pie Jesu Domine."

Offertorium

The boys begin this movement, the full chorus entering at the invocation of Saint Michael, the standard-bearer who will lead the souls into the holy light. Setting "Quam olim Abrahae" as a fugue is an old tradition, and Britten follows it. Here he also quotes himself. In 1952 he had written—for Pears, contralto Kathleen Ferrier, and himself—a canticle, *Abraham and Isaac*, based on the Chester Miracle Play, and the fugue subject in "Quam olim Abrahae" is taken from that touching work. But Wilfred Owen, too, had his sinister take on the story of God's testing of

Abraham's faith, and now, almost without a shift of pace, the music moves into the chamber orchestra and the recounting by the tenor and the baritone of *The Parable of the Old Man and the Young*. It is an inspired textual connection. The music for "When lo! An angel called him out of heaven" is the voice-of-God music from the canticle, but with the tenor, Abraham in the earlier work, now taking the part of Isaac. With the shocking turn of the poem when Abraham ignores the angel's command to sacrifice the ram—"But the old man would not so, but slew his son, / And half the seed of Europe, one by one"—the music returns to the now brutish-sounding fugue. As it recedes, we become aware of the boys serenely intoning the "Hostias."

Sanctus

Against the whirring of high-pitched percussion, the soprano declaims the opening words in the grandest vocal style. The chorus, chanting softly on monotones, seems to want to deny the very possibility of such a style, but as layer upon layer is added, the music builds a huge crescendo of wonder and praise. The "Hosanna" is brilliant, the Benedictus, again with soprano, more conversational. A quick return of the "Hosanna" is abruptly cut off to make way for Owen's *The End*, the earth's protest: "Mine ancient scars shall not be glorified, / Nor my titanic tears, the sea, be dried."

Agnus Dei

Against hushed sixteenth-notes, five of them to a bar, the tenor sings *At a Calvary Near the Ancre*:

> The scribes on all the people shove
> And bawl allegiance to the state,
> But they who love the greater love
> Lay down their life; they do not hate.

The chorus, using the music of the tenor's accompaniment, sings the Agnus Dei. Britten's timing of these quiet choral interventions—after the end of Owen's first stanza, next overlapping the last two words of the second stanza, then overlapping the ends of the final stanza's second and fourth lines—creates a subtle intensification in the unfolding of the song/chant, but without any increase in volume. When the music appears to be over, with the barely audible chorus holding the final sound of "sempiternam," the tenor crosses the language border to add his own "Dona nobis pacem." This prayer for peace closes the Agnus Dei in the Ordinary of the Mass, but not in the Mass for the Dead: the textual variant here is Britten's own. Most of the music in this Agnus Dei consists of alternations of segments of B-minor and C-major scales; for the tenor's haunting envoi, Britten offers a variation or extension of that idea: five notes of the B-minor scale (which can also be heard as five notes of a scale of F-sharp), then five notes of a C-minor scale, with the line finally coming to rest on F-sharp. It makes another version of the F-sharp/C combination of which we hear so much in the *War Requiem*.

"Libera me"

The *War Requiem* is full of marches—dangerous Mahlerian nightmare marches—and this final prayer begins with one of them. What the double basses play after the introductory measure of the drums is a variant of the music that accompanied "What passing-bells" in the first movement. The chorus keens its plea, the music gathers speed and sonority up to the explosion on "ignem" (fire), the soprano—in another reminiscence of Verdi—stammers "Tremens factus sum ego" (I am made to tremble). The "Dies irae" returns, building up to an outcry more piercing than any we have heard until now. After that, all physical energy is spent. Finally, nothing remains save a B-flat-major chord for the strings of the chamber orchestra, *pianissimo*. Britten marks it *cold*.

Against this, the tenor begins the final interpolation, *Strange Meeting*, the poem most often cited as the summit of Owen's achievement. Two dead soldiers speak, enemies in life, friends in death, joined in their mourning for "the undone years"—the English tenor, the German baritone. "I am the enemy you killed, my friend."[7] As they interweave their lines on the closing words "Let us sleep now"—they were an afterthought of Owen's—the boys add their gentle "In paradisum deducant te Angeli" (also heard in Fauré's Requiem, but not in those of Mozart, Berlioz, or Verdi). Gradually the boys pull the full chorus, the soprano, and the orchestra into their music. They themselves withdraw from the mounting mass of sound, at last to reenter with the first words we heard, "Requiem aeternam dona eis." Their notes are F-sharp and C. The great liturgy and the testimony of one poet-soldier have merged into one music. And now we hear for the last time that mysterious choral progression with bells, the

---

[7]Fischer-Dieskau, born in 1925, describes in his memoirs how shattered he was by this combination of music and poetry. Pears, older and with childhood memories of what some Englishmen of his generation still dubbed the Great War, recalled that he could hardly get his colleague to stand and leave the choir stalls at the end of the Coventry performance.

progression from the acid unrest of the F-sharp/C tritone to the quiet of the closing chord of F major: "Requiescant in pace. Amen."

The last word must go to Peter Pears, the artist who, except for Britten himself, knew and understood the *War Requiem* more profoundly than anyone else: "It *isn't* the end, we haven't escaped, we must still think about it, we are not allowed to end in a peaceful dream."

Luigi Cherubini

Luigi Carlo Zanobi Salvadore Maria Cherubini was born in Florence, Tuscany, on 14 September 1760 and died in Paris on 15 March 1842.

Requiem in C Minor

Cherubini's C-Minor Requiem, composed in 1816, was first heard under the composer's direction in the abbey church of Saint Denis on the outskirts of Paris. For centuries, Saint Denis had been the burial place for French monarchs, but their graves had been vandalized during the Revolution. The date of the first performance, 21 January 1817, was the twenty-fifth anniversary of the guillotining of King Louis XVI.

Mixed four-part chorus. Two oboes, two clarinets, two bassoons, two horns, two trumpets, three trombones, tam-tam, timpani, and strings.

Poor Cherubini! He has never quite recovered from Berlioz's burlesque of him in the *Memoirs*. Of course, Cherubini in his late sixties and the twenty-five-year-old Berlioz were not made to get along, but still, as David Cairns puts it in his biography of Berlioz,

> there is a strip-cartoon, Tom-and-Jerry air about the way Berlioz presents [this] relationship . . . from their original encounter in the Conservatoire

library over the full score of [Gluck's] *Alceste*—when Cherubini and the porter chase him round the table because he has not come in by the authorized entrance—to the neat trick by which Cherubini persuades Berlioz not to apply for a vacant professorship of harmony.

For Berlioz, Cherubini was both the representative of an older generation and a man whose adroitness when it came to working the system had enabled him to maintain influence and power through all changes of political climate—and there had been plenty of those since the revolution that began fourteen years before Berlioz was born. As director of the Conservatory—and that was a position whose importance and influence in French musical life you cannot begin to imagine by thinking, say, about the presidency of Juilliard or Eastman—Cherubini was a bit of a pedant and certainly a stickler for rules, musical and administrative. For Berlioz, who had no political skills and was never in tune with anything that spelled Power and Establishment, such a person was automatically an object of suspicion. That after forty years in Paris Cherubini still spoke French with a pungent Florentine accent made him a fit subject for comedy as well. And however scrupulous Berlioz was about not letting problematic personal relationships interfere with his musical judgment, when it came to personalities no holds were barred in his exuberant and brilliantly written *Memoirs*.

If, on the other hand, we go to witnesses less flamboyant than Berlioz, we can find a Cherubini who, beneath his exceedingly thin skin and concomitant irritability, was a keen amateur botanist, a dedicated card player, and a man with a generous capacity for friendship, tenderness, and love.[1] For example, Adolphe Adam, the composer of *Giselle* and *O Holy Night*, remembered a man "whose fine old face" would, after some initial grumpiness, be mantled with a "sensitive, mischievous smile" and in whom "good nature prevailed, the spoiled child disappeared, and [who] grew kindly in spite of himself. He opened his heart to you, and then you could resist him no longer." Two other elective Parisians, Rossini and Chopin, delighted in visiting their senior colleague, and Cherubini was bound in close friendship to Jean-Auguste-Dominique Ingres, whose beautiful portrait of him hangs in the Louvre.[2]

---

[1] One beneficiary of his kindness was the boy Louis Braille. Cherubini arranged for him to be given organ lessons when everyone had written off the idea of such training for a blind boy as a waste of time.

[2] After Ingres had shown the portrait to his sitter, he added the figure of a Muse in the act of laying a wreath on the composer's head. Cherubini was furious, declaring that Ingres had no business deciding who should be crowned by the Muses, and for weeks he refused to speak to the painter. Only after Ingres sent an apology did Cherubini relent: as a peace offering, he sent a three-voiced canon inscribed to "Ingres amabile, pittor chiarissimo." That page for the "most renowned painter" was in fact his very last composition.

The account of Cherubini in the *Memoirs*, so vivid, so amusing, so often cited, blots out something that Berlioz came to recognize and acknowledge fervently—namely, that Cherubini at his best was a powerful composer. The obituary Berlioz wrote for him was generous, and the paragraph on the C-Minor Requiem is full of such phrases as "wealth of ideas, grandeur of form, nobility of style," "truth of expression," and "immeasurable worth." Commenting on the *Marche religieuse* in the "Coronation" Mass for Charles X, Berlioz wrote that "its transcendental calm . . . brings tears to the eyes of the listener. . . . If ever the use of the word 'sublime' needs to be justified, it surely can be when applied to Cherubini's *Marche religieuse.*"

We also do well to remember that Beethoven revered Cherubini as the greatest composer among his contemporaries, saying he was more satisfied with Cherubini's Requiem than with Mozart's, and indeed, it was Cherubini's work that was sung at a memorial service for Beethoven in Vienna's Saint Charles Church ten days after his death.[3] Verdi found the work well worth studying; Mendelssohn, another admirer and conductor of the Requiem, praised the operatic Cherubini for "his sparkling fire, his clever and unexpected transitions, and the neatness and grace with which he writes"; Schumann declared that the C-Minor Requiem "stands without an equal in the world"; and Bruckner copied out movements of Cherubini's Masses for study. Brahms kept likenesses of just three composers in his study: a picture of Bach, a bust of Beethoven, and a reproduction of the Ingres portrait of Cherubini.[4] Wagner, not surprisingly, was more reserved, but even so, he called Cherubini "certainly the greatest of musical architects, a kind of Palladio, rather stiffly symmetrical, but so beautiful and so assured."

Louis XVIII, younger brother of the unfortunate Louis XVI, reclaimed the French throne in 1814 after Napoleon's defeat, abdication, and banishment to Elba.[5] The former emperor's dramatic return forced the king to flee to Ghent, but when the famous "hundred days" had run their course, Louis reclaimed the throne, retaining it until his death in 1824. He wished to see the anniversary of his brother's execution observed, and it was for one of those dark commemorations that Cherubini was commissioned to compose this Requiem in C minor. Given his

---

[3]Their admiration for Beethoven and Gluck is one of the few things about which Cherubini and Berlioz would have agreed.

[4]Brahms conducted the C-Minor Requiem on several occasions. He, too, hated that Ingres Muse and covered her up with a piece of cardboard.

[5]Well might you wonder about Louis XVII. The son of Louis XVI and Marie Antoinette, he became titular king of France when his father was beheaded in 1793. He spent his entire "reign" in prison, seriously ill, and died in June 1795. He had just turned ten.

essentially right-wing bent, Cherubini was happy about the restoration of the monarchy, and he sensed this assignment as a great honor.

An aesthetic of solemnity and classical austerity moved Cherubini to use no vocal solos in the Requiem. The opening, with its plain unisons, its silences, and its dark orchestral coloration, is immediately impressive, and the dynamics, with their crescendos and *sforzandi*, leave no doubt that Cherubini wanted us to sense passion beneath the austerity. At first we hear just cellos and bassoons. Violas, divided into two sections, join in when the chorus begins to sing, and after a while we come to realize that we are not going to hear violins at all in this movement.[6] In accordance with tradition for the orchestration of Requiem Masses, Cherubini also omits flutes. Moreover, the timpani, when they enter a few measures later, are muted by means of a piece of felt.

To begin with, the text is declaimed in block chords, but at "Te decet hymnus" Cherubini enlivens the choral texture with counterpoint, the orchestra adding poignant commentary. The prayer for eternal light to shine on the souls of the departed, "Et lux perpetua," elicits a still more elaborate and beautiful interweaving of lines in chorus and orchestra, and anxious sighs accompany the prayer for divine mercy, "Kyrie eleison."

Composers of Requiems differ in the ways they divide the text into separate movements and even about what to include at all. Unlike the Ordinary of the Mass, the Requiem is not a firmly set text. Cherubini follows his Introitus et Kyrie with a setting of words from Psalm 112, a text rarely included in a Requiem: "In memoria aeterna erit justus, ab auditione mala non timebit" (The righteous shall be in everlasting remembrance. He shall not be afraid of evil tidings).[7] The music for this is a broadly flowing movement in triple meter, still without violins.

The close of that section is soft, but the quiet is shattered by *fortissimo* blasts for horns, trumpets, and trombones. That, in turn, is punctuated by a tremendous crash on the tam-tam, a sound we will not hear again in the Requiem. I imagine Cherubini excitedly exclaiming "Ç'a frappé! Ç'a frappé!" (That hit home!), as he used to do backstage at particularly effective strokes in his operas. Timpani, when they come in, are no longer muffled. The scene is set for the "Dies irae," the fearsome depiction of the Day of Judgment. Even as the last reverberations of the gong vanish into the air, strings, in threatening *pianissimo*, begin a furious

[6]I feel sure that this influenced Brahms in his decision to exclude violins from the first movement of his *German Requiem*. For that matter, I should not be surprised to learn that Bruckner's notable appreciation of violas in the orchestra owed something to his study of Cherubini's C-Minor Requiem.

[7]Cherubini includes this verse in his other Requiem, in D minor, and it is found as well in settings by Victoria and Cimarosa. I am indebted to Anne Montague for unearthing this information.

buzzing and scurrying that suggests the assembly of the dead on this day of days. Over their agitated figurations, the chorus, with the men echoing the women at a distance of one measure, begins to sing.

The "Dies irae" is a big poem: eighteen rhyming tercets, followed by the "Lacrimosa," fifty-seven lines in all. Most composers divide it up into several movements—Verdi as many as ten. Cherubini, however, sets it as a single piece, articulating it powerfully and vividly. His responses to the details of the text are the traditional ones: for example, a huge, brass-dominated climax for the "Tuba mirum," the sounding of the Last Trumpet, and an awed hush at "Mors stupebit," the evocation of death itself amazed at the sight of all creation rising at the summons of the Judge. At the prayer to the fount of pity for salvation, "Salva me, fons pietatis," the singers, their *pianissimo* lines descending in imitation through three and a half octaves, bare their hearts in music of deep pathos. At "Recordare, Jesu pie," the plea for Jesus to remember that "I was the reason for your journey," the violins, firsts and seconds in alternation, support the singing with those descending pairs of notes that in Cherubini's time were called "soupirs" or "Seufzer"—sighs.[8] Musical thoughts are revisited in ways suggested by the text: "Rex tremendae majestatis" (King of tremendous majesty), for example, brings back the massive sound of the opening of the "Dies irae," and at "Voca me cum benedictis" (Call me with the blessed), Cherubini recapitulates the touching plea of "Salva me, fons pietatis." It is in this movement particularly that Cherubini shows the mastery of composition that earned him the admiration of Beethoven and Brahms, a mastery sharpened by his knowledge and experience of opera.

The pace seems to slow. Actually the tempo does not change, but there are fewer events per measure, and so the inner rhythm calms down. This eventually leads to a literal slowing. For the last six lines of the "Dies irae," "Lacrimosa dies illa" (On that day of weeping), Cherubini leaves the previous *Allegro maestoso* and goes into a grandly spacious *Largo*. He scores this music with a wonderful sense of magnificent sonority, though most of it is in fact quiet. The violins add an unrelenting accompaniment in groups of three notes. This is quite a test for the conductor: Are these just patterns of sixteenth-notes or are they, as one can hear so clearly in Toscanini's extraordinary 1950 recording, expressions of fervent, anguished pleading?

It is time now for a deep breath. The Offertorio—"Domine, Jesu Christe"—begins softly and at a moderate pace, but flying arpeggios for

---

[8]For these sighs to make their effect, first and second violins must sit on opposite sides of the stage in the classical way.

the violins light up the evocation of the King of Glory, "Rex gloriae." The prayer that the souls of the departed may be freed from the pains of hell— "de poenis inferni"—is emphasized by fierce whipping figures in the strings, and the image of the deep pit—"profundo lacu"—is set before us by the stammering of the basses and a dramatic darkening of the harmony. This prayer offers a composer wonderful opportunities, and Cherubini responds sensitively to each, from the shuddering fear of descent into darkness—"ne cadant in obscurum"—to the softly radiant music for the holy standard-bearer Michael, who will lead the dead into holy light—"Sed signifer sanctus Michael repraesentet eas in lucem sanctam."

"Quam olim Abrahae," the recollection of God's promise to Abraham, is traditionally set as a fugue, and Cherubini here outdoes his colleagues, past and future, by giving us a big, virtuosically written, highly energized, and splendid-sounding triple fugue on three subjects. The "Hostias" (Sacrifices) brings a broader tempo, a simpler texture, and a change to triple meter, after which the Offertorio concludes with a return to the "Quam olim Abrahae" fugue. An odd and interesting detail: Cherubini changes the word "facimus" to "faciemus" for the sake of a more resonant climax, *e* sounding much brighter than *i*.[9]

The Sanctus is majestic and grandly celebratory. The "Pie Jesu," which follows it, is quietly reverent, and here Cherubini returns to the Requiem's first sonority: divided violas and no violins. An unusual touch, one emulated by Fauré, who knew this work well, is to give the chorus sopranos and later the tenors miniature arias to sing while the rest of the chorus remains silent. The end of this "Pie Jesu," with ever-wider intervals between words and, for the orchestra, a drawn-out series of closing chords descending all the way to *ppp*, is for me an especially memorable and touching page.

Cherubini combines the Agnus Dei and the final "Communio—Lux aeterna luceat eis" (Let everlasting light shine upon them)—into a single movement. Perhaps it is here—in its last minutes—that we find the most inspired and the most heartfelt music in this neglected masterpiece, as the chorus repeats "luceat eis," dominated by deep and solemn tolling C's in the voices and the orchestra's lowest and darkest instruments.

Postscript: Earlier I mentioned Cherubini's other Requiem, the D-Minor of 1836. This, too, is powerfully impressive both as composition and prayer, and much worth knowing. As he did in the one in C minor, Cherubini

---

[9]Opera buffs who know their *Don Giovanni* will perhaps recall hearing some Donna Elviras in "Mi tradì" adjust "infelice" to "infelioce" to avoid having to sing the fairly high A-flat on the dark *i* vowel.

eschews soloists, and the work takes on an extra measure of austerity because the chorus consists of men's voices only. Cherubini had hoped that the C-Minor Requiem, of which he was understandably proud, would be the music at his own funeral. But before it came to that, he made an unhappy discovery. The work was to be sung in 1834 at the state funeral in the Invalides of France's leading opera composer, Adrien Boieldieu, but the archbishop of Paris forbade the use of women in a musical performance in a liturgical setting. Therefore, to ensure that he could be buried to the sound of his own music, Cherubini composed a second Requiem to whose scoring the archbishop could not object. It stands with Mozart's Requiem, Alban Berg's Violin Concerto, and Stravinsky's *Requiem Canticles* as a work written by a composer with his own death in mind, and it was indeed sung at Cherubini's obsequies in 1842.

Cherubini and his wife Cécile are buried in Paris's Père Lachaise cemetery, quite near Chopin, and Cherubini would be furious to know that his tomb was modeled on the Ingres portrait, objectionable Muse and all. In his native city of Florence, the church of Santa Croce erected a monument to him in the probably vain hope that some day, like his friend Rossini, he might be moved from Père Lachaise to that great church and so come home to join his fellow Florentines Galileo, Ghiberti, Machiavelli, and Michelangelo.

Luigi Dallapiccola

Luigi Dallapiccola was born on 3 February 1904 in Pisino d'Istria, then in the Austro-Hungarian Empire (now Pazin, Croatia), and died in Florence on 19 February 1975.

Canti di prigionia (Songs of Captivity), for Chorus and Some Instruments

Dallapiccola composed the first section of the *Canti*, *Preghiera di Maria Stuarda* (Prayer of Mary Stuart), as an independent piece in 1938; it was first performed under the direction of Léonce Gras in Brussels on 10 April 1940. After that performance, the composer added the *Invocazione di Boezio* (Invocation of Boethius), completing it on 14 July, and also the *Congedo di Girolamo Savonarola* (Girolamo Savonarola's Farewell), which he finished on 13 October 1941. The complete *Canti* had their first performance in Rome on 11 December 1941, Fernando Previtali conducting. *Preghiera di Maria Stuarda* is dedicated to Paul Collaer, music director of the Belgian Radio and a strong supporter of new music. *Invocazione di Boezio* is inscribed to the conductor Ernest Ansermet, and *Congedo di Girolamo Savonarola* to Sandro and Luisa Materassi, Sandro, a violinist, being Dallapiccola's recital partner from 1930 into the 1970s.

Four-part chorus. The "alcuni strumenti" are two pianos, two harps, timpani, xylomarimba, vibraphone, tubular bells, suspended cymbals, crash cymbals, three tam-tams (small, medium, and large), triangle, snare drum, and bass drum.[1]

When my son Sebastian was born, Dallapiccola, whom I had come to know when I was a Fulbright student in Italy and later when he was visiting professor at Queens College, New York, sent him a postcard as a welcome into this world. On it he had inscribed a musical quote from Debussy's *Martyrdom of Saint Sebastian* and written out these lines from C. P. Cavafy's *Ithaca* (as far as I know, the English translation was Dallapiccola's own):

> The Laestrygones and the Cyclops,
> And angry Poseidon you shall not meet
> If you carry them not in your soul,
> If your soul sets them not up before you.

Which he followed with a stern "Memento!" The composer of the *Canti di prigionia*, the opera *Il prigioniero*, and the *Canti di liberazione*, had himself seen them, the Laestrygones, those cannibal giants who devoured Odysseus' crew, but he carried them not in his soul. Still, oppression and imprisonment, oppression's companion and consequence, were themes ever present in Luigi Dallapiccola's mind.

Experience came early. His birthplace, Pisino, some thirty miles south of Trieste on the Istrian peninsula, was in one of those ever-conflict-ridden European border territories, and he recalled how, when the train from Trieste to Pola stopped at its tiny station, the conductor would call out "Mitterburg, Pisino, Pazin." In 1915, when Italy declared war on Austria-Hungary, the Hapsburg authorities cracked down on the Italian minorities in the empire, and these were eventually deported from their borderland homes and forced to relocate in the center. Pio Dallapiccola, the future composer's father, was the principal of Pisino's only Italian high school as well as a teacher of Latin and Greek. Known to sympathize with the Irredentists, the group that wanted to liberate Italian territories under foreign rule, he was classified as "politically unreliable," and the whole family was made to move under police escort to Graz, some 150 miles northeast.

[1]Stressing that he had been concerned with "comprehension" rather than "success [or] the possibility of frequent performances," Dallapiccola remarked many years later on his having "called for the vibraphone because it was necessary, although I knew that in 1938 there was not one to be found in all of Italy."

It was a kind of *prigionia*, and it lasted twenty months, until the end of the war in November 1918. On the other hand, Graz also provided the boy with opportunities for musical experiences that would not have come his way in Pisino, particularly performances of Wagner and other non-Italian music. He always remembered 18 May 1917, the evening his father took him to *The Flying Dutchman*: "Even before the Overture came to an end I had decided to become a musician."

After the family returned to Istria, he worked hard at music, but at his father's insistence continued his general education. Dallapiccola became a man of wide and deep knowledge, curious and erudite—a profoundly religious humanist who lived intimately with the work of Proust, Joyce, and Mann, but who liked to say that his real teachers were the medieval mystics; who knew the Greek and Roman classics, Dante, Shakespeare, and Goethe; who loved Blake, Donne, the cross-shaped poems of George Herbert, and what he called the "adamantine words" of the First Letter to the Corinthians[2]; who was fluent in classical tongues and also in French, German, and English, all spoken with a resounding Florentine accent; who revered Webern for his purity but found relatively little to take from his compositions; who was an analytic intellectual nonetheless in love with the physical sensation of music[3]; who was pained by corruption and slovenliness in language or wherever he found it; who viewed the world tragically and with compassion.

A second critical event in Dallapiccola's musical development was his encounter at seventeen with Schoenberg—not just the music, but also the wide-ranging and speculative treatise *Harmonielehre*, both having come to his attention through a violent attack on them in an essay by the composer Ildebrando Pizzetti. To this there was a touching sequel three years later, when Schoenberg conducted his *Pierrot lunaire* at the Pitti Palace in Florence, the city Dallapiccola had chosen as his home, mainly—and how characteristic a decision this was for him—because of its associations with Dante. Two members of the tiny audience in the *sala bianca* had brought pocket scores of *Pierrot*: one was the twenty-year-old Dallapiccola; the other was Puccini, close to death from throat cancer. Himself too shy to approach Schoenberg, Dallapiccola watched in awe—an awe one could hear in his voice as he told the story decades later—as the two great composers conversed quietly in the corner for a long time after the performance.

---

[2]Cross-shaped notations occur in Dallapiccola's music, too: imagine the appearance on the page of a long melody for a single instrument punctuated by a chord for the entire ensemble. The passage in the Pauline epistle he was particularly thinking of was the first verse of chapter 13, which begins, "Though I speak with the tongues of men and of angels . . ."

[3]When he visited Boston in 1967, and the New England Conservatory Orchestra devoted most of a concert to his music, Dallapiccola asked Frederik Prausnitz, the conductor, to end the program with Ravel's *Boléro*.

The connection to Schoenberg became vital toward the end of the next decade as Dallapiccola became ever more curious about serial music. The *Canti di prigionia* was one of the first works in which he explored the possibilities of that world. He felt at one with the sense of order it provided, and it gave strong bones to his natural lyric bent.

The thirties began well: Dallapiccola succeeded his teacher, Ernesto Consolo, as professor of piano at the Cherubini Conservatory in Florence; his compositions began to circulate and be heard at important festivals such as the Venice Biennale; travels to northern Europe afforded him new discoveries such as the music of Mahler and, thanks to a *Simon Boccanegra* in Berlin, the recognition of Verdi not just as a popular composer but as one of stunning greatness.[4] The encounter in Venice with the composer Gian Francesco Malipiero gave him another guiding star in matters of artistry and artistic morality, and he was especially struck by the contrast between Malipiero's *Canzone del tempo*, with its sense of life's passing, and the compulsory optimism and cult of youth that were sweeping Fascist Italy, whose new national anthem was called *Giovinezza* (Youth).

For, yes, there was Mussolini. Like many of his countrymen, Dallapiccola in his twenties had felt some enthusiasm for the dictator who made the trains run on time, but in the next decade he sensed the dangers as Mussolini came ever more under Hitler's spell and drew closer in his political actions to those of the Führer.[5] What Fascism meant hit home when he began living with a Jewish woman, Laura Coen Luzzatto, who became his wife in April 1938. In July of that year, a group of university professors published a manifesto declaring that Italians were pure Nordic Aryans, and two months later, Mussolini proclaimed racial laws similar to those promulgated in Germany. Laura Dallapiccola spent much of the war in hiding.

In 1938, when these disastrous changes occurred, Dallapiccola was writing an opera, *Volo di notte* (*Night Flight*), based on the novel by Antoine de Saint-Exupéry, best remembered for *The Little Prince*. He interrupted work on *Volo di notte* and in four days set to music the prayer Mary, Queen of Scots, wrote in her prison cell at Fotheringay Castle the night before her execution in 1587. He had found the text in Stefan Zweig's biography of that complex woman, so hungry for power and for men, so filled with energy and courage, so unwise, and so unfortunate.[6]

It was some time after composing the *Preghiera di Maria Stuarda* that Dallapiccola began to think of it as the first panel of a triptych on words of condemned prisoners. He decided on two who had shared Mary's

[4]Dallapiccola's writings about Verdi are among the most stimulating and original we have.
[5]In the vehemence of his anti-Fascism, Dallapiccola in retrospect sometimes antedated his political turnaround.
[6]Was Mary Stuart ever in Shakespeare's mind when he limned his Cleopatra just nineteen or twenty years after the queen's death?

fate, death at the hands of their political enemies. All three victims were betrayed and sentenced in trials involving forgeries or false witnesses or testimony elicited under torture.

The idea for the second part of the triptych, the *Invocation of Boethius*, developed quickly, but planning the finale took more time as Dallapiccola made several false starts in choosing a text. He had sketched music for a seventeenth-century madrigal, but the imbalance of following two Latin texts with one in Italian bothered him. Plato's account of the last hours of Socrates moved him deeply, but he found the Latin translations "cold and unapproachable." A letter of John Calvin's contemporary and opponent, Sébastien Castellion, "looked promising" but in the event proved unsuitable.

It was Hitler who led Dallapiccola toward a solution. A bellicose speech about the bombardment of England "reminded me of the horrors Girolamo Savonarola had prophesied. . . . Sir Samuel Hoare, then [British] Foreign Secretary, in answering Hitler exhorted the people to pray." These associations prompted Dallapiccola to remember Savonarola's leave-taking prayer, and with that he completed his *Canti di prigionia*. It was Dallapiccola's first essay in what would come to be called "engaged music," and in later years he was proud to have made a contribution that could stand alongside Karl Amadeus Hartmann's opera *Simplicius Simplicissimus*, Wladimir Vogel's oratorio *Thyl Claes*, and Schoenberg's *Ode to Napoleon Buonaparte* and *Survivor from Warsaw*.

One way that Italy maintained some independence from Germany was in her cultural politics. Attempts by Dallapiccola's publisher to get *Volo di notte* staged in Germany, whose opera houses had once been so hospitable to new works, were harshly rejected by Goebbels's Propaganda-Ministerium. The opera was, however, mounted in Florence in May 1940, just three weeks before Italy declared war on Great Britain and France, and it even got a new production in Rome as late as 1942.[7] The momentum of that success made it possible for the *Canti di prigionia*, unmistakable though their meaning was, to be introduced in Rome on an uncommonly chilly winter day, a day when the main news was that Italy had declared war on the United States. In 1944, with Rome liberated from the Germans, some of Dallapiccola's settings of Greek lyrics were performed in the capital, and when a daughter was born to the Dallapiccolas at the end of that year, her parents named her Annalibera.[8]

---

[7]The Rome production was part of a contemporary opera season that included Alban Berg's *Wozzeck*, long forbidden in Germany.

[8]Dr. Annalibera Dallapiccola is a distinguished philologist and scholar of Indian languages and literature.

The *Canti di prigionia* have a sequel. In 1955, by which time Dallapiccola was an internationally revered figure who drew students to Florence from many nations and continents, he completed a triptych of *Canti di liberazione*. One of the texts, along with words from Exodus and Saint Augustine, was the Castellion letter the composer had originally considered for the last section of the *Canti di prigionia*.

As I write these words twenty-nine years after his death, Dallapiccola is in eclipse—too "uptown" for the taste of the moment, perhaps, and, in spite of the delicacy of sound and texture so characteristic of his music, too rich for the blood and the digestive systems of many people. He will be rediscovered with amazement: the perfection of his text settings (and he is most significant as a composer of vocal music), his wonderfully Italianate lyricism, and the sheer beauty of the sound surface of his pieces make him such a treasurable composer that I cannot imagine him absent for long. I often recall what he once wrote to his friend and colleague Roger Sessions: "Si sa che il nostro mestiere è la scuola della pazienza" (We know that our profession is the school of patience).

This is the final prayer of Mary, Queen of Scots:

> O Domine Deus! speravi in Te.
> O care mi Jesu! nunc libera me.
> In dura catena, in misera poena, desidero Te.
> Languendo, gemendo et genu flectendo,
> Adoro, imploro, ut liberes me.
>
> O Lord God! I trusted in Thee.
> O my dear Jesus, now set me free.
> In harsh chains, in grievous pain, I long for Thee.
> Languishing, sighing, and bending my knee,
> I entreat, I implore you to set me free.

For Dallapiccola, these words reflected "a permanent human condition. . . . For this reason I transformed the Queen's personal prayer into a collective song: I wanted everyone to shout the divine word *libera*." But before we get to that word—or any word—we hear an "Introduzione." Only instruments take part at first, but this, too, is vocal music, for the melody played *pianissimo* by harp and timpani at the very beginning and which then spreads through the entire ensemble is the "Dies irae" from the Gregorian Mass for the Dead. Most listeners will recognize it because, quoted so often in such works as Berlioz's *Symphonie fantastique*, many pieces by Rachmaninoff, and the *Danse macabre* of Saint-Saëns, it has become a musical emblem of death. "Given the world situation a few weeks after the Munich Conference, it did not seem inappropriate to think about the Last Judgment," Dallapiccola wrote.

What also appealed to him was the reach across the years from his own mid-twentieth-century language back to the Middle Ages: that, for him, was symbolic of the universality of his theme. The "Dies irae" and the tonal pattern in the particular ordering of the twelve notes we hear at the same time provide the material for all three *Canti*, different though they are in sound, character, and expression.

Against the instrumental "Dies irae," the chorus quietly makes its presence felt, at first in toneless, murmuring speech, then in humming. From a nearly inaudible beginning the music rises to *fortissimo* (marked *con angoscia*—anguished), then recedes once more. So far we have heard just three words, "O Domine Deus!" Now the full prayer can begin. The tempo is still slow, and the orchestra persists in its bell-like accompaniment. This section, too, arrives at a fierce climax, the pianists being directed to hammer out their notes ferociously. Again, the music recedes into silence, and as the sound of tam-tams and bass drum slowly fades from earshot the last words to hang in the air are "O Domine Deus!"

Boethius (c. 480–524) was a Roman scholar, philosopher, and statesman who brought knowledge of classical texts and ideals into the Middle Ages, translated Aristotle, and wrote treatises on theology, mathematics, astronomy, and music. He became an adviser to Theodoric the Great, but eventually fell afoul of that cruel and violent monarch and was executed on charges of treason and necromancy. In prison, he wrote *De Consolatione Philosophiae*, a work in which he maintained that in spite of all injustices there was a *summum bonum*, an overall good. Second only to the Bible, the *Consolatione*, widely translated (into English by Chaucer), was the most read book of its era. These are the lines Dallapiccola chose for the *Canti di prigionia*:

> Felix qui potuit boni
> Fontem visere lucidum,
> Felix qui potuit gravis
> Terrae solvere vincula.
>
> Happy the man who once
> Could clearly see the fount of good;
> Happy he who could leave behind
> The chains of life on earth.

Dallapiccola described this movement as "a kind of scherzo, with an instrumental introduction to which the *pianissimo* dynamic lends an 'apocalyptic' quality." The tempo is *prestissimo*, and over the continuous metallic rustle of cymbals, piano arpeggios race up and down across six octaves. Deep in the bass, harps and timpani intone the Dies irae, which eventually moves into the middle register as well. "Rats' feet over broken glass": terrifying prison music, surely the most powerful since *Fidelio*, and the more telling for that held-in *pianissimo*.

When the voices enter—only the women sing in this movement—it is with fiery *fortissimo* shouts of "Felix" set against pounding chords for harps and pianos. The emphasis is all on the memory and the idea of happiness. With the return of the ghostly prison music, the singers complete Boethius's first couplet. The music quiets down, and the singers give us the last two lines, lift them to an immense crest, and, back in *pianissimo*, persist for a long time with these words, pronounced now in a rebellious, under-cover hush.

Girolamo Savonarola (1452–1498) was a Dominican monk of legendary severity who set out to eliminate corruption both in the church, his aims being similar to those of Martin Luther a generation later, and in the city government of Florence. Through the fire-and-brimstone sermons in which he prophesied universal destruction, Savonarola won a large following and could take considerable credit for helping to topple the Medicis. For a time, he was virtual dictator of Florence.[9] The church, however, rallied its forces, enemies rose against Savonarola, and he was tortured, brought to trial, and put to death.

> Premat mundus, insurgant hostes, nihil timeo
> Quoniam in Te Domine speravi,
> Quoniam Tu es spes mea,
> Quoniam Tu altissimum posuisti refugium Tuum.

> Let the world oppress, let the foe rise up, I fear nothing
> For I have trusted, Lord, in Thee,
> For Thou art my hope,
> For Thou hast placed Thy refuge on the summit.

This is very different from the tenderness of Mary Stuart's prayer and the glow of light behind the words of Boethius. The music matches the words. The first two defiant lines rise in a mighty shout by the chorus in unison and octaves, and the pianos and harps intone "Dies irae, dies illa" with all their might. The first part of this *canto* is fueled by rage, but when the condemned monk utters the crucial words "Quoniam in Te Domine speravi," the tempo broadens and the declamation becomes

---

[9]The phrase "bonfire of the vanities" originated when Savonarola ordered a public burning of personal ornaments, showy clothing, playing cards, and books and pictures deemed lewd.

more flexible as well as *pianissimo*. The instrumental music that surrounds the singing remains intense and *espressivo*. Impassioned repetitions of the words "Quoniam Tu" initiate a great crescendo. In this movement as well, a dramatic falling away follows the attainment of the peak. At the end, we can just make out the rumble of drums and gongs, the vanishing of the last piano and harp chords, as the men in the chorus stammer out one final in "Te Domine." And when silence has arrived, Dallapiccola's meditation on imprisonment and faith is over.

Antonín Dvořák

Antonín Leopold Dvořák was born at Mühlhausen (Nela-
hozeves), Bohemia, on 8 September 1841 and died in Prague
on 1 May 1904.

Stabat Mater, op. 58

Dvořák sketched his *Stabat Mater* between 19 February and 7 May 1876 and worked out the score in full in the autumn of the following year, completing it on 13 November 1877. The first performance took place in Prague on 23 December 1880 at a concert of the Association of Musical Artists, and the score is dedicated to that group. Adolf Čech conducted, and the soloists were Eleanora Ehrenberg, Betty Fibich, Antonín Vávra, and Karel Čech. Dvořák called the *Stabat Mater* his Opus 28, but Simrock, his German publisher, sometimes liked to assign higher opus numbers to the composer's scores so as to create the impression that they represented more recent and more mature work.

Soprano, alto, tenor, and bass soloists, four-part mixed chorus. Two flutes, two oboes and English horn, two clarinets, two bassoons, four horns, two trumpets, three trombones, tuba, timpani, organ, and strings.

In the 1830s, the German poet Friedrich Rückert mourned the deaths of his young children, Ernst and Luise, in a series of 423 poems. *Kindertotenlieder* he called them, and in 1901 and 1904 Gustav Mahler famously and beautifully set five of them to music. This *Stabat Mater* is Dvořák's *Kindertotenlied*. In September 1875, he lost his two-day-old daughter Josefa, named for his wife's sister, Josefina Čermaková, the woman for whom he carried a torch all his life. Five months later, in response to that death, Dvořák, a devout Catholic, sketched the *Stabat Mater*. Aside from a Mass (or maybe two) he had written as a teenager and subsequently destroyed, this was his first grappling with a sacred text in Latin. In May 1876, he laid his *Stabat Mater* drafts aside in order to concentrate on other projects that were pending or had recently come up, among them the *Moravian Duets* for soprano and contralto, the Piano Concerto, the opera *The Cunning Peasant*, and the *Symphonic Variations*. Then, in the late summer of 1877, death again invaded the Dvořák household: the eleven-month-old Růžena died in August after accidentally drinking poison, and less than a month later, on 8 September, the composer's thirty-sixth birthday, the Dvořáks' firstborn, three-and-a-half-year-old Otakar, succumbed to smallpox, leaving his parents childless.[1] It was in the midst of this new onslaught of grief that Dvořák came back to the *Stabat Mater*, which he then completed in about five weeks.

"Stabat mater dolorosa" (The grieving mother stood): those words begin a long poem—twenty stanzas, three lines each—whose subject is the Virgin Mary as she beholds her Son on the cross. For the devout Catholic this is the ultimate *Kindertotenlied*. The text goes beyond description of the scene, exhorting the believer to partake of the mother's grief as a path to grace. It became part of the liturgy in the fifteenth century, was thrown out by the Council of Trent about a hundred years later, and was restored in 1727 as part of the services for the feast of the Seven Sorrows of Mary, observed on 15 September.

The author of the poem was long believed to be a certain Jacopone da Todi, a prosperous Umbrian merchant who became a Franciscan monk after the death of his young wife. Jacopone's authorship is now doubted, but it does appear that the poem came out of the Franciscan world sometime in the thirteenth century.

It is not an easy text to set: the persistent note of pathos is hard to sustain, and the jog-trot monotony of its trochees and thumping rhymes

---

[1]In due course there would be six more children, all but one living to a ripe old age. The exception was Otilie, called Otilka, who died in 1905 at twenty-seven. She had married the composer Josef Suk, who made a beautiful *tombeau* for her in his *Asrael Symphony*.

creates huge rhythmic difficulties for a composer. The poignant image of the grieving mother has inspired countless painters and sculptors in their depictions of the crucifixion, the deposition, and the *pietà*. It has not been quite so universally appealing to musicians; still, the *Stabat Mater* has attracted some interesting and a few great composers. One of the first was the mysterious and wonderful John Browne at the end of the fifteenth century, and among his successors we find Palestrina, Lassus, both Scarlattis, Pergolesi, Rossini, Liszt, Verdi, Szymanowski, Poulenc, and Pärt. Pergolesi's *Stabat Mater* was long the most popular of all sacred compositions; it is perhaps too pretty to meet the challenge of the text but also too appealing to deserve its current neglect. Liszt created some of his noblest music for this text. His setting is part of his huge oratorio *Christus*, and it would be highly worthwhile for an enterprising conductor to excerpt it from that context. Szymanowski's *Stabat Mater* is a fragrant and compelling work.

Dvořák wrote his *Stabat Mater* as a grieving father and a devout Roman Catholic, but it also turned out to be a landmark in his life as a composer. He had become famous at home in 1873 thanks to his cantata *The Heirs of the White Mountain*, lamenting the catastrophe of the defeat of the Bohemians by Austria in 1620 and the subsequent absorption of Bohemia into the Austrian Empire, and calling for a rebirth of national pride. In 1878, Dvořák's reputation began to spread abroad when, on Brahms's recommendation, the Berlin publisher Simrock took him on. Then the first performances of the *Stabat Mater* in Bohemia and Moravia, including one at Brno conducted by Janáček, made a huge impression, and over the next few years the work was sung widely, carrying Dvořák's name across Europe with glory, and reaching the United States (Pittsburgh and New York) in 1884.

In London, a performance conducted by Joseph Barnby in 1883 was so successful that the composer was invited to lead the work himself the following year. This was the event that marked the beginning of the love affair between Dvořák and the flourishing English choral world, something that came close to equaling the fervent British Mendelssohn-mania earlier in the century. The cantatas *The Spectre's Bride* (1884) and *Saint Ludmila* (1886) and the Requiem (1890) were all written for England or stimulated by association with English choral societies. The Requiem contains much impressive music, and some critics, among them Dvořák's excellent biographer John Clapham, rank it higher than the *Stabat Mater*, but I find it less personal and communicative than the earlier work.[2]

---

[2]Probably I was too early and too firmly influenced by George Bernard Shaw, who expressed his amazement "that any critic should mistake this paltry piece of musical confectionery for a serious composition," and who unleashed his wicked wit on the Requiem on several occasions.

Dvořák divides the *Stabat Mater* text into ten movements, of which the first is much the biggest. Violas, cellos, and one horn quietly sound the F-sharp below middle-C, and this note, softly sustained, gives birth to other, higher F-sharps, rising eventually into the upper register of violins and flute. Clapham is persuasive when he suggests that these rising octaves "lead the eye upwards to the figure of Christ on the Cross," while the chromatic descents that follow them "disclose to us the sight of Mary weeping beneath." But even if you are not inclined to be so visual in your listening, these opening minutes of the *Stabat Mater*, in their breadth, with their poignant chromatics, and their *fortissimo* outbursts (attesting to Dvořák's love of Schubert, particularly the "Unfinished" Symphony) compellingly draw us into the agony-filled atmosphere of this scene.

With the music continuing on the path Dvořák has found, the tenors of the chorus introduce the first words, adopting the chromatic descent for "juxta crucem lacrimosa" (weeping by the Cross). Dvořák devotes many measures and many minutes to the first tercet: there is much to see in the mind's eye, and much to contemplate. One of the things Dvořák has learned from Schubert is that, in spite of the stereotypical image of minor=dark/major=bright, to move from minor to major can sometimes heighten pathos, and he does just that—B minor to D major—for "Cujus animam gementem" (whose soul, groaning), the lines that describe Mary's heart pierced by the sword of grief. It is the solo tenor who sings these words, the other soloists taking over one by one, and with the chorus punctuating their utterances. The harmonies begin to range widely and the textures become more complex. It is like the development in a symphonic movement, whose tensions are relieved by the arrival at a recapitulation. The upward-striving F-sharps return, and so do the first words of the poem, and this great opening portion of the *Stabat Mater* arrives at a quiet close in B major.

The tempo of the first section was *Andante con moto*; what follows in "Quis est homo" (Who is the man) is another *Andante*, this one *Andante sostenuto*. The dark nature of the text leads Dvořák into a lot of slow music: The only movements that are not *Andantes* are *Largo* or *Larghetto*. Thoughtless (and perhaps excessively reverent performance) can lead to monotony, but Dvořák has in fact taken pains to differentiate distinct types of *Andante* (*sostenuto, con moto,* and so on), indicating specific tempos through metronome marks, and also varying metrical patterns. A sensitive conductor not averse to flexibility and with a truly comprehensive view of the entire score knows how to make the work breathe and flow. The great Rafael Kubelik was a stellar example, as was Václav Tálich, and Jiří Bělohlávek is one who has this skill today. (All three of these conductors have made beautiful recordings of the *Stabat Mater*.)

Dvořák also gave careful thought to varying weight and texture. Having used all the vocal forces in the first section, he makes "Quis est homo" a movement for solo quartet. The text is poignantly presented, and the expressive phrase to which the opening words are set powerfully dominates this movement. Dvořák responds vividly to the recollection of our sins ("Pro peccatis") with a sudden crescendo of tremolando strings and trombones, joined by ominous beats on the timpani, and to "tormentis" with trumpets joining the voices of the women soloists. There is remarkable freedom in the way the voices relate to one another, and Dvořák's orchestral skill is strikingly in evidence right at the beginning, with its phrases for a mixture of English horn, clarinet, and bassoon contrasted with the rich, dark sound of divided violas and cellos. At the end, the words are pronounced on a monotone, as though the singers were themselves too grief-stricken for melody, and the long, last word is given to the orchestra alone.

The next movement, "Eja, Mater" (O Mother), brings the chorus back, and now the solo voices are silent. This is a dark funeral march in C minor, a key whose first appearance gives the impression of coming from a great distance.

"Fac, ut ardeat cor meum" (Cause my heart to burn) is an extraordinary movement. Set for bass and chorus, it brings a grandly declamatory and dramatic music we have not heard before in the *Stabat Mater*, though this is alternated with passages of sweet tenderness. The accompaniment often adds an independent voice to the singing, and altogether the orchestral writing is wonderfully imaginative.

"Tui Nati vulnerati" (By Thy glorious death and passion) introduces a new kind of motion, a flowing, gently lilting 6/8 meter. The word "poenas" (sufferings) is the occasion for an outburst of muscular *forte*.

The next movement, "Fac me vere tecum flere" (At Thy feet in adoration) is another march, and Dvořák begins by lifting and dropping us into what seems a startlingly new harmonic world. Actually it is B major, the key where the first movement ended, but we have moved so far away from it since then that the first chords of this section come in with dramatic effect. This is music for the tenor soloist, whose prayer that he may be granted the power of empathy is seconded by the chorus in a series of ever more complex interventions. The powerful climax on "in planctu desidero" (I wish [to join] in your weeping) is one of the most gripping passages in the *Stabat Mater*.

"Virgo virginum praeclara" (Virgin, outstanding among virgins) is another piece for chorus without soloists. Here, Dvořák for the first time approaches an *a cappella* style as he effectively sets chorus and orchestra apart. The close of this section, a sudden hush after one last *fortissimo* outburst from the orchestra, is an amazing moment—something to stop the breath.

Over a restless accompaniment, predominantly in pizzicato strings, but with occasional encouragement from horns and timpani, woodwinds begin the next section, "Fac, ut portem Christi mortem" (Make me bear Christ's death), a duet for soprano and tenor. Again we experience Dvořák's free and inspired art of duetting, the lines spun forward and forward in unpredictable and inventive ways.

The "Inflammatus" (In flames), an alto aria, totally flummoxed me when once I happened upon it on the radio. Something Baroque, with its walking bass and stubborn eighth-notes? No, more likely *faux*-Baroque. Mendelssohn perhaps? Then a puzzling departure into undiluted Romanticism. Dvořák, I admit, never came to mind. A strange essay in *stile antico*, this is not at all in Dvořák's personal voice, the voice that makes most of the *Stabat Mater* so lovable for me, but still a splendid opportunity for a contralto with a powerful vocal presence and a lively sense of rhetoric.

Then we come back to the probing, aspiring, mysterious ascending F-sharps we heard at the start. For his close—"Quando corpus morietur" (When my body dies), for all forces—Dvořák has returned to his beginning, which is to say he is using the same materials to create a new movement that grows into a magnificently eloquent setting of the final tercet. Had Dvořák heard Verdi's recent Requiem, or did he at one point simply hit on a phrase hauntingly close to the touching sequences to which Verdi had set the words "Dona eis, Domine"? But a work Dvořák surely knew was Beethoven's *Missa solemnis*, and to that he pays moving tribute in his "Amen" with its excitingly swift-moving harmonies. It is not only the harmonies that move swiftly: for the first time in the *Stabat Mater* Dvořák attains a fast tempo, *Allegro molto*. Now the work roars energetically toward its conclusion. *A cappella*, the chorus utters one last and grand proclamation of the prayer that the supplicant's soul be received in Paradise. Then the orchestra returns and leads the music to a serene close, *molto tranquillo* and *pianississimo*.

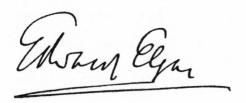

Edward Elgar

Edward William Elgar, Sir Edward after being knighted by King Edward VII on 4 July 1904, was born at Broadheath, Worcestershire, England, on 2 June 1857 and died in Worcester on 23 February 1934.

The Dream of Gerontius by Cardinal Newman, Set to Music for Mezzo-Soprano, Tenor, and Bass Soli, Chorus and Orchestra, op. 38

Using some sketches he had made in 1898, Elgar began *The Dream of Gerontius* in 1899, completed the work in vocal score on 6 June that year, and finished the full score on 3 August. The first performance took place at the Birmingham Festival on 3 October 1900: Hans Richter conducted, and the soloists were Marie Brema, Edward Lloyd, and Harry Plunket Greene.

Mixed chorus and semi-chorus to represent Assistants, Demons, Angelicals, and Souls; mezzo-soprano (Angel), tenor (Gerontius and the Soul of Gerontius), and bass (Priest and Angel of the Agony). Three flutes, two oboes and English horn, two clarinets and bass clarinet, two bassoons and contrabassoon, four horns, three trumpets, three trombones, tuba, two harps, organ, timpani, tam-tam, glockenspiel, jingles, snare drum, cymbals, triangle, and strings (much divided, occasionally even into fifteen, eighteen, and twenty parts). The dedication is "A.M.D.G." (*Ad Majorem Dei Gloriam*—"For the greater glory of God").

This spiritual drama is the greatest work of sacred music that we have in the half-century between the Verdi Requiem and Stravinsky's *Symphony of Psalms*. A truly complete response to a poem of immense religious, in-tellectual, and literary complexity—complete both as an avowal of faith and as a work of human art—*The Dream of Gerontius* is, as Elgar's biogra-pher Michael Kennedy has written, one of those "masterpieces in which the words acquired an extra dimension and became inseparable from the marvelous music to which they were set."[1] Touchingly, Kennedy has also declared that "somewhere in music's pantheon there should be a statue of Father Knight of Worcester, who gave Elgar a copy of New-man's *The Dream of Gerontius* as a wedding present." Alas for Kennedy's sweet thought, it turns out that Elgar had read Newman's poem long before his marriage to Alice Roberts in 1889.

John Henry Newman's *Dream of Gerontius* describes the death of a man and the passage of his soul from the moment it is liberated from the body until its arrival in Purgatory. The long poem, which Newman wrote in 1865 at the age of sixty-four, is one of the glories of English verse, its language as fragrant as the smoke rising from the thuribles in the churches that had become his spiritual home after he was received into the Roman Catholic faith twenty years before. The poem enshrines the poet-priest's devoted friendship with Father John Joseph Gordon; his visit to his friend's deathbed in 1853 was one of the crucial experiences of his life. Newman dedicated *Gerontius* to Gordon's memory.

The road to that moment of profound fulfillment that Elgar's *Gerontius* now represents for us was not a smooth one. With good rea-son, we think of this composer as one of the slowest of music's slow starters. He was about to turn forty when his *Imperial March* in celebra-tion of Queen Victoria's Diamond Jubilee brought him his first success; it would be another two years before Hans Richter's performance of the "Enigma" Variations established him indisputably as a master. But if London had spurned him, or at least ignored him, Elgar had made real headway in establishing a reputation in the provinces, thanks to that

---

[1]The name comes from the Greek *gerōn* ("old man"), the same root that gives us *gerontology*. The *Oxford English Dictionary* says a soft *g* (as in gem) is the preferred pronunciation, but notes that "many scholars would pronounce the initial letter" with a hard *g* (as in gold). English musicians seem to prefer the hard *g*.

very English institution, the choral festival. The most important of these, the Three Choirs Festival, took place annually, rotating among the Anglican cathedrals of Hereford, Gloucester, and Worcester, Elgar's hometown. Elgar's robust and assured concert overture, *Froissart*, named for the fourteenth-century author of history and romances, had made an impression at Worcester in 1890, and performances had followed of the cantata *The Black Knight* (Worcester, 1893) and the oratorios *The Light of Life* (Worcester, 1896), *King Olaf* (North Staffordshire Festival, 1896), and *Caractacus* (Leeds, 1898).

Still more important than what these performances did for Elgar's reputation was what their composition afforded him in experience, in the strengthening of craft: the stunning mastery of the "Enigma" Variations and *The Dream of Gerontius* did not suddenly materialize from nowhere. And given Elgar's increasingly sure standing in the world of the English festivals, it is not surprising that in 1898 the directors of the Birmingham Festival, who had been especially impressed by *Caractacus*, asked for a major new work to be presented in the fall of 1900.[2]

Elgar's first idea for Birmingham was an oratorio about Saint Augustine, but that, as he feared, was rejected as "too controversial"—meaning "too Catholic." Catholics were still a tiny minority in England, and anti-Roman sentiment there was still fierce: it was only in 1830, for example, that Catholics were allowed to sit in the House of Commons, and the passage, by a narrow margin, of that Catholic Relief Act cost the government the next election. In the 1850s, a prime minister, speaking in the Commons, could refer to Catholicism as "mummery and idolatry." For Elgar himself, being Catholic was, along with being poor and lacking an Oxbridge education, part of the complex of factors that kept him edgy and aggrieved all his life.

His next plan was a work about the Apostles—the figure of Judas Iscariot was especially fascinating to him—but what he imagined was something too big to be accomplished by the deadline.[3] *The Dream of Gerontius* was thus a third choice, but a third choice that engaged Elgar passionately, so much so that he had already discussed permission for use and the necessary cutting of the nine-hundred-line poem with Father Richard Bellasis, trustee of Newman's literary estate, and had indeed

[2]Birmingham, whose festival had been founded in 1784, had previously commissioned Gounod's *Rédemption* and *The Spectre's Bride* by Dvořák, but undoubtedly its greatest coup had been Mendelssohn's *Elijah*.

[3]Elgar eventually returned to that idea, and his oratorio *The Apostles* was performed at the Birmingham Festival in 1903. The great musical depictions of and meditations on Judas are found in Bach's *Saint Matthew Passion* and Frank Martin's *Polyptyche* for violin with double string orchestra. It was left to Michael Tippett to set a monument to the great fifth-century thinker in his powerful cantata *The Vision of Saint Augustine* (1965).

written much of the music even before a formal agreement between himself and the Birmingham Festival had been reached.

In light of the rejection of the Saint Augustine idea, I don't know whether to call Elgar's proposal of *The Dream of Gerontius* bold, bloodyminded, or quixotic.[4] His own publisher tried to move him away from the *Gerontius* plan, not only because of the issue of Catholicism but also because it did not include a soprano solo: this meant there was no role for the Canadian soprano Emma Albani, an artist so popular—and for the best of reasons—that it was all but illegal to launch a new oratorio or a major festival without her. At one point, Elgar was so disheartened he offered to withdraw from the project entirely. But Newman's poem was burningly important to him: it had been in his life for a long time, it bore the happy connection with Father Knight and his wedding day, and he and Alice had often read it together.

The poem had also acquired special resonance for thousands of people in England because of its association with General Charles "Chinese" Gordon, whom Simon Winchester describes in *The Meaning of Everything* as "a half-mad, alcoholic, but inescapably heroic Christian imperialist . . . remembered still by British schoolboys, along with other tragic heroes like Scott, Oates, and Lord Cardigan of Crimea." Gordon had been besieged at Khartoum in the Sudan for eleven months in 1884–1885 and, along with the rest of his garrison, was slaughtered by the troops of the Mahdi (Muhammad Ahmad) when he was finally forced to surrender. Toward the end of the siege, Gordon, a Catholic, had sent his copy of *The Dream of Gerontius* back to England with a journalist, who then wrote how essential this book was in sustaining the general's spirit, also revealing which passages Gordon had underlined as especially meaningful to him. Like many of their compatriots, Edward and Alice Elgar had been deeply affected by this story, and they entered Gordon's underlinings into their own copy of the book. Some years later, Elgar even contemplated writing a "Gordon" Symphony.

In the end, it was G. H. Johnstone, chairman of the Birmingham Festival Committee, a skilled businessman (dealing with Elgar's publisher, Novello, promised to be complex), a natural diplomat and gentleman, a man who cared deeply about music and understood it, *and* a Roman Catholic, who saved the day. At New Year's 1900, the Johnstones visited the Elgars at Malvern and went to Mass with them. The next day, Elgar sent a telegram formally accepting the contract, and plans proceeded for the first performance, an event that turned out to be one of the famous disasters in English musical history.

[4]In 1886, a rumor had circulated in the London musical world that Dvořák planned to set *Gerontius* for Birmingham. It was unfounded, but Elgar, who had heard it, believed that Dvořák had dropped the idea for fear of anti-Catholic reaction to it.

What the concert had going for it was the magisterial presence of Hans Richter, the festival's music director: One of the great maestros of his generation, he had led the first *Ring* at Bayreuth in 1876, had been principal conductor at the Vienna Opera and Philharmonic, and was immensely beloved in England, where he had worked regularly since 1877 and had recently taken over the Hallé Orchestra in Manchester. It was also he who had led the triumphant premiere of the "Enigma" Variations the year before. On the other side of the ledger, Elgar was far behind schedule for such a complex undertaking, the publishers were slow in getting copies out, and Richter did not receive a full score in final form until 23 September, ten days before the first performance.

Before that, a catastrophe had occurred when Charles Swinnerton Heap, the festival's superb chorus master, died suddenly on 11 June at only fifty-three. His replacement was W. C. Stockley, the former conductor of the Birmingham Orchestra, under whom the twenty-four-year-old Elgar had been a section violinist. The aging Stockley, lured from retirement in this emergency, was tired, thoroughly out of sympathy with the highly chromatic and highly colored modern music his former violinist had taken to writing, and, as a Nonconformist who would have found even the Church of England too close to Rome, repelled by Newman's text and Elgar's response to it. Stockley didn't sabotage the performance, but he did a poor job with the chorus. *The Dream of Gerontius* is hard to sing, and Elgar, increasingly nervous about what he was hearing (and not hearing), did not help matters by getting up at the dress rehearsal and telling the singers that what they were doing was "no better than a drawing-room ballad." When 3 October arrived, they simply were not ready.[5]

Moreover, the soloists, all renowned, were ill-chosen. Edward Lloyd, a couple of months away from retirement, had been an elegant oratorio tenor, but was utterly at sea in a role that calls for an interpreter of great spiritual depth and a specialist in suffering. As the lieder recordings he made to his own piano accompaniments at the age of sixty-nine attest, Harry Plunket Greene was a great artist, but on this occasion he had pitch trouble and in any case lacked the sheer grandeur of voice that his double assignment as Priest and Angel of the Agony called for. Marie Brema was an imposingly dramatic Wagner mezzo, but the part of the Angel wants a soothing beauty of timbre she never possessed.[6]

---

[5]*Gerontius* was not the only piece to suffer at that festival: Accounts in the press and by such witnesses as Ralph Vaughan Williams tell us that the choral singing in other works such as the *Saint Matthew Passion* and Parry's *De Profundis* was horrendous, too.

[6]For my generation, Janet Baker was the ideal *Gerontius* Angel. You can hear her on Sir John Barbirolli's 1964 recording. Sad to say, there is no recording by Kathleen Ferrier, who sang the Angel many times and must have been wonderful in that part.

The first choral entrance is *a cappella*. The singers' pitch immediately began to drop, and by the time the violas and cellos entered a few bars later, chorus and orchestra were hopelessly out of tune with one another and remained so. It was a wretched start to a wretched occasion. Richter was of course chagrined, but he recovered his spirits and, in his distinctive brand of English, wrote in Elgar's copy of the score: "Let drop the Chorus, let drop everybody—but let *not* drop the wings of your original Genius." He went on to make amends in several fine performances of *Gerontius* with his own Hallé Orchestra in Manchester over the succeeding years, and he was on the podium in 1908 when Elgar enjoyed the most jubilant triumph of his life, the premiere of his First Symphony.

Remarkably, many people in Birmingham that October day heard *through* the performance to discern the stature of *Gerontius*.

Elgar himself was bitter about his Birmingham experience, and six days after the performance he wrote to his friend August Jaeger,[7] the "Nimrod" of the "Enigma" Variations:

> I have worked hard for forty years &, at the last Providence denies me a decent hearing of my work: so I submit—I always said God was against art & I still believe it. Anything obscene or trivial is blessed in this world & has a reward—I ask for no reward—only to live & to hear my work. I still hear it in my heart & in my head so I must be content. Still it is curious to be treated by the old-fashioned people as a criminal because my thoughts & ways are beyond them. I am very well & what is called "fit" & had my golf in good style yesterday & am not ill or pessimistic—don't think it: but I have allowed my heart to open once—it is now shut against every religious feeling & every soft, gentle impulse *for ever.*

Jaeger's reply is missing, but he told one of his fellow-variations, "Dorabella" (Dora Penny), that he had written to Elgar to tell him "it was *weak* and *wicked* to write like that. . . . I told him to look at the Introduction & first Allegro of Beethoven's *Pathétique* (Sonata). That is the mood in which to look adverse circumstances in the face & *defy* them." Elgar back-pedaled a bit, explaining that he had been upset because his wife

---

[7]A treasured friend, Jaeger was also in Elgar's life as musical and literary adviser, publicist, and sounding board. It was he who arranged what seems to have been a wonderful performance of *Gerontius* in Dusseldorf under Julius Buths in May 1902. That event made a tremendous impression on Richard Strauss, who, at a celebratory lunch the next day, proposed a toast "to the welfare and success of the first English progressivist, Meister Edward Elgar, and of the young progressive school of English composers." (Elgar was just about to turn forty-five, and Strauss would be thirty-eight a few weeks later.) A projected post-war collaboration between the two composers, an orchestration of Bach's Fantasy and Fugue in C Minor for organ, with each composer to do one movement, did not come to pass: Strauss did not deliver, and Elgar ended up scoring the entire piece.

was sick; still, he felt no rapport with the church after this: on his deathbed, he told his physician that he had no faith in an afterlife—"I believe there is nothing but complete oblivion"—and he shocked his devout friends by his insistence on being cremated. Of course, Elgar's drive to compose prevailed in 1900, and the next three years saw the achievement of the incidental music to George Moore and W. B. Yeats's *Grania and Diarmid*, the first three *Pomp and Circumstance* marches, the *Cockaigne Overture*, *The Apostles*, *In the South*, and the *Introduction and Allegro for Strings*.

About the poet: John Henry Newman was a powerful figure, extraordinarily controversial and extraordinarily admired in the religious and intellectual life of nineteenth-century England. Born in 1801, he was educated at Oxford and in 1828 became vicar of Saint Mary's Anglican Church there. It was about this time that the Oxford Movement began in the university town, a movement of resistance against what its founders saw as the threat of secularization in England, which they feared would lead to the disestablishment of the Church of England as the country's official church. Newman found himself caught up in the movement and, as editor of *Tracts for the Times*, a series of publications in which its principles were expressed, and author of about one quarter of them, was soon recognized as its intellectual leader. The aim of the movement was to establish that the Church of England, standing between Catholicism on one side and what Newman called the "popular Protestants" on the other, was the true heir of the original Christian church. But even as Newman labored on behalf of this idea, there began what a priest friend of mine calls his "dance with Rome." The *Tracts* moved ever further in that direction, leading finally to the appearance in 1841 of *Tract 90*, in which Newman sought to reconcile the Thirty-Nine Articles of the Anglican Book of Common Prayer with principles laid down by the Catholic church at the Council of Trent in the sixteenth century. The bishop of Oxford suspended publication of the *Tracts* and Newman was threatened with excommunication. Depressed and confused, he withdrew from Saint Mary's to a quiet situation in the country. He was shocked in the spring of 1843 when some adherents of the Oxford Movement, taking the lesson of *Tract 90* to its logical conclusion, converted to Rome, but only a few months later he himself preached his last Anglican sermon—it was titled "The Parting of Friends"—and in 1845 was received into the Catholic Church and went to Rome to be ordained as a priest.

His new life was not free of difficulties: he was intellectually too curious and too restless to fit into his new spiritual home with perfect comfort, and he continued to be attacked for what some perceived as his treason against the Church of England. The need finally to defend himself against those attacks led to the writing in 1864 of his most important work, the *Apologia pro Vita Sua*. *The Dream of Gerontius* followed a year later. By 1870, when he published *An Essay in Aid of a Grammar of Assent*, a rich and difficult meditation on the nature of faith, Newman had achieved his most significant theological and literary endeavors. He spent most of his later years at the Birmingham Oratory, was made a cardinal by Pope Leo XIII in 1879, and died in 1890. As we can see in Herbert Barraud's famous photograph, Newman's was one of the most beautiful faces in English history, and this particular readership will perhaps be pleased to know that he was a great lover of music and a fine violinist. "I could find solace in music from week to week's end," he wrote, and he recounted that while playing Beethoven quartets he had been obliged "to lay down the instrument and literally cry out with delight."

Aware of the need for the listener to enter the world of *Gerontius* in a calm and focused condition, Elgar gives us a spacious orchestral prelude. It accomplishes that goal and it also introduces themes which we shall hear more of as the work unfolds, themes associated with such concepts as prayer, judgment, and despair. The idea of such associations is, of course, Wagnerian, and to the new listener to *The Dream of Gerontius* I would say what I have often said to new listeners to *Tristan and Isolde* or *The Nibelung's Ring*: Don't worry about it. Whatever is necessary by way of linking these musical themes to religious concepts or mental states will enter the attentive listener's mind without special effort. Some of these connections are made easily; others are more elusive, and if your response to these connections becomes richer over time, that is your reward for nurturing your relationship to this great work and returning to it again and again.

One difference between Wagner and Elgar: Wagner never endorsed the labeling of his themes and the use of those leitmotif tables you sometimes find in scores, handbooks, and CD boxes, whereas Elgar, even though he surely assumed that a libretto and open ears were all you really needed, did give his blessing to his friend Jaeger's detailed "analytical and descriptive notes" on *The Dream of Gerontius* (a booklet published by Novello, still in print, excellent and useful). Wagner was one of Elgar's great musical loves, and he is sometimes a vivid presence in Elgar's work: a Wagner-aficionado will immediately recognize a warm and fragrant *Parsifal* sound in the *Gerontius* Prelude. And staying for a moment with this line of associations, if you listen to Elgar's own conducting of parts of *Gerontius* you will be struck by how impassioned and Wagnerian and unoratoriolike it is.

The Prelude, then, offers a rich procession of varied and vividly pro-filed themes, ending, as it had begun, with a single line for violas and low woodwinds, very still and full of agony.[8] A burst of energy charges through the music, something that always occurs when Gerontius on his painful deathbed rouses himself to speak. His first words—"Jesu, Maria, I am near to death"—are underlined by a viola tremolo and a triple *piano* tim-pani roll executed with wooden sticks, a touch of color that alone would suffice to set Elgar apart from the standard English school (Parry, Stan-ford, et al.) of his day. "Maria" would of course have sent an unpleasant jolt through anyone inclined to be rattled by the Catholic atmosphere of *Gerontius*: other flashpoints were references to purgatory and to saints, and for performances in the Anglican Worcester Cathedral, Elgar had to consent to modifications of Newman's text.[9]

Gerontius in effect sings two simultaneous soliloquies: his observa-tions on his condition, above all the growing fear that possesses him; and his interjections of prayer. He begs his friends to pray for him, and the semi-chorus responds with the "Kyrie eleison" (Lord, have mercy) and prayers to Holy Mary and other heavenly powers to intercede for him. These prayers strengthen Gerontius's spirit, and he exhorts himself to "prepare to meet thy God" and "ere afresh the ruin on me fall, [to] use well the interval." Now the full chorus enters with prayers on the dying man's behalf, and Gerontius responds with still greater strength as he both prays for mercy and powerfully asserts his credo, homely English al-ternating with grandly hieratic Latin. The realization dawns on Gerontius that the end of his life on earth is truly nigh: "I can no more," set against an awe-inspiring sequence of chords for strings divided into fifteen parts, quadruple *piano*—a sequence we first heard when Gerontius described the process of dying, the "strange innermost abandonment. . . . This emptying out of each constituent / And natural force." This rises to an immense peak as Gerontius prays for the arrival of the angel who visited

[8]The origin of one of these themes is surprising for this solemn context, yet characteristically Elgarian. In No.11 of the "Enigma" Variations, "G.R.S.", Elgar portrays Dan, the bulldog of his friend Dr. George Sinclair, organist at Hereford Cathedral, as he slides into the river Wye and joyfully scrambles onto land again—the best dog music since Haydn's *Seasons*. Elgar, who loved animals, dogs most of all, in fact wrote many themes associated with Dan, and one of them is a dark phrase he inscribed in Sinclair's visitors' book on 19 April 1898 that represented Dan's musing on an order to be muzzled. A little more than a minute into the Prelude you hear a chordal passage for woodwinds (it is where the harp first comes in). In *Gerontius* it is associated with the idea of prayer, but originally it was Dan's melancholic meditation. If you have read any of Elgar's letters and seen the drawings with which he illustrated them you will not be surprised by this confounding of the comic and the deeply serious.
[9]One can still encounter resistance to *Gerontius*. When I gave some preconcert talks about it in 2000, I was amazed by how many people expressed theological difficulties with it or just bluntly said things to the effect of "I had to shut my ears to the words in order to enjoy the music."

Jesus in his agony. The chorus fervently supports Gerontius. The last hour has come—"Novissima hora est"—and Gerontius dies, his last prayer interrupted by the end of breath and life: "Into Thy hands, O Lord, into Thy hands."

Silence. Then a new voice, a new atmosphere, a new sound. Backed by the grand sonorities of horns and trombones, the Priest sends the soul on its imponderable journey. Here again the words are Latin, leading us from the particularity of Gerontius's deathbed into universality.[10] This wish is taken up—in English—by the chorus in a magnificent litany, each of whose clauses begins with "Go, in the Name of," and it is with this glorious music that Part I of *The Dream of Gerontius* reaches its close.[11]

We are now, literally, in another world. A quietly moving and brief Prelude sets the scene, then the Soul of Gerontius, marvelously refreshed— "I feel in me / An inexpressive lightness, and a sense / Of freedom, as I were at length myself, / And ne'er had been before"—seeks to understand its new condition of being. It hears singing, but "cannot of that music rightly say / Whether I hear, or touch, or taste the tones." The singing is revealed to be that of the Angel who has been chosen as the Soul's Guide ("he" in the poem, but an alto in Elgar). The Soul learns that "with extremest speed" it is being carried to "the Just and Holy Judge." It is free of fear now because Gerontius, God-fearing while alive, had "forestalled the agony."

As the Soul and the Angel approach the judgment court, they encounter howling demons, ready to gather souls to take to hell. Elgar raises a fierce noise in his portrayal of that perpetually raging crowd. It has been a commonplace of criticism to say that this passage is the one failure in Elgar's score, but the fault is more in conductors and choruses. I have certainly heard performances in which the demonic passages were powerful, and interestingly enough, they were all with conductors—most notably John Barbirolli, Britten, Donald Runnicles, David Zinman—who did not grow up in the oratorio tradition.[12] But what the Soul cares about is whether it will see "my dearest Master, when I reach His throne." And with that we come to the part of Newman's poem that posed the greatest

---

[10]As Elgar had requested, his own ashes were interred without ceremony and without music next to his beloved Alice in the village cemetery of Little Malvern, but in Worcester Cathedral there is a window in his memory and a plaque with the first words of the *Gerontius* Priest: PROFICISCERE, ANIMA CHRISTIANA, DE HOC MUNDO! (Go forth upon thy journey, Christian soul, from this world!).

[11]In this closing chorus, Elgar uses a theme he had originally drafted for the projected but abandoned "Gordon" Symphony.

[12]Only grudgingly did Elgar allow his publisher to include *Gerontius* in their oratorio list; he firmly refused ever to apply that designation to the work himself.

challenge to Elgar. The Angel tells the Soul that "for one moment" it shall indeed "see thy Lord," but goes on to warn how fearful and agonizing that moment will be, also telling the story of Saint Francis's reception of the stigmata: "Learn that the flame of the Everlasting Love / Doth burn ere it transform."

The chorus softly intones the hymn *Praise to the Holiest*.[13] As Soul and Angel cross the threshold, *Praise to the Holiest* is heard again, but this time with utmost might. This grows to be a choral movement of immense proportions, and it ends as it had begun, in a glorious blaze of C major. Now the music is full of mystery. The horizon expands vastly as, in the distance, we hear the "Proficiscere": Gerontius's friends pray at his bedside, even while his Soul, which can hear them, is about to meet its Maker. The Angel of the Agony, whose presence Gerontius had longed for in his last moments on earth, intercedes in music of gigantic eloquence, and the chorus echoes his prayer.

But how do you compose the sight of God? This is as daunting a challenge as any composer ever faced. Elgar did not want to face it, but Nimrod would not desist from his exhortations. The Soul's Guardian Angel sings ecstatic Alleluias, and then, with brass and woodwinds striding across vast harmonic vistas and with string figurations rising up like flames, an immense crescendo leads to a shattering crash. "For one moment," Elgar directs in a footnote, every instrument must "exert its fullest force." It is what Elgar called "the one glimpse into the Unexpressible." The Soul, "consumed, yet quickened, by the glance of God," begs now to be taken away to "the lowest deep." Purgatory is entered and the immeasurable wait is begun.[14] As the Soul embarks on that wait in purgatory, "motionless and happy in my pain," the Angel gives comfort in a lullaby, "Softly and gently, dearly-ransomed soul." Here are serenity and calm—and a lovely and generous animal warmth. *The Dream of Gerontius* ends in a sound both huge and soft, and in "Amens" imbued with the promise of peace.

In June 1900, as the work neared completion, Elgar wrote to his friend Nicholas Kilburn: "I am not suggesting that I have risen to the heights of the poem for one moment—but on our hillside night after night looking across our 'illimitable' horizon (pleonasm!) I've seen in thought the Soul go

[13]This hymn has taken on a life of its own in both Catholic and Protestant churches. Newman's best-known hymn is *Lead, Kindly Light*, which he wrote as a young man while becalmed at sea.
[14]About the Angel's alleluias: Ralph Vaughan Williams, who had been at the first performance of *Gerontius* and acknowledged that a phrase in it had inspired a passage in his *London Symphony*, paid tribute to Elgar's work by referring to these Alleluias in his own beautiful hymn *For All the Saints*. He brought the melody to radiant life again many years later in his Symphony in D (No. 5).

up & have written my own heart's blood into the score." A few weeks later, when the score was completely done, Elgar looked for words to inscribe on the last page and found them in a book he had treasured since he had received it as a gift fourteen years before, John Ruskin's *Sesame and Lilies*: "This is the best of me; for the rest, I ate, and drank, and slept, loved and hated, like another; my life was as the vapour, and is not; but this I saw and knew: this, if anything of mine, is worth your memory."

Gabriel Fauré

Gabriel Urbain Fauré was born in Pamiers, department of
Ariège, in the South of France, on 12 May 1845 and died in
Paris on 4 November 1924.

Requiem, op. 48

In 1877, Fauré wrote a *Libera me* for baritone and organ; this, orchestrated, was eventually incorporated into the Requiem and is thus the
earliest music in that work. In 1887–1888, Fauré composed what he
called "a little Requiem" in five movements: Introit and Kyrie, Sanctus,
"Pie Jesu," Agnus Dei, and "In Paradisum," but not including the old
Libera me. This was first performed on 16 January 1888 under the composer's direction in one of the grandest and most unattractive churches
in Paris, La Madeleine. The occasion was what is listed in the church records as a "first-class funeral" service for a certain M. La Soufaché, an ar-
chitect. Fauré conducted, and the treble soloist was Louis Aubert, who
went on to study with Fauré and became quite a good composer himself.
The Requiem's first hearing that was not part of a service occurred at
the Madeleine on 4 May 1888, but the composer asked the friends
whom he had invited not "to sit *together* lest it begin to look like a PER-
FORMANCE!!!" In 1889, Fauré added the "Hostias" portion of the Offertory, and in 1890 he expanded the Offertory again and brought in his

old *Libera me*. The *Libera me* was sung by the baritone Louis Ballard at a concert at the church of Saint Gervais, Paris, on 28 January 1892; the expanded version of the Requiem was first done at the Madeleine under the composer's direction on 21 January 1893. In 1899–1900, at the request of his publisher, Hamelle, Fauré reworked the Requiem for full orchestra. (Actually there is some question about the extent to which Fauré himself was involved in this reworking.) This version, in effect the only one in which the work was known until the 1980s, was introduced in Lille on 6 April 1900, Eugène Ysaÿe conducting.

The original score of the Requiem calls for solo boy soprano, mixed chorus, and an orchestra consisting of harp, timpani, organ, and strings (solo violin, divided violas, divided cellos, and basses). The second version of 1890 adds a baritone—a "quiet bass-baritone, the *cantor* type," Fauré said—as well as four horns, two trumpets, and three trombones. And "the more violas the better," Fauré told Ysaÿe. The final version is scored for the same two soloists and chorus, now with an orchestra consisting of two flutes and two clarinets (only in the "Pie Jesu"), two bassoons, four horns, two trumpets (only in the Kyrie and Sanctus), three trombones and timpani (only in the "Libera me"), harp, organ, and strings (with just a single section of violins but, as before, with divided violas and cellos).

Fauré's Requiem is like no other. That is literally so in that it omits the "Dies irae," the centerpiece of most Requiem settings, and, equally unusually, includes the "In Paradisum" from the Office for the Dead.[1] In a larger sense, it differs from the Requiems of, for example, Mozart, Cherubini, Berlioz, Dvořák, and Verdi in its atmosphere. In part, what accounts for this is the elimination of the "Dies irae" except for the brief reference to it in the "Libera me." Berlioz and Verdi have shown what stupendous opera can be made of that dramatic depiction of the Day of Judgment, but Requiem as drama was an idea to which Fauré was profoundly antipathetic. He particularly disliked the Berlioz Requiem, which he characterized as a work "in which a taste for large-scale dramatic effects and an indifference towards religious music . . . may find equal satisfaction." Of his own Requiem he said in 1921 that "everything I managed to entertain by way of religious illusion I put into my Requiem, which moreover is dominated from beginning to end by a very human

---

[1]Britten also included this text in his *War Requiem*.

feeling of faith in eternal rest." To Ysaÿe he wrote that his Requiem was "as GENTLE as I am myself!!" And indeed, it is Fauré's own GENTLEness that makes it what it is, even if some irony is conveyed by those capital letters.[2]

When Fauré wrote the second—and most representative—version of the Requiem, he was some ten years past the halfway mark of his long and quiet life. On the assumption that he would become a church organist, this youngest son of a provincial schoolteacher with no music anywhere in his pedigree was sent to the École Niedermeyer in Paris. This was an institution founded by Louis Niedermeyer, a Swiss composer whose idea was to train church musicians by giving them a firm grounding in Gregorian chant and the sacred polyphony of the age of Palestrina. Fauré was a student there when Niedermeyer died in 1861. The new director was the twenty-five-year-old Camille Saint-Saëns, who promptly brought the school into the nineteenth century, introducing students to the heady sounds of Chopin and Schumann, both of whom Niedermeyer had thought unsuitable for the young, and, still more radically, to Liszt and Wagner. Saint-Saëns also became a lifelong and unshakably loyal friend to Fauré, even though in the 1890s he began to feel alienated from his former pupil's ever-more exploratory and individual music.

It was also in the 1890s that Fauré began gradually to emerge from obscurity. There were more performances, and in more important venues. In 1896, he was appointed professor of composition at the Paris Conservatory, the institution he would vigorously head beginning in 1905 and where his zeal for reform caused him to be known as "Robespierre." Ravel, Enescu, Koechlin, Florent Schmitt, and Nadia Boulanger were among his students. They learned more technique from teachers such as the famed counterpoint wizard André Gédalge, but Fauré offered something else. Enescu recalled: "On the purely technical side, [Fauré's] teaching was brief. He was not in the strict technical sense of the word a teacher, but from him came an aura: He was inspiring, and this inspiration was contagious. We adored him!"

Also in 1896, Fauré became principal organist at the Madeleine, and it would still be some years before he could afford to give up what he called his "mercenary" work as a church musician. The pressure to earn

[2]In setting Fauré's Requiem apart from others, I am thinking of settings with orchestra from Mozart on, not those of Renaissance masters such as Brumel, Lassus, Palestrina, and Victoria. Another and more recent exception is the 1947 Requiem by Maurice Duruflé, composed in undisguised and unmistakable (perhaps too undisguised and unmistakable) emulation of Fauré's masterpiece.

a dependable living had been increased by his marriage to Marie Frémiet in 1883 and the birth of his sons at the end of that year and in 1889. Like Mahler, Fauré was obliged to be a summer composer most of his life.[3]

He was among the composers with an unrequited love for the theater. His opera *Pénélope*, dedicated to Saint-Saëns and produced at Monte Carlo in 1913, is a treasure trove of beautiful music and has something of a cult following, and the incidental music he wrote for a London production of Maurice Maeterlinck's *Pelléas et Mélisande* at least lives as a lovely concert piece.

Fauré's last years were darkened by the failure of his hearing. Sound grew ever more dim, but worse, what he could hear was distorted in pitch, low notes being perceived as lower than their proper location and high ones as higher. Undeterred, he kept working, and some of his most compelling and original song cycles and pieces for solo piano and various chamber combinations date from those difficult years.

I referred to Fauré's life as "quiet." Externally it was that, but, even aside from financial anxiety, it was not free from inner turmoil. He was not happy being a summer composer, not happy with the amount of travel that his activities as a private teacher and, for a while, as Inspector of Conservatories imposed on him. While he was stoic and most of the time tactful about it, he was jealous of the greater recognition afforded musicians whom, rightly, he thought his inferiors, notably Théodore Dubois, his predecessor as organist at the Madeleine and as director of the Paris Conservatory, who was elected to the French Academy long before he was. Fauré was both proud of and frustrated by his temperamental lack of gift for self-promotion. Not least, as a man both attractive and susceptible to women, he several times found himself in agitation in that department, notably in his passion for Emma Bardac, who inspired him to compose *La Bonne Chanson*, his most beautiful set of love songs, and who eventually left her banker husband for Debussy. Later, Fauré had a long relationship with the intelligent and beautiful pianist Marguerite Hasselmans.[4]

Fauré's music ranges in style from exquisitely fashioned, almost-salon songs like *Nell* and *Après un rêve* to works we could well call esoteric, such as his Piano Quintet No. 2, his only string quartet, and the

[3]Fauré's father-in-law, Emmanuel Frémiet, was a sculptor of international fame. His equestrian statue of Colonel John Eager Howard stands in Mount Vernon Square, Baltimore.
[4]In his exquisite Fauré essay in *A French Song Companion*, Graham Johnson writes that "it took many decades for it to emerge" that the daughter born to Emma Bardac during her first marriage was probably Fauré's. Fauré wrote an endearing set of piano duet pieces for Dolly Bardac and called them the *Dolly Suite*. Dolly, whose given name was Hélène, was also the inspiration for Debussy's delightful *Children's Corner Suite*.

song cycles *La Chanson d'Ève* and *Le Jardin clos*. It is fascinating that such a piece as Stravinsky's *Rite of Spring*, which seemed the last word in outrageous modernism when it was new, has become a popularly assimilated classic, while what Fauré composed at roughly the same time, and with far less harmonic and rhythmic dissonance, remains stubbornly "modern" and challenging. Much like some of Beethoven's late music, one might add, a comparison that would have pleased Fauré, who in his late String Quartet—the date is 1924—used his fellow-sufferer in deafness as a model.

The Requiem stands toward the "easy" end of this spectrum. Today it is the best known of his large works, even though it is most often quite poorly represented in church performances. What surprises is how long it took to become popular outside France: its first hearing in the United States was at a student concert at the Curtis Institute in Philadelphia in 1931, and it did not reach England until 1936. It is now coming to be known in its original sonorous guise, original in both senses, which allows it far more character and flavor than the version for large orchestra.

There are many Fauré compositions on sacred texts, but the Requiem stands alone in the depth of the impression it makes. There was no external occasion for its composition, only the desire to join the composers who had written Requiems. It happened that Fauré's mother died on New Year's Eve 1887, but by then he had already begun the work which, he later declared, "was composed *for nothing* . . . for fun, if I may be permitted to say so!"

The beginning is somber, *Molto largo*, with the chorus declaiming the opening prayer in simple block harmonies. The orchestra provides punctuation and shifts the harmonic perspective between phrases. A more fluid tempo brings a new and soaring melody, to which the tenors sing the next verse, "Te decet hymnus," and the sopranos continue it. These solo arias for single sections of the choir are a distinctive and lovely feature of the Requiem. Fauré imagined the soprano line sung by a children's chorus, himself training such a group at the Madeleine, and children's voices can make a special and wonderful effect throughout the work. The full chorus enters and sweeps us into the brief "Kyrie eleison." Years later, writing to the composer about Fauré's Violin Sonata No. 2, Paul Dukas said that "here at last is music that restores music to its rightful place . . . and in which the reasons of the mind blend with the reasons of the heart without preventing it from taking wing, from moving and delighting us." Listening to this music that says so much with such minimal effort and "effect," one understands exactly what the generous and perceptive composer of *The Sorcerer's Apprentice* meant.

The Offertory begins with music in which canonic imitations for two voices alternate with passages in simple octaves. This was one of the last additions to the Requiem, and it is one of the few moments when the texture is contrapuntal. The baritone soloist enters to sing the "Hostias." The first music returns, and a beautifully swirled brief coda, sung as softly as possible, brings this movement to a close.

In 1900, Fauré wrote to Ysaÿe, who was preparing to conduct the newest version of the Requiem: "You'll see after all those violas, how angelic the violins sound in the *Sanctus!!!*" Still more angelic is the original scoring in which a single violin, heard only here, floats in quiet ecstasy high above the sopranos. And here is another place where a children's chorus can make magic. As though weightlessly, the harmonies move from key to key.

Of the next section, Saint-Saëns declared that "just as Mozart's is the only *Ave verum corpus*, this is the only *Pie Jesu.*" Here is an inspired melody of breathtaking simplicity. The solo soprano, boy or woman, sings it, and Fauré was delighted when Mlle. Torrès had to repeat it as an encore at the Paris premiere of the large-orchestra edition at the Trocadéro in 1900. The number of times this movement has been sung at funerals since then is far beyond reckoning.

As the Agnus Dei begins, the music takes flight in a winged melody every note of which declares "by Gabriel Fauré." The tenors continue with a new and gloriously lyrical idea of their own. The entrance of the chorus sopranos on the word "lux" (light) is a heart-stopping wonder. The appeal to the Lamb of God grows more urgent, and the harmonies darken. The opening music of the Requiem returns for a moment. Then the melody that began the Agnus Dei comes back for seven measures of orchestral postlude, but suffused with the new glow of a different key, a subtly brighter D major. It is a beautiful effect, framing music in the Requiem's central key of D minor between a prelude in F, the relative major, and a postlude in the tonic major.[5]

Then comes the old *Libera me* from 1877, with the baritone singing this quietly fervent melody over an anxious heartbeat in the orchestral bass. Here it is especially important that, as Fauré put it, the singer be cantorial, not operatic.[6] For one brief moment the dread vision of the Day of Wrath is invoked, but this is far removed from the

[5]D major is also brighter because it brings more of the violins' and violas' open strings into play, and their sympathetic vibration adds resonance and glow.

[6]Fauré was furious about the soloist at the Trocadéro performance in 1900: "execrable—a real opera singer who did not begin to understand the *composure* and gravity of his part." To come from the world of French *mélodie* is good, too: Gérard Souzay, for example, was incomparable in this music.

dramatic visions of Berlioz and Verdi. The baritone recalls his prayer, and the chorus in a few measures of the simplest speaking sort of music concludes this section.

Fauré ends by setting words that are not part of the Mass for the Dead at all but an antiphon from the burial service. "In Paradisum deducant angeli" is a sweet and touching text, perhaps because the sudden appearance of a personal name, Lazarus, makes it so, and because, unlike in the "Requiem aeternam" Introit, the dead are not "they" but "you." It is, of course, also deeply consonant with the hope for eternal rest that was central to Fauré's Requiem idea. Over an accompaniment whose sixteenth-notes suggest the flutter of angels' wings, the sopranos—again, one longs for the sound of children's voices—sing a melody of lovely simplicity, one that begins with the singers serenely ascending the notes that make up the chord of D major. The chorus joins only for a few measures between verses, and again for the last words: "aeternam habeas requiem" (may you eternally have rest).

Once I was giving a preconcert talk on the Fauré Requiem in the beautiful Mechanics Hall in Worcester, Massachusetts, and as I came to the end, I heard myself say something I had not planned to say, had not remotely thought about. I found myself remembering Dietrich Bonhoeffer, the Lutheran theologian who was executed in 1945 for his involvement in the July 1944 plot to assassinate Hitler. A priest walked with him to the place of execution, and Bonhoeffer parted from his companion with the words, "In five minutes, Father, I shall know more than you." And I said that this music tells me Gabriel Fauré already knew.

George Frideric Handel

George Frideric Handel was born Georg Friderich Händel in Halle-an-der-Saale, then in the electorate of Brandenburg, on 23 February 1685, and died in London on 14 April 1759.

Messiah, A Sacred Oratorio

Handel composed *Messiah* in twenty-four days in the late summer of 1741, beginning on 22 August and completing its three parts respectively on 28 August, 6 September, and 14 September. A small part of what enabled him to work at such speed was his habit of creative borrowing from his own earlier scores—and sometimes, though not here, from those of others. Handel tried out a few numbers in rehearsal in Chester on his way to Ireland in November 1741, then led the work in a public rehearsal on 9 April 1742 at Neale's Music Hall in Fishamble Street, Dublin, and in its official premiere on 13 April. He thought Neale's Hall "a charming room" in which "the Musick sounds delightfully." The soloists at the first performance included three singers Handel had brought with him from London, the soprano Christina Maria Avoglio (or Avolio) and Mr. and Mrs. Maclaine (an organist and his wife); Susanna Maria Cibber, who took the alto numbers; and James Baily, William Lambe, Joseph Ward, John Hill, and John Mason, all members of the choirs at Dublin's Christ Church or Saint Patrick's Cathedral or both. The concertmaster, whom Handel credited with the excellent string playing, was Matthew Dubourg, Master and Composer of State Music in Ireland.

Messiah is a moving target. Until 1754, Handel changed it every time he revived it, which was often; in fact, even the first performance departed from what he had originally written. Note that, as the text makes clear in any case, Handel intended *Messiah* as a piece for Eastertide, not Christmas, and that all performances in Handel's lifetime were given in March or April.

Messiah has solos for the familiar lineup of soprano, contralto, tenor, and bass. Handel himself performed it sometimes with four, sometimes with five soloists (and in Dublin even more), at least once including a boy soprano and using both female and male altos, the latter being castrati borrowed from the world of Italian opera. For the rest, the work calls for four-part chorus and an orchestra of two oboes and bassoon to double the choral lines (Handel whenever possible used four of each), two trumpets, timpani, and strings, plus harpsichord and organ for the continuo. From account books we learn that Handel sometimes used a pair of French horns, but we are not sure exactly what they played.

Messiah—and Handel's title does not include the definite article we often add—is the most loved of all classical works with voices and, indeed, one of the most loved of all compositions. Insofar as Handel would ever have imagined his oratorios to be the foundation of his lasting fame, he probably would have put his money on *Samson* (composed within weeks of completing *Messiah*), *Saul, Israel in Egypt, Judas Maccabeus, Solomon,* or *Theodora.* Oratorio was essentially transposed opera for him, the chief musical difference being the greater role of the chorus. The typical Handel oratorio is a work with dramatic action, not necessarily sacred in subject. *Messiah* and *Israel in Egypt* are the only two with texts based directly on Scripture; *Messiah* and *Theodora* are the only two whose message is specifically Christian. *Messiah,* being wholly contemplative, and having no external action at all and no story in the theatrical sense, stands alone among Handel's oratorios—indeed, within his life's work. Handel, to whom *Messiah* was of immense importance both as a religious and an artistic testament, would be happy and probably amazed to know how present and alive it is, at least in English-speaking countries, nearly two and a half centuries after his death. That this one composition, great as it is, became canonized at the expense of most of the rest of his total achievement—in sum, the equation Handel-*Messiah*—would have appalled him.

The lively history of *Messiah* unfolds in five stages:

- *1741–1745*: This is when the idea for the work was born in the mind of Charles Jennens, its eventual librettist, when he assembled the word-book, Handel composed the music, the first and immensely successful performances were given in Dublin, it met with an indifferent reception in London in 1743 and 1745, and it disappeared from the repertoire for a time.
- *1749–1759*: Beginning with a well-received revival at the Covent Garden opera house, this is the period of annual performances in London under Handel's direction, involving many changes in the score, at least in the first few years.
- *1759–1784*: This is the first phase of the work's posthumous history. The tradition of annual *Messiahs* in London continued, culminating in the 1784 performances in Westminster Abbey to commemorate the twenty-fifth anniversary of Handel's burial in the Abbey and the centenary of his birth, mistakenly believed to have occurred in 1684. Those concerts, enlisting 261 singers, 229 players, and 3 conductors, set the gigantesque *Messiah* performance style that prevailed for the next century and a half, and they completed the transformation of *Messiah* from a sublime "Musical Entertainment," as Handel had billed his Dublin concerts, to a religious and patriotic totem.
- *1784–c.1959, the two-hundredth anniversary of Handel's death*: These are the years that demonstrated the truth of the observation by the art historian Leo Steinberg that interpretation proceeds "independent of the object interpreted." Mozart's beautiful distortion of *Messiah* (1789; see page 150)—and it is both beautiful and a distortion—is a landmark. It was followed by many other editions, Ebenezer Prout's (1902) being the most often heard, and the one by Sir Eugene Goossens (1958), memorably recorded by Sir Thomas Beecham for the 1959 bicentenary of Handel's death, being the most over-the-top. One thing to be said for Goossens and Beecham is that they certainly swept aside the idea, prevalent through the nineteenth century and the first half of the twentieth, that *Messiah* is solemn and dark brown.
- *c.1959–present*: The return to the presumed letter, and through the letter to the presumed spirit of *Messiah* as Handel imagined it and as it was given in his lifetime. Decisions about tempo, articulation, vocal embellishment (long felt to be sacrilegious and unthinkable), weight and color of sonority, all contributed to this process. Sir Adrian Boult, Sir Colin Davis, Thomas Dunn, Sir Charles Mackerras, Alfred

Mann, Hermann Scherchen, and Robert Shaw were the conductors who most powerfully effected this re-examination.

A physician who met Handel in Dublin remarked that "with his other excellences [he] was possessed of a great stock of humor; no man ever told a story with more. But it was required for the hearer to have a competent knowledge of at least four languages: English, French, Italian, and German; for in his narratives he made use of them all." (He also cursed fluently in all four, as well as in Latin.)[1] Like Handel himself, his music was polyglot and vigorous. He had his first training in Halle and his first job in Hamburg, after which he spent almost five years in Italy. Having taken a position in Hanover, he found himself much drawn to England, which he visited in 1710–1711 and where he settled in the fall of 1712, becoming naturalized in 1726. Experience and natural gift alike propelled him toward the theater, and for some years his chief efforts in his new country were in Italian opera. Soon, though, he became involved as well in the world of music for religious and state ceremonies.

In fact, the British public was beginning to tire of Italian opera, though Handel was amazingly stubborn about ignoring that: in 1741, the year of *Messiah*, he also produced *Deidamia*, his thirty-fifth opera for London. He fell into his new calling as an oratorio composer by accident, the backstage hero of that story being Edmund Gibson, bishop of London (who had intended no such role for himself). To celebrate Handel's birthday in 1732, the children of the Chapel Royal under the direction of their Master, Bernard Gates, mounted a production of *Esther*, a masque based on Racine and first performed in 1718. It pleased so much that plans were made for a series of public performances at the King's Theatre. This was when the bishop intervened. The theater, as far as he was concerned, was a site of sin and not a fit place for the presentation of a work based, however remotely, on the Bible. The upshot was that *Esther* was given in concert as an oratorio. This genre was then unknown in England, but the public took to it at once, and over the next ten years Handel composed eight such works, including *Messiah*.

Handel's journey to Dublin, a welcome escape from the stress associated with producing opera in London, came about through an invitation from the duke of Devonshire, who was also the Lord Lieutenant of Ireland. Handel's music was popular in Dublin, and presumably the duke promised patronage and assured him of success. Knowing Handel to be

[1]Imagining what kind of man Handel was, we must not ignore how thin-skinned and vulnerable he was in many ways, and that the tussle of managing his professional life in London's highly competitive and volatile musical climate took an enormous toll on his physical and mental health.

famously generous, he also requested a new work to be presented for the benefit of some of Dublin's major charities. After being welcomed at a special service at Saint Andrew's Church, Handel presided over performances of *L'Allegro, il Penseroso ed il Moderato*; *Acis and Galatea*; the *Ode for Saint Cecilia's Day*; *Esther*; *Alexander's Feast*; the opera *Imeneo* (in concert); a good many concertos; and as the climax of a successful season, *Messiah*. All the concerts were sold out, the composer reporting in Handelian English: "I needed not sell one single Ticket at the Door."

The first *Messiah* performance was given "for Relief of the Prisoners in the several Gaols, and for the support of Mercer's Hospital in Stephen's Street, and of the Charitable Infirmary of the Inn's Quay." A large crowd being expected, the concert announcement requested "the Favour of the Ladies not to come with Hoops this Day . . . the Gentlemen [were] desired to come without their Swords." After a public rehearsal, Faulkner's *Dublin Journal* declared that *Messiah* "was allowed by the greatest Judges to be the finest Composition of Musick that ever was heard." Reviewing the performance itself, the *Journal* could not really top that, but with no letup in enthusiasm it reported: "Words are wanting to express the exquisite delight it afforded to the admiring, crouded Audience. The Sublime, the Grand, and the Tender, adapted to the most elevated, majestick and moving Words, conspired to transport and charm the ravished Heart and Ear."

The most famous of *Messiah* stories originated at the Dublin concert. The contralto soloist was Susanna Cibber, sister of Thomas Arne, the composer of *Rule, Britannia!* Mrs. Cibber had been famous as an actress in London, but she and her playwright husband, son of the more famous dramatist Colley Cibber, became embroiled in a messy divorce. The younger Mr. Cibber lost in the court of law, but his wife was the loser in the court of public opinion, and so she moved to Dublin for a time. Dubliners had their reservations about divorcées, too, but when Mrs. Cibber concluded her deeply felt singing of "He Was Despised and Rejected," the Reverend Dr. Patrick Delany, rector of Saint Andrew's, stood and exclaimed: "Woman, for this, all thy sins be forgiven thee!"[2]

The Cibber phenomenon seems to have contributed to London's reserved reception of *Messiah*. Not only was she one of the soloists there, she was joined in the cast by an equally scandalous personality, Mrs. Kitty Clive, a comic actress of distinctly naughty bent whose background was the music hall, but who had recently enjoyed success as a saucy

---

[2]The exact wording is reported variously. For that matter, the story may well be apocryphal, but anyone who has ever heard this air sung by an artist such as Muriel Brunskill, Kathleen Ferrier, or Janet Baker might well be disposed to believe it.

Delilah in Handel's *Samson*. Even aside from moral doubts surrounding those particular singers, there was some unease about having a sacred work presented in a secular venue such as Covent Garden. In London, Handel produced *Messiah* three times in March 1743 and twice more in April 1745. Wishing to avoid giving offense with a title explicitly tied to the New Testament, Handel billed those first London performances as *The Sacred Oratorio*. The small number of performances and the failure of the publisher John Walsh to issue an album of favorite airs both attest to the fact that the work did not please.

In March 1749, Handel revived *Messiah* at Covent Garden, now calling the work by its proper name. By then opposition had evaporated, and *Messiah* became established. Thereafter it was given every season at Covent Garden, and on 1 May 1750 Handel conducted the first of what would become his annual benefit performance for his favorite charity, the Foundling Hospital. By 1759, *Messiah* was sufficiently popular to warrant three hearings at Covent Garden. At the third, on 6 April, Handel, now blind and nearly crippled by a series of strokes, made his last public appearance. Too weak to go through with his proposed journey to Bath for the waters there, he took to his bed that night and died eight days later. He left his conducting score and all performance materials of *Messiah* to the Foundling Hospital.

The compiler of the *Messiah* text, Charles Jennens, was a Leicestershire squire whose name first enters the Handel chronicle in 1725 as one of the subscribers to the score of the opera *Rodelinda*. His *Messiah* is one of the great achievements in Christian literature. Handel, who, as he once pointed out to the archbishop of Canterbury, had read his Bible very well, may also have taken part in the preparation of the book, but we have no firm knowledge about that. Jennens was rather dissatisfied with Handel's treatment of his book. "He made a fine Entertainment of it," he wrote, "tho' not near so good as he might and ought to have done. I have with great difficulty made him correct some of the grossest faults in the composition. . . ." Word of this naturally reached to Handel, who felt much wounded.[3]

Jennens cast his book in three parts. (Only in *Messiah* does Handel call the divisions of an oratorio "parts" rather than "acts.") The first presents the announcement of God's plan for redemption, and at its center stands the story of the birth of Christ. The subject of the second part is the complex one of redemption through Jesus' sacrifice, mankind's rejection of that sacrifice, and, after suffering, the victory of the resurrection.

---

[3]Handel and Jennens collaborated once more, in 1744, on the oratorio *Belshazzar*, and it was Jennens who in 1756 commissioned the famous Thomas Hudson portrait of Handel that now hangs in the National Portrait Gallery in London.

The third and final part deals with the vanquishing of death, and with redemption and resurrection. If we think about all this, we can see that the
question of *Messiah* versus *The Messiah* goes beyond nit-picking. Jennens
and Handel intended the broadest possible contemplation of the messianic idea of redemption; calling the work *The Messiah* narrows the focus
to the story of Jesus Christ, from the large to the particular.

Jennens imbues his presentation of the messianic idea with depth
and mystery by using mainly the words of prophet and psalmist. In some
places he adds comment from the Epistles, and Part III is drawn almost
entirely from the New Testament. Direct narration occurs only in the
presentation of the Nativity story in the familiar verses from Luke, and
their effect is especially touching because they are so different from everything that surrounds them.

Handel had a beautifully shaped libretto to work with, and he took
it on with the relish and skill of a great master of musical theater. Harmony is one of his primary means, and here, as in all things, Handel has a
powerful command of the grand, simple effect. His harmony is rarely as
colorful as Bach's, with its dissonances, chromatics, and pungent "false
relations," but he has a sure sense for the big strategy. *Messiah* is not exactly "in a key" as we might say a Classical symphony is, but by the time
we have completed the journey from the Overture to "Amen," it is clear
that D is a powerful center of gravity.

Handel actually begins somewhere quite different. The Overture, or
Sinfonia, is in E minor, and this leads into the softly radiant E major
of the first pair of vocal numbers, "Comfort Ye" and "Ev'ry Valley."
That minor-to-major contrast, which helps articulate a deeper contrast
between the formal and the deeply and tenderly personal, is one of the
most magical moments in all music. (The tune with which the strings begin "Comfort Ye" is so simple we can for a few seconds almost believe it
to be something we could have thought of ourselves.)

Then Handel moves in a powerful sequence of quasi–dominant-to-
tonic relationships from E to A ("And the Glory of the Lord Shall Be Re-
vealed"), to D minor ("Thus Saith the Lord"/"But Who May Abide the
Day of His Coming?"), to G minor ("And He Shall Purify the Sons of
Levi"). D is the first key to which he returns (in "O Thou That Tellest
Good Tidings to Zion"), a move to which he lends emphasis by going immediately to a pair of pieces in the closest minor key, B minor ("For Behold, Darkness Shall Cover the Earth"/"The People That Walked in
Darkness"). D is also the key in which we first hear trumpets ("Glory to
God"). After the brightness of that chorus Handel turns into another di-
rection for the remainder of Part I. The melodies of the soprano aria "Rejoice Greatly" are sprightly and the rhythms dance, but the new harmonic

world we have entered—B-flat major—sheds a softer light. With the chorus "His Yoke Is Easy," Part I ends in gentle understatement, which is
also a clear declaration: "This is not over."

Handel's resources are also simple when it comes to the actual sound
of *Messiah*. His orchestra consists basically of strings, with oboes and
bassoons providing reinforcement in the choruses, and with harpsichord
and organ to help fill out the harmony. Within his string group Handel
gets variety by using solo players much of the time, for example, in most
of the arias ("Ev'ry Valley" and "The Trumpet Shall Sound" are the ex-
ceptions) and even for the beginnings of most of the choruses.

The nearest he comes to a special orchestral effect is his use of
trumpets and kettledrums. He is economical with these and, as a result,
stunningly effective. The first time we hear trumpets, about two-thirds
of the way into Part I in "Glory to God," they are directed to play "from
a distance and rather quietly." Their next appearance is in "Hallelujah!".
Handel begins even this tremendous piece with solo strings, expands
to full strings with oboes and bassoons after the voices come in, and
holds the trumpets in reserve—and the drums for their first entrance
at all—until after the first proclamation that "the Lord God Omnipotent reigneth." When at last these emblems of glory do strike in, the impact is more thrilling than anything achieved by more glamorous and
costly reorchestrators.

Part I of *Messiah* deals with God's promise and God's comfort, and
its season is Advent and Christmas. I have tried to describe the wonder of
"Comfort Ye," and this is followed by an ecstatic aria, "Ev'ry Valley
Shall Be Exalted," ecstasy being expressed in vocal brilliance. With the
plunge into a dark and dramatic D minor, the tone changes drastically in
the bass recitative "Thus Saith the Lord," with its colorful evocation of
the shaking of the heavens and the earth. Here, too, we are struck by how
much power there is in simplicity: Bach, with his lust for complexity,
could not have made this gripping declaration. Handel's delight in illustration, a penchant he certainly shares with Bach, comes to the fore in the
music he writes to make us see the flames of the refiner's fire.

We get the first hint of the Nativity, but first we must experience the
darkness that Isaiah tells us "shall cover the earth." Here is another of
Handel's minor-to-major miracles—that wondrous change when he takes
us from "darkness shall cover the earth, and gross darkness the people"
to "but the Lord shall arise upon thee." And so, by way of the stern air
"The People That Walked in Darkness," Handel propels us into the pure
joy of the chorus "For unto Us a Child Is Born" with those exclamations
of "Wonderful, Counsellor," whose thrill never palls. This is one of the
"borrowed" movements, an adaptation of an Italian duet Handel had

written in the summer of 1741, and the same is true of the choruses "And He Shall Purify" and "His Yoke Is Easy."

The Nativity recitatives, introduced by a brief "Pastoral Symphony," are vivid, especially the flames that surround the soprano's "And suddenly there was with the angel a multitude of the heav'nly host." The center of gravity of this section is in a piece most familiar to us as a double aria for alto and soprano, that division actually being an inspired late change. After a recitative, "Then shall the eyes of the blind be opened," the alto, to the most gentle and consoling music, sings the words of Isaiah: "He shall feed his flock like a shepherd," but for the continuation in the words of Matthew, "Come unto him, all ye that labour," a bright soprano takes over, and in a new key. This is one of Jennens's most beautiful marriages of texts from far-apart sections of the Bible.

With Part II we arrive at the darkest portion of *Messiah*. Its subject is Christ's suffering and Passion, human scorn, the descent to hell, and eventually victory and triumph, with an interlude devoted to the spreading of the Gospel. The season is Passiontide and Easter.

Handel begins with a chorus, "Behold the Lamb of God," whose grand formality corresponds to that of the Sinfonia that opens Part I, and he follows this with that most immediate and personal of arias, "He Was Despised." Handel has reserved his most somber harmonies and his most tenebrous key, F minor, for "Surely He Has Borne Our Griefs" and "And with His Stripes We Are Healed."[4] The latter chorus is based on a theme that is a cliché of seventeenth- and eighteenth-century music, one that combines a minor triad with a piercing diminished seventh (D-flat/E-natural): we can find literally hundreds of examples, in Bach's *Well-tempered Clavier* and *Musical Offering*,[5] in Haydn's quartets, the Mozart Requiem, and more. From "And with His Stripes" Handel, with his sense for contrast, moves into the brightness of "All We Like Sheep Have Gone Astray," another transformation of one of his Italian chamber duets, only to present us with a greater and even shocking change of atmosphere when the giddiness of the straying sheep suddenly gives way to a dark *Adagio* full of disturbing chromatic harmonies: "For the Lord hath laid on him the iniquity of us all." We have arrived at the central point.

Now divine suffering is pitted against human scorn. Handel makes the most of the difference between the savage jeering of "He Trusted in

[4]By "darkest" I mean farthest on the flat side of the harmonic spectrum. In his operas, F minor is a key Handel never uses casually, always associating it with deeply tragic moments, often with scenes of madness.

[5]In the *Musical Offering* the theme itself was actually invented and supplied by Frederick the Great.

God that He Would Deliver Him" and the poignant lament of "Behold, and See if There Be Any Sorrow Like Unto His Sorrow" (the first in C minor, the other in E minor, a grinding juxtaposition). The recitative that connects these two pieces, "Thy Rebuke Hath Broken His Heart," is Handel's most special excursion in *Messiah* into intense and mysterious chromatic harmony. In these few measures we reach the highest point of pathos in the work. After that, the brightness of the A-major air "But Thou Didst Not Leave His Soul in Hell" follows like a wiping away of tears. The juxtaposition of this psalm verse with "He was cut off out of the land of the living; for the transgression of Thy people was He stricken" is one of the most beautiful touches of the *Messiah* text.

With the chorus "Let All the Angels of God Worship Him," Handel gives us a welcome sight of his eventual redeeming musical destination, D major. The sequence of the chorus "The Lord Gave the Word," the aria "How Beautiful Are the Feet of Them That Preach the Gospel of Peace," and the magnificently vigorous chorus "Their Sound Is Gone Out," with its grand depiction of words traveling "to the ends of the world," portray the spreading of the gospel. Then conflict: "Why Do the Nations Rage So Furiously Together," a powerful bass aria (if it occurred in an opera it would be called a "Rage Aria"), the tight and intense chorus "Let Us Break Their Bonds Asunder," and the fiery tenor aria "Thou Shalt Break Them with a Rod of Iron"—all prepare the magnificent D-major confirmation of the radiant "Hallelujah!" that concludes Part II.[6]

But "Hallelujah!" is not the end. The promise of redemption and resurrection, which is the most important part of the *Messiah* text, is yet to come. The season for Part III is Ascension and Pentecost, the celebration of the descent of the Holy Spirit. Harmony is the means by which Handel can surpass the trumpets-and-drums blaze of the Hallelujah Chorus, and the E-major glow of the gently confident soprano air, "I Know that My Redeemer Liveth," accomplishes the heightening that is now

---

[6]The custom, piously observed in the United States, of standing for the Hallelujah Chorus was begun by King George II at one of the first London performances of *Messiah* (unless this story, too, is apocryphal). When the king stood, everyone had to stand. Robert Shaw used to maintain that His Majesty's rising was caused not by religious or musical emotion but by a more direct physical need, as he did not realize how close the next intermission was. Nowadays the arrival at the Hallelujah Chorus is often the occasion for a silent showdown between the secularists who resolutely refuse to stand for what has been dubbed "the national anthem of heaven" and the traditionalists who rebuke them with looks of poison.

At the Handel commemoration of 1784, the then-reigning monarch, George III, added something else to the Hallelujah Chorus which fortunately has not become a tradition, and that is an encore. At the first *Messiah* performance at the festival he commanded the Earl of Sandwich to give the sign, but at the second, as we learn from Dr. Charles Burney's account, "his Majesty was pleased to make the sign himself, with a gentle motion of his right hand in which was the printed book of the words."

needed. Next comes the grave passage, its text familiar from so many funerals, "Since by Man Came Death," extraordinarily arresting because it
is the only music for unaccompanied voices in all of *Messiah*. "The
Trumpet Shall Sound" is a D-major air, and the double choral finale,
"Worthy Is the Lamb"/"Amen," brings *Messiah* harmonically home. But
on the way we meet another of Handel's quiet miracles, the combination
of duet and chorus, "O Death, Where Is Thy Sting?"/"But Thanks Be to
God," music that seems to come from another, more German and deeply
spiritual world, and then the gloriously inventive aria, "If God Be for Us,
Who Can Be Against Us?"

In a way the "Amen" chorus has to compete with "Hallelujah!", but
Handel achieves the wonder of finding music still grander, still more jubilant. He can do this because, master strategist that he is, he has held in
reserve for these last minutes another source of torrential musical energy, namely, a massive laying out of contrapuntal virtuosity. Several choruses, beginning with "And He Shall Purify," have reminded us that this
resource is indeed in Handel's vocabulary, but the "Amen" chorus goes
far beyond any of these. Handel would have been aware of the reputation
for contrapuntal wizardry of his contemporary, J. S. Bach, and I like to
imagine that at this moment, sitting at his table in Brook Street, he
thought to himself, "Ach, I can do this, too," and then proceeded, at high
speed, to nail this magnificent peroration.

As I mentioned earlier, during the fourteen seasons of *Messiah* performances under Handel's supervision the score underwent substantial
changes. Because of the limitations of some of the local singers, even what
was heard at the premiere differed from what was in the score Handel
took to Dublin. Over the years pieces were shortened or lengthened,
eliminated or added, recomposed entirely, or transposed into other keys
and for other voices. Thus two ways of performing *Messiah* are available.
You can reconstruct one of the forms in which the work was actually
given by Handel between 1742 and 1759 (or, for that matter, the 1741
score), or you can treat *Messiah* with its variants as a sort of kit from
which to build an edition of your own. Most conductors take the latter,
synthetic approach.

A few comments on some of the possible variants are in order. "But
Who May Abide the Day of His Coming?" was first composed as a bass
aria in D minor and 3/8 time, beginning much like the version most familiar today. It strikes us as an exceedingly mild piece, but even so, the
Dublin bass could not manage it to the satisfaction of the composer, who
provided a recitative in its stead. The first London performances alternated between the original aria and the recitative. In 1750 Handel used

the castrato Gaetano Guadagni for the first time, and it was for this virtuoso that he wrote the aria with the ferocious *prestissimo* coloratura
passages on the words "for He is like a refiner's fire."[7] Later, Handel
transposed it into several other keys for different altos and the soprano
Christina Passerini. Older readers will remember hearing this version
of the aria sung by basses, a transposition that was Mozart's doing, not
Handel's.

Handel originally composed the "Pastoral Symphony" before the
Nativity recitatives as a prelude only eleven measures long. In Dublin he
expanded it by adding a middle section and a *da capo*, though reverting to
the short form in 1754 and possibly thereafter. Handel calls it *Pifa*, indicating that it should suggest the sound of *pifferi*, or shepherds' pipes. (In
the Nativity sequence itself, as we shall see in a moment, Handel also provided an engaging new variant to suit Kitty Clive's special gifts, which,
like Mrs. Cibber's, were more verbal than vocal.)

"Rejoice Greatly" is another aria that was strikingly transformed.
Originally it was a very long piece in 12/8 gigue tempo. Handel soon
shortened this, and the original was never sung in his lifetime. Later he
made what is probably the more familiar version with the meter changed
from 12/8 to 4/4, the passagework becoming the more brilliant thereby.
Both versions were sung at various times by tenor or soprano, but more
often by the latter.

The recitative "Then Shall the Eyes of the Blind Be Opened" exists
in versions for soprano and for alto. The aria it introduces, "He Shall
Feed His Flock," was originally written for soprano. I mentioned Handel's inspired revision for two singers earlier.

The recitative/aria pair "Thy Rebuke Hath Broken His Heart"/"Behold, and See If There Be Any Sorrow" exists in versions for tenor and
soprano—identical except for the choice of register.

Of "Thou Art Gone Up on High" there are two different versions,
both of them existing in soprano and alto keys.

The lovely *siciliano* "How Beautiful Are the Feet" was originally for
soprano in G minor, but on occasion Handel had it sung in C minor by
an alto. There is also a dramatically different and very beautiful variant,
even with a somewhat different text, for two altos, culminating in a chorus, "Break Forth into Joy."

For the bass aria "Why Do the Nations So Furiously Rage Together" we have two strikingly dissimilar versions. The original is a broad
da capo piece, but in the 1750s Handel changed his mind about that,

[7]Guadagni, just twenty when he sang his first *Messiah*, went on to enjoy a distinguished international career in opera. Gluck wrote *Orfeo* for him.

making a brief and powerful recitative on the words "The kings of the earth rise up and the rulers take counsel together against the Lord and His Anointed." The sudden irruption of recitative is immensely dramatic, and it makes for an electrifying transition into the chorus "Let Us Break Their Bonds Asunder."

The alternative versions of the textually most complex and musically most subtle aria in *Messiah*, "If God Be for Us," are a matter only of choosing between soprano in G minor and alto in C minor.

Der Messias, A Sacred Oratorio, Arranged by Wolfgang Amadè Mozart, K. 572

Mozart arranged Handel's *Messiah*, composed for the most part in 1741, for Baron Gottfried van Swieten ("Baron Suiten" to Mozart) in February and March 1789. With Mozart presiding at the fortepiano, Ignaz Umlauf conducted performances of this version on 6 March and 7 April 1789 at the Vienna town house of Count Johann Esterházy. The work was sung in German. There was a chorus of twelve, and the soloists were Mozart's sister-in-law Aloysia Lange, Katharina von Altamonte (or Altomonte), Valentin Joseph Adamberger, and Ignaz Saal. Mozart's *Messiah* edition soon began to be encrusted with alien accretions of its own, and it was not published in a reliable score until the appearance of the *Neue Mozart-Ausgabe* in 1961.

Mozart's *Messiah* orchestra consists of two flutes and piccolo, two oboes, two clarinets, two bassoons, two horns, three trombones, timpani, keyboard (presumably fortepiano), and strings (Mozart's additions to Handel are given in italics). Unlike Handel, Mozart gave the oboes and bassoons independent rather than doubling parts. He gave the trombones independent parts in the Overture and the chorus "Since By Man Came Death," and in accordance with Viennese practice of his day he also used them to double the altos, tenors, and basses of the chorus.

Though he might dislike many specific things that editors and arrangers have done to *Messiah* since his death, Handel, himself a vigorous—even cavalier—arranger, adapter, and appropriator, would be neither surprised nor disapproving that eight or so generations of musicians have felt the need to do *something*. The idea that one should perform "ancient music" (as it used to be called) in its own style and according to the practices of its time, rather than adapting it to current customs and expectations, is a modern one. What mattered was that a performance worked. Handel would not have minded even an attempt to perform *Messiah* in 2004 in the manner of 1750, provided the audience felt that the effect was to bring them closer to the work, not to shut them out. And he would have understood the point of what the Leipzig publishers Breitkopf & Härtel put on the title page of Mozart's *Messiah* edition in 1802: "Händel's *Messiah* / Arranged for Greater Serviceability for Our Day / By W. A. Mozart."

Mozart, for his part, might well be surprised that to find "his" *Messiah* in any sense deemed serviceable two hundred years after he devised it. It was meant for 1789, and if he ever gave a moment's thought to a performance of *Messiah* in the twenty-first century, he would have assumed that we would have our own arrangers to make this bizarrely out-of-date music palatable.

So why the Mozart *Messiah* today? We don't need it by way of accommodation to current taste as Baron van Swieten's club of Associierte needed it in 1789, as *Messiah* devotees in the first half of the twentieth century needed the additional accompaniments of Dr. Ebenezer Prout (which incorporated some details of Mozart's), or as Sir Thomas Beecham thought in 1959 that the world needed the gaudy glosses of Eugene Goossens. Most of today's *Messiah*-loving public is content with unretouched Handel, and there are no practical reasons for departing from Handel's own score: we have the right instruments, singers practiced in mid-eighteenth-century style and technique, keyboard players adept at playing continuo parts, and trumpeters for whom "The Trumpet Shall Sound" is a piece of cake.

I see three reasons to produce Mozart's *Messiah*. The first and most important is that it is beautiful. And if you say, "But it isn't Handel," I would answer, "Granted, but think of it as the wonderful gift of a new piece by Mozart." Another important reason is that hearing a familiar work in a new guise helps us to experience it afresh. To most of us *Messiah* is extremely familiar. Hearing it has taken on the quality of ritual, with the result that we are in danger of no longer *listening* to it, but rather registering—with satisfaction and comfort—that a performance of *Messiah* is taking place. A final reason is that the "Mozart *Messiah*" is part of the biography of a beloved work and, more broadly considered, a fascinating document in the history of taste.

How did Mozart come to make this arrangement? I have told the story of Baron van Swieten's near-obsession with Bach and Handel in the essay on Mozart's Mass in C Minor. In 1780, he organized a group of wealthy patrons who called themselves the Associierte, and it was for their private concerts that Mozart rescored *Messiah* in 1789 as well as Handel's *Acis and Galatea* the year before and *Ode for Saint Cecilia's Day* and *Alexander's Feast* the year after. Still later it was the Associierte who sponsored Haydn's choral version of his *Seven Last Words* as well as the composition and performance of *The Creation* and *The Seasons*.

In Vienna, Handel was no national demigod, and van Swieten and his friends put on *Messiah* for their musical delight, not like the Londoners of the 1780s, who used it as a puissant symbol of the glory and might of the state and its earthly king. Mozart led *Messiah* in a room of modest size and with fewer performers than Handel ever assembled. No organ was available, the art of florid, high trumpet playing (of which "The Trumpet Shall Sound" is a modest example compared to what one finds in Bach) was lost, and the singers had neither the inclination nor the skill to improvise embellishments for *da capos* and at cadences. These are technical matters, though taste enters as well in the question of the vocal embellishments, which were in fact called "notes of taste."

And taste is of central importance here. Handel's *Messiah* sound is remarkably plain, not just compared to *Don Giovanni* but to Handel's own operas and other oratorios. My guess is that he kept his *Messiah* orchestra so simple because he was unsure of what he would find in Dublin, where the premiere took place. His deployment of his simple resources is wonderfully effective, but it would have seemed impossibly thin to Viennese ears in 1789, just as it continued to seem impossibly thin to conductors well into the twentieth century. Audiences, of course, never had a chance to find out until Handel's own scoring came back into circulation in the second half of the twentieth century.[1] One of van Swieten's charges to his pet arranger was to color the piece up a bit.

Before getting to a few details of Mozart's *Messiah* Coloring Book, let us look at the question of language. English, the language of Handel's text, was relatively unfamiliar to the Viennese and carried no emotional or cultural resonance for them. It was therefore taken for granted that *Messiah*, like the other works performed for the Associierte, would be sung in German. Mozart had to make a few musical changes to accommodate the German text, which is primarily the work of Christoph Daniel Ebeling, a Hamburg theologian who drew both on the German Bible and on Friedrich Gottlieb Klopstock's sacred epic *Der Messias*. Performers today can re-adapt Mozart to fit the English words or go with Mozart all the way and use the German text. The latter course tends to

---

[1]There was an oft-repeated story about the viola player who dreamed he was playing *Messiah* in the original orchestration and woke up to find that he was.

provoke considerable resentment from British and American audiences, some of whose members assume that God speaks only English.

Now here are some of the differences you will hear:

In the Overture, Mozart adds horns, trombones, and bassoons to the *Grave* introduction.

"Ev'ry Valley" gets delicious new flute and clarinet parts, now doubling, now imitating, sometimes playing what Handel himself might have added at the harpsichord.

"But Who May Abide the Day of His Coming" is assigned by Mozart to the bass, a plan retained by Prout and others, remaining standard practice until the 1960s, and he adds flutes, oboes, and bassoons to striking effect.

"O Thou That Tellest Good Tidings to Zion" brings Mozart's most elaborate additions thus far. Before the chorus comes in, Handel uses only violins and continuo; Mozart adds flutes, clarinets, bassoons, and horns, and calls on the full string section, inventing an especially beautiful new part for the violas.

In "The People That Walked in Darkness," Mozart outdoes even his work in the previous aria. Handel writes an austere line for violins and violas in unison. Mozart sees that the bass line allows for the possibility of chromatic harmonization. He accepts that invitation enthusiastically and gives free rein to his fantasy in purple-patch harmony, instrumental color (flute, clarinets, bassoons, and again a new viola line), and intricate imitative figurations. Isaiah's apocalyptic darkness has become the darkness of the courtyard of Donna Anna's palace, that *bujo loco* where Donna Elvira finds herself alone and with a palpitating heart.

"All We Like Sheep" brings a remarkable change of sound with its enchanting popping wind chords and new swirling figurations for "We have turned every one to his own way."

"But Thou Didst Not Leave His Soul in Hell," here assigned to the soprano, gets lovely woodwind doublings right out of *Figaro*, the flute often going with the violins an octave higher, the bassoon with the voice an octave lower. This is one of the subtlest bits of Mozart in *Messiah*.

A little later Mozart—or more probably van Swieten—makes an unfortunate cut. Jennens-Handel have a thrilling sequence from Paul's Epistle to the Hebrews. In recitative, the tenor sings: "Unto which of the angels said He at any time, Thou art my Son, this day I have begotten Thee?" To which the chorus replies: "Let all the angels of God worship Him." Van Swieten-Mozart omits the choral reply as well as the ensuing aria "Thou Art Gone Up on High," skipping to the chorus "The Lord Gave the Word." This cut is made in many *Messiah* performances today.

"How Beautiful Are the Feet," given in its most familiar form as a soprano aria, becomes another exceptionally lovely bit of Mozart, with elaborated string parts and delicate woodwind additions, a little freer than those in "But Thou Didst Not Leave His Soul in Hell."

Mozart makes "Why Do the Nations Rage So Furiously Together" a big piece with trumpets and drums. He uses Handel's original, long form.

"Thou Shalt Break Them with a Rod of Iron" is one of Mozart's most stunning transformations. He adds only a single flute, two clarinets, and two bassoons, but he uses them astonishingly, running a sequence of long notes and rapid chromatic descents through the orchestral introduction, devising all kinds of pungent punctuation and commentary, and breaking out in the closing ritornello in an amazing dance of imitative figuration.

"Since by Man Came Death," unaccompanied in Handel, gets a powerful backing of oboes, clarinets, bassoons, and trombones (in their first obbligato passage since the Overture).

Now we get a big change, and one that cost Mozart much trouble. This is "The Trumpet Shall Sound," and the final version represents Mozart's third attempt. Vienna had no trumpeter who could manage Handel's obbligato. In any case, as those who know Brahms's *German Requiem* will remember, Luther's Bible translation tells us that the Great Summons will be sounded on the *letzte Posaune*, the last trombone, equally impractical for eighteenth-century Vienna, and Mozart ended up giving the solo in somewhat simplified form to the French horn. Mozart makes a cut in the main part of the aria and omits the middle section ("For this corruptible must put on incorruption") altogether, theologically an unsound decision but—I will risk the ire of the Handel police—musically a good one.

The duet "O Death, Where Is Thy Sting?" is gorgeously enriched with a characteristically Mozartian double-viola part.

Now comes the boldest change of all. Van Swieten found Handel's aria "If God Be for Us, Who Can Be Against Us?" "dry," in which he was deeply wrong. He did, however want to keep this important and beautiful text from the Epistle to the Romans, and therefore commanded Mozart to set it anew, in recitative. Here then is the one passage that is pure Mozart and has nothing to do with Handel. This extraordinary moment, when the Countess Almaviva meets the Apostle Paul, is one of Mozart's most rapturously beautiful pages—with a breathtaking slip from major into minor at "It is Christ that died"—and it exemplifies most acutely the daring charm of that seductive hybrid that is "Mozart's *Messiah*."

Franz Joseph Haydn

Franz Joseph Haydn was born in Rohrau-on-the-Leitha, Lower Austria, on 31 March 1732 and died in Vienna on 31 May 1809.

Harmoniemesse (Wind-Band Mass) in B-flat

Haydn composed this Mass in 1802 and it was first performed in the Mountain Church at Eisenstadt, Hungary (now Austria), on 8 September that year.

Soprano, alto, tenor, and bass solos, four-part mixed chorus. Flute, two oboes, two clarinets, two bassoons, two horns, two trumpets, timpani, organ, and strings.

Prince Anton, mostly remembered for disbanding his orchestra and thus freeing Haydn to go off to Vienna and London, was the exception among Esterházy princes in that he had no interest in music or any of the arts. But Prince Nikolaus, who succeeded him in 1799, reverted to the style and tastes of his great-grandfather, Prince Paul Anton, for whom Haydn had gone to work as Vice-Capellmeister in 1761, and his grandfather, another Prince Nikolaus and Haydn's employer for twenty-eight years. The grandfather played an odd string instrument called the baryton on which

Haydn lavished hundreds of pages of beautiful music; the grandson played the clarinet, at least if we are to believe a portrait of him by Joseph Fischer.

Like his music- and art-loving forebears, the later Prince Nikolaus spent fortunes on those pleasures of his, among other things reconstituting the orchestra his father had done away with. Nikolaus loved his wife, Maria Josepha Hermenegild, a former Princess von Liechtenstein, and beginning in 1796, he commissioned a full-scale Mass with soloists, chorus, and orchestra every year for her name day, 12 September. He thus provided rewarding work for two great composers (Haydn and Beethoven) and one very good one (Johann Nepomuk Hummel), and at the same time gave pleasure to his wife, to his church-music-loving self, to God, and to many generations of singers, players, conductors, and listeners.[1]

Turning to Haydn was an obvious choice for the prince. One reason was Haydn's long history in the Esterházy household, for which, along with all those symphonies, operas, baryton trios, and so on, he had written six Masses during his years there. No less important was Haydn's uncontested standing as the greatest living composer, a place he himself would unhesitatingly have assigned to his beloved Mozart until the latter's death at the end of 1791. It must have given Haydn special pleasure to return to the Esterházy estates at Eisenstadt, no longer a servant but an eminence, and the holder, to boot, of an honorary doctorate from Oxford University. Part of his pleasure, too, would have lain in writing for the warmly gracious princess, who not only valued his art but, now that his dear Viennese friend Marianne von Genzinger was gone, knew better than anyone how to provide for the creature comforts of an aging composer, making sure that the supply of Malaga and Tokay did not run out and that the occasional medical bills were discreetly taken care of.

In this second chapter of his Esterházy life, Haydn composed six Masses; Hummel, the Esterházy Concertmeister from 1804 to 1811 (with a brief interruption in 1808), contributed three; and Beethoven wrote his Mass in C for this series in 1807.[2] To say that these late Haydn Masses all hew to one basic pattern is to do no more than to make a similar observation about, say, Haydn's symphonies for London: The six Masses are as distinct in personality, even in sonority, as those twelve great symphonies.

The *Harmoniemesse* is the last of Haydn's six. I wish there were space to includes essays on all of them, especially the first of them, *Missa in*

---

[1]The Esterházys seem not to have been strict about celebrating precisely on the day; at least, the performances of Haydn's and Beethoven's Masses took place on various September dates, none of them the twelfth.

[2]Hummel was in effect Capellmeister, but could not hold that title since Haydn had been granted it for life.

tempore belli (Mass in Time of War), written in the fourth year of the Napoleonic wars, with Austria suffering defeat after defeat at the hands of the twenty-seven-year-old French general, and the *Missa in angustiis* (Mass in a Time of Anxiety)—also known as the "Nelson" Mass, composed two years later, when Lord Nelson's victory at Abukir gave the Alliance one of its few bright moments. If I absolutely had to name one of the Masses as the high point of this wondrous late harvest—and that would not be easy at all—I think I would be torn between the *Harmoniemesse* and the brightly sharp-edged "Nelson" Mass. The *Harmoniemesse* occupies a special place because it was the last one Haydn completed, and perhaps that is why I have chosen it for inclusion here, to stand, as it were, for that whole miraculous group of works. Haydn worried about this Mass and, as he wrote to the prince in June 1802, he labored very hard at it, "but even more, I was FEARFUL," anxious to see whether he could still earn some applause. He reached the summit in this work, but soon afterwards, mental exhaustion set in, and a string quartet he began in the following year, 1803, remained a two-movement fragment.

Haydn did get the *Beyfall,* the applause he had hoped for. We have the testimony of Prince Ludwig Starhemberg, the Austrian ambassador to England, who was present for the first performance and who noted in his diary (in French):

> Wednesday, 8 September. This was the name day of the Princess; therefore at 10 in the morning we went to wait on her, attired in the grand Eisenstadt dress uniform, and afterwards to Mass in a great convoy of carriages. Superb Mass, new and excellent music by Haydn and conducted by him (he is still in the service of the Prince). Nothing could have been more beautiful or better performed.

Harmonie is an old word for wind band, and the *Harmoniemesse* takes its name, which it acquired in the nineteenth century, from the prominence of wind sonorities in it. Except for the presence of a flute, the orchestra is actually no more "windy" than the one in three of the previous Masses, the "Nelson" and "Theresia" Masses being quite spare in that department, but the actual scoring of the *Harmoniemesse,* strikingly rich, is tilted more in that direction.

The Kyrie is a slow movement, and one could take it for the introduction of a symphony. Haydn begins with purely formal gestures, but as early as the fifth measure the darkening shadow of a G-flat falls across the scene. It is not enough to send the piece clear into B-flat minor, but the shadow is one that keeps returning, lending impressive gravity as well as a characteristically Haydnesque ambiguity of feeling to what we hear.

The first entrance of human voices, nearly a minute into the piece, is stunning. When the chorus pronounces its first invocation of "Lord, have mercy upon us," it does so in powerful *forte*—in fact *forte assai*, very strong—on the keynote, B-flat, but the harmony that supports that cry is not the tonic chord of B-flat major, which is what you would expect at such a crucial marker. Instead, Haydn gives us a poignant dissonance—E-natural/B-flat/D-flat/G—which he resolves only two measures later into a regular B-flat cadence. This vocal entrance continues the musical agenda that was set in the opening music for orchestra alone: a constant alternation of B-flat-major clarity with shadows—G-flat shadows in that introduction. When the voices begin to sing, the shadow is different, that is, it is made of different notes, but the dramatic darkening effect is the same. This is what we experience throughout the first "Kyrie" and the "Christe eleison."

Haydn sets the text as a single movement, but the return of "Kyrie" after "Christe" heralds new departures, notably a more elaborately contrapuntal imitative texture and a more florid style for the solo quartet, including some lovely flights in thirds, first for the two women, then for the two men. Haydn gives us something like a recapitulation of the opening music, one of whose striking variants is that this time the choir's B-flat is harmonized with a chord of B-flat. The closing section of the movement expands gloriously, with the orchestra becoming ever more active. This is the grandest of Haydn's Kyries and a token of that care and diligence of which he spoke in his letter to the prince.

The solo soprano leads off in the Gloria, which goes at a brilliant tempo, *Vivace assai*. To become a bit quiet for the words "et in terra pax" is convention, but here Haydn, in the eleventh year of war, is dark as well as quiet, something he achieves with the combination of the stark unison for the first syllables and the move toward F minor for the subsequent harmonies. For "laudamus" and "glorificamus," the music reverts to its initial brightness.

"Gratias agimus tibi" begins a new section, a little slower, and with the text entrusted to the solo alto. The sound is of Mozartian sensuousness, thanks especially to the prominence of the clarinets. In due course, soprano, tenor, and bass (in duet with the tenor) take the vocal line. At "Qui tollis peccata mundi" the chorus enters and the orchestra becomes very active. With the final section, "Quoniam tu solus sanctus," fast and spirited music returns. To set "in gloria Dei Patris" as a fugue is another convention, but in this Mass Haydn gives us a hugely energetic double fugue—more assurance to his patron of *Mühe* and *Fleiss*—taking pains and working hard—but also a show of exuberant energy of which the seventy-year-old composer was obviously and justly proud. The fugue moves with extraordinary swing and thrust, amazing us over and again with new extensions and explorations, and delighting us with the vocal brilliance of the writing and, of course, with its syncopated "Amens."

Like the Gloria, the Credo moves off at a great pace, and with the orchestra more joyously enterprising than ever. "Et incarnatus est" is a lyric *Adagio* begun by the solo soprano, turning toward the distant region of G-flat major at "et homo factus est." A most touching detail: the return of the soprano soloist for one more repetition of the words "passus et sepultus est." The resurrection is proclaimed in a powerful C minor—an unusual touch, that minor key for those words. Haydn moves briskly through the doctrinal clauses in the third part of the Creed, closing the movement with a fiery fugue for "et vitam venturi saeculi, Amen."

The Sanctus is a solemn *Adagio*, with a change to a quicker tempo for "Pleni sunt coeli." The Benedictus is a surprise. In Austrian Masses of this period, including Haydn's earlier ones, this text is most often set as a friendly *Allegretto*; here, however, Haydn decrees a really fast tempo, *Molto allegro*, and writes a movement of real brilliance, including a vigorous fugal episode. This leads to a quick return of the "Osanna."

Agnus Dei, another *Adagio*, enters with a wonderful sense of freshness because the key, G major, is one as good as untouched up to now. Here Haydn quotes his own oratorio, *The Seasons*, completed and introduced the year before, and the reference is apt, for it is to the great chorus of supplication, "Sei nun gnädig" (Be gracious). With the repeated pleas of "miserere," the music moves once again to dark harmonic places.

Haydn always sets the closing "Dona nobis pacem" as a spirited *Allegro*, as though giving thanks for a prayer already answered. In his writings on music, D. F. Tovey many times referred to Samuel Johnson's friend Oliver Edwards, "whose efforts at philosophy were frustrated by cheerfulness breaking through." Like Tovey, I can only suppose that something like this happened to Haydn as he approached the end of a Mass. It certainly is a beautiful *Allegro* that Haydn writes here, and its ebullient close is set in neat relief by the single moment of reverent hush just a few measures before the final double bar.

The Two Great Oratorios

It is rare for an artist to experience the most significant turning point in his life near the end of his sixth decade. It happened to Haydn: the critical event was the death on 28 September 1790 of Prince Nikolaus Esterházy, his patron and employer for the past twenty-eight years. Haydn was twenty-nine when he entered the service of Nikolaus's older brother, Prince Paul Anton, as Vice-Capellmeister on 1 May 1761, and he was fifty-eight when the circumstances of his life changed so drastically. Not caring for music, Nikolaus's son, Prince Anton, dismissed most of his players; Haydn and his Concertmeister, Luigi Tomasini, were kept on full salary and retained their titles, but strictly as sinecures.[1]

Haydn lost no time moving to Vienna. In recent visits to the residence there of Peter and Marianne von Genzinger—he was Prince Nikolaus's physician, she was a cultivated amateur musician and a woman of exceptional warmth and understanding—he had found not only the pleasure of stimulating and sympathetic company and delightful creature comforts, but also a keen sense of how restricted his life at Eszterháza had been. Only two weeks after his arrival in Vienna, a stranger appeared unannounced at his door one December morning and declared: "I am Salomon from London and I have come to fetch you. Tomorrow we shall conclude an agreement."

In brief, Haydn went to London for two extended stays, enjoying an extraordinary rush of professional, social, and even romantic success. His last symphonies are a happy monument to those happy times. Haydn's English harvest was not, however, to be assessed only in terms of material gains and prestige; the impact on his music and his musical growth, as vigorous as ever as he entered his sixties, was immense. In 1803, mental exhaustion obliged him to put away his pen, although he continued to be tormented by musical thoughts he could not find the strength and concentration to set down. Until that time, however, he was open to new ideas, delighted by the conquest of new territories, and not less by the stimulus of finding ever-new responses to old challenges. England, with its welcoming and willing—indeed, demanding—public, had made the old man young and ever more inventive and progressive.

Having spent his career in the service of private music *chez* Esterházy and before that in the households of Baron Fürnberg and Count Morzin, Haydn was deeply susceptible to the appeal of public musical life as he met it in England. With profound emotion he recalled hearing a procession of four thousand charity children sing a hymn in Saint Paul's Cathedral in 1792: "No music moved me so greatly in my whole

---

[1]Anton died in 1799, and his successor was another Prince Nikolaus, who figures in the story of Haydn's *Harmoniemesse*, page 155.

life as this, innocent and full of devotion," he told his biographer Griesinger, and sang the melody to him, more than a dozen years after the event. And Haydn treasured no composition of his own more than the Emperor's hymn, *Gott erhalte Franz den Kaiser,* which he wrote in the winter of 1796–1797. Within twenty years it was republished with more than forty different texts, and it has been adopted by institutions ranging from the Third Reich to various Protestant churches to Columbia University. The desire to present to his own country and his own sovereign the gift of a national hymn arose when he heard an English crowd sing their own national anthem to the words "God save great George, our King."

Had someone told Haydn ten years earlier that he would close and cap his career as a composer of choral music he would have been thoroughly surprised, if not out-and-out incredulous. But he did, and that too came out of his English experience. He was excited and stirred to the roots of his being by the Handel Festival in Westminster Abbey in May 1791. There he heard *Israel in Egypt, Messiah,* extracts from several other oratorios, various anthems including *Zadok the Priest,* and some concertos. He had heard some of Handel's vocal works in Vienna, including *Messiah* in Mozart's orchestration, but that was at private performances that left him with no inkling of the rhetorical force and emotional impact of *Israel in Egypt* and *Messiah* sung and played by more than a thousand performers in a great national shrine which was also the composer's burial place, and in the presence of the king and queen, who rose for the Hallelujah Chorus, just like their subjects.

In Vienna, Baron Gottfried van Swieten, prefect of the Imperial Library, president of the Court Commission on Education and Censorship, and one of the most vigorously imaginative and effective patrons in the history of music, had tried to interest Haydn in writing an oratorio "in the manner and spirit of Handel," but without success, and Johann Baptist von Alzinger's libretto on *The Deification of Hercules* with which he tried to tempt the composer did not help his cause. But Handel in London set Haydn aflame, his newly developed sense of box office not less than his spirit, and the central problem now was finding a suitable subject.

Van Swieten was not known to be self-effacing; even so, he might be astonished by how profoundly he affected the course of Western music and how often—indeed, how inevitably—historians and critics invoke his name when they speak and write about his occasional protégés, Haydn and Mozart. Born in 1733 in the university town of Leiden in the Netherlands, birthplace also of the painters Rembrandt,

Jan Steen, and Gabriel Metsu, van Swieten moved to Vienna when his father was appointed personal physician to the Empress Maria Theresa. He himself chose a career in the diplomatic corps, holding appointments first in Brussels, Paris, and Warsaw, then, in 1770, becoming Her Majesty's ambassador in Berlin. In 1777 he returned to Vienna, where he died in 1803.

He was a keen amateur musician, and three of his wanly competent symphonies are among the countless spurious works published in the eighteenth century under Haydn's name, but obviously it was not as a composer that van Swieten made his mark. In Berlin, when he was not busy negotiating with Frederick the Great over the partition of Poland, he became friends with Carl Philipp Emanuel Bach and with the king's sister, Princess Anna Amalia, herself a pupil in composition of Johann Sebastian Bach's student, Johann Philipp Kirnberger. In these circles van Swieten came to know the work of J. S. Bach and Handel. That knowledge became a passion, an obsession, and the occasion of relentless propagation of the faith. Mozart would remark in 1782 that at the Sunday musicales in van Swieten's apartments "nothing but Handel and Bach" was played, and it was for the baron's oratorio evenings that Mozart made those fantastical hybrids, his reorchestrations of Handel's *Messiah*, *Alexander's Feast*, *Acis and Galatea*, and the *Ode for Saint Cecilia's Day*. It was chiefly through van Swieten that Haydn and Mozart learned their Handel and Bach, and it is the infusion of those influences into their language that defines the Classical style they perfected and that Beethoven would continue. It is nicely fitting that after the turn of the century van Swieten became the dedicatee not only of Beethoven's First Symphony, which symbolizes the voice of the future, but also of Johann Nikolaus Forkel's Bach biography, a crucial work in history and criticism that looks both backward and forward.

It was probably through Mozart that Haydn was introduced into the van Swieten circle, and after Haydn's return to Vienna in August 1795 after his second stay in London, there were three significant contacts between the two men, all to do with the baron's determination to turn Haydn into an oratorio composer. First, van Swieten prepared the text for the choral version of *The Seven Last Words of the Savior upon the Cross*, which Haydn had written as a set of orchestral meditations for the Cathedral of Cadiz in 1785. Almost immediately after that, in the winter of 1795–1796, the baron translated and edited the text of an oratorio on the subject of the Creation, followed by work on another oratorio based on James Thomson's *The Seasons*. Those last two stories are told in the two essays that follow.

Die Schöpfung (The Creation)

Haydn began work on this oratorio in 1796 and completed the score at the beginning of April 1798. The first performance, a private one, was led by Haydn at the Palais Schwarzenberg in Vienna on 29 April 1798, the solo parts being taken by Christine Gerardi, Mathias Rathmeyer, and Ignaz Saal. The first public performance, also under the composer's direction, took place at the Burgtheater in Vienna on 19 March 1799, again with Rathmeyer and Saal, but with Gerardi replaced by Saal's daughter Therese.

Soprano soloist in the roles of the Archangel Gabriel and Eve, tenor soloist as the Archangel Uriel, and bass soloist as the Archangel Raphael and Adam, although some conductors prefer to bring on a new soprano and bass for Eve and Adam; four-part mixed chorus (with four measures for alto solo in the final movement). Three flutes, two oboes, two clarinets, two bassoons and contrabassoon, two horns, two trumpets, three trombones, timpani, and strings. A fortepiano or harpsichord is needed for the recitatives.

There is a charming and characteristic story that was told in 1878 to Sir George Grove by the then–seventy-nine-year-old singer and composer C. H. Purday, whose father had been a friend of François-Hippolyte Barthélemon. Barthélemon, a violinist, composer, and noted Swedenborgian who was on warmly cordial terms with Haydn in London, was asked by the composer for advice on what he might do to write a work similar to Handel's *Messiah*. "Barthélemon took up a Bible which was lying near and said, 'This is the book: Begin at the beginning.'"

Considering how celebrated the composer and how beloved the work, we know dismayingly little about the genesis, so to speak, of *The Creation*. What we do know is that when Haydn left for England for the second time in August 1795, he had in his baggage a libretto in English on the subject of the Creation, given him by the impresario Johann Peter Salomon with the idea that Haydn might set it to music for some future concerts in London. We also know that Haydn had at first felt too uncertain of his English to set the text, that he accepted Baron van Swieten's offer to translate it into German as well as to edit it down to a suitable length, and that, equipped not only with the new German libretto and a revision of the English one, but also with copious suggestions from van Swieten on *how* to set the text, he began to compose *The Creation* early in 1796.

The original libretto disappeared, presumably into the baron's wastebasket during the course of editing and translating. Van Swieten wrote a letter to a Leipzig journal in 1798 in which he described his share in the work as "somewhat more than a translation, though by no means something I could regard as *my own*." He corrected another writer's assertion that it was by Dryden, adding that it was the work of "an unnamed author who compiled it largely from *Milton's* poem *Paradise Lost* and who had intended it for Handel." To his biographer Griesinger, Haydn imparted the information that the idea for *The Creation* belonged to an Englishman, Lidley by name. No one has ever found Lidley; however, Donald Tovey plausibly suggested that "Lidley is only Linley with a cold in his head." That would be Thomas Linley Sr. (1733–1795), father-in-law to Richard Brinsley Sheridan and, at the time of Haydn's London visits, co-director of the Drury Lane oratorio concerts. In an incisive article on "The Origin and Libretto of Haydn's *Creation*," Edward Ollesen suggests that, while Linley is an unlikely author for the libretto, he may well have "passed to Haydn a libretto from the library (or from the lumber room) of the Drury Lane oratorios." As for the connection with Handel, Ollesen points out that Linley was the successor at Drury Lane to John Christopher Smith the Younger, who had taken part in Handel's own oratorio performances and who had inherited from his father, Handel's copyist and amanuensis, a considerable legacy of Handel manuscripts. Ollesen proposes that possible candidates as *Creation* author are Charles Jennens, Handel's librettist for *Saul*, *Messiah*, *Belshazzar*, and the faithfully Miltonian *L'Allegro, il Penseroso ed il Moderato*; or Newburgh Hamilton, who wrote the texts for Handel's *Occasional Oratorio*, *Alexander's Feast*, probably *Semele*, and certainly his other Miltonian oratorio, *Samson*.

It has been generally supposed that Haydn's eye while composing *The Creation* was chiefly on van Swieten's German text. It is noteworthy, though, that the first publication of the score, undertaken in 1800 by Haydn himself, was bilingual, on its title page as well as in the sung texts. *The Creation* is in fact the first large-scale work published in an edition designed to allow for performance in two languages. The correspondence of instrumental foreshadowings and doublings of vocal lines to the shape of the English text has led the musicologist Nicholas Temperley to conclude that Haydn really did intend to produce a *Creation* quite as much as a *Schöpfung*, that the English text has more legitimacy than has hitherto been granted it, and that the issue of performances in

English for English-speaking audiences—and in a version as close as possible to the 1800 text—is due for renewed scrutiny.

The text, whoever wrote it and in whichever language we hear it, is organized in this fashion: Part I represents the first four days of Creation; Part II represents the fifth and sixth days; Part III represents Adam and Eve leading all Earth's creatures in thanksgiving and conveys the couple's bliss.

Each of the six days begins with a narrative from the Book of Genesis, includes some descriptive or lyrical commentary, and concludes with a chorus. The commentary is based on *Paradise Lost*, particularly the account of the Creation given to Adam by "the affable Archangel" Raphael in Books VII and VIII, with some details drawn from the description of the Garden in Book IV.[1] Of the closing choruses, all but the first are hymns of praise and several of them are psalm paraphrases. Part III has nothing from Scripture but does draw on the Morning Hymn that Milton puts into the mouths of Adam and Eve in Book V of *Paradise Lost*: "more tuneable than needed lute or harp / To add more sweetness. . . ."

Part I

The most enormous challenge Haydn faced was his first, "The Representation of Chaos," which is the title he gave to his orchestral prelude: his response was also his greatest achievement in orchestral music. He had always been a bold harmonist, but by leaps rather than by slides; now he embraced Mozart's vocabulary and syntax of chromatic harmony, and, limning for us as no painter could the image of an earth "without form, and void," he invented music of incomparable and daring originality. The majestic, seemingly timeless swirl of the harmonies, each step leading to a destination, unknown, unguessed at, yet the whole held firmly, classically, within the bounds of C minor— it is this element that evokes the most intense and awed sense of wonder. The orchestral fantasy of the muted strings (especially their effect in *forte* and *fortissimo*), the adumbrations of life in those strange climbing arpeggios and in the sudden two-octave clarinet scale, the crescendo string chords placed so disturbingly just before the beat, are no less marvelous.

---

[1]As virtually every commentator on *The Creation* has pointed out, the mysterious librettist knew his Milton very well indeed, and the musician or music lover who comes to *Paradise Lost* knowing Haydn's oratorio first will find Milton's epic "full of quotations."

When this music has settled, the Archangel Raphael begins the story: "In the beginning God created the heaven and the earth."[2] The voices of the chorus join his as the Spirit of God moves upon the face of the waters. For the miracle of the creation of light, Haydn uses the most powerful of all possible gestures, which is also the simplest. He played that one close to the vest: it was the one passage that no one, not even the perpetually inquisitive van Swieten, had seen before the first rehearsal. The uninhibitedly responsive audiences of Haydn's day applauded this moment at every performance.[3] And Haydn knows what to do not only *with* the creation of light but also *after* it: chaos and darkness were described by Raphael, the bass, but when the narrative is continued after the first blaze of light floods the earth, it is in the brightness of Uriel's tenor that we hear the words "And God saw that it was good."

Even beyond that, for the gentle aria "Nun schwanden vor dem heiligen Strahle"? "Now Vanish Before the Holy Beams," Haydn adds yet more light of another kind by moving into softly luminous A major, harmonic territory so far unexplored. "Nun schwanden" begins amiably, but the wealth of detail and the breadth of the orchestral introduction serve notice that Haydn has more in mind than affable lyricism. The flight of hell's spirit moves the music suddenly into C minor, something in fact like a speeded-up recollection of chaos, and the chorus enters—"Verzweiflung, Wut und Schrecken" (despair, rage, and terror)— with a fugue of marked severity. That in turn beautifully sets off the smiling, hymnic phrases that evoke the new-created world sprung up at God's command. And do not miss the violins and the flute behind those mellifluous phrases. "And the evening and the morning were the first day."

On the second day, God created weather. Here is the first occasion to clarify a point that sometimes confuses listeners: Almost without exception in the descriptive recitatives, the music comes first, the verbal explanations afterwards. The praises of this day are sung in another combination

---

[2]The Archangels Raphael, Gabriel, and Uriel are part of the Miltonic apparatus in *The Creation*. Raphael is sent by God "to admonish [Adam] of his obedience, of his free estate, of his enemy," and it is he who describes to Adam God's creation of a new world. Raphael occurs in the apocryphal books of the Bible and in the Kabbalah. Gabriel is in charge of the Gate of Paradise and is guardian to Adam and Eve. Declared by Pope Pius XII the patron saint of television and other electronic means of communication, Gabriel is prominent in the Old and New Testaments as well as in the Koran. Uriel, regent of the sun, warns Gabriel of the escape of an evil spirit from the deep and of that spirit's invasion of Paradise. He first appears in postbiblical writings, both in the Jewish and Gnostic Christian literatures.

[3]Haydn enjoyed telling people that the pizzicatos just before the blaze depicted God striking a match.

of chorus and aria, a renewed affirmation of C major, and for the first time we hear the shining soprano of Gabriel.

The third day brings an expansion of the now familiar pattern. There are two cycles of biblical narrative and lyric commentary, first the creation of land and sea, with Raphael's aria "Rollend in schäumenden Wellen"/ "Rolling in Foaming Billows," then the appearance of grass and trees, giving rise to the most famous and beloved aria in *The Creation*, Gabriel's "Nun beut die Flur"/ "With Verdure Clad."[4] Raphael's grand aria is another instance of one of those surprise conclusions Haydn delights in and that is here invited by the contrast between the boisterous sea and the purling, limpid brook. The chorus "Stimmt an die Saiten"/ "Awake the Harp" handsomely sounds the praises of the third day.

Haydn's fourth day is brief and wonderful: a famous sunrise, a magical depiction of the moon gliding across the vast and silent night sky, and one of the greatest of choruses, drawn from Psalm 19: "The heavens declare the glory of God: And the firmament sheweth his handywork."[5]

Part II

For the fifth day, the scriptural narrative is again presented in two stages. Gabriel's "Auf starkem Fittiche"/ "On Mighty Pens" is another piece full of surprises, beginning with the expansive and varied introduction, continuing with the range of musical characters encountered in this aviary air, and embracing the complex textures at the beginning of the second stanza, "Aus jedem Busch"/ "From Ev'ry Bush." Haydn made a few revisions between the first private performance of *The Creation* and its introduction in public concert eleven months later; the most imaginative of these was adding the beautiful (and Mozartian) accompaniment for divided violas and divided cellos to the recitative about the great whales. The celebration of this day is double: first a lyric trio, then a trio-cum-chorus of exceptional verve and brilliance.

---

[4]Here is a good example of one of the ways the librettist uses Milton. After a paraphrase of Genesis, "Let the earth bring forth grass," Milton continues: "He scarce had said when the bare Earth, till then / Desert and bare, unsightly, unadorn'd, / Brought forth the tender Grass, whose verdure clad / Her Universal Face with pleasant green" (Book VII, 313–16).

[5]Haydn the populist would be gratified to know that the melody of this chorus made its way into hymnals as early as about 1810. It is still there, sung usually to Joseph Addison's verse "The spacious firmament on high," a paraphrase of Psalm 19. To link another pair of threads: One of Addison's most notable achievements in the magazine *The Spectator*, which he edited with Richard Steele in 1711–1712, was a series of weekly articles on *Paradise Lost*.

The labors of the sixth day are great indeed. First comes one of the most celebrated of Haydn's pages: the parade, at once amusing and touching, of cheerful, roaring lion, flexible tiger, nimble stag, noble steed, grazing cattle, sheep so plentiful they seem to have been sown, buzzing insects, and things that creep in *adagio* and even unto low D. Again, the words are verification of what the music tells you first. Then comes the human creature, the librettist drawing for a moment on the account in the second chapter of Genesis, the famous tenor aria "Mit Würd' und Hoheit angetan"/ "In Native Worth and Honor Clad" being another of those pieces in which Haydn travels to destinations the demure opening does not lead us to expect.[6]

"Vollendet ist das grosse Werk"/ "Achieved is the Glorious Work" seems at first to be the most terse of the hymns of praise, but in fact its end after a mere thirty-seven measures is no conclusion at all. In an *Adagio* scored for winds alone, Gabriel and Uriel introduce a new note of prayerful humility. When the strings at last enter—low strings only, in unison, with an ominous darkening of the harmony and the soft pounding of a fear-straitened heart—they do so to allow Raphael to evoke the dread moment when God turns His face away. (We shall meet another such shadow in the dead of Haydn's Winter in *The Seasons*.) The spirit of Mozart is never absent from Haydn's spirit and memory at such moments, and the measures that lead back to the reprise of this trio—"Den Odem hauchst du wieder aus"/ "Thou sendest forth thy breath again"—are all but a quotation from *The Magic Flute*. After this extraordinary trio, Haydn is ready to return to his chorus and, expanding it and infusing it with still greater contrapuntal vigor, he brings to a close the events and the praise of the sixth day.

Part III

Genesis makes less fuss than *Paradise Lost* does over the creation of human beings. The scriptural account, after the creation of "the beasts of

---

[6]Except for playing the *Emperor's Hymn* on his piano, something that greatly sustained his spirit in the dreadful war days of May 1809, "Mit Würd' und Hoheit" was the last music Haydn heard. On 24 May 1809, a week before his death, a French officer called on him and, finding him in lively form, sang the air to him in Italian translation. The piano builder Andreas Streicher tells us that "the officer sang in such a manly way, with such sublimity, and with such truth of expression and genuine feeling for music that Haydn could not hold back tears of joy, and not only told the singer but afterwards other people as well that he could recall no voice and no song that had given him so much and such real pleasure. After half an hour the officer got on his horse and rode off to fight the enemy. He left his address, which, as far as one can tell, reads 'Sulimy, Capitaine des Hussards.' Let us hope this noble gentleman learns that it was he to whom Haydn owed his last musical pleasure."

the earth . . . cattle . . . and everything that creepeth," simply continues: "And God said, 'Let us make man in our image.'" But in Milton
we read:

> There wanted yet the master work, the end
> Of all yet done—a Creature who, not prone
> And Brute as other Creatures, but endu'd
> With Sanctity of Reason, might erect
> His Stature, And, upright with Front serene
> Govern the rest, self-knowing, and from thence
> Magnanimous to correspond with Heav'n,
> But grateful to acknowledge whence his good
> Descends, thither with heart, and voice, and eyes
> Directed in Devotion, to adore
> And worship God Supreme, who made him chief
> Of all his works. Therefore th'Omnipotent
> Eternal Father (for where is not He
> Present?) thus to his Son audibly spake:
> "Let us make now Man in our image . . ."[7]

And this is reflected in Raphael's aria "Nun scheint in vollem Glanze
der Himmel"/ "Now Heaven in Fullest Glory Shone" near the end of
Part II, which introduces the idea that "There wanted yet that wondrous being, / That, grateful, should God's power admire, / With heart
and voice His goodness praise."

In sum, for Milton and for the *Creation* librettist, the appearance of
the human creature is a necessary end to this work of God's. It therefore
needs expanding upon, and that is why we have Part III with its drastic
change of location and tone.

Haydn achieved a miracle. Part III brings the subtlest, most fragrant music in *The Creation*, also the grandest and the headiest. But
one also imagines that after five quarter-hours of the words of God
and the songs of archangels and the heavenly choir, the shift to the
new-created world of "the blissful pair" cannot at first have been altogether easy for him.

Always an ingeniously imaginative writer for orchestra, Haydn
nonetheless came back to Vienna from London with fresh and expanded
mastery in that area, and the Introduction to Part III with its trio of
flutes is one of his most beautiful orchestral conceptions. And new for
The Creation is the exotically scented key of E major. The music of this
Introduction continues into Uriel's recitative, to give way eventually to

[7]*Paradise Lost*, VII, 505–19.

more neutral gestures as the glorious duet with chorus "Von deiner Güt'"/ "By Thee with Bliss" approaches. Here Adam and Eve "with songs / And choral symphonies" lead all creation in a hymn of praise. It is Haydn's mightiest musical achievement. He begins with a duet with oboe obbligato and quiet choral affirmations, cousin to Tamino and Pamina's "Wir wandeln durch des Tones Macht" (We walk, by music's power), and, together with that rapturous page, the model for Leonore's "O Gott! Welch' ein Augenblick!" (O God, what a moment!) in the finale of *Fidelio*.[8] Haydn's accompaniment is a marvel of economy and color, especially the woodwind punctuations and those softly shuddering drumstrokes when the chorus enters. The grandest cathedral is an apt setting for these pages. The music for the second stanza, "Der Sterne hellster"/ "Of stars the fairest," is the music of domestic orisons. It is, after all, Adam and Eve "under shady arborous roof . . . [at] dayspring." And again Haydn astonishes us with the range of his design and the energy of his invention.

Above all, the harmonic surge of the music is of immense potency. In the course of the prelude and Uriel's opening recitative, Haydn has already made the voyage from exotic E major to G. The great duet with chorus began in C, and now, at Adam's "Der Sterne hellster," it is in F. Haydn continues his thrust toward the flat side of the harmonic spectrum, and by the fourth stanza, Adam's "Ihr Elemente"/ "Ye mighty elements," he has traveled all the way to A-flat, as removed in one direction from central C as exotic E major had been in the other. Then Haydn begins the journey to C major and home, which he reaches with the last choral stanza, "Heil dir, O Gott"/ "Hail! Bounteous Lord!" What is characteristic for Haydn as well as crucial in affirming our sense of the spaciousness and grandeur of the design is the tensely hushed return to that darker, more mysterious world of A-flats and E-flats. He gives it only eight measures, perhaps ten seconds by the clock, but the effect inspires awe.

What follows is lovely epilogue. Adam and Eve turn from praise and thanksgiving to contemplation of each other and of their still-innocent earthly bliss, first in a richly detailed recitative, then in a confidently expansive and deliciously scored duet. With this movement Haydn also leaves "divine" C major to close in "human" E-flat and B-flat. And what he closes with, after an ominous hint by the Archangel Uriel of a

[8]Beethoven's oboe melody in this passage goes back to 1790 and his *Cantata on the Death of Emperor Joseph II*, antedating both *The Magic Flute* and *The Creation*, but in *Fidelio* Beethoven sets this melody into a completely different, newly elevated, and, I feel sure, Mozart- and Haydn-inspired compositional context.

tale to be told on another occasion, is one final, vibrantly joyous paean of glory, laud, and honor.

Die Jahreszeiten (The Seasons)

Haydn started work on *The Seasons* at the beginning of 1799 and completed the score early in 1801. The first performance, a private one, was given under the composer's direction in the Schwarzenberg Palace, Vienna, on 24 April 1801. The soloists, all of whom had sung in the public premiere of *The Creation* two years earlier, were the soprano Therese Saal, the tenor Mathias Rathmayer, and the bass Ignaz Saal (Therese's father). The first public performance of *The Seasons* followed five weeks later, on 29 May 1801, in Vienna's Redoutensaal, with the same soloists and again with Haydn conducting.

Three vocal soloists, namely a bass as Simon, a farmer; a soprano for Hanne, his daughter; and a tenor as Lucas, a young farm laborer; a four-part chorus, split into a double chorus for the final movement. Two flutes and piccolo, two oboes, two clarinets, two bassoons and contrabassoon, four horns, three trumpets, three trombones, timpani, triangle, tambourine, strings, and a keyboard instrument (preferably a fortepiano) for the recitatives.

After *The Creation* had enjoyed stupendous success both at its private premiere and its first public outing a year later, Baron Gottfried van Swieten, who had been an essential force behind those events, was determined to consolidate what he undoubtedly thought of as his and Haydn's triumph. He therefore promptly came up with a scheme for another oratorio, this, too, based on a British source, James Thomson's blank-verse poem *The Seasons*. Into the German libretto he drew from that work he interpolated the *Spinning Song* by Gottfried August Bürger as well as a little ballad by J. F. Weiss about the maid "who kept her honor clean."

"I should never have written it, I overtaxed myself," said the seventy-three-year-old composer some four years after the first performances of *The Seasons*. And he never ceased to blame the collapse of his health in 1802 on the effort it had cost him to complete this second great oratorio of his last years. Yet he had undertaken the task with enthusiasm, and he completed the score at a high, often exalted, level of inspiration.[1] He had also resented some of the details van Swieten had insisted on, such as the pictorial imitation of lambs and fishes, birds and bees in "O wie lieblich" (Oh, how lovely), the trio with chorus that concludes Spring: "French trash" (*französischer Quark*), he called it. But it turns out that he had also taken his patron and librettist's advice on many points, among them, in that very number, the magnificent change of key, that sudden invasion of B-flat, *fortissimo*, at the exclamation "Ewiger, mächtiger Gott" (Eternal, mighty God).

Van Swieten was as right in the feeling that led him to see in *The Seasons* perfect material for Haydn as he was culpably clumsy in his adaptation of that wonderful poem by James Thomson. Born in Scotland in 1700, Thomson settled in London in 1725, earning his bread as a private tutor.[2] One of his poems became popular to the point of assuming virtually the status of folk art, something so taken for granted that we don't even think to ask who wrote it: *Rule, Britannia!*, which occurs in his 1740 masque *Alfred*. *The Seasons* is earlier, begun with *Winter* in 1726, completed by the appearance of *Autumn* in 1730, but often and extensively revised almost until Thomson's death in 1748.

A plotless poem on an immense scale—in its final version it comes close to five thousand lines—it is original in conception as well as beautiful in both the Miltonic breadth of its rhythm and the loving specificity of detail in its observation of nature. Little remains of these qualities in the Van Swieten's *Jahreszeiten*, now thudding, now arch. Moreover, Thomson, who thought blood sports and booze were brutal and brutish, would have been outraged by the baron's three cheers for those pastimes. Then again, who would want Haydn not to have composed the amazing set of pieces that concludes *Autumn*: the Hound-Dog Aria "Seht auf die breiten Wiesen hin" (Look upon the broad meadows), the Hunting Chorus "Hört, das laute Getön" (Hark, the loud clangor), and the Drinking Chorus "Juchhe, der Wein ist da" (Whoopee, the wine is here). That genre triptych alone ensures for Haydn a premier place with Titian, Michelangelo, and Turner, Goethe and Mann, Verdi, Stravinsky, and

---

[1]Haydn's grumpiness about *The Seasons* has had an effect on the reception of the work. Even Donald Tovey, than whom no writer has done more for the love and understanding of Haydn, seems sometimes to regard *The Seasons* as a not quite successful, somewhat tired and effortful sequel to *The Creation*. I do not hear this. One thing I do hear is that Thomson–van Swieten is a less inspiring book than Genesis–Milton–van Swieten. Another is that in some of the longer duets and trios, Haydn was reverting to the expansive manner of his operas.

[2]This Thomson should not be confused with a later Scots poet of the same name who wrote the once-immensely popular poem *The City of Dreadful Night*.

Carter, as one of those rare artists to whom old age brings the gift of ever-bolder invention.

Spring

Spring begins in a most unspringlike manner, with a slow descent down the first part of a scale of G minor, each note *fortissimo* and with an accent.[3] Those four stern bars introduce a fiery, even wild *Vivace* that is like a fiercely compressed version of one of Haydn's "London" Symphony first movements. Haydn never wrote a more exciting symphonic *Allegro*. What is happening here? If we had no indicator but the bald announcement of "Spring" in the program book, we would be very puzzled, indeed. The printed score, however, tells us that this "introduction represents the transition from winter to spring," and when at last we hear a human voice, Simon's, it bids us in powerful recitative in tempo to "watch severe Winter flee." It is a gripping beginning and perhaps a serving of notice that much of what is to come will be deeply serious.

On the whole, though, *Spring* is an amiable season, and the nicely swinging opening chorus, "Komm, holder Lenz!" (Come, lovely spring!), establishes that mood. (Even so, it has its moments of darkly chromatic Mozartian shadows that pass over the landscape.) This chorus is followed by one of the most famous numbers in *The Seasons*, "Schon eilet froh der Ackermann" (The farmer hurries with joy), a song that describes a plowman going about his work. It is perhaps so familiar that we could easily overlook how original it is, with its witty counterpoint and spicy scoring (were we expecting that piccolo?), not to forget the charming self-quotation from the "Surprise" Symphony. The great supplication that follows, "Sei nun gnädig" (Be now gracious), does not exactly quote but certainly harks back to the sublime *Adagio* of the Symphony No. 98. Almost the first music Haydn wrote after receiving the news of Mozart's death, that movement alludes to the *Andante* of the "Jupiter" Symphony. In this chorus, the association for Haydn is again with Mozart, and this time, with the fugue on "Uns spriesset Überfluss" (All grows in plenty), it leads him into a variant of "Quam olim Abrahae" in his beloved friend's Requiem. Haydn's *Spring* is, on the whole, gracious rather than intense, but in this movement and in the so-splendidly laid out concluding chorus we begin to get a sense of the spacious worlds his *Seasons* comprehends.

---

[3]Here is a model, surely, for Beethoven's Second and Third *Leonore* Overtures.

Summer

Here we have another dark introduction, a C-minor *Adagio* depicting "morning twilight." (These little explanatory glosses at the beginning of each season were van Swieten's idea.) Daybreak and cockcrow make for a charming and evocative scene. Then Haydn has to compete with himself in depicting a sunrise, for he had already done it so beautifully in *The Creation*; once again, he achieves it with moving splendor. Then comes an unforgettable depiction of numbing noonday heat. What miracles he achieves with his two woodwinds, who play scarcely a dozen notes between them, his muted strings, and the magical effect of removing the mutes for the last two bars of the tenor's aria, "Dem Druck erlieget die Natur" (Nature succumbs to oppression). The tense waiting for the release of a thunderstorm is another of Haydn's extraordinary moments; this, too, is managed just with the continuo group, then pizzicato strings, and two brief and distant drumrolls. A few years later, Beethoven composed a famous storm scene of his own: he had listened carefully to Haydn's. The terrors of the storm have passed, and it is time for bed and a peaceful close, cushioned in soft E-flat major.

Autumn

Autumn begins with a sunny Introduction, whose "subject is the farmer's happy feelings at the abundant harvest." With the arrival of this third season, Haydn ascends to a new level of inspiration. He complained about van Swieten's hymn in praise of hard work, "So lohnet die Natur den Fleiss" (Thus does nature reward diligence), but it drew from him marvels of scoring, especially in the endlessly inventive deployment of solo flute, oboe, and bassoon, and demonstrated his most magisterial hold on design.

In the three genre pieces already mentioned, Haydn surpasses himself. First, the Hound-Dog or Pointer Aria, in which he again shows his fondness for hard-edged and spare polyphony, though what we remember most vividly is the snuffling bassoon, the gunshot, and the bird's plunge to earth. About this time, Haydn had managed to acquire a score of Bach's B-Minor Mass, and I am sure that the "Quoniam" in that work, such a marvelous study in low-register sonorities, served as model for the sound world of this aria. After the single hunter with his dog comes the crowd scene, Brueghel set to music, the big Hunting Chorus with its wonderful art of continuously unfolding and surprising variation. Beginning in D but ending in E-flat, it also revels in the reckless abandoning of Classical harmonic decorum. All those hunting calls, blared lustily by four horns in unison, are real ones![4] Finally, *Autumn* ends with that giddy chorus of drinkers reeling from key to key, a piece I always think of as the one in which Haydn invents Mahler.[5]

Winter

Winter begins with another of *The Seasons'* great instrumental movements, an elegiac page in C minor, cousin to Mozart's *Masonic Funeral Music.* We are told that it "depicts the thick fogs with which Winter begins," but it is hard not to feel that something more than murky weather is on the aging composer's mind and pressing on his soul. Simon's opening recitative continues in this dark mood. A harsh chord of A major interrupts it, and Hanne foretells the arrival of winter "from Lapland's vaults." Her brief aria, "Licht und Leben sind geschwächet" (Light and life are weakened), just after this, is a perfect evocation of sun-deprived depression. There follows a set of three famous, much-loved genre scenes: the description of the traveler lost in the snow (with a tragic ending in Thomson, but a happy one here), the proto–*Flying Dutchman* Spinning Song, and the story of the young woman who is so resourceful in dealing with a young lord of less-than-honorable intentions.

Haydn has shown us a broad range. He has been funny, grandiloquent, touching, and uncannily adept at conjuring up weathers and smells and textures, times of day and movement, people and places. But he has even more to give us: the last pages of *The Seasons* take us to new profundities and new heights. Winter is Old Age, and here, once again, and now with overwhelming pathos, Haydn's thoughts turn to the beloved friend who, ten years before, had died two months short of his thirty-sixth birthday. It is Simon who tells us that "Winter's victory is now achieved."[6] The orchestra is full of sighs. We are invited to reflect on the quick passing of life and that ever-confounding question of "What

---

[4]Daniel Heartz has written a fascinating study of this subject titled "The Hunting Chorus in Haydn's *Jahreszeiten* and the '*dirs de chasses*' in the *Encyclopédie*," in *Eighteenth-Century Studies* 9 (1976).

[5]The progression from D to E-flat in the Hunting Chorus is itself a Mahlerian maneuver; see *Ich hab' ein glühend Messer* in the *Songs of a Wayfarer* and the recapitulation of the *Frère Jacques* movement in the Symphony No. 1 (both D to E-flat), and the Fifth Symphony as a whole (rising by a semitone from C-sharp to D). The Ninth Symphony reverses the procedure by going from D to D-flat. And around the corner waits Carl Nielsen.

[6]Simon is a formidable assignment for a singer. He must have an easy top as well as powerfully sonorous low notes, show an authoritative command of coloratura, be an arresting narrator, persuade in the friendly comedy of the plowman's song, and now, in *Winter*, assume both the gravity of the role of the Speaker in *The Magic Flute* and convey the noble pathos of Haydn's melancholy.

happened to all those plans, those noble resolutions?" At last the music grows in energy, only to suspend all motion as the singer points to virtue as the way to salvation and to the holy mount. But now it is free to open up into the luminous C major of the final chorus, a movement imbued with an energy born of mastery and faith, vast in its splendor of sound and spirit—ending with "Amen," sure, vigorous, twice, and in tempo.

Arthur Honegger

Arthur Honegger was born in Le Havre, France, on 10 March 1892 and died in Paris on 27 November 1955.

Le Roi David (King David), Symphonic Psalm in Three Parts after the Biblical Drama by René Morax

There are three versions of *King David*. Version I consists of twenty-seven numbers of incidental music for the eponymous play by René Morax. Honegger composed this between 25 February and 28 April 1921, completing the orchestration on 20 May. Marcelle Cheridjian-Charrey, accompanied by her husband, sang six of the solo movements with piano at a Paris concert on 2 June 1921, and Georges Hubbard sang three more at a concert on 7 June. The original *King David* was a spectacle that took more than four hours, about one hour of it being given over to music. Beginning on 11 June 1921, this was presented ten times that month and in July at the Théâtre du Jorat at Mézières in the canton of Vaud, Switzerland, with the composer conducting. The percussionist at these performances was the eighteen-year-old Maurice de Abravanel, who in his long career (without the "de") as conductor would be one of Honegger's most prominent interpreters.

Version II, which Honegger called a "Symphonic Psalm," is an oratorio using the music of Version I but with the multiple spoken roles of the original version reduced into a part for one narrator and with the order of a few of the numbers changed. This was introduced in Lyon on 21 January 1923, Georges Witkowski conducting.

Version III expands the orchestration of II for large orchestra. Honegger accomplished this between 17 July and 20 August 1923, and the first performance was given in Hans Reinhart's German translation on 2 December that year at Winterthur, with Ernst Seidel conducting the chorus and orchestra of the Winterthur Municipal Theater and soloists Clara Wirz-Wyss, Lisa Appenzeller, and Carl Seidel. The first performance with the original French text was given in Paris on 14 March 1924, conducted by Robert Siohan and distinguished by the participation of the baritone Charles Panzéra (singing the tenor solos) and, as narrator, of the director and actor Jacques Copeau. The second and third versions both bear the dedication "TO MY PARENTS."

Version I: soprano, contralto, and tenor soloists; mixed chorus; male choir. Two flutes (second doubling piccolo), oboe (doubling English horn), two clarinets (second doubling bass clarinet), bassoon, horn, two trumpets, trombone, celesta, piano, harmonium, timpani, cymbals, snare drum, bass drum, tam-tam, tambourine, and bass (cello ad libitum).

Version II: Same as above, but adds a speaker.

Version III: Same voices as II, but with an orchestra of two flutes, two oboes, two clarinets, two bassoons, four horns, two trumpets, three trombones, tuba, timpani, bass drum, snare drum, tambourine, tam-tam, triangle, celesta, harp, organ, and strings, plus offstage piccolo, English horn, bass clarinet, and contrabassoon.

Saul: first king of Israel at the end of the eleventh century B.C.E., heroic in battle and a resolute defender of his country against the neighboring Philistines, with whom Israel was all but permanently at war. He was also tragically unstable, often childlike, impulsive, capricious, a victim of deep depressions, given to literally murderous rages, and consumed by jealousy toward his brilliant son-in-law David. After Israel's defeat by the Philistines at Gilboa and the death of three of his sons on that battlefield, Saul took his own life.

David: Saul's charismatic successor to the throne, "cunning in playing [the harp], and a mighty valiant man, and a man of war, and prudent in matters, and a comely person" (I Samuel 16:18), fortunate in beginning his career in boyhood with the stunning coup of vanquishing the Philistine giant Goliath. David was also ruthless when his own interests and sexual desires were at stake, but late in life he was beset with guilt and sorrows even as he rejoiced in his triumphs.

The Old Testament shows us no figures more complex and more fascinating than these two larger-than-life monarchs, nor are there any two in that richly peopled gallery whose relationship was as problematic. It is surprising that so few composers have taken them on. There are Saul oratorios by some minor Italians, but besides Honegger's work, just two significant compositions have been written on this subject: Handel's oratorio *Saul* and Carl Nielsen's opera *Saul and David*. Mozart's cantata *Davidde penitente*, a setting of Italian versions of parts of the Penitential Psalms, is an odd supplement to this exceedingly short list. The music, some of it lifted from the Mass in C Minor, some of it new, is beautiful, but here Mozart, that great examiner and portrayer of human souls, does not engage with this challenge at all.[1]

The more reason, then, to be grateful to René Morax for having called Honegger's *King David* into being. In 1908 with his brother Jean, an artist, Morax had started what was essentially a theater festival in the small market town of Mézières, some twenty miles north of Lausanne on Lake Geneva. Despite Switzerland's neutrality in World War I, its economy suffered, and Morax suspended the festival in 1915. In 1921, when it was feasible to resume, he decided to do so in grand style with a huge spectacle on the subject of King David. I imagine he had been stimulated and encouraged by the success of the Hofmannsthal-Reinhardt *Everyman* at the 1920 Salzburg Festival.

As in the prewar Mézières productions, music was to play an important part in *King David*, but somehow—and I have never quite understood this part of the story—Morax neglected to do anything about getting a score written until it was dangerously late. Because of the tight deadline, Gustave Doret, a distinguished musician (he had conducted the first performance of Debussy's *Afternoon of a Faun*) who had been virtually the Mézières house composer, turned Morax down. So did the second choice, Jean Dupérier. Morax then asked Ernest Ansermet, the conductor of the Orchestre de la Suisse Romande in Geneva, for advice. Ansermet unhesitatingly recommended the twenty-eight-year-old Arthur Honegger, a choice endorsed by Stravinsky, then living in Morges, just west of Lausanne. At that moment Stravinsky's thoughts must have gone back to 1909 when his own career was jump-started by the inability of

---

[1]The collection of harpsichord sonatas titled *Musical Representation of Some Bible Stories* (1700) by Bach's predecessor at Leipzig, Johann Kuhnau, includes a depiction of David's slaying of Goliath.

Anatol Liadov and Nikolai Tcherepnin to punctually provide Sergei Diaghilev with a score for *The Firebird*.

Honegger, born in France to Swiss parents, was primarily trained in Paris. In 1921 he was already a prolific composer if not yet a very well known one, though his *Pastorale d'été*, just introduced in Paris, had favorable attention. Those who followed new music would have recognized Honegger's name as one of Les Six, a group of composers who had little in common except that the critic Henri Collet happened to meet them all one evening at the apartment of Darius Milhaud (the others, in addition to Milhaud, were Georges Auric, Louis Durey, Francis Poulenc, and Germaine Tailleferre) and subsequently wrote an article in which he dubbed them with that label. Aesthetically the grouping made little sense, but, not least because Jean Cocteau appointed himself propagandist for these young musicians, it was invaluable for publicity. It was in fact *King David* that would put Honegger prominently on the map.

Honegger was young, energetic, and confident, but even so, he was daunted by the task of inventing an hour of music in less than two months. The chorus at Mézières was made up of amateurs—talented, hardworking, and prepared by a superb musician, Paul Boepple (who went on to a distinguished career as teacher and conductor in America), but still, amateurs they were. So, indeed, were most of the instrumentalists. They needed the music as soon as possible, which meant that Honegger had to send each piece off as soon as it was finished, with never a moment to look back, reconsider, or revise. For that matter, in a world before photocopy machines, he couldn't even keep a copy of what he had written for reference. What worried him most was the technical problem of balancing a large chorus and an orchestra of sixteen. It was Stravinsky who came to the rescue. "Imagine," he said to his young colleague, "that it was *your* idea." That advice worked.

The performances at Mézières were a huge success, and soon there was talk of giving *King David* elsewhere. Morax and Honegger decided that the music would work virtually unaltered in concert: to create a concert version of his immense drama, he reduced it to a compact narration for a single speaker.[2] Honegger left the original orchestration untouched, but was persuaded also to make what the score calls a *version augmentée* more suitable for large halls. This became so popular that the original instrumentation virtually disappeared from view until the 1960s, when choruses for whom a full orchestra was out of financial reach realized that they could afford an ensemble of sixteen. Honegger himself always

[2]Perhaps it is too compact. The conductor Philip Brunelle puts it this way: "You get past Goliath and it's all over: the audience doesn't know the rest of the story and the narration makes overly generous assumptions on that score."

preferred the original score, although his own recording is of the *version augmentée*. The advantages of that edition for large choruses in large halls are obvious; however, it does not always avoid bombast and it is somehow more "ordinary" than the original score with its edgy and highly spiced sound.

In his book *I Am a Composer*, Honegger recalled the writing of *King David* as a time of contentment: "The subject perfectly suited my 'Biblical' tastes. I cherish among my best memories these performances and especially the preparation of the work. Happy period! Students, peasants, professionals co-operated in the enjoyment. . . . We had chariots drawn by real horses!"

But only a few pages before, we find Honegger in one of the sour moods of his late years: "You want to know where I begin to grow bored? I can tell you precisely." He goes on to identify the point in *King David* "at which I doze off peacefully." He does, however, concede his relative satisfaction with "The Dance Before the Ark," the "Chorus of Penitence," and the ending.

Most of the twenty-seven movements that make up *King David* are very short. That, of course, reflects their original function as musical incidents within a much larger and nonmusical context—in fact, "incidental music." As a result, the few longer sections—the "Lamentations of Gilboa" that closes Part I, "The Dance Before the Ark," which comprises almost all of Part II, and "The Death of David"—stand out strikingly.

The Introduction, with beating drums and a wailing oboe, carries us back across three thousand years. The Narrator's first words, taken from I Samuel 16, send us immediately to the seed of the conflict between Saul and David. The Old Testament Lord, who in his caprices and vengefulness is a character hardly more admirable than the two earthly monarchs, has repented making the difficult Saul a king: "The spirit of the Lord departed from Saul, and an evil spirit from the Lord troubled him." The Lord commands his servants to find the young David, son of Jesse and still a boy looking after his father's sheep, and to anoint him. We meet David himself in a song of sweet lyricism, "L'Éternel est mon berger" (The Everlasting One is my shepherd), given a special coloration by the part for high bassoon. The score says contralto, but Honegger preferred a boy's voice here, and that is the casting that has become customary.

Next comes the first in a series of psalm settings, "Loué soit le Seigneur" (Praised be the Lord), derived from Psalm 9 and given in the verse paraphrase by the sixteenth-century poet Clément Marot. The chorus sings the tune in unison, and the orchestra with a prominent trumpet part chugs along in energetic sixteenth-notes: the effect is very eighteenth-century, but also not far from some of what Hindemith was writing around this time and what we will meet again in the Overture of Weill's *Threepenny Opera*.

To go through the entire oratorio movement by movement would be fatiguing and not terribly useful. Let me instead point to what are for me some of the high moments:

No. 6. The setting of a version of Psalm 11, "Ne crains rien et mets la foi en l'Éternel" (Fear nothing and put your trust in the Lord). David has killed Goliath, found favor at the court of Saul, struck up a friendship of extraordinary intensity with Saul's son Jonathan (one of those male-to-male relationships that everybody today wants to misread), and has fallen in love with and married Saul's daughter Michal. But the people's chants of "Saul slew his thousands, and David his ten thousands" inflame Saul's jealousy, and he attempts to kill David even while the young man is singing and playing in an attempt to soothe him. David flees into the desert. The psalm, in Honegger's most appealing lyric vein, is a solo for the tenor with a French horn obbligato and some arresting woodwind punctuations. The flight of the arrow of the wicked, mentioned by the psalmist, is vivid.

No. 7. "Ah! Si j'avais des ailes de colombe" (Oh, had I the wings of a dove), a text from Psalm 55 and given to the soprano, who is accompanied by ornate instrumental lines with the flute most prominent.

No. 8. "The Song of the Prophets" is a brief piece for the chorus tenors and held in the orchestra to the low register with a persistent beating of the tam-tam. I find it strong and impressive even though it is the movement that made the composer "doze off peacefully." David has an opportunity to kill Saul in his sleep but refuses to avail himself of the chance.

No. 12. This is the great scene in which Saul, seeing his own army vastly outnumbered by the host of the Philistines and feeling abandoned by all, goes to the Witch of Endor to command her to summon the spirit of Samuel. The woman is frightened because Saul has forbidden necromancy, and she fears a trap. This is a speaking part set across a terrifying musical background full of Honegger's most adventurous harmonies, and it is a glorious and enviable opportunity for an actress. (It is worth finding the Vanguard recording conducted by Maurice Abravanel to hear Honegger's old friend, the amazing Madeleine Milhaud, let go in this scene.)

Nos. 13 and 14. Samuel prophesies that the Philistine armies will prevail over the Israelites. The fierce March of the Philistines makes this only too believable. At Mount Gilboa, they kill Saul's three sons, among them the beloved Jonathan. "And the battle went sore against Saul, and the archers hit him; and he was sore wounded of the archers." Saul commands his armor-bearer to kill him, "lest these uncircumcised come and thrust me through and abuse me," but the armor-bearer refuses. Saul then throws himself on his own sword but fails to kill himself. The young man who finally delivers the coup de grace carries the news of Saul's death to David, who, enraged—"How wast thou not afraid to stretch forth thine hand to destroy the Lord's anointed?"—has him killed. Then David "took hold on his [own] clothes and rent them; and [with his men], mourned and wept and fasted."

Honegger's *Lamentations of Gilboa* is the most eloquent music yet to appear in the oratorio and indeed one of the most wrenching threnodies in all music. What we hear is anguished keenings—Yemenite? Hebrew?—by the soprano and contralto soloists, their lament being then taken up by the women of the chorus. The narrator, speaking across these wordless cries, gives voice to David's cry (II Samuel 1:19–20):

> The beauty of Israel is slain upon thy high places:
> How are the mighty fallen!
> Tell it not in Gath,
> Publish it not in the streets of Askelon.

And that heart-piercing music brings the first part of *King David* to an end, and with it the story of the tragic King Saul.

Nos. 15-16. David is king. That is something to celebrate, and so is the return of the Ark of God, recaptured from the Philistines. "And David danced before the Lord with all his might." Danced and leaped nearly naked, furthermore, earning him the contempt of Michal, his wife. David's response: "And I will yet be more vile than thus . . . and of the maidservants, of them shall I be had in honour." But that is the future; the present is the dance, over which there hangs no shadow. Introduced, as Honegger's biographer Harry Halbreich puts it, "by the luminous narthex" of the women's "Festival Song," this, at ten minutes or so, is the longest number in the work. It is a magnificently imaginative piece. The chorus sings and the orchestra builds a mighty crescendo, rising in pitch as well as in volume, traversing many keys, and vigorously inventive in harmonic and orchestral detail. An angel, the soprano soloist, foretells that it is not David but his yet-unborn son who will build a great house for the Lord. The chorus greets this with ecstatic Alleluias, each entry carrying the song to a higher plane. This is music that we shall hear again.

Nos. 19 and 20. David, walking on the roof of his palace, sees the beautiful Bath-sheba at her bath. He desires her, summons her, and sends her husband, Uriah, to certain death in battle. The prophet Nathan comes to reprove David, who responds with two Penitential Psalms, both texts being drawn from Psalm 51, "Miséricorde, o Dieu, pitié selon de ta grande compassion" (Have mercy upon me, O God, according to thy lovingkindness), and Honegger sets it as a dialogue between the men and the women of the chorus over steadily repeated chords. He follows this with "Je fus conçu dans le péché" (I was conceived in sin), whose constant changes make it one of the most subtle and interesting movements in *King David*. The melody is by the sixteenth-century Huguenot composer Claude Goudimel. Honegger ends the movement with a brief but intensely expressive instrumental postlude—just three bars, but marvelous in its effect.

No. 21. Punishment falls on the house of David, and the king pleads, "Je lève mes regards vers la montagne. D'où me vient le secours?" (I will lift up mine eyes unto the hills, From whence cometh my help). This setting of Psalm 121 is a miniature recitative and aria for the tenor.

No. 22. "O forêt d'Ephraïm" (O forest of Ephraim) is a response to the death in that forest of the lawless and violent Absalom, nonetheless deeply loved by his father, David. Set for female voices with the pulse of the tambourine prominent among the instruments, it is surprisingly sweet and could almost be an early song by Fauré. It is of extraordinary loveliness.

No. 23. The Israelites now get a fine march, as though to make up for the one given to the Philistines in Part I.

No. 24. The story moves rapidly forward to David's old age and death. The words are derived from Psalm 18 and from David's song in II Samuel 22. This, "Je t'aimerai, Seigneur, d'un amour tendre" (I will love Thee, Lord, with a tender love), is another of Clément Marot's paraphrases, and it evokes some of Honegger's most lyrical music as it progresses from a single voice to the song of the whole chorus.

Nos. 26–27. David commits a final act of hubris in commanding a census of his people, and once again Jerusalem is punished by the Angel of Death. He proclaims Solomon, his son by Bath-sheba, king of Israel, and as Nathan anoints the new ruler, David climbs to look upon the Temple one last time. The crowning of Solomon is described by the narrator's voice, speaking over grave orchestral music. David's last words, the invention of René Morax, shoot forward into the world of the New Testament, predicting the birth of Jesus, like David a descendant of Jesse, and then giving thanks for his own life.[3] It is this beatific passage of thanksgiving, spoken by Jean Hervé in transcendent ecstasy in Honegger's own recording, that made me fall in love with this work as a teenager.

---

[3]Benjamin Britten's opera *The Rape of Lucretia* ends with a similar leap into the Christian world, affecting for many, disturbing for others.

An angel echoes and expands on David's prophecy—"Dieu te dit: un jour viendra" (God tells you: a day will come)—and the chorus repeats the words after the angel. It is here, with the chorale melody, cousin to the Lutheran chorales *Wachet auf* (Sleepers, awake) and *Wie schön leuchtet der Morgenstern* (How beautifully the morning star shines) but actually Honegger's own, that we most keenly sense not only the presence of Bach but the composer's own resolute Protestantism. Onto this chorale melody other voices sprinkle gentle Alleluias, the return of the music of David's "Dance before the Ark." Those Alleluias, as they were sung by the musical amateurs of Mézières, were Honegger's most joyous *King David* memory. And this exalted chorale-fantasy brings the story to a grand close.

A brief postscript on Handel's *Saul* (1739) and Nielsen's *Saul and David* (1901), two works by sharp-eyed observers of the human condition, and both very much worth knowing:

The libretto of *Saul* was written by the excellent Charles Jennens, who a few years later would put the *Messiah* book together. I don't get the impression that Handel was hugely interested in David or Jonathan, but he does characterize David's wife, Michal, and Saul's hard-edged daughter Merab nicely. The Witch of Endor is a lively presence, too. The glory here is in the portrayal of Saul. Handel was no stranger to melancholia, and the scenes of the tragic king's rages and depressions are very powerful indeed. Not least, *Saul* offers plenty of examples of Handel's handsomest choral writing, both the dark kind and the festive, the latter including an exuberant Hallelujah chorus.

I have sometimes been a little bit sorry that Nielsen wrote *Saul and David* as early as he did: what a thing he might have made of it in the 1920s, when his style had reached its wild apogee. But even early, around the time of the Symphony No. 2, *The Four Temperaments*, Nielsen had much to bring to the task. He and his librettist, Einar Christiansen, do a superb job of initial scene-setting to tell us what Saul's transgressions were that caused the spirit of the Lord to depart from him. Saul's defiant monologues, David's fight with Goliath (which Nielsen presents as it is imagined by Michal and her attendants), the scene at Endor, and especially the final scene of mourning for Saul and Jonathan are magnificent moments.

Leoš Janáček

Leoš Janáček was born in Hochwald (Hukvaldy) in Northern Moravia, then part of the Austrian Empire, on 3 July 1854 and died in Moravská Ostrava, Czechoslovakia, on 12 August 1928.

Glagolitic Mass

D rawing in part on material from a Latin Mass he had started in 1908, Janáček drafted his *Glagolitic Mass* between 2 and 17 August 1926, completing the work on 15 October. The movement for organ solo was a late addition to the score, being drafted and composed between October and early December. Janáček made many more revisions of details in November and December 1927 while preparations for the premiere were under way. Among the revisions was a name change from *Misa slavnija* (*Missa solemnis*) to *Missa glagolskaja* (*Missa solemnis*). Adding *Missa solemnis* to the title was a bow to Beethoven, whose great Mass Janáček had conducted in Brno in 1879. The final title, *Mša glagolskaja*, was the choice of Miloš Weingart, professor of Slavonic studies at the University of Prague, who was responsible for making sure the Church Slavonic text was correct. The first performance was given on 5 December 1927 in the concert hall of the Sokol Municipal Stadium in Brno, the capital of what was then the Czechoslovakian province of Moravia. Jaroslav Kapil conducted, the two principal soloists were soprano Alexandra Čvánová and tenor Stanislav Tauber, the alto was Marie Hloušková, and the bass was Ladislav Němeček. The orchestra came from the Brno Opera, the chorus was that of the Brno Friendly Society, and the organist was Bohumil Holub.

Soprano, alto, tenor, and bass solos; four-part chorus. Four flutes (three doubling piccolo), two oboes and English horn, three clarinets (one doubling bass clarinet) plus three offstage clarinets, three bassoons (one doubling contrabassoon), four horns, four trumpets, three trombones, tuba, timpani, snare drum, triangle, tam-tam, cymbals, bells, two harps, celesta, organ (with an important solo part), and strings.

It was understandable, wrote the pianist and critic Ludvík Kundera in the Prague magazine *Tempo* in 1927, that Janáček, as an old man, should feel the need to have a large religious work in his catalogue.[1] The seventy-three-year-old composer put his reply on a postcard: "Not an old man, not a believer. Not till I see for myself."

Who was this unbeliever, and how did he come to write so fervent, so excited a setting of a sacred text? Moravia, now part of the Czech Republic, had been a great kingdom in the Middle Ages; in the nineteenth century it was an Austrian crown land. Hukvaldy, where Jiří Janáček was the schoolteacher and organist, is a village about 150 miles east of Prague. The nearest market town was Příbor, or Freiberg, where Sigmund Freud was born just two years after Jiři's son Leoš. The boy went to school in Hukvaldy until, at eleven, he was sent to the Augustinian monastery in Brno, becoming a pupil of Pavel Křižkovský, an admired composer of church music. As part of what we would now call a work-study program, Leoš worked in the monastery's gardens, where his supervisor was Gregor Mendel, the father of modern genetics.[2] After further schooling in Brno and Prague, as well a spell of unpaid teaching, Janáček returned to Brno, where he began to make a name for himself as a conductor. By 1877 he was also composing seriously, but, unsure of his technique, he took time for further studies in Leipzig and Vienna. Home once more, he founded the Brno Organ School in 1881, staying on as director until 1919. He continued to compose, but insofar as he was known outside Brno at all, it was as a teacher and administrator.

[1]Ludvík Kundera (1891–1971) was the father of the novelist Milan Kundera.
[2]The garden was the very one where Mendel conducted his crucial experiments with the hybridization of garden peas. Mendel became the monastery's abbot in 1868.

All this changed dramatically in 1916 when, in consequence of a series of implausible chances, his opera *Její pastorkyňa* was produced at the Prague National Theater, and with smashing success. *Její pastorkyňa* (Her Foster Daughter, but known and produced outside Czechoslovakia as *Jenufa*) had been in the repertory in Brno for twelve years, but Brno was a provincial capital, and success there meant nothing to the wider world outside. Prague, on the other hand, was a major music center, and the impact of *Její pastorkyňa* there quickly led to a production at the even more prestigious Court Opera in Vienna. Someone who played a major role in these developments was Max Brod, the leading intellectual in Prague's German-speaking community, the translator into German of *Jenufa*, and a tireless champion of Janáček's work.[3]

At sixty-two, Janáček found himself famous. He became a significant figure in the cultural life of the ill-fated republic that was established with so much optimism in 1918, and in his last years he composed with more vigor and freshness of invention than ever. During that time, Janáček's spirits and inspiration were wildly fired up by his love for Kamila Stösslová, a married woman he met when he was sixty-three and long married, and she was twenty-five.[4] She did not return his love and seems not to have had the foggiest notion of the stature of the man on whom she had such an electrifying effect. Undeterred, Janáček wrote her hundreds of letters as though she were the most intellectually stimulating partner in the world. Empty-headed as she seems to have been, we owe Stösslová an immense debt. The harvests of the 1920s included the operas *Káta Kabanová*, *The Cunning Little Vixen*, *The Makropulos Affair*, and *From the House of the Dead*; the *Glagolitic Mass*; the *Sinfonietta*; the tone poem *Taras Bulba*; the Concertino for Piano; the wind sextet *Youth*; and the two string quartets titled *Kreutzer Sonata* and *Intimate Letters*.

Janáček was a complex and temperamental man, many of whose statements about his work and about life in general are contradictory and downright cranky. In spite of the postcard to Kundera, he was—in his fashion—religious; certainly he had a vivid sense of what the text of the Mass was all about. He detested churches and stayed out of the way of official ecclesiastical life, but he dedicated the *Glagolitic Mass* to

---

[3]Brod is most famous for his efforts on behalf of Franz Kafka, particularly for refusing to heed Kafka's request that his unpublished manuscripts be destroyed after his death. Those who enjoy coincidences, as well as those who deny that there are coincidences, will perhaps find it interesting that outside of his own writings, Brod's energies were so intensely tied to the lives of two great and idiosyncratic artists who shared a birthday, 3 July.

[4]This was not Janáček's first extramarital passion, the most intense, flagrant, and hurtful to his wife being the one with Gabriela Horvátová, who had sung the title role in the first Prague production of *Jenufa*. Stösslová was alone in having fulfilled, albeit unknowingly, the role of Muse.

Archbishop Prečan of Olomouc.[5] He had previously bemoaned to Prečan the poverty of recent sacred music and then wrote the Mass in response to the archbishop's challenge to compose "something better."

Janáček had composed sacred music before, mostly around the turn of the century and including the unfinished Latin Mass in 1908 that he later raided for the *Glagolitic Mass*. His decision now, at seventy-two, to come back to that field was based on a mixture of public and private considerations. "I wanted to express faith in the certainty (the certainty of survival, that is) of the nation," he wrote, "not on a religious basis, but on a moral one which calls God to witness." Again, Janáček is anxious to explain that the Mass is not "religious"; yet, as probably every commentator has pointed out, God finds his way into the very sentence that denies the work's religiosity.

What set Janáček to thinking about these questions was the impending tenth anniversary of the founding of the republic of Czechoslovakia. He deplored the omission in the commemoration plans of any tribute to what he called "the spirit of Cyril and Methodius," and he meant his Mass specifically to fill that gap as well as to serve more generally as a contribution to the decennial. Saints Cyril (c. 827–869) and Methodius (c. 825–884) were brothers from Thessalonica, Methodius being the abbot of a Greek monastery and Cyril a philosopher at the University of Constantinople. The conflicts between East and West that eventually led to the Schism of 1054 already troubled the church in the ninth century, and in 862 Prince Rostislav of Great Moravia, wishing to strengthen his position against German political and ecclesiastical influence, asked Byzantine Emperor Michael III and Patriarch Photius to send missionaries. Thus it was that Cyril and Methodius came to Moravia. Cyril died while both brothers were on a visit to Rome; Methodius returned to his mission, was appointed archbishop of Pannonia and Moravia, and, in spite of continued harassment from rival German bishops, persisted in his calling until his death.[6]

Cyril and Methodius brought the Danubian Slavs not only the Gospel but literacy as well. One of the issues in the East-West conflict was the right to use the Slavic language and liturgy rather than the Latin; therefore, the translation of the liturgy and much of the Bible into the language now known as Old Church Slavonic was one of the brothers' most urgent tasks and one for which, as superb theologians, scholars, and linguists, they were ideally equipped. Cyril invented an alphabet for the

[5]Prečan's most celebrated predecessor at Olomouc was Beethoven's pupil Archduke Rudolph, for whose installation as archbishop that composer wrote his *Missa solemnis*.
[6]Pannonia was a Roman province in territory that comprises what are now parts of Hungary, Austria, Slovenia, and Croatia.

purpose. Just which alphabet it was is lost in the mists of more than eleven centuries; it seems likelier, however, to have been the graphically charming Glagolitic than the Greek-based Cyrillic that bears his name and is still used in Bulgarian, Serbian, and the various Russian languages.[7] It is also possible Cyril invented both. The two saints are among the most revered in Czechoslovak lands, Bulgaria, and the former Yugoslavia, and Janáček himself retained vivid memories of taking part as a boy of five in the thousandth-anniversary commemoration of Cyril's death.

Old Church Slavonic stayed alive in the Russian Orthodox Church, which still permits its use on 5 July, the feast of Saints Cyril and Methodius. At the same time, modern Slavic languages have moved away from it by about the same distance that separates present-day American from the English of the King James Bible, and in many of them the Latin alphabet has long replaced the Glagolitic. One could say that since Janáček worked from a text in the Latin alphabet, his Mass ought properly to be called *Old Slavonic* rather than *Glagolitic*; the fact, however, is that, principally because of his reverence for Cyril and Methodius, he called it *Glagolitic Mass*. Just as Beethoven was careful to inform himself about the meaning and accentuation of Latin when he worked on his *Missa solemnis*, so did Janáček take great pains to get his Old Church Slavonic right, asking a pupil, Father Josef Martínek, to find him a copy of the text in which the accented syllables were set in bold type. He also read scholarly articles and finally had both text and music scrutinized by an eminent philologist, Miloš Weingart.

A week before the first performance, Janáček published in a Brno newspaper a characteristically mystical, almost pantheistic article (with the apposite musical illustrations) about the writing of the Mass:

> Why did I compose it?
> It pours, the Luhačovice rain pours down. From the window I look up to the glowering Komoň mountain.
> Clouds roll past; the gale-force wind tears them apart, scatters them far and wide. . . .
> It grows darker and darker. Already I am looking into the black night; flashes of lightning cut through it.
> I switch on the flickering electric light in the high ceiling.
> I sketch nothing more than the quiet motive of a desperate frame of mind to the words "*Gospodi pomiluj*" [Lord, have mercy].
> Nothing more than the joyous shout "*Slava, Slava!*" [Glory!].

[7]Glagolitic letters, quite original in their formation, resemble those symbols for telephones, implements of cutlery, and so forth, that one sees in European hotel and restaurant guides. The name *Glagolitic* comes from the Old Church Slavonic word *glagolal*, meaning "he said," which occurs in the Creed of the Mass.

Nothing more than the heart-rending anguish in the motive *"Rozpet že ny, mǔcen i pogreben jest!"* [and was crucified also for us, he suffered and was buried].

Nothing more than the steadfastness of faith and the swearing of allegiance in the motive *"Věrruju!"* [I believe].

And all the fervor and excitement of the expressive ending "Amen, amen!"

The holy reverence in the motives *"Svät, svät!"* [Holy], *"Blagoslovljen"* [Blessed], and *"Agneče Božij!"* [O Lamb of God!].

Without the gloom of medieval monastery cells in its motives,

without the sound of the usual imitative procedures

without the sound of Bachian fugal tangles,

without the sound of Beethovenian pathos,

without Haydn's playfulness. . . .

against the paper barriers of Witt's reforms. . . . [8]

Tonight the moon in the lofty canopy lights up my small pieces of paper, full of notes—

tomorrow the sun will steal in inquisitively.

At length the warm air streamed in through the open window into my frozen fingers.

Always the scent of the moist Luhačovice woods—that was the incense.

A cathedral grew before me in the colossal expanse of the hills and the vault of the sky, covered in mist into the distance; its little bells were rung by a flock of sheep.

I hear in the tenor solo some sort of high priest,

in the soprano solo a maiden-angel,

in the chorus our people.

The candles are high fir trees in the wood, lit up by stars; and in the ritual somewhere out there I see a vision of the princely Saint Wenceslas.

And the language is that of the missionaries Cyril and Methodius.

And before the evenings of three Luhačovice weeks had flown past, the work was finished. . . . [9]

In April 1926 Janáček had written his fiercely brilliant Sinfonietta. With its aggressive repetitions, astonishing abruptions, dazzling sonorities, and command of dramatic gestures, it was a perfect springboard for the attack on the Mass. If we think about what other music was around in the middle 1920s—and it doesn't really make any difference whether we think about the Puccini-Strauss end of the spectrum or what the advance-guard

---

[8]Franz Xaver Witt (1834–1888), a German musician and priest, was a leading apostle of the Cecilian movement, which sought to get instruments out of church music and restore the Palestrinian *a cappella* style.

[9]Cited in Paul Wingfield, *Janáček: Glagolitic Mass* (Cambridge University Press, 1992). Typing these words of Janáček's, I am struck anew by the similarity between his short-phrased, percussive prose style and his musical language.

was producing in its various flavors—it is no surprise that people were thrown by those repetitions and abruptions, by nearly everything about the pace at which Janáček used and metabolized musical material—his syntax, his rhythm, his rhetoric.

Czech audiences by and large understood and responded; elsewhere, the Mass was mostly rejected as incoherent.[10] Occasionally it was patronizingly received as babble from a primitive world that was, thank goodness, located at some remove and that one would not often have to deal with. Surprisingly, Nicolas Slonimsky's classic, ever-entertaining, and ever–thought-provoking Lexicon of Musical Invective includes nothing about Janáček, but the early reviews of the Glagolitic Mass would have provided rich examples of not hearing and not understanding. The growing availability of recordings made a big difference, but it was really not until the 1960s that the work came to be widely recognized as not only one of the most personal but one of the great monuments in the history of sacred music.

Following Moravian tradition, Janáček encloses his Mass between fanfares, and the first music we hear is an Introduction that could well be a movement of the Sinfonietta.

"Gospodi pomiluj," corresponding to the Kyrie in the Latin liturgy, emphasizes intervals that give it a pungently modal flavor. The music reflects the ternary structure of the text, with the solo soprano coming in to dominate the invocation to Christ. The return to "Gospodi pomiluj" is sharply abbreviated.

In the "Slava," analogous to the Latin Gloria, the soprano takes the lead, and at the highest level of intensity. The tenor enters with even greater urgency on the words "Sčdec o desnuju otca" (Thou that sittest at the right hand of the Father) and later leads the way into the God-intoxicated sequence of "Amin, amin!"

The "Věruju," or Credo, begins with one of Janáček's most dramatic contrasts as the drumming bass clarinet and low strings give way to the quietly ecstatic chords on which the choir sings the first word: "I believe!" A string trill, begun by the violas and gradually picked up by the other instruments, whirs through the texture. Janáček's use of the orchestra is always remarkable, as much for his idea of orchestral independence in a vocal work as for his rich Bartókian fantasy in matters of instrumental detail. Between the clause about the incarnation and the account of the crucifixion, he inserts an extraordinary symphonic interlude in three parts.

---

[10]For years, Janáček's music, like Musorgsky's, was routinely disparaged and dismissed as technically insufficient.

Kundera offered a most specific exegesis of these pages, and Janáček offered no denial. According to Kundera, the flute recitative and the continuing music for clarinets and strings (for a long time just violas and cellos) represent Jesus praying in the desert; the fanfares over the ostinato bass depict Christ as sower of the seeds of bliss; the dissonant, disjointed organ solo evokes his agony upon the cross. The crucifixion is announced in a single angry shout. The resurrection is expounded in processional music as austerely stiff as a Byzantine icon.

A violin solo sets a silvery dome over the serene music of the "Svät, svät," or Sanctus—a recollection surely of the same sound in the Benedictus of Beethoven's *Missa solemnis*. Kundera also suggests a pictorial interpretation of the brief "Blagoslovjen" as Christ walking in the streets with the crowd throwing flowers in his path and crying out "Benedictus!"

The "Agneče Božij," corresponding to the Agnus Dei, brings the slowest and simplest music in the Mass as passages for *a cappella* chorus alternate with strings and woodwinds, the instrumental groups themselves speaking antiphonally to each other. In the middle of the movement, the four vocal soloists are briefly heard once more.

Next comes Janáček's afterthought, the bravura organ solo, an excited ostinato. And to conclude, an Intrada or processional—in this instance functioning more like a recessional—for the orchestra at its most brilliant. Janáček's biographer Jaroslav Vogel, who was also a conductor, calls it "a marching entry into life strengthened by the preceding display of power and faith in the Slav spirit."

Zoltán Kodály (signature)

Zoltán Kodály

Zoltán Kodály was born at Kecskemét, Hungary, on 16 December 1882 and died in Budapest on 6 March 1967.

Psalmus hungaricus for Tenor Solo, Chorus, and Orchestra, op. 13

Kodály composed the *Psalmus hungaricus* in 1923 for a concert to celebrate the fiftieth anniversary of the union of the cities of Buda, Óbuda, and Pest as Budapest. The text is Psalm 55, translated into Hungarian by the sixteenth-century poet and preacher Mihály Vég of Kecskemét. With Ferenc Székelyhidy as tenor soloist, Ernö Dohnányi conducted the first performance in Budapest on 19 November 1923. Dohnányi's own *Festive Overture* and Béla Bartók's *Dance Suite* were introduced on the same occasion.

Solo tenor, mixed chorus, boys' chorus (optional). Three flutes, two oboes, two clarinets, two bassoons, four horns, three trumpets, three trombones, timpani, cymbals, harp, organ, and strings.

When Zoltán Kodály died at eighty-four, he was the most loved man in Hungary. Recognition had come to him with two events. One was the first performance of *Psalmus hungaricus*, and the other was the premiere three years later of his opera *Háry János*. They were the works that established

Kodály as creator of a national music; the *Psalmus* and especially the concert suite he drew from *Háry János* were also the ones that carried his
fame abroad. And with the Amsterdam premiere of the *Psalmus hungaricus* in 1927, Kodály began his fourth career (after composer, ethnomusi-
cologist, and teacher) as an effective conductor of his own music. The
Háry János Suite pleads Kodály's case charmingly and effectively, and one
can say the same for some of the other works that show up on concert
programs with some frequency—the *Dances from Galánta*, the Duo for
Violin and Cello, and the dramatic Sonata for Cello Solo, for example—
but not to know his work for chorus is to have a blinkered view of his
achievement. That includes an enormous amount of unaccompanied
choral music, much of it for children, and if there was a cause even closer
to Kodály's heart than helping to create a Hungarian national music, it
was the musical education of the young.[1] His large-scale choral works
with orchestra include a handsome *Te Deum*, but the most powerful of
them is the fervent *Psalmus hungaricus*.

Kodály's father was a stationmaster for the Austro-Hungarian Imperial and Royal Railways. As a civil servant he was moved about a good
deal, and so Zoltán grew up in a succession of small towns in Hungary
and Slovakia. Wherever he went, he absorbed the local folk music, and
from his parents, who sang and played violin and piano, he picked up
something of classical music. He himself became proficient on the piano,
violin, viola, and cello. Studying the music that was sung and played at
home, in church, and at school, he taught himself how to compose, and
at fifteen he was even able to hear a piece of his own, an Overture in
D minor, played by the school orchestra at Nagyszombat (now Trnava,
Slovakia).

At seventeen, Kodály went to Budapest, studying Hungarian and
German literature at the university and at last beginning his formal musical education at the Academy of Music. His composition teacher was
Hans Koessler, as German and conservative as could be, but also a man to
instill an unshakable sense of craft and responsibility in his students,
who included Ernö Dohnányi, Béla Bartók, and Leo Weiner, the most
important Hungarian composers of Kodály's generation. The young
Kodály was serious—so serious that when Koessler suggested he begin in
his second-year class, he refused: he did not want to miss any opportunity to firm up his technical muscles.

At the university, Kodály also began systematic investigation of long-
familiar and beloved terrain, Hungarian folk music, and he eventually

---

[1]On a panel at Dartmouth College in the 1960s, Kodály was asked at what age a child's musical
education should begin. His answer was crisp: "Nine months before the birth of the mother."

wrote his doctoral dissertation on that subject. In the middle 1890s, a philologist by name of Béla Vikár had gone into the field with a (more or less) portable phonograph. Kodály now followed his example, as did the slightly older Bartók, and there began for the two of them a lifetime of collecting, transcribing, and editing folk music, as well as a loving, nourishing friendship that was never disturbed by the fact that as composers they came to tread markedly different stylistic paths. After getting his degree in 1906, Kodály received a grant that allowed him to go abroad for half a year—four months in Berlin and two in Paris. The most important thing that happened to him was his encounter in Paris with the music of Claude Debussy, and he returned home with a suitcase full of new scores. Naturally he shared these discoveries with Bartók, and both went on to find their quite-distinct voices in a marriage of Western European art music with the folk idiom of Central and Eastern Europe. They had already gleaned one crucial fact from their folk music studies, and Debussy, coming from quite another angle, now confirmed it for them: there was life beyond major and minor scales.

Kodály's and Bartók's devotion to folk music was part of the process of learning to be Hungarian, and that, decidedly, was something that had to be learned. Since the end of the seventeenth century, Hungary had been a minority nation within the huge and disorderly Hapsburg empire. The Hungarians were in a privileged position within the empire when one compares their lot with, say, that of the Czechs; nonetheless, their culture, customs, and language were always submerged to some extent. Even in his art music, as distinct from what he wrote chiefly with educational purposes in view, Kodály tended to choose material calculated to call his fellow Hungarians unto themselves and to an awareness of national consciousness. *Psalmus hungaricus* and *Háry János*, the summits of the sacred and secular, the serious and comic parts of Kodály's work, exemplify this intention.

The union of Óbuda, Buda, and Pest in 1873 had given the Hungarians a larger city than any they had had before (the combined population then was something like 280,000), and it was a place they could think of as a real political, economic, and cultural capital. The fiftieth anniversary of the founding of Budapest, which had become one of Europe's most elegant cities, was therefore something to celebrate, and the need to celebrate was all the greater because Hungary's recent past had been so wretched. The war that had begun in 1914 was lost, the king (who was also emperor of Austria) was deposed, and a Socialist republic had been proclaimed. But Serbian, Rumanian, and Czech troops occupied the country, the economy was in disarray, and an attempted Communist takeover created further dissension. It was a perfect setup for a right-wing counterrevolution, and this came late in 1919 in the form of an invasion under the leadership of Admiral Miklós Horthy, who in 1920 took the title of Regent after Parliament reinstated the monarchy (a short-lived absurdity), and who remained as dictator until 1944.

Kodály found himself caught in these swings between Red terror and White terror. Like Dohnányi and Bartók, he was identified with the 1918 republic, having been appointed deputy director of his alma mater, the Budapest Academy of Music. After the fall of the Socialist government and its replacement by the Horthy regency, the new musical power in the land was the violinist and composer Jenö Hubay, an effective teacher whose students included Joseph Szigeti, Jelly d'Arányi, Zoltán Székely, and Sándor Végh, but an extreme conservative in his political and musical views as well as a vengeful man. Dohnányi had enjoyed international fame as a composer and pianist since before the turn of the century, and Bartók's renown abroad had just begun. The government preferred not to get involved in attacks that would give it a bad name elsewhere in Europe; Kodály, on the other hand, was someone who could be gone after with impunity. He was fired from the academy and kept from teaching for two years, and the performance of his music was discouraged with a heavy hand. Bartók was able to come to the rescue in that he persuaded Universal, his Vienna-based publisher and one of the most prestigious houses in Europe, to add his friend's works to their list. Once that sponsorship was established, the siege against Kodály at home was lifted.

In this context it is amazing that in organizing the musical part of the Budapest jubilee the government chose artistic quality in the persons of Bartók, Dohnányi, and Kodály, rather than ideological rectitude. Bartók's *Dance Suite* was a huge success, but it also made political waves. At a time of political chauvinism, Bartók had been attacked for want of patriotism because of scholarly articles he had written about the folk music of Hungary's enemy, Romania; defiantly, his new work celebrated Romanian and Arabian dances as well as Hungarian. Dohnányi's *Festive Overture* would be forgotten were it not mentioned sometimes in connection with the Jubilee concert. Kodály's *Psalmus* stirred the audience deeply, and, hailed as a great national totem, it immediately assumed a status beyond musical considerations.

Kodály had not intended to write such a work at all. Forty years later, in the course of a conversation about Bartók, he told the Belgian musicologist Denijs Dille:

As for my relations with Bartók, I can only say that from the moment I recognized his genius I felt the need to smooth his path and to clear it of all obstacles. Thus I always avoided competing with him, always strove to do something different from what he was doing. When we got this commission . . . I asked him what he was going to do, and he told me he was going to do a suite of dances. I had had the idea of doing the *Dances from Marosszék* and *Dances from Galánta*, but since he was doing [dances] I chose another theme, the *Psalmus*. This was a poem absolutely unknown except to literary historians. And so you see how the lines that one follows all one's life, even unconsciously, finally come together. If I had not studied ancient Hungarian literature I would never have done the *Psalmus* because I would never have found the text.[2]

Kodály had weathered the storms of 1920–1921 with impressive dignity and forbearance, but he was hurt, angry, and glad of a chance to turn his Budapest commission into a statement. Psalm 55 is a bitter lament, and the sixteenth-century verse-paraphrase by Mihály Vég of Kecskemét, Kodály's own birthplace, lends it special poignancy of expression. The text is replete with themes of mischief and betrayal, violence and strife. To that first Budapest audience in 1923 these words, their effect heightened by the nobly eloquent music, were full of resonance—of the history of an oppressed people, of the Turkish occupation of Hungary, of the Protestant Reformation, of the events of the last five years, of the composer's own well-known recent experiences. *Psalmus hungaricus* has not lost its relevance for Hungarian listeners. Nor is it parochial in its appeal, for its theme is timeless.

An impassioned, anguished orchestral introduction prepares the first entrance of the chorus, contained and tight-lipped in its grief. The melody to which the singers intone "Mikoron Dávid" is the principal theme of the *Psalmus hungaricus*, one to which the music will return five times. The orchestral music resumes, now to introduce the tenor protagonist. He too begins quietly, but where the chorus was instructed to sing *sotto voce*, his part is marked *espressivo*. It is not in him to stay calm, and his song is a flood of pain. The music sweeps forward, and the varied and intense verses, for the most part dominated by the tenor, are anchored by the choral refrain. Silence, more shattering than music itself, punctuates the singing. Suddenly the atmosphere changes. From a long silence there emerges the calm of a chord of A-flat major, magically scored for strings and harp. A flute suspends a serene melody across this tapestry of sound and is joined by a single violin. When the voices come back after this, the longest orchestral interlude in the psalm, they do so in the calm and

[2]Kodály got around to the Marosszék and Galánta dances in 1930 and 1933 respectively.

confidence engendered by the closing prayer. The music rises to a great crest, its earlier modal harmonies clarified into a brilliant A major, but after that the work closes quietly, the chorus returning to the *pianissimo* unison with which it had begun and with the psalmist reflecting—as Kodály himself must have reflected—that he has made his grief into song.

Felix Mendelssohn-Bartholdy

Jakob Ludwig Felix Mendelssohn was born on 3 February 1809 in Hamburg, then under Napoleonic rule, and died in Leipzig, Saxony, on 4 November 1847. Bartholdy was the name of his maternal uncle Jakob, who had changed his own surname from Salomon and taken on Bartholdy from the previous owner of a piece of real estate he had bought in Berlin. Bartholdy was added to the Mendelssohn family name to distinguish the Lutheran Mendelssohns from the Jewish ones when Felix's father was baptized in 1822. The children—Felix, his older sister Fanny, and his younger siblings Rebekka and Paul—had already been baptized at Uncle Jakob's urging.

Elias (Elijah), Oratorio on Words of the Old Testament, op. 70

The *Elijah* project was on Mendelssohn's mind as early as 1837, but he began work on the score only when he received an invitation in the summer of 1845 to compose an oratorio for the Birmingham Festival. He completed the score on 11 August 1846, just in time for the first performance in Birmingham on the twenty-sixth of that month. Although he had composed the work in German as *Elias*, it was first heard in William Bartholomew's English translation as *Elijah*. Mendelssohn himself conducted, Joseph Staudigl was Elijah, and the other soloists were Maria Caradori-Allan, Maria Hawes, and Charles Lockey. The program also included arias by Mozart and Cimarosa as well as one of Handel's Coronation Anthems. Four arias and four choruses of *Elijah* were encored. During the following winter, Mendelssohn spent some time revising the score so as to make parts of it, particularly the section with the Widow, "more weighty and mystical." He then led the first performance of the revised version in London on 16 April 1847.

When *Elijah* was introduced in America on 8 November 1847 at the Broadway Tabernacle, New York, readers of the *Brooklyn Eagle* could learn the next day that

> the music, judged by the rules of art, is of the highest importance, but it is clearly too elaborately scientific for the public ear. It is, besides, too heavy in its general character, and wants relief of a proper proportion of lightness and melody. There is scarcely a striking or pleasant air in it. To a mere musician, however, it would offer study and delight for years. Although the audience was large and sat out the performance, it was evident that no great degree of pleasure was derived from it.

That review is of more than ordinary interest because its author was a twenty-seven-year-old aficionado of Italian opera named Walt Whitman.

The score calls for four soloists. The bass is Elijah himself, and other singers represent specific characters from time to time: the soprano, the Widow; the contralto, the Angel and Queen Jezebel; the tenor, Obadiah and King Ahab. In addition, the part of the boy who is told by Elijah to watch for rain is often assigned to a boy soprano. There are also some movements that involve a double quartet, and the second quartet is usually drawn from the chorus. Two flutes, two oboes, two clarinets, two bassoons, four horns, three trombones, ophicleide (usually replaced today by the fatter-sounding tuba), timpani, organ, and strings.

> I picture Elijah as a grand and mighty prophet of a kind we would do well to have in our own day—powerful, zealous, but also harsh and angry and saturnine; a striking contrast to the court sycophants and the rabble; in antithesis, in fact, virtually to the whole world; yet borne on the wings of angels.
> —Mendelssohn to the Reverend Julius Schubring, 2 November 1838

In his memoir of Mendelssohn, the composer Ferdinand Hiller, a friend since boyhood, recounts how one evening he "found Mendelssohn deep in the Bible. 'Listen,' he said, and then he read to me, in a gentle and agitated voice, the passage from the First Book of Kings, beginning with the words, 'And behold, the Lord passed by.' 'Would that not be splendid for an oratorio?' he exclaimed.'" And that, at least according to Hiller's recollection nearly forty years later, was the start of the process that led to the composition of *Elijah*.

What Mendelssohn is most famous for, other than his own music, is his role in the revival of interest in the music of Johann Sebastian Bach. That story has been much romanticized over the years, but there is no doubt that the performances of the *Saint Matthew Passion* Mendelssohn conducted in Berlin in March 1829—he had just turned twenty—made considerable impact. He had begun rehearsing the *Passion* a year and a half before, but his own preparation, not only for the exploration of that great work but also for a life that would include splendid contributions of his own to the choral repertory, had begun when, as a boy of ten, he entered Carl Friedrich Zelter's Berlin Singakademie, a chorus with something of an educational bias.

Zelter, mostly remembered now as Goethe's highly conservative adviser on musical matters, had studied with Carl Fasch, who had been both colleague of and successor to Carl Philipp Emanuel Bach at the court of Frederick the Great, and he succeeded Fasch as director of the Singakademie.[1] Given Zelter's temperament and age (he was born in 1758, two years after Mozart), the Singakademie was not an institution in which to learn about Beethoven or Schubert, to say nothing of really dangerous modernists like Weber and Berlioz, both of whom he bad-mouthed to Goethe. It was, on the other hand, the right place for immersion in Haydn and, to some extent, Mozart (not as sympathetic and comprehensible a figure to Zelter), Handel, and especially J. S. Bach, as well as in the music of several generations of Italian composers from Palestrina to Pergolesi.

The history of the sacred and semisacred oratorio is a spotty affair. Handel wrote his last one, *Jephtha*, in 1752. A little more than twenty years later, Haydn composed *Il ritorno di Tobia*, too interesting a work to be as neglected as it is. Ten years after that, Mozart recycled some of the music of his unfinished C-Minor Mass as *Davidde penitente*.[2] Then,

[1]Zelter's father was a building contractor and stonemason responsible for the construction and even some of the design of Sanssouci, Frederick the Great's charming rococo summer palace at Potsdam. Zelter himself was trained as a master stonemason and worked at that profession until he was well into his thirties.
[2]In the nineteenth century, *Davidde penitente* was actually better known than the Mass itself. For that story, see my essay on the C-Minor Mass, p. 212.

just on either side of the turn of the century, come the two works that represent the high-water mark of the genre after Handel, Haydn's *The Creation* and *The Seasons*. Beethoven's *Christ on the Mount of Olives* is fascinating as a preview of *Fidelio* and the two Masses, but it does not add up to a convincing experience. Schubert's *Lazarus* has wonderful moments but, abandoned halfway through, it is a frustrating torso.

Mendelssohn's upbringing as a Christian convert together with his Singakademie experience made him eager to compose worthy and large-scale successors to the Bach Passions and the oratorios of Handel and Haydn. The Cecilia Society in Frankfurt asked him for an oratorio in 1831, but it was not until the winter of 1835–1836 that he took the plunge and composed *Paulus* (*Saint Paul*). Twenty-six when he began that work, he was the newly appointed conductor of the Leipzig Gewandhaus Orchestra and the experienced composer of operas, church music, lieder, and some of his best-known instrumental works, among them the *Hebrides* and *Becalmed at Sea and Prosperous Voyage Overtures*, the "Italian" and "Reformation" Symphonies, the Piano Concerto No. 1, the String Octet, the String Quartets, opp. 12 and 13, and quite a few of the *Songs Without Words*.

Mendelssohn introduced *Paulus* at the Lower Rhine Music Festival in Dusseldorf in May 1836. It was sung, mostly in Germany and England, more than fifty times in the next year and a half. In October 1838 it came to New York, where it aroused the enthusiasm of Walt Whitman, who would be so critical of *Elijah* nine years later.[3] It seemed as though Mendelssohn was indeed the man to pick up on where Haydn had left off.

But he was a strange mixture of confident and hesitant. Most of the time he was one of the most fluent musicians who ever lived, but he could get surprisingly stuck. The *Hebrides Overture* went through revision after revision, the "Scotch" Symphony was nearly thirteen years in the making, and to the end of his life he was dissatisfied with the "Italian" Symphony and would not publish it. Thus, despite being buoyed by the acclaim that had greeted *Paulus*, and though *Elijah* was never completely out of his thoughts, he only began work on his second oratorio nine years

[3]Dissenting about *Saint Paul* was Mendelssohn's friend Robert Schumann, who was disturbed by what he sensed as a populist trend in the work. However, he went on to write: "Let us remember that Beethoven, who wrote *Christ on the Mount of Olives*, also composed the *Missa solemnis*; and let us trust that, as the youth Mendelssohn has written one oratorio, the man will write another." (Schumann, by the way, was a year younger than Mendelssohn.) Many years later, Schumann added a footnote to this review: "Mendelssohn fulfilled this prophecy in *Elijah*."

after the success of the first, and then only when he was importuned by Joseph Moore, the director of the Birmingham Festival. Birmingham, where Mendelssohn had conducted several times, was his favorite British city after London, and he even knew to pronounce it "Brum" in the authentic local way.

Casting about for suitable material, he was torn between Elijah and Peter. For counsel he went to Julius Schubring, a friend since childhood, now a Lutheran pastor in Dessau and his librettist for *Saint Paul*.[4] Mendelssohn decided on Elijah, partly on Schubring's advice, partly because he liked the idea of focusing on an Old Testament figure this time, and partly because the subject, with its fire, rain, tempest, and earthquake, offered opportunities to be picturesque. What Hiller recounts of Mendelssohn's fascination with the possibilities of "And behold, the Lord passed by" is part of that story. Mendelssohn tried to get Karl Klingemann, his friend and travel companion through the British Isles, to write the libretto for him. When Klingemann declined, he himself assembled the text on the basis of Schubring's suggestions, discovering as he worked how difficult it is to select the most suitable episodes and to give shape and drive to the whole.[5]

The Mendelssohn who labored over the score of *Elijah* was a different man from the buoyant young composer of *Saint Paul*. He was only in his middle thirties, but his health had begun to fail and he was losing his zest for travel and for playing the piano and conducting. Many in the Birmingham audience were shocked by his appearance: disturbingly thin, sallow, and balding. Still, the work on *Elijah* had gone well and had given him pleasure.

The concert itself, he reported, was the best first performance he had ever had, and the audience, which demanded and got encores of eight numbers and which cheered the composer unstintingly, was thrilled. Staudigl, the Elijah, described by Berlioz as having a voice "smooth and sumptuous as velvet, at once suave and powerful," was splendid. Mendelssohn was especially happy with his tenor soloist, the young Charles Lockey. He had hoped to have the great Jenny Lind as his soprano and had written the part with her in mind, but she was quarreling with a manager in England and refused to travel to that country. Mendelssohn's one major disappointment, therefore, was the enforced

[4]Indirectly, Schubring had also been involved in the 1829 *Saint Matthew Passion* revival. He was convinced that Bach was nothing but dry mathematics, and a considerable part of what spurred Mendelssohn was his desire to change his friend's mind.
[5]Brahms's *German Requiem*, Elgar's *Dream of Gerontius*, and Vaughan Wiliams's *Sancta Civitas* are counterexamples of strong librettos assembled by composers.

collaboration with Maria Caradori-Allan, worn of voice and arrogant of temperament.[6]

The end came shockingly soon. Mendelssohn spent the winter of 1846–1847 in poor health, and it was all he could do to bring himself to undertake his tenth and last visit to England for another round of *Elijah* performances, now reintroducing the work in its revised and final form. "Gray on gray" was his response when someone asked him how he felt. In May, five days after his return home, his sister Fanny, herself just forty-one, suffered a stroke and died. She was at the piano, playing Bach's *Well-Tempered Clavier*, which she had memorized as a girl of thirteen, for she, too, was a brilliant musician, though like Virginia Woolf's imagined Judith Shakespeare, she had no chance to make much of her gifts. Modern attitudes and insights make it clear that Felix's relationship to her was in many ways exploitative and patronizing. Be that as it may, she was the person to whom he had felt closest all his life. She meant more to him than parents, wife, and children, and his spirit did not survive her loss. In the summer of 1847 he found the energy to complete his dark String Quartet in F minor. At the beginning of November, burned out, he died. On his desk were sketches for a third oratorio, *Christus*.

Paulus brings us some impressive moments; for example, Jesus' words of reproach, "Saul, Saul, why do you persecute me?", so imaginatively scored. The work still has its advocates, but it has pretty much dropped from view. *Elijah*, by contrast, maintains a place at the center of the repertory; in Britain and America it is second only to *Messiah* in popularity. It can be thrilling to sing, and it includes some of Mendelssohn's finest music. It is the work of a master, and if it is flawed it is, ironically, because Mendelssohn himself lacked those gritty qualities—"powerful, zealous, but also harsh and angry and saturnine"—that he cited in his letter to Schubring as so profoundly impressing him in the figure of Elijah.

Elijah was a prophet in Israel in the ninth century B.C.E. His chief cause was maintaining the worship of Jehovah as opposed to that of foreign gods—in sum, the defense of the First Commandment. Ahab, king of Israel from 874 to 853 B.C.E., was a powerful antagonist, and so, even more, was his queen, Jezebel, a Phoenician princess who had brought the worship of Baal with her from Tyre and had introduced her husband and his people to its ways. Baal, I learn from an essay by P. Kyle McCarter Jr. in the invaluable

[6]Lind sang in *Elijah* often after Mendelssohn's death, and beautifully. She also organized a benefit performance of *Elijah* to create a Mendelssohn Scholarship to send an English musician to study at the Leipzig Conservatory. The first Mendelssohn Scholar was the sixteen-year-old Arthur Sullivan.

Harper's Bible Commentary, was used by the authors of the Bible as a generic name for foreign gods. The specific god central to Jezebel's practices would have been Melcarth, a rain god, a significant detail in light of the importance in the Elijah stories of the lifting of a drought.[7]

Elijah's accomplishments, his complex relationship with Ahab, and his persecution by Jezebel, are recounted in I Kings, and portions of that book provide the main narrative thread of Schubring's *Elijah* libretto. Just as the libretto for Handel's *Messiah* combines narrative, prophecy, and commentary to powerful effect, so is the *Elijah* text interlarded with verses from the prophetic books, the Psalms, and the Pentateuch. The Bible itself is full of such references back and forth, Elijah himself in many respects being a kind of reincarnation of Moses. Schubring and Mendelssohn also present him as a precursor to Christ.

We see—or rather, we hear, and imagine that we see—Elijah pronouncing the threat of drought, telling Ahab that it is he, Ahab, not Elijah, who is the troubler of Israel's peace, then instructing the king to assemble the people on Mount Carmel for a contest between Jehovah and Baal. It is, of course, Jehovah who wins this contest by bringing fire to the altar—loaded historiography. Part I concludes with the bringing of rain to the parched land. Part II shows us the prophet on his journey through the wilderness, his despair at what he believes to be the failure of his mission, and the restoration of his strength with the appearance to him of the Lord—not in the tempest, not in the earthquake, not in the fire, but in the still, small voice—and of the host of seraphim.

Space does not permit a description of all the musical events of *Elijah*. It is hardly necessary, anyway. Attention to the words will open the way to the music, just as, conversely, the music illuminates the texts and the events. Let me pick just a few details for comment.

Except for *The Creation*, no oratorio has a more striking opening than *Elijah*. McCarter points out that in the Bible Elijah enters Ahab's story "suddenly and without preparation." Out of nowhere, a new chapter begins: "And Elijah the Tishbite . . . said unto Ahab, 'As the Lord God of Israel liveth, before whom I stand, there shall not be dew nor rain these years, but according to my word.'" (This could be dramatic flair on the part of the author; it could also be that something is missing.) Mendelssohn, after just one measure of dark chords for woodwind and brass, also starts right in with a grave—and Handelian—recitative on that

[7]Jezebel, who was responsible for many deaths among the righteous, got hers in the end. She survived Ahab, who fell in battle, until Jehu, a former lieutenant of Ahab's, became king in 842 B.C.E. One of his first deeds was to extirpate whoever remained of the house of Ahab. He ordered Jezebel to be thrown out of a window, had her trampled by horses, and fed her remains to his dogs.

very verse. An arresting detail: the descending, angular diminished fifths on the words "there shall not be dew nor rain." Mendelssohn made them arresting on purpose: he wanted you to remember them, because they will recur in association with the idea of punishment for apostasy.

After this beginning comes the Overture, a potent example of Mendelssohn in his most serious, severe vein (one in which his endeavors sometimes misfire). This is nervously agitated, intense fugal writing; the color comes from Mozart in this same key of D minor: the great Piano Concerto, K. 466, and *Don Giovanni.* Wind instruments keep cutting through with what is literally a "speaking" commentary, for their phrases are reiterations of the last words Elijah had sung, "Ich sage es denn." The impact is lost in performances in English because William Bartholomew, the translator, was too reverent about keeping the language of the King James Version, and the rhythm of "but according to my word" does not correspond to that of the German. It would be easy to change Elijah's words to something like "Till I speak the word" (Tovey's suggestion), and the gain would be immense. Which brings us to the question: In which language do we sing *Elias/Elijah?* This is an unusual situation: a work composed in one language but given its first performance in another, and in a translation in part overseen and certainly approved by the composer, whose English was very good. The case here for using English in English-speaking countries is strong.

The Overture rises to a mighty climax, then spills without a break into the opening chorus, "Hilf, Herr!"/ "Help, Lord!" Bartholomew gets some of the credit for this striking sequence of events. It was Mendelssohn's idea to begin immediately with Elijah's curse, but it was Bartholomew who suggested: "Then let an Introductory movement be played, expressive, descriptive of the misery of the famine—for the chorus (I always thought) comes so very quickly and suddenly after the curse, that there seems to elapse no time to produce its results."

The chorus itself impressively combines power (in sheer rhythmic energy) and pathos (the prayers for an end to the drought), and the agitation in the orchestra at the question "Will denn der Herr nicht mehr Gott sein in Zion?"/ "Will then the Lord be no more God in Zion?" is most affecting. But most impressive of all is the way this movement ends, namely, with a choral recitative in which each section singly voices its despairing plea.

The tenor aria "So ihr mich von ganzem Herzen suchet"/ "If with All Your Hearts" is a prime example of Mendelssohn's lyricism, and the scoring is both soft-grained and sumptuous. One can always count on Mendelssohn to devise elegant entries into a reprise; this one is exceptionally lovely, as is the enriched orchestration that follows. This gentle song is also an effective foil for the powerful C-minor chorus that follows, "Aber der Herr sieht es nicht"/ "Yet Doth the Lord See It Not." Here Mendelssohn has another surprise in store: the sudden incursion of a passage in the simple four-part harmony of a chorale, after which the chorus concludes in confident major.

Elijah's mockery of the priests of Baal when their god fails to answer their appeal provides the occasion for a delightful detail (and, I suppose, the only moment of humor in *Elijah*): the sharp, mocking woodwind chords that echo the Prophet's sardonic "Rufet lauter!"/ "Call him louder!" The music for the unfortunate adherents of Baal is not Mendelssohn's strongest, and I find myself wondering whether the composer intended to stack the deck or whether it was just not in him to write something appropriately pagan and savage.

In Elijah's aria "Ist nicht des Herrn Wort wie ein Feuer?"/ "Is Not His Word like a Fire," you hear how carefully Mendelssohn studied Handel, and how effectively.

The extended scene in which Elijah prays for rain—so suspenseful, with the boy being sent again and again to scan the sky (an echo, in reverse, of Noah?)—is planned and worked in masterly fashion. It is a fine opportunity for a conductor with a knack for theatrical timing. No wonder the Birmingham audience demanded a repetition of this episode before they broke for intermission.

Mendelssohn opens Part II with one of his Jenny Lind arias, "Höre, Israel"/ "Hear Ye, Israel." A very Bachian piece it is, too, and I am sure Mendelssohn was remembering his beloved *Saint Matthew Passion* when he decided to place a B-minor aria in 3/8 time for female voice just there. F-sharp was Mendelssohn's favorite note in Lind's voice, and that note would inevitably be especially prominent in a B-minor/major aria. I imagine, too, that the scoring, with pairs of flutes, oboes, and clarinets, gives us an idea of what Mendelssohn's lost reorchestration of Bach must have sounded like. Wholly original is the way the aria continues: via a transitional recitative into a new and more vigorous verse in major, and then directly into the next chorus. The effect of the key change from B major, where the aria ends, to the G major of the "Fürchte dich nicht"/ "Be Not Afraid" chorus is strong.

A splendid sequence of musical numbers begins with Elijah's intense recitative, "Der Herr hat dich erhoben"/ "The Lord hath exalted thee." Soon after that, Jezebel speaks: "Habt ihr's gehört, wie er geweissagt hat wider dieses Volk?"/ "Have ye not heard he hath prophesied against all Israel?" The nineteenth-century critic H. F. Chorley, a shrewd observer of singers and singing, remarked that this recitative had always "passed unnoticed" until the great Pauline Viardot-García declaimed it.

Clearly there are moments in *Elijah* when the reverential English oratorio tradition wants to be shot through with some fire, and these moments do not occur only in the title role.

Elijah's aria "Es ist genug!"/ "It Is Enough!", with its cello solo, is one of the most Bachian pieces in the work, designed to evoke the alto aria with viola da gamba obbligato, "Es ist vollbracht" (It is accomplished), in the *Saint John Passion*. The trio of angels, for two sopranos and alto *a cappella*, "Hebe deine Augen auf zu den Bergen"/ "Lift Thine Eyes to the Mountains," is a justly admired page. So is the tenderly lyric chorus to which it leads, "Siehe, der Hüter Israels schläft noch schlummert nicht"/ "He, Watching over Israel, Slumbers Not, nor Sleeps," remarkable for the euphony of the murmuring strings, the delicate role entrusted to the timpani, and the wonderful surprise of the six *a cappella* measures at the close. I am sure I am not the only listener whose favorite moment in *Elijah* this is. And the contralto aria that follows, "Sei stille dem Herrn"/ "O Rest in the Lord," is one of the most famous moments in the oratorio literature.

Then comes the verse that sparked Elijah, "Der Herr ging vorüber!"/ "Behold, God the Lord Passed By!" This initiates the other great dramatic sequence in the work, the one parallel to the rain miracle at the end of Part I, and it is no less gripping. The powerfully uprushing opening music comes by courtesy of Ludwig van Beethoven's "Pathétique" Sonata.

Still more of Mendelssohn's finest music is yet ahead: Elijah's aria with oboe obbligato, "Ja, es sollen wohl Berge weichen"/ "For the Mountains Shall Depart," full of unpredictable detail, preceded by another beautiful recitative for chorus; the majestic, *Fidelio*-like chorus, "Und der Prophet Elias brach hervor"/ "Then Did Elijah the Prophet Break Forth"; the gentle tenor aria "Dann werden die Gerechten leuchten"/ "Then Shall the Righteous Shine Forth," another of the score's most famous—and justly famous—numbers; and so, by way of the quartet "Wohlan, alle, die ihr durstig seid" /"O Come, Everyone That Thirsteth," richly scored for divided violas and cellos, all the way to the full-bodied final chorus, "Alsdann wird euer Licht hervorbrechen"/ "And Then Shall Your Light Break Forth."

Wolfgang Amadè Mozart

Joannes Chrisostomus Wolfgang Gottlieb Mozart, who began to call himself Wolfgango Amadeo about 1770 and Wolfgang Amadè in 1777—but never Amadeus except in jest—was born in Salzburg, Austria, on 27 January 1756 and died in Vienna on 5 December 1791.

The K numbers refer to the chronological catalogue of Mozart's works published in 1862 by Ludwig, Ritter von Köchel, an Austrian botanist, mineralogist, and music bibliographer. His catalogue has several times been revised in the light of new knowledge, and when a K number appears with a second number in parentheses next to it, for example, K. 427(417a), the first is Köchel's original, the other is the one in the most recent editions of the catalogue.

The Shorter Choral Works

The eminent physicist Freeman Dyson, son of the composer Sir George Dyson, is supposed to have said as a child that "music is nice but too long." Those words could have been the motto of Hieronymus Colloredo, prince-archbishop of Salzburg from 1772 until 1801, and Mozart's employer from his enthronement until 8 June 1781, when his chamberlain, Count Arco, propelled the twenty-five-year-old composer into unemployment and freedom with, literally, a kick in the pants. The *Vesperae solennes de confessore*, Mozart's last church piece for Salzburg, reflects the archbishop's preference for music that gets it over with quickly—here, nearly two hundred lines of Latin text disposed of in about twenty-five minutes.

In the Catholic liturgy there are eight daily prayer services or "hours," as distinct from the Mass. Vespers, from the Latin *vespera* (evening), is the seventh of these and is held at sunset. We do not know of any particular occasion for which this lovely and joyous work was written. Its title tells us that it is designed to fit the Vespers service for a day on which a confessor saint is celebrated.[1] There are many of these, and nothing gives us any more detailed clues. The Vespers liturgy differs slightly according to whether the confessor was a pope or not. The choice of texts here indicates the latter.

The musical portion of a Vespers service for nonpapal confessors includes settings of Psalms 110, 111, 112, 113, and 117, plus the *Magnificat* canticle from chapter I of the Gospel of Luke. The exquisite jewel in this bright and attractive work is the setting of Psalm 117, *Laudate Dominum*, a soprano solo familiar to many who have never heard a note of the context in which it occurs. The music, which moves in a gentle 6/8 meter, anticipates both the "Incarnatus" in the C-Minor Mass and Susanna's "Deh vieni, non tardar" in *Le nozze di Figaro*. The family resemblance to the latter is uncanny and especially lovely, down to the sighing violins at "Laudate eum." The chorus takes over for the Doxology— "Gloria Patri et Filio et Spiritui Sancto"—and the solo soprano returns for the final "Amen." The music abounds in beautiful detail, such as the not-quite-exact doubling of the chorus sopranos by the violins at "Sicut erat in principio" and "saecula." And only in this movement of the *Vesperae* is the bassoon emancipated from being just part of the bass apparatus and given an expressive obbligato.

Mozart spent some time in Munich at the beginning of 1781 in order to supervise the first performances of his opera *Idomeneo*, a commission from the Elector Carl Theodor. Increasingly unhappy in Salzburg, he hoped to parlay the success of *Idomeneo* into a permanent appointment in Munich and thought to strengthen his position by providing an example of his skill at church music, a *Kyrie eleison*, K. 341. Nothing came of Mozart's hopes for Munich, but the *Kyrie* is one of his most powerful compositions in any genre. It is in D minor, the key later associated with the darkness and the passions of the Piano Concerto, K. 466, *Don Giovanni*, and finally the unfinished Requiem. The plea for mercy is dramatic and intense, and the

---

[1]In the early history of the church, confessors were those who asserted their faith even when doing so was dangerous, but who did not actually become martyrs. From about the fourth century on, the term was applied more generally to those who had lived a life of heroism and virtue, and had died a holy but peaceful death.

sound itself—four-part chorus, with an orchestra of pairs of woodwinds with four horns, two trumpets, organ, and strings—is magnificent.

And finally there is the *Ave, verum corpus*, K. 618, whose manuscript is dated 18 June 1791. It was Mozart's first piece of sacred music since abandoning the C-Minor Mass in 1783. Here is another perfect jewel, this one cut for Anton Stoll, a choirmaster at Baden, the spa town outside Vienna where Mozart's wife took a number of cures in this, the last year of the composer's life. The liturgical occasion would be the summer feast of Corpus Christi, the Thursday following Trinity Sunday.

Futile as it is, we sometimes find ourselves wondering where Mozart would have gone musically had he lived longer. A specific question: Was he perhaps, as his last piano concerto, the *Ave, verum corpus*, and parts of *The Magic Flute* suggest, on his way to a simpler manner?[2] The *Ave, verum corpus* is the essence of utter simplicity. The harmonies are plain, the texture hardly less so, yet in his whole life—chronologically so short, artistically so long—Mozart never invented anything more affecting than these forty-six perfect measures.

Mass in C Minor, K. 427(417a)

Mozart worked on his C-Minor Mass in 1782–1783 and led the first performance of the Kyrie, Gloria, Sanctus, and Benedictus at Saint Peter's, Salzburg, on 23 October 1783.

Two soprano, tenor, and bass solos; mixed chorus divided variously into four, five, and eight parts. Flute, two oboes, two bassoons, two horns, two trumpets, three trombones, timpani, organ, and strings.

The Requiem is the most famous of Mozart's many unfinished works, but the Mass in C Minor is no less veiled in mystery. Why was it not finished? We know that death cut off work on the Requiem. We know that Mozart stopped work on the Concerto for Violin and Piano, 315f, and the Sinfonia Concertante for Violin, Viola, and Cello, K. 320e, because the concerts for which they were intended were canceled for court

---

[2]The exact same question, also forever unanswerable, is brought to mind by Beethoven's very last works.

mourning. Sometimes we can make an intelligent guess, surmising, for example, that the C-Major Suite for Piano, K. 385i(399), often called "Suite in the Manner of Handel," was a style-study that had served its purpose when Mozart broke off after the Courante. As for the C-Minor Mass, Alfred Einstein, one of the twentieth century's most important Mozart scholars, blames it on Mozart's wife, pointing out that virtually all the works written for or associated with Constanze are unfinished. That is true, but Einstein's Mozart biography glows in the dark with its author's dislike of Constanze, his almost equal contempt for her sister Aloysia, the one Mozart had really wanted to marry in the first place, and his even greater loathing for their mother. Fascinating, but as an explanation not good enough.

Here, in brief, is what we know about the history of the C-Minor Mass. We need to go back to 1777, when Mozart, then twenty-one, visited Mannheim and fell thunderously in love with the fifteen-year-old Aloysia Weber. Aloysia, whose disorganized father worked as a singer and copyist, was already on her way to becoming a brilliant soprano— Mozart later wrote one of the bravura parts in *The Impresario* for her as well as seven other arias—and there is no doubt that her musical accomplishment and promise were crucial in inspiring Mozart's passion. But when Mozart and Aloysia met again a year later in Munich, where she and her father were now employed, she made it clear that she was not interested.

Then, in the spring of 1781, when Mozart made his permanent move from Salzburg to Vienna, he found that the Webers had preceded him to the capital, Aloysia as a singer and her father, who had meanwhile died, as a box-office clerk.[1] For five months Mozart lodged at the Webers', discovering that Aloysia was even now not a matter of indifference to him and coming actually to welcome the protection afforded by her husband's vigilance. (Aloysia's husband was Joseph Lange, whose unfinished portrait of Mozart is the most sensitive that has come down to us.)

Frau Weber, meanwhile, maneuvered Mozart and her third daughter, Constanze, also a soprano of some promise, toward marriage. Mozart's father was, as always, ready with advice, animadversions, and warnings. Wolfgang's and Constanze's wedding day, 4 August 1782, was the end of an exhausting trail. Not even the real end, because the task of reconciling old Leopold Mozart was not easy and not over: his formal consent arrived

---

[1]The eldest Weber daughter, Josepha, also a soprano, was the first Queen of the Night in *The Magic Flute.*

the day after the ceremony. Out of that background came Mozart's vow to compose a Mass for performance in Salzburg on his and Constanze's first visit.

Mozart began the composition in the summer of 1782, and on 4 January 1783 reported to his father that he had "the score of half a Mass . . . lying here waiting to be finished." (Other projects that occupied him about this time included the "Haffner" Symphony, the C-Minor Serenade for Wind Instruments, the Piano Concertos, K. 413–415, and the first three of the six string quartets dedicated to Haydn.) The trouble is that "half a Mass" is still all we have. It is possible that Mozart finished the work between January 1783 and his and Constanze's visit to Salzburg that October, and that most of the Credo and Agnus Dei are lost. Certainly there was no trace of these movements in 1840 when the score was first published. It is also possible that he never took the work beyond the halfway stage, and that at the Salzburg performance in October he filled in with other music, presumably from Masses of his own. The performance of an incomplete Mass in a liturgical setting would have been unthinkable. That even the "complete" movements are not always quite finished—they run from beginning to end, but are missing lines and parts in the "Credo," "Incarnatus," and "Osanna"—suggests that the latter hypothesis is more likely.

At any rate, a fragment it is, and we are faced not only with the frustration of missing what would have been Mozart's grandest and boldest setting of a sacred text, but also with the vexing question of "What happened?" That question is unanswerable and will remain so except in the unlikely event that the missing movements show up. Still, it is hard to refrain from wondering, and Einstein's observation about the works for Constanze is not to be dismissed.

This problem also wants to be considered in the light of Mozart's attitude toward religion. He was a religious man, but he was not, most of his life, an intensely believing or devoutly observing Catholic; George Bernard Shaw's remark that *The Magic Flute* was Mozart's great religious composition is not frivolous. But shortly after his wedding, Mozart wrote to his father: "For quite a time we have gone to Mass and confession and communion together, and I found that I have never prayed so fervently or confessed or communicated so devoutly as at [Constanze's] side, and it was the same for her." This is not Mozart's usual tone, and, aside from speculating that Mozart was writing to placate and please his father—always something to keep in mind when reading his letters—it may be that some months into his marriage his observances cooled into their previous less-fervent and less-devout temperature, with the consequence that he found it impossible to continue

with his only liturgical work written not on commission or contract but
ex voto.

Another line of investigation concerns the music itself. It is obvious
that the C-Minor Mass embraces an extraordinary diversity of style and
manner, whose extremes could be defined by the severity of the Handelian "Qui tollis" and the "Cum Sancto Spiritu" fugue at one end of the
spectrum and the operatically virtuosic and sensuous "Et incarnatus est"
at the other. Seventeen-eighty-two was the critical year in which Mozart
got to know the music of Handel and Johann Sebastian Bach, an event that
brought about an enormous stretching of his musical language through
the addition of the resources of Baroque contrapuntal technique to the
galant manner he had inherited from Bach's youngest son, Johann Christian, and others of that generation.[2] The end result of that fusion was the
easy, totally integrated contrapuntal mastery of the late piano concertos,
operas, and symphonies.

But before there could be a first movement of the C-Major Piano
Concerto, K. 503, or of the "Prague" Symphony, Mozart had to find his
way in a series of works in which he tried his hand at the newfound old
style and explored its possibilities. It meant that for awhile he wrote
fugues—compositions, in other words, in which the Baroque element
was isolated rather than wed to and absorbed into Mozart's normal language. It also led him to the occasional curious style-exercises like the
Handelian keyboard suite I mentioned earlier. Psychiatrists might be glad
to know that, around this time, Mozart also composed a solidly chordal
Marche funèbre del Sigr Maestro Contrapuncto.[3]

Mozart's "Baroque" works include, along with a few dry pieces,
some unfinished ones: an exercise had served its purpose, or Mozart saw
that he was on an unprofitable tack, or, maneuvering about strange territory, he was simply perplexed by the question of how to continue. It is
not difficult to imagine him, early in 1783, looking through the growing
pile of manuscript pages of the C-Minor Mass, scratching his head,
wondering where in the world this monster wanted to go, and then, in
the absence of a strong inner compulsion to move forward, deciding either to put off thinking about the problem for a while or to abandon the
project then and there. After all, there was so much else to do, and
surely the problem of what to perform in Salzburg would solve itself
somehow.

[2]For more on Mozart's encounter with the music of J. S. Bach and Handel, see the Haydn essay,
The Two Great Oratorios, p. 159.
[3]Mozart wrote this into the album of Barbara Ployer, his student in piano and counterpoint,
perhaps at the party to celebrate her performance of his G-Major Piano Concerto, K. 453, at her
father's house on 13 June 1784.

The music of the C-Minor Mass makes one additional appearance in Mozart's career. In January 1785 the Viennese Society of Musicians asked him for a choral work to be sung at a pair of concerts in March. He was extremely busy that winter: his father was visiting Vienna, as was Haydn; there were the two quartet sessions at which his six quartets dedicated to Haydn were introduced; and, not least, between New Year's and mid-March he took part in eleven public concerts, which included the premieres of the just completed D-Minor and C-Major Concertos, K.466 and 467. Even Mozart would have had to practice hard. No wonder he had to tell the society he would be unable to produce a whole new Psalm as promised. To meet his obligation, he took the Kyrie and Gloria of the C-Minor Mass, which had not yet been heard outside Salzburg, added two arias and an insert for solo voices before the final chorus, and adapted the whole to Italian verse-paraphrases of the Penitential Psalms (these were the work of Lorenzo da Ponte, later celebrated as Mozart's librettist for *Le nozze di Figaro*, *Don Giovanni*, *and Così fan tutte*). And thus it was that *Davidde penitente*, K. 469, came into being.

There is a curious postscript to the story of *Davidde penitente*. When the English composer Vincent Novello and his wife visited Mozart's widow and son in Salzburg in 1829, one of their many questions concerned that work, and Novello recorded this in his travel diary: "The 'Davidde penitente' originally a grand Mass which [Mozart] wrote in consequence of a vow that he made to do so, on [his wife's] safe recovery after the birth of their first child—relative to whom he had been particularly anxious. This Mass was performed in the Cathedral at Salzburg and Madame Mozart herself sang all the principal solos." It is interesting that Constanze Nissen, as she was by then, failed to remember that the vow concerned not the birth of a child but her husband's bringing her to his home town as his bride—her forgetfulness the counterpart of Mozart's failure to finish the Mass.

In many respects the C-Minor Mass stands in isolation in Mozart's church music. Its greatness is anticipated only in the isolated D-Minor *Kyrie*, K. 341, written for Munich in 1781, and afterward Mozart set no more sacred Latin texts until the *Ave, verum corpus*, K. 618, and the Requiem, both in the last months of his life. Moreover, the C-Minor Mass is uniquely expansive in scale: complete, it would amount to more than an hour and a half of music. Mozart's procedure is to take clauses of text and turn them into separate arias, ensembles, or choruses. Bach's B-Minor Mass is the example more familiar to us now of such a setting, but Mozart would have known models by Austrian church musicians of his own generation and the one preceding.

* * *

The gentler major-mode soprano solo for the "Christe eleison" relieves the deep solemnity of the "Kyrie eleison." The solo writing here and later tells us that Constanze was no mean singer: formidable feats are asked in range, including a downward extension to A below middle C (*Figaro's* Susanna has the same bottom note), and the singer is expected to have a perfect command of large skips, arpeggios, scales, and chains of trills. Mozart was something of a vocal coach to Constanze, and her "Christe eleison" solo in fact includes phrases from a vocal solfège exercise he had written for her a couple of years before.

The Gloria is a brilliant C-major trumpets-and-drums chorus, but with room for a more yielding music in response to "bonae voluntatis." It ends quietly, preparing the way for the florid soprano aria on "Laudamus te." The "Gratias agimus tibi" chorus, with its dotted rhythms and pungent harmonies, looks back to the Baroque. Mozart also expands the sonority by writing for a five-part chorus with two sections of sopranos. "Domine Deus," a duet, is archaic in its spare polyphony, but toward the end, when the soprano voices cross so that we hear two high B-flats and then two A's in succession, but sung by the women in alternation, we have one of Mozart's most seductive moments of sheer sensuous beauty. "Qui tollis" is Handelian in the grandest way—a magnificent double chorus with splendidly imagined tensions between the sustained vocal lines and the sharply dotted rhythms in the strings. The harmonies become intensely chromatic, and this moment is one of the summits of classical church music. The "Quoniam trio" and the fugue on "Cum Sancto Spiritu"— the two separated by a huge outburst on the name "Jesu Christe"—join brilliance to learning.

With the Credo, things get problematic for the editor and the conductor because now there are obvious gaps. For all intents and purposes the C-Minor Mass had disappeared into oblivion during the nineteenth century, although its curious pendant *Davidde penitente* continued to show up in performance every once in a while. In 1901, the Mass surfaced again and became known to modern audiences when it was performed in Dresden in an edition by Alois Schmitt and Ernst Lewicki. The Schmitt-Lewicki edition supplements Mozart's incomplete score with music from other works by Mozart and by the early-eighteenth-century composer and organist Johann Ernst Eberlin.

For the Mozart bicentennial in 1956, H. C. Robbins Landon prepared an edition, published by Breitkopf & Härtel, in which he filled in some of the gaps. He approached his task as a scholar, doing only the minimum of what would make the incomplete movements work in performance. In 1986, as a supplement to the complete critical edition of

Mozart's works (*Neue Mozart-Ausgabe*), Bärenreiter commissioned a version from the Salzburg composer Helmut Eder, who, as the title page has it, "reconstructed and completed" the "Credo," "Et incarnatus est," "Sanctus," and "Osanna." Eder was in effect asked to do what Mozart's pupil Franz Xaver Süssmayr had done for the Requiem, what Franco Alfano did for Puccini's *Turandot*, and what Deryck Cooke (and others) did for the Mahler Tenth Symphony, to name a few of the most famous examples. Eder approached the job as a composer, not with the intention of placing his own stamp on the Mass as, for example, Mozart did when he made his wonderful and thoroughly un-Handelian edition of *Messiah*, but using his invention and skill to go beyond the minimum and, when necessary, to do some real composing.

The "Credo in unum Deum" is another movement in vigorous trumpets-and-drums C-major style, even though those instruments themselves are for the moment absent. Here it is especially the second-violin and viola parts that have to be supplied as well as almost all the orchestration for the closing measures.

"Et incarnatus est" is one of the greatest pages in Mozart, and one that has given offense to those who believe sacred music is one thing and secular another. Mozart has written a sublime quartet for Constanze (though she did not get to sing it in Salzburg) with flute, oboe, and bassoon, accompanied by soft strings and organ. In a completely formal manner, the music draws to a halt on a six-four chord, that unmistakable sound that introduces cadenzas in Classical concertos, and the quartet does indeed take off on a most beautiful, fully written-out cadenza, concluding trill and all. In this aria—Susanna goes to church—Mozart puts brilliance to work in the service of lyric ecstasy. Here, too, the string parts are missing from the first vocal entrance until after the cadenza, and Eder has written parts modeled on Mozart's own introductory measures rather than contenting himself with the simple punctuating chords in Schmitt-Lewicki and Robbins Landon. Mozart's autograph has two unused and unmarked staves. The Bärenreiter editors have speculated that these were perhaps intended for French horns, and Eder has supplied a few measures for those instruments. I must say that I find his realization beautiful.[4]

Nothing further exists of the Credo; the next movement, therefore, is the Sanctus. This is another grand piece for double chorus, though in fact most of Chorus II is missing from the sources and has had to be supplied. The Benedictus gives us the sound of the full solo quartet for

---

[4]It can be heard on recordings by Claudio Abbado (Sony Classical) and Helmuth Rilling (Haenssler).

the first time, and it leads to a reprise of the joyous double-chorus "Os-anna." And there it ends.

Requiem, K. 626

Mozart worked on his Requiem during the second half of 1791. His labors proceeded in three stages. He began in July or early August, inter-rupting himself in late August to supervise and conduct the premiere of *La clemenza di Tito* in Prague. He resumed work at the end of September, but stopped in mid-October at the behest of his wife, who, worried about both his physical and mental well-being and, associating his condition with his growing obsession with the Requiem, took the score away from him. He returned to it one last time at the end of November and may still have been at work on the score as late as 3 December, two days before his death. The first movement—in two sections, "Requiem aeternam" and "Kyrie eleison"—was sung at a Requiem Mass for Mozart in Saint Michael's Church, Vienna, on 10 December 1791, five days after his death. Almost certainly it was Mozart's Requiem as completed by his student Franz Xaver Süssmayr that was performed in Vienna on 2 January 1793 at a benefit concert for the composer's widow and two sons, arranged by Baron Gottfried van Swieten. For certain, the work was performed—under strange circumstances, of which more below—in Wiener Neustadt on 14 December 1793.

Soprano, alto, tenor, and bass solos; four-part chorus. Two basset horns, two bassoons, two trumpets, three trombones, timpani, organ, and strings.

Moviegoers' alert: Antonio Salieri had nothing to do with it. Thanks to the activities of a long succession of persons, from Franz Count von Walsegg, Constanze Mozart, and Franz Xaver Süssmayr in the 1790s to Peter Shaffer and Milos Forman nearly two hundred years later, no musi-cal composition has had its history so befogged in myth and error as Mozart's Requiem. These people—and many others I have not named here—were motivated variously by vanity; plain dishonesty; the need for money; fading or excessively inventive memories; hatred of Jews, Jesuits, and Freemasons; faulty scholarship; and artistic exuberance. Of the many obfuscators en route, one who merits particular mention is Alexan-der Pushkin, whose 1830 play *Mozart and Salieri,* made into an opera by

Rimsky-Korsakov in 1898, gave wide currency and even a certain respectability to the already-current slander that Salieri had poisoned his younger rival.

The unfinished state of the Requiem together with the desire to perform and hear it has also given employment to several generations of musicians and scholars, from Süssmayr, who was probably right there at Mozart's deathbed, to two other composers in Mozart's circle, Franz Jakob Freystädtler and Joseph Leopold Eybler, and on to such present-day figures as Franz Beyer, Duncan Druce, H. C. Robbins Landon, Robert Levin, and Richard Maunder, all of whom have tried to turn what Mozart left at his death into a practicable edition of the Requiem. "Confusion" hardly begins to do justice to the situation.

Let me begin with what we know for sure. The first event is the death on 14 February 1791 of the twenty-year-old Countess Anna von Walsegg. Her husband, Franz Count von Walsegg, then twenty-seven, wished to commemorate her with two monuments, one in marble and granite, for which he paid the sculptor Johann Martin Fischer three thousand florins, and a Requiem Mass by Mozart. The price for the Requiem, proposed by the composer and agreed to by the count's agent, was 225 florins, or 50 ducats, about half the fee Mozart usually got for an opera. Twenty-five ducats were paid down, with the remainder to come upon delivery of the score. Too much has changed in economic structures to make a sensible translation into modern dollar values, but perhaps it helps to cite Andrew Steptoe's account in H. C. Robbins Landon's *Mozart Compendium*, according to which "tradespeople and middle-class professionals would receive 200–1000 fl. [annually], while large merchants and senior government officials would have earned between 1,000 and 10,000 fl."

Now the complications begin. Count Walsegg liked to commission works secretly in order eventually to present them under his own name. He particularly enjoyed having them performed anonymously, then asking his friends to guess the composer. Most of them knew their role in this game. Because this was his plan for the Requiem, the commission was tendered to Mozart with the stipulation that he must not attempt to uncover its source. The man who called at Mozart's lodgings at 970 Rauhensteingasse in the center of Vienna sometime in the summer of 1791 to make the arrangement did not identify himself, but was probably a clerk in the office of Walsegg's lawyer. Now myth and fantasy enter the picture as well. Someone, in telling the story, costumed the messenger in a gray cloak, and someone invented a tale that this "gray messenger" appeared just as the Mozarts were about to leave for Prague for the premiere of *La clemenza di Tito* at the end of August, plucked at Constanze Mozart's skirt, and in sinister tones whispered, "What about the Requiem?"

The second half of 1791 was a busy time for Mozart. As well as getting *La clemenza di Tito* ready for performance on 6 September as part of the festivities surrounding the coronation of Emperor Leopold II as king of Bohemia, he had to finish *The Magic Flute*, begun earlier in the year, in time for its premiere in Vienna on 30 September. Early in October Mozart also completed a clarinet concerto for his friend Anton Stadler. In addition, he took a break from the Requiem by writing a cantata to celebrate the opening of a new temple for his Masonic lodge. It is an appropriately bright piece, the handwriting in the manuscript is firm and sure, and everyone loved it when it was sung on 17 November. It was the last item he entered in the catalogue of his works he had kept up scrupulously since 1784.

Mozart enjoyed the success of *The Magic Flute*, conducting the first performance and going to several others, sometimes taking his mother-in-law, his son Karl, and various friends, among them Salieri, the soprano Caterina Cavalieri, and the cheese merchant Joseph Leutgeb, who was also the virtuoso for whom he had written his horn concertos. He was pleased that it was hard even for him to get tickets. He was busy with a heap of projects and full of good resolutions about keeping the family finances on a more even keel.

At the same time, he had not felt consistently well since returning from Prague in mid-September and, by no means for the first time, he was occasionally depressed. At moments he was convinced that he was being poisoned by *acqua toffana*, a slow-acting mixture of arsenic, antimony, and lead. It was in one of these low periods that Constanze Mozart took the score of the Requiem away, not least because from time to time Mozart was gripped by the idea that he was writing the work for his own death. Around 20 November, he felt sick enough to take to his bed, and at the beginning of December his illness became suddenly acute, with high fever, projectile vomiting, and swelling and inflammation of hands and feet to the point of near-immobilization. Most scholars now accept the diagnosis of acute rheumatic fever proposed by Carl Bär in his book *Mozart: Krankheit, Tod, Begräbnis* (Mozart: Illness, Death, and Funeral), but new theories will undoubtedly keep coming along. Mozart died at 12:55 A.M. on 5 December and was buried at the Saint Marx Cemetery late the following day or possibly early in the morning on the seventh.

Much picturesque detail has accumulated about Mozart's last days, and because most of it entered the literature years after his death we cannot always distinguish history from invention. It may well be true that parts of the Requiem were sung at Mozart's bedside the day before his death by a group that included Constanze Mozart, Süssmayr, Mozart's sister-in-law Josepha Hofer, Benedikt Schak, and Franz Xaver Gerl (re-spectively, the last three were the Queen of the Night, Tamino, and Saras-tro in *The Magic Flute*). Mozart's other sister-in-law, Sophie Haibel, recounts that in the last hours he mimicked timpani passages from the Requiem with his mouth. The reliability of that is more difficult to as-sess, as is the story of the delirium in which he thought himself at a *Magic Flute* performance ("Quiet! Hofer is just taking her high F!"), but both stories are firmly entrenched in Mozart Requiem mythology.

Then there is the hard-to-demolish myth about Mozart's funeral, in-vesting with immense pathos his interment in an unmarked group grave instead of, as George Bernard Shaw wrote, "having a respectable vault all to himself to moulder in for the edification of the British tourist." This simply reflects ignorance of Viennese burial customs during the reign of the austere Joseph II. In his Mozart biography, Maynard Solomon also makes the point that the family, intensely concerned for the composer's welfare in those last days, are likely to have known what kind of funeral he wanted—or did not want. Nicolas Slonimsky, by the simple expedient of checking the records of the Vienna meteorological bureau, invalidated the long-cherished story that the weather on the day of the funeral was so bad that visitors had to turn back before the coffin reached the gravesite. (A still better version I read as a child amends this to "everyone except Mozart's little dog.") But the story itself, with its invocation of the pa-thetic fallacy, is characteristic of this kind of myth-making—"tapping into underlying archaic verities," as Solomon puts it.[1]

The immediate practical question right after Mozart's death was what to do about getting a score of the Requiem to Walsegg so that Con-stanze could claim the second half of the commission fee, everyone as-suming that the count would only pay for a complete work. Who was to do what Mozart had left undone? Just one section was truly complete, the opening "Requiem aeternam," but what the "Kyrie" needed was so clear as to present no problem. Mozart's pupil and friend Freystädtler—kidded and immortalized in a delightful Mozart canon, *Lieber Freystädtler, lieber Gaulimauli*, K. 232(509a)—was able to perform that task in time for the memorial service five days after the composer's death. But for the "Dies irae," "Tuba mirum," "Rex tremendae majestatis," "Recor-dare," "Confutatis maledictis," "Lacrimosa," "Domine Jesu," and "Hos-tias," Mozart left only fragments in various stages of completeness. In some cases one can more or less infer how things ought to go on, and for-tunately at least the vocal parts exist for most of those movements, but

---

[1]See, for example, the discussion of the supposed eclipse at Jesus' crucifixion in Dominic Crossan's *Who Killed Jesus?* (Harper Collins, 1995).

the "Lacrimosa" breaks off completely after only nine wondrously beautiful measures. And from the Sanctus to the end—Sanctus, Benedictus, Agnus Dei, "Lux aeterna," and "Cum sanctis tuis"—we have nothing at all. A formidable lot of work needed to be done, and done well enough to persuade von Walsegg of seamless continuity.

Constanze Mozart first turned to Freystädtler, who had helped out with the *Kyrie*, but he wanted no further part of the project. She next asked Joseph Leopold Eybler, a student of Mozart's and in his day a highly regarded composer.[2] He accepted, promising to finish the score by the middle of Lent, but he soon withdrew, either because he got cold feet at the thought of continuing, to say nothing of "completing," Mozart's fragmentary beginnings, or because he was too busy with projects of his own. (By strange chance, his public career came to an end in 1833 when he suffered a stroke while conducting Mozart's Requiem.)

Enter the twenty-five-year-old Franz Xaver Süssmayr. A fairly recent acquaintance who had begun studying with Mozart in 1791, he was a not-excessively-gifted pupil, but he had made himself useful by writing some of the *secco* recitatives in *La clemenza di Tito* when Mozart saw himself beginning to run out of time. Süssmayr, who would also die young (in 1803, at thirty-seven), later had some success as an opera composer, but his work on the Requiem, an endeavor that would have been a challenge to a far-more-talented and experienced musician, shows him to be slipshod in technique and certainly inadequate in invention.

At least, though, he was willing, and he did what needed to be done.[3] He completed his task in February 1792, having newly copied all the pages Mozart himself had written so as not to arouse von Walsegg's suspicion with a score in two different handwritings. Two copies of Süssmayr's score were made for Constanze Mozart. Possibly with Constanze's encouragement, Süssmayr muddied the waters by forging Mozart's signature on the manuscript and, oddly, dating it 1792.

In February 1800, Süssmayr told the story of his involvement with the Requiem in a letter, not free of self-serving exaggeration, to the publisher Breitkopf & Härtel, who had recently begun an *Oeuvres complettes* of Mozart. He wrote, in part: "The task was finally referred to me because it was known that during Mozart's lifetime I had often played and sung through the finished movements with him, that he had frequently

[2]Eybler sometimes gets a footnote because a Viennese critic, reviewing and disliking Beethoven's *Eroica* at its first performance, held up a symphony of Eybler's as an example of how to do this sort of thing so much better.

[3]For a somewhat similar story, see my account in *The Symphony: A Listener's Guide* (Oxford University Press, 1995) of the various attempts to produce a performable edition of Mahler's unfinished Symphony No. 10.

discussed the working out of this piece with me, and that he had indicated to me the basis and plan for his instrumentation." Again, it is hard to assess exactly how true all this is. Süssmayr explains that Mozart's last completed verse was "qua resurget ex favilla" (the second line of the "Lacrimosa"), and that he, Süssmayr, had completed the "Dies irae" and Offertorium from sketches, but that the Sanctus, Benedictus, and Agnus Dei were "ganz neu von mir." In order to give the work a sense of unity and, as he claimed, in accordance with Mozart's instructions, he repeated the "Kyrie" fugue for the concluding "cum sanctis tuis in aeternum." That would actually have been in accordance with the custom of many Requiem composers at this time.

As for Count Walsegg, he made a manuscript copy of his own from the Süssmayr score and labeled it *Requiem composto del Conte Walsegg*. On 14 December 1793, he himself led what he believed, probably erroneously, to be the first performance at the Cistercian monastery in Wiener Neustadt.

No one has been completely happy with the Mozart-Süssmayr Requiem. Süssmayr's pages have faults of voice-leading and grammar, perhaps attesting to the deadline pressure he was under; in any case, few of us have ears so delicate as to be offended by his occasional parallel fifths and octaves. What is more frustrating to the attentive listener is the feebleness of his invention. We would of course feel that less if we did not constantly have Mozart right at hand to measure it against. Even so, not until the last quarter of the twentieth century were serious attempts made to come up with alternatives to Süssmayr; today, however, a conductor planning a performance of the Requiem has a quite a choice of completions, continuations, performing versions, or whatever you want to call them.

Interestingly, the Süssmayr version has never lost its primacy. Conductors of the generation of Victor de Sabata and Bruno Walter had no practical alternatives in print, and apparently it did not occur to any of them to try something on their own.[4] Among the more recent champions of Süssmayr are Claudio Abbado, Leonard Bernstein, Sir Colin Davis, Carlo Maria Giulini, Bernard Haitink, Herbert von Karajan, Sir Neville Marriner, Sir Georg Solti, and Michael Tilson Thomas, and the list even includes conductors with more than a passing interest in textual and other musicological questions, among them William Christie, Sir John Eliot Gardiner, and Andrew Parrott.

[4]De Sabata was a composer of some skill, and Walter certainly had some competence in that area. Sir Thomas Beecham, that intrepid fixer-up of Handel, never published an edition of the Requiem, but he prepared one for his own use and recorded it in 1956. Its most eccentric feature—within a context of relative chastity—is the replacement in the "Tuba mirum" of the trombone by a solo cello.

If we wonder about Süssmayr's continuing hold, we would have to conclude that his authority rests on the fact that he was, after all, in steady and often close contact with Mozart in 1791, and on his claim that many of his decisions were based on verbal instructions from Mozart as well as, less certainly, on Constanze Mozart's assertions years after the event that she had turned over to him various scraps of paper with drafts and sketches by Mozart. And Christoph Wolff gives us something to think about when he writes in his valuable book *Mozart's Requiem*:

> The manuscript that was delivered to Count Walsegg has remained to this day the last witness—the only surviving and incorruptible witness—of the confusion that reigned in the days immediately before and after Mozart's death. And this score is unique in representing and embodying in its physical fabric the original and essential musical truth of the unfinished work. In its often abrupt opposition and imperfect union of the finished and the unfinished, it draws us spellbound into the situation of the last days of 1791; into the oppression weighing upon Mozart's family and friends as they looked on the unfinished Requiem and faced the responsibility of dealing with their daunting musical legacy—only too conscious that they could not do it.

The principal alternatives to Süssmayr, whose score was presented in exemplary fashion in 1877 by Johannes Brahms in the old Breitkopf & Härtel complete Mozart edition, are the versions by Franz Beyer (Kunzelmann, 1979), H. C. Robbins Landon (Breitkopf & Härtel, 1987), R.C.F. Maunder (Oxford University Press, 1988), and Robert Levin (Haenssler, 1994).[5] Of these, Beyer's and Robbins Landon's are the most conservative, sticking most closely to Süssmayr, and Maunder's is the most interventionist. I shall comment on these as I go through the movements of the Requiem.

The opening is a marvel. It makes one ache to think what the Requiem might have become. Against an accompaniment of quiet, detached single notes and chords in the strings, two bassoons and two basset horns weave a tissue of sustained lines.[6] Tenderly expressive dissonances occur in their crisscrossing. The music is dark in color, prayerful, and deeply private. I also sense here the presence of Mozart the dramatist, the opera

[5]Recordings become unavailable and new ones appear all the time, but even so, I hope it is useful to the inquisitive to say that the Robbins Landon version has been recorded by Roy Goodman (Nimbus) and Bruno Weil (Sony), Maunder's by Christopher Hogwood (L'Oiseau-Lyre), and Levin's by Martin Pearlman (Telarc).

[6]The basset horn is an alto clarinet, more delicate in sound, less chocolaty than the regular clarinet. It virtually vanished from the scene after Mozart, but beginning with Richard Strauss in *Elektra*, several twentieth-century composers found interesting and effective ways of using it.

composer with the uncanny gift of setting a character onstage through the suggestive power of an aria's orchestral introduction alone. The whole world of "Requiem aeternam dona eis, Domine" is here, completely here, before the choristers have uttered a word.

Then, in the eighth slow measure, we hear those first words, pronounced in a powerful *forte*, backed by trombones and the four woodwinds, the strings lending urgency to this utterance with their tense syncopations. The music becomes more lyrical, and the solo soprano intones the words "Te decet hymnus." She does so to a plainsong melody you might recognize because Bach also uses it in his *Magnificat*.

The movement gains in power as the strings accentuate the melody with tense dotted rhythms, finally to arrive at a quiet half-close.

The excitingly vigorous "Kyrie eleison" is Mozart's take on a Handelian choral fugue. The fugue subject itself is an eighteenth-century cliché. Two components shape it: the outline or at least the adumbration of a minor triad and a spiky descending diminished seventh. We can find examples of this in, among many others, Bach (the A-minor fugue in Book II of *The Well-tempered Clavier* as well as *The Musical Offering*), Handel ("And With His Stripes" in *Messiah*), and Haydn (Quartet in F minor, op. 20, no. 5).[7]

---

[7]The *Musical Offering* theme is not Bach's own but one handed to him by Frederick the Great of Prussia, a musical monarch who came up with an eloquent variant of a current cliché.

Mozart actually gives us a double fugue, an athletic subject in virtuosic sixteenth-notes running alongside the principal Handelian theme, and he works out the movement with overwhelming energy, strength, and sense of direction. The movement ends with a bow to "ancient music" in that the last chord is neither minor nor major but a stark open fifth, just D and A. And that is the last movement that is all—or virtually all—Mozart.

"Dies irae" is a fiery chorus. Mozart has left us the complete vocal part and enough of the string parts in the orchestra to guide us in filling out the rest. Doubling the choral lines with trombones is sound eighteenth-century church-music practice. Süssmayr has the woodwinds double the voices throughout as well and adds effective parts for trumpets and drums. Both Maunder and Robbins Landon conspicuously lighten the wind writing.

Mozart begins the "Tuba mirum," the depiction of the Last Trumpet calling the dead to judgment, with a stern summons in the voice of the trombone—fair enough, because the German Bible speaks of "die letzte Posaune" (the last trombone). Unlike Berlioz and Verdi, his great successors in Requiem-writing, Mozart does not give us a dramatic scene; rather, he has the bass sing a solemn declamatory aria, while the trombone adds a lyric (and difficult) obbligato. Moving into an impassioned F minor, the solo tenor picks up the text at "Mors stupebit," and it is here that Süssmayr makes his first serious mistake by keeping the trombone solo going: a double mistake because any reason in the text for the use of the trombone has now gone by and because what he gives the trombone to play is shapeless and weak. All the post-Süssmayr editors drop the trombone where Mozart's part for it leaves off and they lighten the woodwind parts.

The situation for "Rex tremendae majestatis" is much like that of the "Dies irae"; that is, we have complete vocal parts and, in the orchestra, complete bass and first-violin parts. Here is another movement of tremendous and exciting thrust. Again, recent editors lighten the wind parts by modifying Süssmayr's habit of having them double the voices mechanically.

In the "Recordare" we find the most intimate, personal text in the Requiem, and Mozart leads off with a beautiful, gentle weave of lines for the basset horns and strings. After that, we have complete vocal parts by Mozart and brief patches of orchestral writing at transitions and cadences. Robbins Landon and Levin again thin out Süssmayr's wind writing, but Maunder creates a richer, more colorful fabric. His idea is to use the orchestral style of the big works from 1791—*La clemenza di Tito* and *The Magic Flute*—as a model, but other scholars have condemned this as misguided because in late-eighteenth-century practice the orchestra is treated very differently in church and opera house, and thus Mozart is unlikely to have gone in this direction.

Like the "Rex tremendae majestatis," "Confutatis maledictis" splendidly alternates powerful assertions and poignant pleas. Levin does some welcome thinning out of Süssmayr's monotonous, mechanical orchestration; Maunder, strangely, cuts ten measures of authentic Mozart.

The "Lacrimosa" follows without a break. Mozart writes two bars of touching, sighing music for strings and gives us six wonderful measures of choral music with a beautifully imagined contrast between the lyric setting of the first three words and the chords that rise powerfully through an octave and a half on "qua resurget ex favilla judicandus homo reus." Except for the mechanically applied wind doublings, Süssmayr continues the movement quite effectively until the end, when he lets us down with a perfunctory two-chord "Amen." But both tradition and a sense of design demand something weightier here, namely a fugue. The confident and technically well-versed Levin, who has completed several Mozart torsos, supplies one all his own. It is an enjoyable movement, full of energy, with no departures from the language of the 1790s, but it is in a voice that is not Mozart's. Unlike all other editors, Maunder goes completely his own way from the point in the "Lacrimosa" where Mozart breaks off. He, too, ends the movement with a substantial new fugue, basing it on a Mozart fragment discovered in the 1960s and using the fugal passages in the F-Minor Fantasy for Mechanical Organ, K. 608, as a model for the continuation. Robbins Landon, standing by his conviction that Mozart's students, Freystädtler, Eybler, and Süssmayr, "are better equipped to complete Mozart's torso than a twentieth-century scholar, however knowledgeable," sticks with Süssmayr's simple two-chord "Amen." I vote for the fugal close.

The "Domine Jesu"—with vocal parts and instrumental bass line by Mozart—floats sweetly by, its simplicity bringing to mind that exquisite jewel from June 1791, the *Ave, verum corpus*, as well as certain elements of *The Magic Flute*. The key, E-flat major, in its relation to the harmonic landscape most of the Requiem has inhabited up to this point, also contributes to the impression of gentleness. Mozart makes beautifully poetic responses to the plea that the dead be saved from the mouth of the lion ("Libera eas de ore leonis") and the invocation of Saint Michael the standard-bearer. Both "ne absorbeat eas tartarus" and "Quam olim Abrahae" lead Mozart to write magnificently vigorous fugal music. A sudden moment of calming-down tells me that Mozart was remembering the magical close—"And the Lord hath lain on Him the iniquity of us all"— of "All We Like Sheep Have Gone Astray" in *Messiah*. The "Hostias" continues in the gentle spirit of the "Domine Jesu," and it leads to a reprise of the "Quam olim Abrahae" fugue.

With the arrival at the Sanctus, we are in trouble. We simply have no clue as to Mozart's intentions. Süssmayr provides some generically festive trumpets-and-drums music in D major, but both this and the "Osanna" fugue that follows are too short for so grandly laid out a work, and too perfunctory. Levin elaborates both the composition itself and the orchestral writing. Maunder's decision is the drastic one of simply omitting both the Sanctus and Benedictus and treating the Requiem as a torso like the C-Minor Mass. This, to me, is the most convincing solution.

The Benedictus, also all Süssmayr, is inclined to ramble. It is a pretty movement, though, as Viennese settings of this text before Beethoven's *Missa solemnis* tended to be. Süssmayr even begins with a musical idea of Mozart's, a phrase he wrote down in 1784 as part of a counterpoint exercise for his student Barbara Ployer. Levin again does what he can to fill Süssmayr's design in a richer, more interesting way. A needless clumsiness, neatly remedied by Levin, is Süssmayr's idea of recapitulating the "Osanna" in B-flat, the key of the Benedictus, instead of in its original key of D.

The Agnus Dei is also all Süssmayr, touching in many details, such as the mournfully expressive string figure that runs through the first eight bars, but it is ill-composed over all. Levin helps by furnishing new string parts. Maunder escapes Süssmayr by using music from the Gloria of Mozart's 1775–1776 Mass in G, K. 220.

For the conclusion, Süssmayr seems to have had clear instructions from Mozart. Accordingly, he goes back to the beginning of the work (actually to measure 19) for the "Lux aeterna," and sets the "Cum sanctis tuis" to the great Handelian fugue we first heard as "Kyrie eleison." And so Mozart does at least have the last word.

Carl Orff

Carl Orff was born on 10 July 1895 in Munich and died there on 29 March 1982.

Carmina burana, Cantiones profanae cantoribus et choris cantandae comitantibus instrumentis atque imaginibus magicis

Orff composed *Carmina burana* in 1935–1936. It was first presented on 8 June 1937 in a production staged by Otto Wälterlin at the Frankfurt Opera, Bertil Wetzelsberger conducting, and with sets and costumes by Ludwig Sievert.

Soprano, tenor, and bass solos, with additional brief solo assignments for two tenors, baritone, and two basses; large mixed chorus, small mixed chorus, and boys' chorus. Three flutes (two doubling piccolo), three oboes (one doubling English horn), three clarinets (one doubling E-flat clarinet, one doubling bass clarinet), two bassoons and contrabassoon, four horns, three trumpets, three trombones, tuba, timpani, three glockenspiels, xylophone, castanets, ratchet, small bells, triangle, antique cymbals, crash cymbals, suspended cymbal, tam-tam, tubular bells, tambourine, snare drum, bass drum, celesta, two pianos, and strings.

Carmina burana—with the accent in *Carmina* falling on the first syllable—means "songs from Beuern," which is a variant of Bayern, the German name for Bavaria. And the rest: "Secular songs to be sung by singers and choruses to the accompaniment of instruments and also of magic pictures."

Beuern here refers specifically to Benediktbeuern, a village in the foothills of the Bavarian Alps about thirty miles south of Munich. It takes its name from a Benedictine monastery founded there in 733. When, as part of the arrangements in a newly forged alliance of Elector Maximilian IV Joseph with Napoleon, all Bavarian monasteries were secularized in 1803, the contents of their libraries went to the Court Library in Munich. In 1847, Johann Andreas Schmeller, the court librarian, published a modern edition of the most remarkable of these acquisitions, an ample and richly il-lustrated parchment manuscript of some three hundred anonymous poems from the thirteenth century, most of them in Latin, but a fair number in Middle High German, with some infusion of French and Greek. Schmeller invented the title *Carmina burana* for his edition. British and American readers first encountered *Carmina burana* in 1884 when the English histo-rian, poet, essayist, and biographer John Addington Symonds published a little volume he called *Wine, Women, and Song*, which included his fragrant translations of forty-six poems from the collection. Orff's lively cantata drew the attention of thousands more to these treasures, and in the 1950s, when Walter Lipphardt, a German scholar, deciphered and transcribed the original melodies, and when the Early Music Quartet and other such groups began to perform and record them, the circle was complete.

Orff encountered *Carmina burana* in Schmeller's edition (which is still in print) and enlisted the help of the poet Michel Hofmann in orga-nizing twenty-four of the poems into a libretto. He did not know the orig-inal melodies; in fact, he did not even know they existed. After the riotously successful premiere of his *Carmina* in 1937 he told the house of Schott, his sole publisher since 1927: "Everything I have written to date, and which you have, unfortunately, printed, can be destroyed. With *Carmina burana* my collected works begin."

He was just about to turn forty-two when he sent that letter. It had been a long, long upbeat. His family background was military; he himself was from childhood passionately interested in music, words, and theater. He got a story published in a children's magazine when he was ten, at which point he was already composing music to go with the puppet plays he had written for a theater he had built himself. He had lessons on the piano, organ, and cello, but his parents said no to the instrument he most wanted to play, the timpani. He had some guidance in composition from Anton Beer-Walbrunn and Hermann Zilcher, and in his middle twenties he studied for a while with Heinrich Kaminski, an interesting composer, but essentially he was self-taught.

He composed prolifically—pieces, one infers, of large ambition and originality of coloring; he worked in theaters in Munich, Mannheim, and Darmstadt as conductor and coach; he devoted much time to the study of Renaissance and early Baroque music as well as to music from Africa; he followed eagerly the development of modern dance, particularly the work of Mary Wigman; with Dorothee Günter he founded a school for music, dance, and gymnastics, making imaginative and productive contributions to music education that were eventually codified in the *Orff-Schulwerk*, published bit by bit beginning in 1930 in collaboration with several of his students; he made versions of several works by Monteverdi for the modern theater and staged such compositions as the *Saint Luke Passion* that was falsely attributed to J. S. Bach and the *Resurrection Oratorio* of Heinrich Schütz. His allegiance was to Expressionism. He absorbed every note of Schoenberg's *Five Pieces for Orchestra* and transcribed the Chamber Symphony No. 1 for piano duet. Franz Werfel was the center of his literary universe. A photograph from 1920 presents Orff to us as the embodiment of W. S. Gilbert's portrayal of Oscar Wilde in *Patience*:

> A most intense young man,
> A soulful-eyed young man,
> An ultra-poetical, super aesthetical,
> Out-of-the-way young man.

All his life, Orff sought privacy. Andreas Liess and Lilo Gersdorf, the authors of the two monographs on Orff published in his lifetime, both make a point of the composer's insistence on their sticking to the music and excluding the life: reading those two books, one would hardly guess that there was such a thing as the Third Reich and that political issues affected Orff's life in any way, then or afterward.[1]

As a man practiced in deceit (I don't know whether that included self-deception), Orff had good reason for his stance. He had a Jewish grandmother, but even so, without ever being an active, virulent Nazi, he found it easy to accommodate himself to the regime, signing letters with "Heil Hitler!" and refusing the offer of his American student Newell Jenkins to help him find a position in the United States. Having successfully deceived the Nazis about his grandmother, Orff was equally anxious after the war to reinvent his past, presenting himself as a victim of Nazi persecution and going so far as to claim that he had been a member of the

[1]Andreas Liess, *Carl Orff* (Atlantis, 1955); Lilo Gersdorf, *Carl Orff* (Rowohlt, 1981).

White Rose resistance group at the University of Munich, a fantastical fiction which not even his widow and daughter were willing to corroborate.

Orff's eagerness to provide new incidental music for A *Midsummer Night's Dream* when Mendelssohn's score had become racially unacceptable has been particularly resented, and it inevitably comes up in any discussion about him. His 1939 score, written for a production in Frankfurt, was in fact one of more than forty composed between 1933 and 1945, almost all of them by forgotten nonentities, Rudolf Wagner-Régeny coming closest to being an exception.

Some new scores for Shakespeare's comedy were commissioned and composed in the 1920s, when Mendelssohn's Romantic music did not suit new production styles then being explored in German theaters; however, as Fred Prieberg points out in his book *Musik im NS-Staat* (Fischer, 1982), it was not plausible after 1933 for a composer to claim that replacing Mendelssohn with a new *Midsummer Night's Dream* score was a purely artistic act innocent of any political implications.[2] After the war— and not surprisingly—we find Orff working to cover his tracks in the matter of the *Midsummer Night's Dream* music, describing what he wrote for Frankfurt in 1939 as the "third version," fudging the fact that the earlier "versions" were insubstantial sketches. Clearly, his intention was to minimize his response to the bid to supplant Mendelssohn. In their books, Liess and Gersdorf connive with him in this deception.[3]

As for Orff's artistic development, over which he also insisted on drawing a veil, we still have no clear knowledge of just what happened in 1935 on the road to Damascus when he came across Schmeller's *Carmina burana* collection and saw what manner of music he had to invent for those poems. The Pauline metaphor is hardly too strong for Orff's instant conversion from his previous compositional concerns to the audacious simplicities of *Carmina burana*. And it was a conversion for life. The "collected works" that begin with *Carmina burana*, almost all for voices and most of them for the stage, are varied in substance, intent, and effect, and they all stand upon the common principle that directness of speech and of access are paramount.

Carmina burana represents integration as well as revolution in Orff's life. The ideal of a direct physicality in music was already central to his

---

[2] Two composers who indignantly turned down *Midsummer Night's Dream* commissions for the purpose of replacing Mendelssohn were Hans Pfitzner, a strong nationalist and often outspokenly anti-Semitic, and Orff's student Werner Egk, not one of the most savory personalities on the German musical scene during those years.

[3] Orff and the other musicians who invented fictitious curricula vitae for the twelve years of the Thousand-Year Reich found ready allies among the musicologists and lexicographers, most of whom were themselves only too eager to rewrite their own life histories and work-lists.

educational endeavors, and he had explored the possibilities of medieval
theater in his adaptation of the *Saint Luke Passion*. He discovered a remarkable gift for writing tunes that sound as though they had always
been there. He leaned heavily on Stravinsky (*Les Noces* [*The Wedding*] and
Oedipus Rex are the principal source works), though removing the wit
and the delight in the unpredictable that make Stravinsky Stravinsky.

Since boyhood, when he had written his puppet theater music for an
ensemble of piano, violin, zither, glockenspiel, and the kitchen stove (literally), Orff had always enjoyed the coloristic side of composition, and
the orchestration lists, full of original and fantastical combinations, that
Liess gives in his book for the suppressed and destroyed pieces from
1912 on make fascinating reading. Orff scored *Carmina burana* with a
sure hand. Here, too—and often in later years—he looks to Stravinsky,
especially to the pianos and percussion of *The Wedding*, but he translates
Stravinsky's brilliant and imaginative economy into a prodigal generosity
with sonorities and confidently brought-off effects, rather like devising a
Les Noces coloring book.[4]

Orff had discovered a winning formula. *Carmina burana* enjoyed an
instant and clamorous public success, although the Nazi musical bureau-
cracy was at first nervous about the erotic tone of some of the poems
and, insofar as they were able to detect it, the Stravinsky influence.[5] Performances by von Karajan and Böhm helped spread the work's fame, and
when, after the war, it was able to get international circulation, it found
an audience it has never lost. *Carmina burana* is one of the few box office
certainties in twentieth-century music. The work also has a life on television and movie screens, with bits of it helping to advertise Nescafé and
Old Spice, and excerpts appearing in several films and trailers.

Undeniably, the constellation of aesthetic and historical considerations that "place" *Carmina burana*—its successful courting of popularity
by the avoidance of harmonic and rhythmic complexities, to say nothing
of the absence of polyphony, plus the unpleasant matter of the composer's political past and his way of dealing with that past—has also
made it a controversial piece. Musicians tend to speak ill of *Carmina burana*, and that includes some famous conductors who have had great success with it.[6] Singers, on the other hand, enjoy it, not least its considerable

[4]I first heard *Carmina burana* in 1953 in Rome in a performance conducted by Hans Schmidt-
Isserstedt, and I still remember how the woman sitting at my left muttered every three or four
minutes, "Ma è più russo che tedesco" (But it's more Russian than German).
[5]The eroticism here is nothing compared to what appeared later in *Catulli Carmina*.
[6]One conductor I shall leave nameless despises *Carmina burana* most of the time, but acknowl-
edges that once in a while it is fun to conduct. He likens this to being in Paris or Rome and having a sudden craving for a Big Mac.

difficulties, though many a baritone must have wished that Orff had not written high G's with such abandon, as though there were no tomorrow. But however suspect one might find the composer's ends and means, you cannot deny his skill at pacing and design, the catchiness of his tunes (so consonant with the blunt end-rhymes of medieval German Latin), the splendid way in which everything "sounds," and even the perverse courage it took to sit down in 1935 or 1936 and write some of those nursery-tune simplicities. Had Orff ever felt called upon to defend his one-dimensional masterpiece, he might have repeated his answer to a question about his preference for "old material" as subjects of his stage works: "I do not feel it to be old, only valid. The dated elements are lost and the spiritual strength remains."

Orff was immediately captivated by O *Fortuna, velut luna* (O Fortune, like the moon), the first poem in the Schmeller edition of *Carmina burana*, and by its accompanying Wheel of Fortune miniature.[7] He saw this bitter meditation as a strong frame, inside which he groups poems in three chapters:

I. *In Springtime* and *On the Green* (pastoral and genre poems);
II. *In the Tavern*;
III. *The Court of Love*, concluding with the ecstatic address to "Blanziflor [Blanchefleur] et Helena."

O *Fortuna* is a massive structural pillar—a brief exordium, then a crescendo and acceleration built over nearly a hundred measures, all of them glued to the insistent tonic, D. *Fortune plango vulnera*, with its chant-like beginning, is a variant of O *Fortuna* on a smaller scale.

The three spring poems introduce brighter colors, although the first two, *Veris leta facies* and *Omnia Sol temperat*, continue with melodies close to chant. With *Ecce gratum* Orff completes the transformation of atmosphere by moving into the major mode.

The sequence on the green begins with a lively dance for the orchestra alone. The harmony sticks to tonic and dominant, as it does virtually throughout the cantata, but here Orff does allow himself some delightful metrical dislocations. *Floret silva* alternates the large and small choruses. The sly slurs on "meus amicus" (my friend) are charming, as is the picture of the lover riding off into the distance—in Latin "hinc equitavit" and "der ist geriten hinnen" in German. Another instrumental dance

---

[7]It turns out that O *Fortuna* was originally not the first poem at all. At some point in its history the manuscript had been taken apart or had just come apart, and when it was rebound its fascicles were assembled in the wrong order.

separates the softly curved "Chramer, gip die varwe mir," the song of the girl out to buy some makeup, from the uninhibited *Swaz hie gat umbe*. In *Were diu werlt alle min*, erotic ambition extends to nothing less than possession of the queen of England, the energetic Eleanor of Provence, wife of Henry III (not Henry II's Eleanor of Aquitaine, as is sometimes stated). This movement is enclosed between fanfares and ends with an exultant shout.

Orff regards the tavern as a male preserve, and he begins with an unbridled setting for baritone of *Estuans interius*. Then comes one of the cantata's most famous and most original numbers, *Olim lacus colueram* (Lament of the roast swan).[8] The bassoon initiates the pitiful keening, which is then continued by a tenor with the sympathetic backing of piccolo, E-flat clarinet, and muted trumpet—with flutes, violas, a muted trombone, and assorted percussion to provide musical gooseflesh (or swanflesh). The Abbot of Cockaigne, who has been partaking of more than just roast swan, lurches forward to pronounce his fierce little credo, whereupon the whole male chorus plunges into its whirling catalogue of toasts and drinkers.[9]

After a pause for breath, we enter the *Cours d'amours* and the delicate sound of flutes and soprano voices, including those of a boys' chorus. In *Dies, nox et omnia*, the baritone bemoans his lovelorn state with larger-than-life pathos and in falsetto flourishes that send him clear up to high B: *tender but always exaggerated* is Orff's direction to him. In *Stetit puella*, the soprano sets before us a picture of a girl in a red dress and with irresistible sexual radiance. *Si puer cum puellula*, which Symonds aptly titles "A Poem of Privacy," is set for six chattering, leering men. *Veni, veni, venias* is a love song full of bird noises. For *In trutina*, the sweet song of the girl who, in the end, will find it not so difficult to choose between *lascivus amor* and *pudicitia*, Orff holds the soprano to her most seductive low register projected against a softly pulsating accompaniment.

---

[8]The great early-nineteenth-century hostesses still served swan on occasion. After Tchaikovsky and Petipa, Saint-Saëns and Pavlova, many of us would find it distinctly odd, not to say repellent, to eat swan. It is not at all easy to come by, except, of course, for shoot-it-yourself shoppers; see Wagner's *Parsifal*, Act I. The "swan" entry in Alan Davidson's *Oxford Companion to Food* is worth a quick read.

[9]Cockaigne is that medieval utopia where, in the words of the *Encyclopaedia Britannica*, "life was a round of luxuriant idleness. . . . The rivers were of wine, the houses were built of cake and barley sugar, the streets were paved with pastry and the shops supplied goods for nothing. Roast geese and fowls wandered about inviting folks to eat them, and buttered larks fell from the sky like manna." The thirteenth-century French poem *The Land of Cockaigne* is a satire on monastic life, and it is in that tradition that our reeling baritone introduces himself as an abbot. The goliards, those wandering students and clerks who were the authors of most of the *Carmina burana*, were fond of satiric imitations of ecclesiastic orders and ceremonies, and the collection includes several "anti-Masses" for drinkers, gamblers, and so on.

It is the loveliest lyric inspiration in the *Carmina*. The baritone and chorus heat things up still more in the restless and vigorous *Tempus est iocundum*, and then, in a beautifully placed musical and dramatic stroke, the girl fulfills the promise of *In trutina*: "Dulcissime" soars *con abbandono*, and to the very highest reaches of the soprano's voice. The brief but sonorous address to *Blanziflor et Helena* makes a bridge to the reprise of the *Fortuna* chorus—about whose ringing final words few of us would guess they exhort, "Mecum omnes plangite!" (Come, all, and weep with me!).

Sergei Rachmaninoff

Sergei Vasilievich Rachmaninoff was born at his father's estate at Oneg, near Semyonovo in the district of Starorusky, Russia, on 1 April 1873 and died in Beverly Hills, California, on 28 March 1943.

The Bells, op. 35

Rachmaninoff began *The Bells*, settings of a poem by Konstantin Balmont after Edgar Allan Poe, in January 1913 and completed the four sections respectively on 28 June, 13 July, 30 July, and 9 August of that year. With soloists E. I. Popova, A. D. Alexandrov, and P. Z. Andreyev, and the chorus and orchestra of the Maryinsky Theater, Saint Petersburg, the composer conducted the first performance on 13 December 1913. The work is dedicated to Willem Mengelberg and the Amsterdam Concertgebouw Orchestra, with whom Rachmaninoff had had an exceptionally happy experience in 1908 in performances of his Piano Concerto No. 2.

Soprano, tenor, and bass soloists, mixed chorus. Three flutes and piccolo, two oboes and English horn, two clarinets and bass clarinet, two bassoons and contrabassoon, six horns, three trumpets, three trombones, tuba, celesta, harp, piano, timpani, glockenspiel, triangle, tambourine,

snare drum, cymbals, chimes, military drum, bass drum, tam-tam, and strings.

The Bells and the *All-Night Vigil* were Rachmaninoff's favorites among his own compositions. The *Vigil*, which consists of more than an hour of music for *a cappella* chorus, was intended for a night-long service in Russian Orthodox churches on the eve of a holy day, and the composer asked to be buried to the sound of its fifth hymn, *Now Lettest Thou Thy Servant Depart in Peace.* The world of secular yearning, melancholia, and virtuosity that dominates the Rachmaninoff of the piano concertos—for most of us the Rachmaninoff we know best—is far away in that rapt masterpiece. Here are chaste harmonies in block chords and simple contrapuntal motion, set out with a wondrous sense of euphony. *The Bells* is not as far removed from the concertos and symphonies, the solo piano pieces, and the songs; even so, to encounter it for the first time is to have one's sense of the composer's range greatly stretched.

Today we know Rachmaninoff best as a composer, and second best as one of the most aristocratic, individual, and rhythmically exciting pianists of his time—one of the greatest in an age of great pianists. Hardly less remarkable as a conductor, he was regarded highly enough to be asked to take over the Boston and Cincinnati Symphonies when he moved to America in 1918 after the Russian Revolution. (He turned down both.) The concentration, clarity, nobility of style, and beauty of sound of the few recordings he made with the Philadelphia Orchestra, his favorite in America—*The Isle of the Dead* and the *Vocalise* in 1929, the Symphony No. 3 ten years later—make believable every glowing account one reads about his work on the podium. Needing to support his family, he did a lot of conducting in his early years, both opera and concert—more conducting than piano-playing, in fact—and it fatigued him as well as sometimes annoyed him because it took time from his composing. After he came to America, he primarily made his living as a pianist, but toward the end of his life he accepted occasional conducting engagements, and *The Bells* was on the program of his last concert with his beloved Philadelphians in December 1939 as well as on the last concert he ever conducted, with the Chicago Symphony in 1941.

From time to time he managed to organize an escape—for example, canceling a good many concerts, in December 1912 he took his family to Switzerland and then to Rome. There they settled in an apartment in the Piazza di Spagna where Piotr and Modest Tchaikovsky had spent Christmas 1880. There Rachmaninoff began *The Bells*. But this Roman idyll did not last. His daughters Irina, ten, and Tatiana, six, both contracted typhoid fever, and the family went to Berlin for better medical treatment than they felt confident of finding in Italy. The girls' convalescence and *The Bells* were completed during the following summer at Ivanovka, the estate that had been part of his wife's family property, where he had written the Piano Concerto No. 3 as well as many songs and the first sets of *Études-Tableaux* for piano, and of which he himself had become the owner in 1910.

The first audiences in Saint Petersburg and Moscow loved *The Bells*. In the latter city, Rachmaninoff had a mysterious fan who sent great bouquets of white lilies whenever he gave a concert there. This time she outdid herself. According to the account in the Rachmaninoff biography by Sergei Bertensson and Jay Leyda, "this usual floral tribute . . . was something exceptional this time; bells of all sizes hanging from a crossbeam attached to a table. These bells were made of solid masses of white lilac blossoms—and it was February."

For that matter, a mysterious woman may have played a part in the genesis of *The Bells*. Mikhail Buknik, a cellist who had been a friend of Rachmaninoff's since they were both students at the Moscow Conservatory, told the story three years after the composer's death:

> I had a cello pupil, a Miss Danilova, who once came to her lesson in great agitation; while she played, she seemed very excited and eager to tell me something. She finally revealed that Balmont's translation of Poe's poem *The Bells* had once made a great impression on her—she could think of it only as music—and who could write it as music but her adored Rachmaninoff! That he must do this became her *idée fixe*, and she wrote anonymously to her idol, suggesting that he read the poem and compose it as music. She excitedly sent off this letter; summer passed, and then in the autumn she came back to Moscow for her studies. What had now happened is that Rachmaninoff had composed an outstanding choral symphony based on Poe's *The Bells* and that it was soon to be performed. Danilova was mad with joy. But someone had to be told her secret—and that's how all her emotions were unloaded during my lesson. She told me the whole story. I was astounded to think that our reserved and quite unsentimental Rachmaninoff could have been capable of being inspired by someone else's advice—to create so important a work! I kept my secret till Rachmaninoff's death.[1]

I have always hoped this story is true. What is certain is that Rachmaninoff *was* fired up by Balmont's version of Poe, and if Miss Danilova

[1]Quoted in Sergei Bertensson and Jay Leyda, *Sergei Rachmaninoff: A Lifetime in Music* (New York University Press, 1956).

was involved, blessings on her. Rachmaninoff was good at bells: their sound is often invoked in his instrumental music, most famously in his Prelude in C-sharp Minor, but no less tellingly in such works as the Suite No. 1 (*Fantaisie-Tableaux*) for two pianos, the finale of the Symphony No. 2, and the *Symphonic Dances*.

Poe's posthumous reputation—he died, aged forty, in 1849—was far greater in Europe than in his own country. Emerson called him "the jingle man" (presumably with *The Bells* in mind), and for James Russell Lowell he was "three fifths genius and two fifths sheer fudge." On the other side of the Atlantic his fellow poets were more responsive to the genius in him. Baudelaire and Mallarmé thought him magnificent and found him inspiring to their own work, as did such English writers as the Rossettis, Swinburne, and Stevenson. Yeats hailed him as "always and for all lands a great lyric poet." Claude Debussy was obsessed for years by his desire to turn *The Fall of the House of Usher* and *The Devil in the Belfry* into operas.

The Russian symbolist poet Konstantin Dimitrievich Balmont, six years older than Rachmaninoff, was another devotee. His verse was known, among other things, for its imaginative sound effects—the poet and critic Nina Berberova wrote that these eventually came to seem "vain"—and in this he had been influenced by Poe's virtuosic onomatopoeia in *The Bells*. Balmont's rendering of Poe is atmospheric and free. Rhythmically it is so independent that it is impossible to fit Poe's words to Rachmaninoff's music. If you want *The Bells* in English, you have to settle for a retranslation from the Russian by Fanny S. Copeland; all in all, you are better off with the gorgeous and satisfyingly chewy sonorities of Balmont's Russian. Rachmaninoff, by the way, acquired most of his English after his move to America. I wonder whether he ever got around to reading *The Bells* in the original.

When he wrote *The Bells*, Rachmaninoff thought of it as a choral symphony and he referred to it as his Third Symphony; however, he never gave it that title officially, and eventually, in 1935–1936, he composed a "real" and purely orchestral Third Symphony. Poe-Balmont is in four parts, and the music follows that design. The first part is about the sound of silvery sleigh-bells, a symbol of the beginning of life and of youth. The scoring of the opening, with its high woodwinds, muted trumpet, triangle, harp, celesta, and piano, is deliciously imaginative, and the crescendo that leads to the first entrance of the solo tenor is superbly plotted. Irregular meters enhance the excitement. Later Rachmaninoff has the chorus hum, which makes me wonder whether one of his recreations in Rome had been to see *Madama Butterfly* with its famous humming chorus. At the climax, violins and violas add a rocking motif; we shall hear it again in *The Bells,* but beyond that, it is an idea we encounter often in Rachmaninoff's music.

Golden wedding bells are the subject of the second movement, begun by muted violins presenting a new version of the rocking theme. We tend to think of wedding music as joyous, but for Rachmaninoff the dominant idea is the solemnity of the sacrament and the human commitment. But passion has a part to play as well, and there are glorious opportunities for the solo soprano to spin out ecstatically stretched musical phrases. Again, Rachmaninoff's orchestral imagination functions at the highest level.

The third movement, the only one without a solo singer, is the imagined symphony's scherzo. The subject is the strident alarm bells that announce the terror of fire. There is nothing comparably wild elsewhere in Rachmaninoff's music.

Finally, there is the evocation of the iron tone of funeral bells. As he ended the work thus, with a slow movement, Rachmaninoff's mind must often have turned to the *Symphonie pathétique* of his beloved Tchaikovsky. It is for this movement that he saves the dark sound of his bass soloist. The bassoon quietly sounds the "Dies irae" from the Catholic Mass for the Dead, a theme that was a lifelong obsession for Rachmaninoff, and which was hinted at even in the wedding music. *The Bells* ends with an eloquent postlude for the orchestra alone.

Franz Schmidt

Franz Schmidt was born in Pozsony, Hungary (now Bratislava, Slovakia) on 22 December 1874 and died in Perchtholdsdorf, a suburb of Vienna, on 11 February 1939.

Das Buch mit sieben Siegeln—aus der Offenbarung des hl. Johannes (The Book with Seven Seals—From the Revelation of Saint John the Divine)

Schmidt began work on *The Book with Seven Seals* in May or June 1935 and completed the score on 23 February 1937. On 15 June 1938, Oswald Kabasta conducted the first performance in Vienna with the Chorus of the Society of the Friends of Music and the Vienna Symphony Orchestra, the organist Franz Schütz, the tenor Rudolf Gerlach as Saint John, and a solo quartet consisting of Erika Rokyta, Enid Szantho, Anton Dermota, and Josef von Manowarda.

Tenor soloist as Saint John[1]; solo quartet of soprano, alto, tenor, and bass; four-part chorus (as large as possible). Organ (both in a virtuoso solo role and an orchestral part), two flutes and piccolo, two oboes and English horn, two clarinets and bass clarinet (doubling clarinet in D), two bassoons and contrabassoon,

---

[1]Schmidt specifies a Wagnerian heldentenor, but the great exponents of this long and taxing role have been lyric Mozart tenors such as Anton Dermota, Peter Schreier, and Fritz Wunderlich, and, with one degree more vocal heft, Thomas Moser and Julius Patzak.

four horns, three trumpets, three trombones, tuba, timpani (three players), bass drum, three tam-tams, cymbals, snare drum, xylophone, and strings (as many as possible). Schmidt also indicates several passages in which, if possible, he wants the woodwind doubled.

I have often recalled a distinction one of my English literature professors made when he spoke about James Boswell. Boswell, he said, was not a great writer, but he *was* the writer of one very great book. I cannot say whether Franz Schmidt was overall a great composer, but I can assert quite surely that he was the composer of two great works, the Fourth Symphony (1932–1933), which was a Requiem for his daughter Emma, dead in childbirth at thirty, and *The Book with Seven Seals* (1935–1937).[2]

Schmidt's first language was Hungarian, and as a boy he planned eventually to take his mother's family name of Ravasz. (His father was also Hungarian on his mother's side.) A scoffing remark by his piano teacher, the eminent Theodor Leschetizky, to the effect that "someone with a name like Schmidt shouldn't become an artist" was enough to make him stick with his homely German patronymic.

Music was his heritage from both parents, and he always maintained that his mother, who had studied with Liszt, was his best piano teacher. She and her successors did a good job: in other musicians' recollections of Schmidt you read over and over that he was the most fascinating pianist they had ever heard, or quite simply the best.[3] Schmidt was also superb on the cello, joining the Vienna Court Opera Orchestra and the Philharmonic as coprincipal at twenty-one, and he was an excellent organist as well. These instrumental skills were at the service of a formidable musical mind and a stunningly capacious memory. Whatever was stored there could travel instantly from brain to fingers to keyboard, and music he had not seen or heard in years could flow from those fingers at the mere mention of the title. At the end of one piano recital in Vienna, he sat down and, on the spur of the moment, played Strauss's *Till Eulenspiegel*—flawlessly. He also taught, and put in several years as rector of the Vienna Staatsakademie and the Musikhochschule.

Through the latter part of the 1920s Schmidt composed much strong and engaging music in various genres. Late Bruckner, early Schoenberg, Mahler, perhaps a bit of Reger as well (that fondness for fugues)—all played a part in the formation of his musical language. He counts as one

[2]For more on Schmidt's life and the Fourth Symphony in particular, see the essay on that work in my book *The Symphony: A Listener's Guide* (Oxford University Press, 1995).
[3]The great Lithuanian keyboard master Leopold Godowsky, when asked who was the greatest living pianist, replied: "Schmidt is the other one."

of the conservatives in the twentieth century's first half, but he was neither ignorant of nor hostile to more modernist trends. At the end of the 1920s, his music seems suddenly to become deeper and wider. For my ear, this extraordinary breakthrough happens in the ecstatic, often startlingly dissonant *Adagio* of his Third Symphony (1928). The brilliantly scored *Variations on a Hussar Song* (1931) is Schmidt's most buoyant piece; the Fourth Symphony is his most dangerously thin-skinned, poignant, and personal work, grand and intimate at the same time.

By 1933, when he completed that great work, Schmidt was in poor health and daily more conscious that his composing days were numbered. He wanted to follow his last symphony with something no less personal and also meaningful for the times. He was always convinced that he was a natural opera composer, but neither *Notre Dame* (1904) nor the musically more ambitious *Fredigundis* (1921) had brought him success.[4] Now, entering his sixties, Schmidt did not have the stomach for one more tilt at the operatic establishment, but he did begin to think about writing some sort of large dramatic work with voices.

Casting around for a subject, Schmidt thought for a while of somehow using *Welt und Leben* (World and Life), a weighty tome by his friend Alexander Wunderer, a Vienna Philharmonic oboist with literary ambitions; the author, though, was not enthusiastic about having his work reduced to an oratorio libretto, and that idea was abandoned. We don't know just how Schmidt arrived at Revelation. One who eagerly sought to take credit for steering Schmidt in that direction was his student Raimund Weissensteiner, both priest and composer, but accounts of Schmidt's life at this time by all other members of his circle are consistently skeptical about this.

Someone who certainly had something to do with it was Oswald Kabasta, conductor at the Austrian Radio and of the Vienna Symphony; he had led the first performance of the Fourth Symphony and would do the same for *The Book with Seven Seals*.[5] It was a time of unrest and anxiety in Austria. Engelbert Dollfuss, the chancellor, was assassinated in July 1934, but not before he had dismantled constitutional government and put an authoritarian state based on Italian Fascist and conservative Catholic principles in its place; moreover, Austria was also under the threat of a German takeover (by no means unwelcomed by all, and to be realized in March 1938). Kabasta sensed that in this uneasy climate a work

[4]*Notre Dame* is a *verismo* opera based on Victor Hugo's *Hunchback of Notre Dame*. Its orchestral Intermezzo, a captivating example of Schmidt's "Hungarian," i.e., Gypsy, style, shows up on concert programs from time to time.
[5]Kabasta was a fascinating conductor, and his recordings are well worth seeking out.

based on a sacred text might be welcome. In characteristically droll manner, he put it to Schmidt that there was "a bull market in Catholicism." At any rate, by the beginning of 1935 Schmidt had acquired several translations of Revelation, including, to the horror of his Catholic friends, Martin Luther's, and he was beginning to think about what he might make of this musically.

By a wide margin the strangest book in the Bible, Revelation is a kind of pastoral letter written to seven churches in Asia Minor by a man on the island of Patmos in the Dodecanese. He identifies himself as John; however, he is not, as was long believed, the Apostle John but another personage now known as Saint John the Divine. The book cannot be dated exactly, but almost certainly it falls into the reign of the emperor Domitian (81–96), who, grandly calling himself *dominus et deus*, was known for the atmosphere of terror that dominated his years on the throne and particularly for the zeal with which he persecuted Christians. The thrust of John's letter is to send words of comfort and reassurance to those Christians under Roman domination by describing both the blessed state that awaits those who keep the faith, even at the cost of their lives, and the punishment, inevitable and imminent, of their persecutors.

The purpose, then, is plain and clear; what is extraordinary is the execution. As David E. Aune observes in his introduction to Revelation in *Harper's Bible Commentary,* "Ancient Jewish and Christian apocalyptic literature is highly symbolic; often the symbolism is bizarre."[6] Among the images John sets before us are a book with seven seals; seven angels sounding seven trumpets to announce seven woes[7]; the four horsemen of the apocalypse (an image that has become part of popular culture); a Lamb that appears to have been killed and which has seven eyes and seven horns; a monster from the sea with seven heads and ten horns; a woman about to be delivered of a boy, herself "clothed with the sun, and the moon under her feet, and upon her head a crown of twelve stars"; and, as her adversary, "a great red dragon, having seven heads and ten horns, and seven crowns upon his heads." It is a cornucopia of dizzying opportunities for an imaginative composer, as indeed it is for a painter, and Schmidt revels in its possibilities.

Ignoring John's warning in the final chapter that "if any man shall add unto these things, God shall add unto him the plagues that are written in

---

[6]*Apocalypse* is a word that has become so firmly tied to the idea of devastation that we tend to forget its primary meaning of "revelation." It is derived from the Greek *apokaluptein,* "to uncover."

[7]As you may already know from such works as the Brahms Requiem, in German Bible translations these "trumpets" are *Posaunen,* trombones. Schmidt concentrates on trombones in these passages, but enlists trumpets, horns, and tuba as well.

this book," he put together a powerful and shapely text whose core is drawn from John's report of his vision, but to which he adds verses from the Psalms as well as words of his own. Unlike Vaughan Williams in *Sancta Civitas*, Schmidt does not focus on the redeeming vision of the Holy City, the new Jerusalem, but makes the book with seven seals the focal point of his apocalyptic oratorio, the proclamations of the seven woes by the seven trumpets being his secondary theme.

Schmidt begins with what he describes in the program note he wrote for the first performance as a "Prologue in Heaven," a designation he borrows from Goethe's *Faust*. John first greets the congregations on his own behalf and that of Jesus Christ, upon which there follows the summons he heard from the Lord: "Come up hither, and I will shew thee things which must be hereafter." Then John sets the scene: the throne in heaven from which radiate "lightnings and thunders and voices" and with one "like a jasper and a sardine stone" seated upon it, surrounded by a rainbow, by twenty-four elders, seven torches, and four beasts. In front of it all there is "a sea of glass like unto crystal."

The music begins with bells—not real bells, but the bright sound of horns and woodwinds, soon joined by strings, imitating a gigantic carillon. (Not by chance, this lasts for seven measures.) Even before this brief prologue within the prologue is up, we hear the ringing tenor voice of John. In contrast, the Lord, who in Revelation is described as speaking in the voice of a trumpet, is a deep bass.[8] After John has resumed his narrative, we hear the solo quartet in a Sanctus, "Holy, holy, holy, Lord God Almighty," and the chorus, representing the twenty-four elders, continues the hymn of praise.

Then comes the crucial vision: "And I saw in the right hand of him that sat on the throne a book . . . sealed with seven seals." A solemn new theme, introduced by the double basses alone, enters here, and it is one we shall hear often—always associated with the book. But who, ask the angels, is worthy to break the seals and open the book? In bleakly spare music it is revealed that "no man in heaven, nor in earth, neither under the earth" can do this, but it is at this moment that "the Lamb, as it had been slain, having seven horns and seven eyes, which are the seven Spirits of God" appears. The tone of the music changes utterly, settling now in a gently lyric G major. This, too, is a melody we shall hear often.

---

[8]Sometimes an extra bass soloist is brought in for the voice of the Lord, although Schmidt was content to have the part sung by the bass in the solo quartet, provided, of course, that he was an artist of stature. That is how it was done at the first performance, and Anton Dermota, the tenor in the original quartet, reports that Josef von Manowarda, the principal exponent of the Wagnerian bass roles at Bayreuth through the 1930s, was "magnificent."

The Lamb accepts the book, eliciting new songs of praise—here is the first time we hear the organ prominently—and what Schmidt calls his "Service of Thanksgiving" comes to a powerful close, its last sound an Amen sung by the chorus alone. These *a cappella* conclusions are a signature sound of this work.

The Prologue over, an organ solo, a meditation in a slow tempo on the book theme, introduces what Schmidt thinks of as the real first part of the oratorio. The narrative thread here is the breaking by the Lamb of the first six seals. The first seal reveals, amid thunder, a rider on a white horse, "and he that sat on him had a bow; and a crown was given unto him: and he went forth conquering, and to conquer." The chorus hails this redeemer figure in jubilant Handelian music.

At the opening of the second seal, a red horse appears, its rider having power "to take peace from the earth, and that they should kill one another." The music sets before us a conflict between warriors determined to destroy, plunder, and slaughter, and mothers begging mercy for their children. Against an agitated march stirred along by the snare drum and obsessed with tense, narrow semitones, we hear the wailing of the women, their agony of spirit expressed in the uncomfortable jagged intervals of the sevenths they must sing. This rises to an immense climax, a moment of catastrophe; then, gradually, the military noises disappear into the distance.

With the opening of the third seal there comes a black horse, whose rider holds a scale in his hand and who decrees: "A measure of wheat and three measures of barley for all." The voice is that of the solo bass. This leads to one of the most poignant passages in the work. The English horn introduces a melancholy music that is taken up, first by bassoons and other woodwinds, then by the soprano and alto soloists representing a mother and daughter desperate for bread in a world where the men are dead and the fields ravaged. The chorus *a cappella* softly reminds: "Be steadfast in sorrow! Then we shall prevail, and our victory is sure."

The Lamb opens the fourth seal, whereupon there appears "a pale horse: and his name that sat on him was Death, and Hell followed with him." The pale rider on the pale horse has power "to kill with sword, and with hunger, and with death." There follows an extraordinary page, a ghostly, sinister music: strings played with the wooden stick of the bow, xylophone, and muted trombones in their lowest register, all set against a continuous *pianissimo* cymbal roll. With this as background, two survivors (tenor and bass solos), amazed to be alive among all the dead, note with horror what they see: the pale horse and his rider, Death, and the riders on the red and black horses, "given power to murder by sword, famine, disease, and wild beasts." But, they recall: "The Lord did vouch-safe us: 'He that endureth to the end, he shall be saved at last.'" For those last words, the spectral orchestra withdraws and is succeeded by the organ, the two singers now heard in calm harmony. This episode, hauntingly prophetic of *Strange Meeting* in Benjamin Britten's *War Requiem*, is the most moving as well as the most astonishing passage in *The Book with Seven Seals*.

The breaking of the fifth seal reveals "the souls of them that were slain for the word of God, and for the testimony which they held." In a choral fugue whose style shows Schmidt close to Beethoven's *Missa solemnis*, with the organ adding virtuosic sixteenth-note scales to the orchestral texture, the martyrs ask: "How long, O Lord, holy and true, dost thou not judge and avenge our blood?" At the end, Schmidt again creates a striking effect by suddenly using the chorus *a cappella*: "Lord, when judgest thou?" Now we hear the voice of the Lord, that sonorous bass, for the second time, now moving in stately quarter-notes: "Rest yet for a little season," and the sins of the persecutors will be avenged.

When the Lamb opens the sixth seal a great earthquake erupts. John's description is magnificent: "The sun became as black as sackcloth of hair, and the moon became as blood; and the stars of heaven fell unto the earth . . . and every mountain and island were moved out of their places." Schmidt responds with a ferocious chorus, all tumultuous sixteenth-notes, wild harmonies, terrified cries. Again, an *a cappella* close: "Who shall be able to stand?" An abrupt upward rush in the orchestra cuts the music off.

The score does not specifically indicate a break at this point, but in his program note Schmidt refers to what follows as "the second part," and this is where, ever since the first performance, conductors have placed an intermission. The music resumes with another organ solo, this one tempestuous, fast, extremely chromatic in its harmonies. The Lamb opens the seventh seal, and "there was silence in heaven about the space of half an hour." Schmidt, however, interprets the great silence as "lasting to the end of the world." In his essay he writes: "During this silence, Saint John tells us . . . the story of the true Faith and of its Church, beginning at the birth of the Savior, continuing with its fight against the worshippers of the devil and their false teaching, and concluding with its final victory."

After the great silence, symbolized by orchestral music of a serenity we have not experienced before in this work, Schmidt turns to the succession of visions: "the woman clothed with the sun" giving birth to a boy; the appearance of the great fire-red dragon; the ascent to heaven of the "man child, who [is] to rule all nations with a rod of iron"; the great battle between the angels of Michael and those of the dragon; and the defeat of the dragon and of Satan, who is "bound for a thousand years, and cast . . . into the bottomless pit." Schmidt's dragon music for dark, low brass is powerfully impressive, and so is the grim battle scene in the orchestra, hugely energized by the composer's contrapuntal skills. The music associated with the Lamb takes on tremendous vigor as the forces of good come to prevail over the forces of Satan.

Six trumpets sound, bringing great woes to the world: hailstorms of blood and fire, a mountain falling into the ocean, the destruction of all ships, water turning to blood, eclipses, craters opening to bring forth black smoke and plagues of locusts. But the seventh trumpet proclaims the Day of Judgment, and for the third time we hear the voice of the Lord: "Behold! I make all things new! And he that overcometh, he shall inherit all things, and I shall be his God." The trumpet proclamations are clothed in music of commanding majesty, and this chapter concludes with the grandest chorus up to this point. Schmidt, however, holds enough in reserve to be able to unleash still greater fury for John's warning that he whose name "is not found in the book of life [is] cast into the lake of fire, the second death"—a gripping climax achieved in terrifying *pianissimo*.

The rest is epilogue. This unfolds in three phases. First comes the most famous part of *The Book with Seven Seals*, its blazing Hallelujah chorus. Here Schmidt speaks and celebrates in the Hungarian tones of his childhood. This is "Hungarian" in the sense in which Schubert, Liszt, and Brahms used the word, the idiom actually being that of Gypsy rather than authentic Hungarian folk music. At the same time, Schmidt's declamation of "Hal-LE-lu-jah," with a strongly accented short note placed on the beat, is distinctly Hungarian.

Ex. 1

Hal - le - lu - jah!_____

He adds another flavorful ethnic characteristic when he introduces the word "Hallelujah!" each time with an upward rush of strings reminiscent of the introductory flourishes we hear in cymbalom playing. It is music of overwhelming jubilance and among the most exciting pages in all choral music.

From there Schmidt moves into another world for a brief prayer of thanksgiving sung quietly by the men of the chorus, unaccompanied and *tranquillo*. This leads to the epilogue within the epilogue. As the seer takes leave and bids farewell—"And I John saw these things and heard them"—the music returns to the pseudo-carillon from the very beginning of the work. The chorus joins him for a single "Amen," loud and firm, after which five powerful measures of cadence—orchestra alone—bring the great oratorio to its close.

Roger Sessions

Roger Sessions

Roger Huntington Sessions was born in Brooklyn, New York, on 28 December 1896 and died in Princeton, New Jersey, on 16 March 1985.

When Lilacs Last in the Dooryard Bloom'd, Cantata after Walt Whitman for Soprano, Contralto, Baritone, Mixed Chorus, and Orchestra

When Lilacs Last in the Dooryard Bloom'd, commissioned by the University of California at Berkeley in celebration of its centenary in 1964, was completed on 2 January 1970. Sessions dedicated the score to the memory of Martin Luther King, Jr., and Robert F. Kennedy, both assassinated in 1968. The first performance was given on 23 May 1971 at Berkeley with Michael Senturia conducting, with the University Symphony Orchestra, the University Chorus, the Repertory Chorus, and soloists Helene Joseph, Stephanie Friedman, and Allen Shearer.

Solo soprano, contralto, and baritone; mixed chorus. Two flutes (one doubling alto flute) and piccolo, two oboes and English horn, two clarinets plus E-flat and bass clarinet, two bassoons and contrabassoon, four horns, two trumpets, three trombones, bass tuba, timpani, vibraphone, xylophone, marimba, glockenspiel, large, medium, and small tam-tams, tenor drum, suspended cymbal,

**maracas, wood block, slapstick, bass drum, tambourine, military drum, tam-
bourin provençal, cymbals, snare drum, Chinese drum, triangle, claves, and
strings.**

When I once asked Sessions about some small differences between the
text of Whitman's elegy for Lincoln as it appears in the published poem
and in his score—"and" for "with," that sort of thing—he allowed that
this had probably happened because he had for the most part set it from
memory. He added that he did of course own a copy of *Leaves of Grass*,
one he had bought at the Harvard Coop in 1911 when he was fourteen
and a freshman. Although born in Brooklyn, his father having settled in
New York as a magazine editor, Sessions was a New Englander by temperament and heritage, and he always referred to Hadley, Massachusetts,
as his "ancestral hangout." Composing began early: at twelve he had
written an opera, *Lancelot and Elaine*—Wagnerian, with leitmotifs—
based on Tennyson's *Idylls of the King.* In later years he thought that the
most satisfying aspect of his time at Harvard had been the opportunity to
hear the Boston Symphony regularly, and its sound defined an orchestral
ideal that remained valid for him all his life. (His ideal conductor was the
musically fiery, physically reined-in Arthur Nikisch, whom he heard in
Boston with the London Symphony in 1912.) The outbreak of war frustrating a plan to study in Paris with Ravel, Sessions settled for Yale and
Horatio Parker, but he always felt that his true musical education began
when, at twenty-two, he started work with Ernest Bloch. Sessions taught
at the Cleveland Institute of Music for awhile, was assistant to Bloch,
and briefly—and unhappily—even served as the Institute's director. He
lived in Paris, Berlin, and France for several years on a series of grants and
prizes, eventually settling at Princeton, where he was on the faculty twice,
with a seven-year interruption at the University of California at Berkeley.

When Lilacs Last in the Dooryard Bloom'd is the grandest and greatest
of the threnodies of this humanist and idealist, which include music in
memory of Franklin D. Roosevelt (Symphony No. 2) and John F.
Kennedy (Piano Sonata No. 3). His operas *The Trial of Lucullus* (1947)
and *Montezuma* (1935–1964) were responses to the large political events
of the day, as was what he thought of as his Vietnam trilogy of symphonies, the Sixth, Seventh, and Eighth. And there were also private acts
of reflection, celebration, and mourning: the *Pages from a Diary* for piano (published, to his distress, as *From My Diary*), the Symphony No. 4
with its elegy for his brother John, whose death in 1948 affected him
more than any other he had experienced until that time; the *Five Pieces
for Piano*, a *tombeau* for Luigi Dallapiccola, his dearest friend among

composers; and the *Canons for String Quartet*, "written on the high seas" *in memoriam* Igor Stravinsky. But if there is much in Sessions of what John Harbison, who studied with him, has characterized as "melancholy without self-indulgence, loneliness without isolation," his vocabulary also encompassed the exuberance of the Second Piano Sonata, the Symphony No. 3, and the Double Concerto for Violin and Cello, not to forget the abundant sensuality and *joie de vivre* of the *Idyll of Theocritus*.

The Civil War, in which Walt Whitman served in the offices of the Paymaster, the Secretary of the Interior, and the Attorney-General, but also as a nurse's aide and "consolant" in military hospitals, was a crucial period in his emotional life, and he always wanted to put together a book in which he might gather that experience. He imagined it as part mosaic and part history, but he never brought it about.[1] Abraham Lincoln was shot on 14 April 1865 and died early the next day. *When Lilacs Last in the Dooryard Bloom'd* was the forty-six-year-old Whitman's response to that death and to the solemn progress of the funeral train as it made its way from Washington to Springfield, Illinois. It was published that fall in *Sequel to Drum-Taps* and eventually incorporated in *Leaves of Grass*.[2]

No American poet has been set to music more often than Walt Whitman: John Adams, Ernst Bacon, Leonard Bernstein, Arthur Bliss, Ernest Bloch, Harry Thacker Burleigh, Elliott Carter, Mario Castelnuovo-Tedesco, George Crumb, Frederick Delius, Norman Dello Joio, Howard Hanson, Roy Harris, Karl Amadeus Hartmann, Hans Werner Henze, Paul Hindemith, Gustav Holst, Benjamin Lees, Charles Martin Loeffler, Otto Luening, Vincent Persichetti, Ned Rorem, Franz Schreker, William Schuman, Charles Villiers Stanford, Michael Tilson Thomas, Fartein Valen, Ralph Vaughan Williams, and Kurt Weill make an incomplete list of composers who have taken on Whitman's texts (and have sometimes, in turn, been undone by them).[3]

Paradoxical as it seems, given how attractive his verse is to composers, Whitman is hard to set to music. The sometimes-inflated rhetoric

---

[1]*Walt Whitman's Civil War*, edited by Walter Lowenfels (Knopf, 1960), who assembled letters, lectures, poems, and journalistic reports, comes close to a realization of this plan.

[2]*Leaves of Grass* grew over a period of thirty-seven years from twelve poems published in 1855 to nearly four hundred. Whitman was fired from his clerkship in the Department of the Interior in June 1865 because Secretary James Harlan thought the collection indecent.

[3]A prime example of failure for me would be Hindemith's much admired but rhythmically straitlaced setting of *When Lilacs Last in the Dooryard Bloom'd*, commissioned by Robert Shaw and composed in 1946 with President Roosevelt's death the previous year in mind. At the other end of the spectrum, Delius, in his lovely *Sea Drift*, delicately and tenderly responsive to Whitman's emotional world, tends toward the dangerously liquid.

can be a trap, and his recklessly large-breathed rhythms (no poet ever had more capacious lungs), based on the diction of the King James Bible, can present grave difficulties. It is just with those grand rhythms that Sessions is especially successful. His own art combines severity and control with the "abundance, sublime willfulness, [and] Dionysian qualities" that Harbison identifies as so centrally characteristic of Sessions's music, and so, projecting the poetry, now in simple chordal declamation, now in those long, high-arched lines of which he was the master, he conveys wonderfully the feel, the pace, and the variety of Whitman's lines.

Sessions considered *Lilacs* (which he always referred to as "my cantata") and *Montezuma* his most important works, and the cantata was, as he put it in a letter to Dallapiccola, "certainly [one] in which I put a good part of myself." He divides the text into three sections. The first, introductory and very short, presents the three symbols around which Whitman builds his poem: lilac, star, and thrush. The second describes the slow journey of the funeral train. It is pageantry and catalogues, public poetry, though it ends in the quiet of "Sing on! sing on! you gray-brown bird!" The third is Whitman's loving contemplation of death. Its focal point is the carol:

> Come, Lovely and soothing Death,
> Undulate round the world, serenely arriving,
>   arriving,
> In the day, in the night, to all, to each,
> Sooner or later, delicate Death.

It is for this moment that Sessions reserves the sound of the solo contralto, a sound he has let us hear just once and briefly, in the second part, at the lines: "O how shall I warble myself for the dead one there I loved? / And how shall I deck my song for the large sweet soul that is gone? / And what shall my perfume be, to adorn the grave of him I Love?"[4]

Sessions has made some cuts in Whitman's text for the second and third parts of the cantata. Those lines of the poem, he pointed out, recapitulate and summarize, and that expressive and structural task is one he has chosen to turn over to the music itself, which can accomplish it even more powerfully and evocatively. From the outset, Sessions establishes musical associations with poetic ideas—the figure the flute and clarinet play in the very first measure, for example, with the lilacs or, more broadly, with April ("fourth-month" in Whitman's Quaker-inspired language) and spring and renewal; a characteristic sequence and flavor of

---

[4]Sessions's ideal alto voice was that of Ernestine Schumann-Heink, whom he heard often at the Metropolitan Opera and in recital until her retirement in 1932.

harmonies with the star in the western sky; the phrases for off-stage flute and piccolo, sometimes with xylophone, that evoke the song of the hermit thrush.[5]

One could point to detail after detail in which that network of associations is elaborated; to the beautifully fluid way Sessions moves the text in and out among the voices of the chorus and the soloists; to the special moments, such as the undulating, swaying violin music for the "sea-winds, blown from east and west"; the vaulted melody with which the violins follow the phrase "Night and day journeys a coffin"; "the tolling, tolling bells' perpetual clang"; the "glad serenades" and dances the poet proposes to Death, and the ecstasy in "I float this carol with joy, with joy to thee, O Death!"; the field after the battle and the obsessive, explosive returns to the word "suffer'd"; the mixture near the end, part doublings, part variants, of chorus and orchestra at "Yet each I keep, and all, retrievements out of the night"; the last magical phrase for bass clarinet, alto flute, trombone, and clarinet, a phrase that does not cease so much as recede out of earshot.

[5]In Andrea Olmstead's *Conversations with Roger Sessions* (Northeastern University Press, 1987), the composer goes at length into the different songs of various kinds of thrush, whistling examples. Of the hermit thrush he says that it is "like a coloratura wood thrush with much more life and exuberance [than the wood thrush and Wilson's thrush]. It starts on a long note, as it does in the cantata. After the cantata was performed in Boston, some of the people in the chorus who were from the western part of Massachusetts said it sounded just like the thrushes in their backyards. But I wasn't trying to reproduce the hermit thrush. I was suggesting the kind of sound that Whitman refers to. That may seem a very fine distinction, but there's nothing that literal about it. In other words, I didn't look it up or anything." Or in still other words, like Beethoven's comment on his "Pastoral" Symphony: "More feeling than painting."

Igor Stravinsky (signature)

Igor Stravinsky

Igor Fedorovich Stravinsky was born on 18 June 1882 in Oranienbaum, now Lomonosov in the Northwest Saint Petersburg Region of the Russian Republic, and died in New York on 6 April 1971.

The Wedding, Russian Choreographic Scenes in Four Tableaux

Stravinsky made the first notations for this music in June 1914 and finished the sketch score on 11 October 1917. The scoring underwent several radical changes, and the first performance of parts of the four extraordinarily interesting preliminary and abandoned versions of the first two tableaux took place at Harvard University on 12 August 1968 under the direction of Claudio Spies. Looking at my now-somewhat-tattered program, I see that the orchestra list for that concert includes the then–twenty-one-year-old future composer John Adams, here playing clarinet. The first complete performance—or as complete as possible—of the 1917 version was given on 11 February 1973, Robert Craft conducting. Stravinsky decided on the final scoring in 1921 and completed the work in Monte Carlo on 6 April or 5 May 1923, depending on whether you prefer to believe the note in the published score or the composer's letter of 6 May 1923 to his publisher. The first public performance, preceded by a private hearing at the house of Princess Edmond de Polignac, was given on 13 June 1923 in Paris by the Ballets Russes, and the score is dedicated to Serge Diaghilev, founder and director of that company. Ernest Ansermet conducted, the choreography was by Bronislava Nijinska, the sets and costumes were by Natalia Goncharova, and Felia Dubrovska and Leon Woizokowski danced the roles of the bride and groom. The pianists were Marcelle Meyer, Édouard Flamand, Georges Auric, and Hélène Lyon. The original plan was for Francis Poulenc and Vittorio Rieti to play two of the pianos, but both were prevented by illness. They did, however, get their chance at the London premiere under Eugene Goossens in 1926, when they were joined by Auric and Vladimir Dukelsky, the latter, under the name of Vernon Duke (George Gershwin's suggestion), becoming reasonably rich and famous in the 1930s as the composer of *April in Paris* and *I Can't Get Started With You*. Composers paying tribute to Stravinsky by playing in *The Wedding* was an idea that took hold. The nineteen-year-old Shostakovich was one of the pianists at the first performance in the Soviet Union, and a remarkable quartet was assembled for the U.S. premiere, given in Carnegie Hall under Leopold Stokowski in 1926: the composer Alfredo Casella, then conductor of the Boston Pops; the composer, violinist, and conductor Georges Enescu; Germaine Tailleferre, one of Les Six; and the harpist and composer Carlos Salzedo. At the last performance that Stravinsky himself conducted, in New York in 1959, the pianists were Samuel Barber, Aaron Copland, Lukas Foss, and Roger Sessions.

The Russian title of this work is *Svadebka*, but because of its Parisian associations, internationally it is still most often called by its French title, *Les Noces*. We have opted here for the English *The Wedding*.

The Wedding calls for soprano, alto, tenor, and bass soloists, mixed chorus. Four pianos, timpani, xylophone, large and small snare drums, large and small side drums without snares, bass drum, cymbals, suspended cymbal, tam-tam, triangle, two tambourines, a bell tuned to B-natural, and antique cymbals on B-natural and C-sharp.

It is in every way an amazing work, this *Wedding*. Joyous and emotionally charged, this masterpiece is not exactly a depiction of a Russian peasant wedding; rather, Stravinsky created a swirl of images by running together fragments of talk and ritual, having assembled the text himself from material in a collection of traditional wedding songs edited by P. J. Kireyevsky. Aptly, he once compared it to Joyce's *Ulysses*, a work-in-progress at the same time (and not many miles away): There, "the reader might seem to be overhearing scraps of conversation without the connecting thread of discourse. But [*The Wedding*] might also be compared to *Ulysses* in the larger sense that both works are trying to *present* rather than to *describe.*"

There are four scenes. In the first, the bride is made ready, and her hair is bound in red and blue ribbons. At the thought of leaving home, she weeps, but she weeps also because that, too, is part of the ritual. The second scene is the parallel one at the house of the groom. Then comes the moment of the bride's actual departure from her house, which leads to the final tableau, the wedding feast itself, a dizzying whirlwind of drinking, talk, toasts, and games. An older couple is chosen to warm the marriage bed, and while the four parents station themselves on a bench outside the door, the bride and groom at last enter the bedroom. The final words we hear are the new husband's declaration of love to his wife.

We learn a few names as the notes fly by—the groom is called Khvetis Pamfilievich and the bride Nastasya Timofeyevna—but the four solo singers do not represent specific characters. The lines of the groom, for example, are sung by the tenor in scene 2, but the closing words in the bedroom are given to the bass. Usually with a vocal work I suggest that the best way in is through the text. I think, though, that if you concentrate on following the text of *The Wedding* word by word, you will miss most of the music. Schumann's song cycle *Dichterliebe*, which takes slightly longer in performance than *The Wedding*, consists of roughly a thousand words, and a Bach cantata of about that length might have something like three hundred. But the Stravinsky text has about 2,500 words, and most of them go by at lightning speed.

It took Stravinsky almost nine years to get from the first sketches to the final double bar. No other work of his was in progress so long. He began *The Wedding* a little more than a year after the premiere of *Le Sacre du printemps* and he had just finished his opera *The Nightingale*, part of which harks back to the time of his studies with Rimsky-Korsakov and the composition of *The Firebird*, and part of which is firmly situated in the adventurous new music of the immediate prewar years. By the time *The Wedding* was completed, Stravinsky had written *The Soldier's Tale*, *Pulcinella*, the *Symphonies of Wind Instruments*, and the Octet for Winds. It was a time, for him, of drastic re-examination of all his ideas about composing; it was, if you like, the period in which the later Stravinsky, the Stravinsky of the works from *Pulcinella* to the *Requiem Canticles*, was born.

The compositional content of *The Wedding* was fixed by the fall of 1917. What took Stravinsky all that time was finding the miraculous, blazingly festive, and wholly new sound of the score in its final form. His first idea in 1914 was to use an orchestra with many wind instruments (he is still in the sound world of *Le Sacre*), but adding the flavorful sound of the Hungarian dulcimer or zither called the cimbalom (anticipating *Renard* of 1915–1916) and, by way of strings, to use only two solo quintets (looking—or hearing—ahead to *Pulcinella* of 1919–1920 and to the spare scores of the later years). The 1915 and 1916 fragments hew to the same basic idea, but with a much smaller ensemble for the former, and a rather larger one, including two flugelhorns and a barytone, in the latter.[1]

In 1919 he came closer. That ensemble consists of harmonium, two cimbaloms, pianola, bass drum, and tambourine, with snare drums, triangles, and cymbals of various sizes. That is an amazing sound, reminiscent of music outside the Western concert tradition such as is made, for example, by a Javanese or Balinese gamelan. The 1919 score is excited and exciting, all nerve endings, but it was the inspiration of the four pianos that added weight and, where needed, solemnity to the buzz. Once that sound was found and fixed, Stravinsky could write down his declaration of love to the world that had formed him—a work in his own first language to a text of his own devising.

Within its twenty-five minutes, *The Wedding* is a work of wondrous variety, from the keening of the bride and the deep seriousness of the invocation of the blessings of saints and the Virgin Mary, through the giddy exuberance of the party music, to that solemnly ecstatic, heart-stopping close, the young husband's words punctuated so unpredictably yet so firmly by the ring of the bell, the antique cymbals, and the four pianos.

With the *Symphony of Psalms*, another celebration of the sound of bells, *The Wedding* is Stravinsky's most moving composition. Thinking about the words, so rich in symbols and untranslatable idioms, Stravinsky once wrote: "I wonder if [*The Wedding*] can ever completely reveal itself to a non-Russian." With respect to the "completely," he was surely right. Still, when words and music get together, the music takes over, always, and I have sometimes thought that Stravinsky, writing that sentence, had forgotten the engulfing power of his own glorious music.

Perséphone, Melodrama in Three Tableaux, by André Gide

Stravinsky began work on *Perséphone* in May 1933, completed a summary sketch on 30 December that year, and finished the orchestration on 24 January 1934. He himself conducted the premiere at the Paris Opéra

---

[1]The flugelhorn, a valved bugle, found a place forty years later in one of Stravinsky's late sacred works, *Threni*. He never did use the barytone (the band instrument, that is, not the short-lived string instrument to which Haydn's patron, Prince Nikolaus Esterházy, was so devoted).

on 30 April 1934. Ida Rubinstein, who had commissioned the work, recited and mimed the title role, and the tenor soloist was René Maison. In 1949, Stravinsky made a few slight revisions, most of which concern metronome marks.

Solo tenor (Eumolpus, the Priest), speaker (Persephone, the Goddess); mixed chorus, children's chorus. Three flutes (third doubling piccolo), three oboes (third doubling English horn), three clarinets (third doubling bass clarinet), three bassoons (third doubling contrabassoon), four horns, four trumpets (include high trumpet in D), three trombones, tuba, timpani, xylophone, bass drum, snare drum, two harps, piano, and strings.

The Rite of Spring and *Perséphone*, separated by twenty-one years, are Stravinsky's two paeans to spring: the one, wild, fiercely ecstatic, revolutionary and a symbol of a new musical era, is the most famous composition to have come out of the twentieth century; the other, all lyric leisure, but with every note what Elliott Carter has called a "Stravinsky-note," is still one of the least known of that century's masterpieces, a hidden treasure.

The choice of story was Ida Rubinstein's. She came from Russia, a tall woman of what has been described as "mysteriously androgynous beauty." She was wealthy and she was demanding: Stravinsky recounts that she commissioned the painter Léon Bakst to arrange the flowers in her Parisian garden—in boxes, so that the design could be changed every few weeks. She kept a black tiger cub, and it was said that she drank champagne out of Madonna lilies. Her real talent was in mime, but she had ambitions to dance, act, and sing. In 1909, Diaghilev introduced her in Michel Fokine's *Cléopâtre*, and she was sensational in a role perfectly suited to her gifts and limitations, as she was again a year later in *Shéhérazade*. Her last performances for the Ballets Russes were in *Shéhérazade* in 1911. After that, she was off on enterprises of her own, *The Martyrdom of Saint Sebastian*, with a text by Gabriele d'Annunzio, music by Debussy, sets and costumes by Bakst, and choreography by Michel Fokine, being the first of what the dance historian Lynn Garafola calls her "genre-defying spectacles." After seeing her as the martyred saint, Proust wrote to his friend Reynaldo Hahn: "I found the legs of Mme. Rubinstein sublime. . . . For me this was everything." In 1928, she formed her own company, the Ballets Ida Rubinstein, with Bronislava Nijinska as her principal choreographer. In 1960, she died in the Provençal town of Vence at seventy-four. Music lovers are profoundly in her debt: aside from her involvement in *Perséphone* and *The Martyrdom of Saint Sebastian*, she commissioned *Joan of Arc at the Stake* from Honegger and *Boléro* from Ravel, and got Stravinsky to compose *Le Baiser de la fée.*

Rubinstein had wanted to stage Stravinsky's *Apollo*, but that score belonged to Diaghilev's company and could not be made available to her. She therefore commissioned *Le Baiser de la fée*, which she produced at the Paris Opéra in November 1928, with choreography by Nijinska. In January 1933, she asked André Gide to approach Stravinsky about a collaboration for a "symphonic ballet" based on André Gide's *Hymn to Demeter.* At the end of January, Gide and Stravinsky met in Wiesbaden to discuss the project. The big news in that agreeable spa town was that Adolf Hitler had become chancellor of Germany that day. In short order a libretto was delivered and the composition begun. The "entente parfaite" Gide noted both in his journal and in a letter to Rubinstein did not last long. Gide tells the story in *Ainsi soit-il* (*So Be It*) and Stravinsky does so in *Memories and Commentaries*, one of his books of conversations with Robert Craft. What exactly happened, or when, does not emerge with ideal clarity, but it is evident that Gide was upset with a proposed staging far less realistic than he had envisioned and than his script implies, and that he was even more disturbed by Stravinsky's treatment of his text. At any rate, after a run-through *chez* Rubinstein he chose to leave Paris for a vacation in Sicily rather than attend the premiere, and indeed disassociated himself from the project altogether. Later he sent Stravinsky a copy of the published libretto with the dedication "In communion," but the two men did not meet again.

In brief, the issue was syllables. The day before the premiere of *Perséphone*, Stravinsky published an article in the Paris *Excelsior*, saying that for his new work he had wanted "only syllables, beautiful, strong syllables—and beyond that, a plot." I do not know how beautiful, strong, and satisfying Stravinsky found Gide's syllables: he did, on one occasion, refer to his collaborator's poetry as "vers de caramel." Stravinsky's love for beautiful, strong syllables as musical, sonorous objects leading a life independent of their communicative function informed his vocal music always, no matter whether he was setting French, his own native Russian, Church Slavonic, Latin, English, or Hebrew. Gide preferred his words to his syllables.

A quarter century later, Stravinsky the critic quarreled with Stravinsky the composer. *Conversations with Stravinsky*, the first of his conversation books with Robert Craft (1959), includes the following exchange:

R.C.: What is the feeling now about the use of music as accompaniment to recitation?

I.S.: Do not ask. Sins cannot be undone, only forgiven.

To which there is a postscript. In January 1961, Stravinsky completed *A Sermon, a Narrative and a Prayer*, one of the most beautiful of his late settings of sacred texts. The Narrative, of the stoning of Saint Stephen, is from the Acts of the Apostles, and much of it is told in spoken recitation with music. The fascinating thing, though, is that the seventy-eight-year-old composer of *A Sermon, a Narrative and a Prayer* had truly and precisely reconsidered the "sin" of the fifty-one-year-old composer of *Perséphone*, and one of the most wonderful features of the later work is the subtle, intensely "composed" dovetailing of speech and bel canto.[1]

Gide, roughly following the second Homeric Hymn (written in the sixth or seventh century B.C.E., and not by Homer), has divided the action into three tableaux:

Persephone Abducted. Eumolpus, chief priest of the Eleusinian rites that honor both Demeter, goddess of fertility, and her daughter, Persephone, offers an invocation.[2] The nymphs in whose care Demeter has placed Persephone praise the beauty of spring. They warn Persephone not to pick the narcissus, for whoever breathes its scent will see the Underworld.[3] As Persephone bends over the cup of the flower, she sees the hopeless, wandering Shades. Eumolpus tells her that they await her coming. Persephone's compassion leads her to go to the Underworld, there to become Pluto's bride and to bring solace to the Shades.

---

[1] In 1944 Stravinsky had used a male speaker in his short cantata *Babel*, but without the fine interplay of speech and song of the later *Narrative*.

[2] Eleusis was the site of a temple a few miles northwest of Athens.

[3] According to Mrs. M. Grieve's classic *Modern Herbal* (Jonathan Cape, 1931; rev. 1973), where she cites Pliny the Elder as her authority, the name "narcissus" is "derived, not as is often said, from the name of the classical youth who met with his death through vainly trying to embrace his image reflected in a clear stream, but from the Greek word *narkao* (to benumb), on account of the narcotic properties which the plant possesses." Mrs. Grieve goes on to point out that "an extract of the bulbs, when applied to open wounds, has produced staggering numbness of the whole nervous system, and paralysis of the heart. . . . Herrick alludes in his *Hesperides* to the Daffodil as a portent of death, probably connecting the flower with the asphodel, and the habit of the ancient Greeks of planting that flower near tombs." Mrs. Grieve notes that various forms and products of the Narcissus (she almost always capitalizes the names of flowers) have been used to good effect in various cultures for "hysterical affections," epilepsy, and as an antispasmodic generally, for bronchial catarrh, epidemic dysentery, leprosy, rheumatism, syphilis, and baldness, and as an aphrodisiac.

Persephone in the Underworld. Persephone sleeps in the Elysian Fields. The Shades ask her to tell them about the earth in spring, but Pluto calls her, and Eumolpus reminds her that she is there to reign over the Underworld, not to show pity. The Shades, the Hours, Mercury himself offer her gifts. She rejects them, but Mercury hopes that, remembering her mother, Persephone will be tempted by a fruit. She succumbs when he offers her a bite of a pomegranate, which brings back a longing for the earth. Gazing into the narcissus, which she has brought with her, Persephone sees the earth held in the grip of winter, and her own mother, Demeter, desperately searching for her. Eumolpus consoles Persephone, telling her that Demophoön, now an infant boy, will teach humankind to till the soil and that he will bring her back to earth to be his terrestrial bride and the Queen of Spring.

Persephone Reborn. Demophoön, now called Triptolemus, removes Demeter's cloak of mourning. Persephone reappears, and roses spring up where her feet touch the earth. She rejoices at her union with Demophoön-Triptolemus and at being restored to her mother. Persephone also understands that her bond with Pluto and the Underworld cannot be broken, that for a certain portion of each year she must descend to her other home. And that is when and why we have winter.

Gide ends the text of *Perséphone* by invoking the words of Jesus as Saint John reports them: "Except a corn of wheat fall into the ground and die, it abideth alone: but if it die, it bringeth forth much fruit."[4] This Christianization of the Persephone myth—the emphasis on Persephone's compassion and on the idea that she descends to the Underworld by her own choice—is Gide's peculiar and touching contribution to the tale. It represents for him a reconciliation of two currents, classicism and Christianity, whose collision had caused him painful conflict as a young man. For Stravinsky, *Perséphone* was a return to the theme of sacrifice for the sake of renewal, brutal and involuntary in *The Rite of Spring*, here a voluntary act of compassion and love.[5]

Let Stravinsky have the last word (from a conversation with Robert Craft, first published in the journal *Perspectives of New Music* in 1962, where he proposes that Auden fit the music with new words!):

> *Perséphone* does start tentatively, the B-flat music in 3/8 meter near the end is long, and the melodramas tend to beget large stretches of *ostinato*. I am no longer able to evaluate such things, or ever again be as I was when I wrote

[4]How much this verse meant to Gide we can infer from his giving his first book of memoirs, published in 1926, the title *Si le grain ne meurt*, published in translation as *If It Die.* . . .
[5]*Oedipus Rex*, whose musical language Stravinsky revisits in *Perséphone*, is also a story of sacrifice for a greater good than that of the individual.

Perséphone. But I still love the music, especially the flutes in Persephone's final speech (this needs stage movement!), and the final chorus (when it is played and sung in tempo, and very quietly without any general crescendo). I love the chord before the C-minor Russian Easter music, too [when the chorus sings "Nous apportons nos offrandes"], and I love, above all, the lullaby *Sur ce lit elle repose*. I composed this *berceuse* for Vera de Bosset in Paris during a heat wave, and I wrote it for her to my own, Russian, words originally. But the whole of Perséphone was inspired by Vera de Bosset, and whatever tenderness or beauty may be found in the music is my poor response to those qualities in her.[6]

Symphony of Psalms

Stravinsky wrote the *Symphony of Psalms* in 1930, completing the score at Charavines-les-Bains near Grenoble on 15 August that year. The work was commissioned by Serge Koussevitzky for the Boston Symphony's fiftieth anniversary, and the title page reads (in French): "This symphony, composed to the glory of GOD, is dedicated to the 'Boston Symphony Orchestra' on the occasion of the fiftieth anniversary of its existence." The premiere was planned for the Boston Symphony concerts of 12–13 December 1930, the new work to be preceded by Mozart's Symphony No. 40 and repeated in the second half between Stravinsky's Capriccio for Piano and Orchestra and Schoenberg's orchestration of Bach's *Saint Anne* fugue. The chorus of the Cecilia Society was prepared by Arthur Fiedler. In the event, Koussevitzky fell ill and Richard Burgin conducted an entirely different program. Koussevitzky did, however, give permission for the European premiere, which thus became the world premiere, to go ahead as planned on 13 December, with Ernest Ansermet conducting the chorus and orchestra of the Brussels Philharmonic Society.

Mixed chorus (Stravinsky preferred children's voices for the soprano and alto parts, though he did not use them in his recordings of the work). Five flutes (one doubling piccolo), four oboes and English horn, three bassoons and contrabassoon, four horns, five trumpets (one of them high trumpet in D), three trombones, tuba, timpani, bass drum, harp, two pianos, cellos, and basses.

[6]Vera de Bosset became Vera Stravinsky on 9 March 1940 in Bedford, Massachusetts. She died in 1983. Not to be missed are two moving and beautiful books, both edited by Robert Craft: *Igor and Vera Stravinsky: A Photograph Album* (Thames & Hudson, 1982) and *Dearest Bubushkin: Selected Letters and Diaries of Vera and Igor Stravinsky* (Thames & Hudson, 1985).

To point out that in the *Symphony of Psalms* Stravinsky uses the word *symphony* in a special way is to be redundant: with Stravinsky everything is a special case. Except for Berlioz, no one composer has given us a more diverse set of suggestions than Stravinsky as to what "symphony" might mean. Among his five symphonies—the Symphony in E-flat Major (1907), *Symphonies of Wind Instruments* (1920), *Symphony of Psalms* (1930), Symphony in C (1940), and *Symphony in Three Movements* (1945)—the *Symphonies of Wind Instruments* and the *Symphony of Psalms* are linked not only by their solemnity (the closing section of the former work was originally a *tombeau* for Claude Debussy) and a certain austerity, but also by the composer's return to the original sense of "symphony" as a mingling of sounds, and by his departure from the Classic-Romantic associations that surround the word.

The Stravinsky-Koussevitzky connection was an old one, the two men having met about 1907 at the house of Stravinsky's teacher, Rimsky-Korsakov. Koussevitzky had conducted *The Rite of Spring* in Moscow and Saint Petersburg as early as February 1914, less than a year after its stormy premiere in Paris. He had given the first performances of the *Symphonies of Wind Instruments* (London, 1921) and the Piano Concerto (Paris, 1924, with Stravinsky as soloist), had invited the composer to introduce the Octet at one of the Concerts Koussevitzky (Paris, 1923), and led the first American performances, all with the Boston Symphony, of the Piano Concerto, *Oedipus Rex*, and the Capriccio. As founder and co-owner with his wife, Natalie, of the Éditions Russes de Musique, he was also Stravinsky's principal publisher of the works from *Petrushka* to *Perséphone*.

In his invitation to Stravinsky, Koussevitzky offered a fee of $3,000 (about $31,500 in 2004 money) and made no stipulations about instrumentation or form. Since Stravinsky, devoutly Russian Orthodox, had had the idea of composing psalm settings in mind for some time, this is what he went ahead with. He first thought of setting the psalms in Old Church Slavonic, and the decision to use Latin came only when he was some way into the work. He began with Psalm 150, and the first idea he wrote down was this rhythmic figure

Ex. 1

which, as "Laudate Dominum," is a forceful presence throughout the quick part of the last movement. "The fast-tempo sections of the Psalms were composed first," said Stravinsky, "and the first and second movements of the symphony followed. The *Alleluia* and the slow music at the beginning of the 150th Psalm, which is an answer to the question in the [39th] Psalm, came last."[1]

That a composition should have unique thematic material is a fairly obvious idea; that it should, or even can, have a unique sonority is more specifically a Stravinskian thought. What Stravinsky calls for in the *Symphony of Psalms* is an altogether special palette with unusual concentration on certain sounds (flutes, trumpets, and pianos) and complete omission of others (clarinets and high strings).

For that matter, even the scoring and spacing of a common chord becomes an adventure.[2] An E-minor chord is a familiar enough object, but Stravinsky puts down measure 1 of the *Symphony of Psalms* as though it were the first triad in the history of the world.

Ex. 2

One of the basics a student learns in an elementary harmony class is that when writing a triad you emphasize in the first place its root and then its fifth. In an E-minor chord, those would be E and B respectively. Stravinsky's sharply articulated opening chord here, as distributed through his orchestra, is singularly underprivileged in B's, and even more in E's. The note of which there is by far the most is G, the third, the one that, according to common practice and academic theory, is the one not to be doubled. Part of this amazing sound also stems from the spacing of the chord: the concentration of flutes, oboes, harp, and pianos at the top, the parallel concentration of bassoons, contrabassoon, trombones, timpani, basses, harp, and pianos at the bottom, and that great gap in between.

Equally characteristic of Stravinsky is what happens after this chord: the scurrying sixteenth-notes in oboe and bassoon. What he does here is directly opposed to the Classic-Romantic way of "modulating" organically

[1]Stravinsky uses the numberings of the Psalms as found in the Vulgate. The corresponding numbers in the King James Version are verses 12 and 13 of Psalm 39, the first three verses of Psalm 40, and Psalm 150.

[2]Beethoven, a composer Stravinsky learned to cherish only very late in life, provides exciting precedents in this matter.

and smoothly from one event to the next. Instead, he proceeds by shock, making a deliberately violent leap from the E-minor chord to the sixteenth-note figuration and then back. Moreover, the two chords the sixteenth-note pattern outlines—going up on B-flat, coming down on G—are not brought into a relationship of mutual relevance but are left as opposed and, for the time being, unreconciled elements.

Another Stravinskian feature is the dynamic marking on that first chord. It is *mezzo forte*. The force of this opening is unmistakable, and almost every other composer would have expressed its electrifying impact with a smashing hammer-blow of sound. But Stravinsky turns its energy inward, and the compacted, held-in nature of his expressive impulses provides an essential clue to the sources of the beauty and power of his music.[3] The intensely moving final pages of the *Symphony of Psalms*, "Laudate Eum in cymbalis benesonantibus . . ." are another manifestation of that same spiritual reserve.

The first Psalm, immensely exciting in its quick, take-no-prisoners ascent to its conclusion, is really one overwhelming crescendo. That crescendo amounts to a single overriding gesture, in spite of the arresting presentation of opposites in the first two bars and of what evolves from that opposition. The destination and conclusion of this movement is a brilliant chord of G major. And now we understand why that first E-minor chord was so G-laden: E minor was the stepping-stone to its relative major, G. That whole first movement has been one big upbeat to the second. And that movement will in turn be revealed as the platform—in musical terms, the dominant—from which to attain the symphony's real tonal center, C. That second movement also ends in its relative major, which is E-flat, and the finale continues the chain with its delicate balance of E-flat (the chorus) and C (the bass). And those two keys are the ones whose dominants, B-flat and G, collided so startlingly in the sixteenth-note oboe-and-bassoon figuration at the very beginning of the symphony.

Clearly, Stravinsky is intensely concerned with unity. Most obviously, the three movements are to be sung and played without pause. The sequence of texts, too, is carefully composed. The 39th Psalm is like an answer to the 38th, and the Alleluia with which the 150th Psalm begins is the "new canticle" of the 39th.

Here is Stravinsky's account of the second movement: "The 'Waiting for the Lord' Psalm makes the most overt use of musical symbolism in any

[3]You can find a parallel instance in the Classical repertory in the two opening chords of Beethoven's "Eroica" Symphony. The gesture is *fortissimo*, as it were, but the marking is *forte*, Beethoven saving actual *fortissimo* for critical climaxes later in the movement.

of my music before *The Flood* [1961?]. An upside-down pyramid of fugues, it begins with a purely instrumental fugue of limited compass and employs only solo instruments." This is the point at which Stravinsky comes closest in austerity to the Byzantine icons that meant so much to him.

Next we hear what Stravinsky calls "the human fugue," which he in fact describes as "the next and higher stage." The voices are first heard with instruments, but eventually they sing *a cappella*. Stravinsky continues: "The human fugue also represents a higher level in the architectural symbolism by the fact that it expands into the bass register. The third stage, the upside-down foundation, unites the two fugues" at "Et immisit in os meum canticum novum" (And he hath put a new song in my mouth).

Stravinsky regards Psalm 150 as "a song to be danced, as David danced before the ark."[4] And when *Dialogues and a Diary* came out in 1963, he astonished many of his listeners and readers with the statement that "the *allegro* in the 150th Psalm was inspired by a vision of Elijah's chariot climbing the heavens [II Kings 2:11]; I do not think I had ever written anything so literal as the triplets for horns and piano to suggest the horses and the chariot. The final hymn of praise must be thought of as issuing from the skies; agitation is followed by the calm of praise."

There is one more great crescendo for the Psalmist's praise of God with timbrel and choir (Stravinsky does not take the biblical hints on orchestration), but for the praise on high-sounding cymbals and cymbals of joy, the music settles into a different, deeply inward kind of ecstasy, whose musical expression here is all timeless, motionless quiet. Great censers swing, and subdued voices fill the air with their adoration. Or, in musical terms, pianos, harp, and timpani move through three notes over and over, while cellos and trumpets—later oboes as well, finally all the winds—in the same register as the voices, spread harmony at once rich and luminous. The "Alleluia," the new canticle, returns for a moment to resolve, with the final "Dominum," everything into a C-major chord, severe and beatific.

Mass

Stravinsky completed the Gloria on 20 December 1944 and the Kyrie at about the same time; the Mass as a whole was finished on 15 March 1948.

4"Tympano et choro," translated in the Douay-Rheims Bible as "timbrel and choir," is given in the King James Version as "timbrel and dance."

On 26 February 1947, Irving Fine conducted the Kyrie and Gloria, accompanied by two pianos, in Boston. The first complete performance was given on 27 October 1948 in Milan, with Ernest Ansermet conducting members of the chorus and orchestra of La Scala.

Four-part mixed chorus, with solo voices occasionally emerging from the chorus, the score indicating that "children's voices should be employed." Two oboes and English horn, two bassoons, two trumpets, and three trombones.

"Must one be a believer to compose [a Mass]?" Robert Craft asked Stravinsky in the *Conversations* they published in 1959. "Certainly," came the unambiguous reply, and not merely a believer in 'symbolic figures,' but in the Person of the Lord, the Person of the Devil, and the Miracles of the Church." In *Stravinsky in Pictures and Documents*, Craft tells us that the composer fulfilled this requirement in the most literal way possible.

The Mass is one of the very few works by Stravinsky composed not in response to a commission but from inner need alone. He had been baptized on the day of his birth and ceremonially received into the Russian Orthodox Church twenty-four days later. In his teens he began to rebel against the religious life, and when he rejoined the church in 1926 he had not been a communicant since 1910. He described joining a group of pilgrims on a journey from Venice to Padua to celebrate the seven-hundredth anniversary of Saint Anthony: "I happened to enter the Basilica just as the Saint's body was exhibited. I saw the coffin, I knelt, and I prayed. I asked that a sign of recognition be given when and if my prayer was answered, and as it was answered, and with the sign, I do not hesitate to call that moment of recognition the most real in my life."

The composition of Stravinsky's first sacred work, an *a cappella* Lord's Prayer in Old Church Slavonic, followed immediately. Over the years there came the *Symphony of Psalms*; a Creed and *Ave Maria* (both in Slavonic, though Stravinsky later made Latin versions, as he did of the Lord's Prayer); the Mass; the *Canticum sacrum*; *A Sermon, a Narrative, and a Prayer*; and the *Requiem Canticles*. There was as well a number of works with nonliturgical texts but wholly or partly on sacred subjects: *Babel*; the Cantata on Elizabethan texts; the setting of T. S. Eliot's *The Dove Descending Breaks the Air*; *The Flood*; *Abraham and Isaac*; and the arrangements of Bach's *Vom Himmel hoch* Variations and three *Sacrae Cantiones* by the sixteenth-century madrigalist Gesualdo. "My Mass," Stravinsky tells Craft in *Expositions and Developments,* a later book of conversations with Craft, "was partly provoked by some Masses of Mozart that I found in a secondhand music store in Los Angeles in 1942 or 1943. As I played through these rococo-operatic sweets-of-sin, I knew I had to write a Mass of my own, but a real one."

Craft explains the "partly" by pointing out that in 1944 Stravinsky had reached a "spiritual crisis," something that was

> evident in his reading, which consisted of Bossuet's *Lettres sur l'Evangile* . . . , Bloy, Bernanos, and parts of the *Summa.* In that year, too, Stravinsky visited Santa Clara, the convent of the Dominican sisters in Sinsinawa, Wisconsin, and he was often with Jacques Maritain. At about the same time, Stravinsky filled the margins of Ramuz's *Questions* with criticisms of its "Protestantism," while endorsing the Roman Catholic view of C.-A. Cingria in the margins of *his* books.[1]

That was the year Stravinsky began the Mass by composing the Kyrie and Gloria. In general, however, to quote Craft again, he "was openly aiming at the commercial market," and he was soon interrupted in his work on the Mass by an invitation from Franz Werfel to write the score for a film then being made of his *Song of Bernadette.* Because the producers failed to provide satisfactory financial and artistic conditions, Stravinsky bowed out of that project. But he had already composed music for the Apparition of the Virgin scene, which he elaborated and joined to something else he had written in 1942, both pieces finding a place in his *Symphony in Three Movements.*[2] In any event, before returning to the Mass, Stravinsky went on to complete the *Symphony* (for the New York Philharmonic-Symphony), to write his *Ebony Concerto* for Woody

---

[1]Vera Stravinsky and Robert Craft, *Stravinsky in Pictures and Documents* (Simon & Schuster, 1978). The French cleric Jacques-Bénigne Bossuet (1627–1704) was an eloquent preacher and an ardent supporter of Louis XIV's campaign to curtail the rights of French Protestants. The novelist and critic Léon Bloy (1846–1917) was a fervent propagandist for the Catholic Church and a spiritual counselor to, among others, the novelist Joris-Karl Huysmans, the philosopher Jacques Maritain, and the painter Georges Rouault. One of Bloy's disciples and successors was Georges Bernanos: in 1950, Robert Bresson made his novel *Diary of a Country Priest* into a memorable film, and Bernanos's film scenario of Gertrud von Le Fort's *The Last at the Scaffold* became the source for Francis Poulenc's opera *The Dialogues of the Carmelites.* The *Summa theologica,* written about 1265–1274, is the central philosophical treatise of Thomas Aquinas. He died before he could finish the work, which is nonetheless regarded as the doctrinal basis for the Catholic Church's theological teachings. C.-F. Ramuz (1878–1947) was a Swiss writer, best remembered for his novel *The Day the Mountain Fell* and by musicians for the scenario and libretto for Stravinsky's *The Soldier's Tale.* C.-A. Cingria (1883–1954), another Swiss writer, was in Craft's opinion "of Stravinsky's friends in Switzerland during World War I . . . the one . . . for whom the composer felt the most affection."

[2]Alfred Newman wrote the score for *The Song of Bernadette* and won the Academy Award for it.

Herman, to compose the Concerto in D for the twentieth anniversary of Paul Sacher's Basel Chamber Orchestra, and to write a new ballet score, *Orpheus,* for George Balanchine. He resumed work on the Mass in the fall of 1947 and wrote the last measures of the Agnus Dei on 15 March 1948.

Stravinsky wrote a Roman Catholic Mass because "I wanted my Mass to be used liturgically, an outright impossibility as far the Russian Church was concerned, as Orthodox tradition proscribes musical instruments in its services—and as I can endure unaccompanied singing in only the most harmonically primitive music." A most odd comment, by the way, from the composer of *Threni.* "My Mass has been used in Catholic services, rarely as yet," Stravinsky said in 1960, "but used nonetheless." Overall, Stravinsky felt disappointed in this respect.

Stravinsky hoped not only that his Mass might be liturgically useful, but that it also might be

> a protest against the Platonic tradition, which has been the Church's tradition through Plotinus and Erigena, of music as antimoral. Of course Lucifer had music. . . . But Lucifer took his music with him from Paradise, and even in Hell, as Bosch shows, music is able to represent Paradise and become "the bride of the cosmos."
>
> "It has been corrupted by musicians," is the Church's answer, the Church, whose musical history is a series of attacks against polyphony, the true musical expression of Western Christendom, until music retired from it in the eighteenth century or confounds it with the theater. The corrupting musicians Bosch means are probably Josquin and Okeghem, the corrupting artifacts the polyphonic marvels of Josquin, Okeghem, Compère, Brumel.

In Stravinsky's Mass, the instruments, as the composer puts it, "tune" the chorus. The Kyrie is music of utter simplicity; the "Christe eleison" introduces slightly more polyphonic elaboration as well as an unmistakably Stravinskian dancelike accompaniment in oboes and bassoons.

The Gloria adds quietly ecstatic flourishes and embellishments to the vocabulary, and two solo voices, alto and soprano, detach themselves from the chorus. The unisons between those two voices are imagined with a beautiful sensitivity to color.

Of the Credo, Stravinsky said that as "one composes a march to facilitate marching men, so with my Credo I hope to provide an aid to the text. The Credo is the longest movement. There is much to believe." Stravinsky introduces it with a plainsong intonation for the words "Credo in unum Deum," just as Renaissance composers used to do in their *a cappella* Masses, a practice also observed occasionally by later composers such as Bruckner and Vaughan Williams.[3] He then proceeds to set the text as simple syllabic chanting whose flat *piano* is relieved only by a crescendo on "cujus regni non erit finis" and firmer pronouncement (but only *poco più forte*) of the words "ecclesiam," "peccatorum," and "mortuorum." The instruments drop away for the six-measure polyphonic Amen.

The Sanctus returns to the more florid style of the Gloria, and the "Hosanna," physically the most energetic part of the score, is to one of those very Russian melodies of Stravinsky's that keep revolving in new permutations around a very few notes. He sets the Agnus Dei as alternations between a kind of intonation for the instruments and *a cappella* treatment of the text.

Canticum Sacrum Ad Honorem Sancti Marci Nominis (Sacred Canticle in Honor of the Name of Saint Mark)

Stravinsky composed the *Canticum Sacrum* in 1955 on commission from the Venice Biennale and conducted the first performance in Saint Mark's Cathedral, Venice, on 13 September 1956. For that concert he also wrote a companion piece as Lutheran as the *Canticum* is Catholic, namely, a beautiful arrangement for chorus and orchestra of Bach's late organ masterpiece, the Canonic Variations on the Christmas song *Vom Himmel hoch*.

Solo tenor and baritone; mixed chorus (the soprano line is marked *discanti*, which suggests that Stravinsky would have preferred boy trebles, as he did in the *Symphony of Psalms* and the Mass). Flute, two oboes and English horn, two bassoons and contrabassoon, three trumpets and bass trumpet, four trombones (two tenor, one bass, one contrabass), harp, organ, violas, and basses. The dedication, in Latin, is "to the City of Venice, in praise of its Patron Saint, the Blessed Mark, Apostle."

[3]Bach's B-minor Mass also makes clear reference to this practice, even though not observing it exactly. What is very strange is that the plainsong introduction is omitted in both of Stravinsky's own recordings of the Mass (1949 and 1960), the Creed therefore beginning in mid-sentence as well as leaving out the clause "I believe in one God." The 1949 recording does, however, use children's voices (the choir of the Church of the Blessed Sacrament, New York). Stravinsky, at least at that time, felt strongly about this, writing to Nadia Boulanger on 18 March 1949: "Unfortunately, [the children on the recording] were not all first-rate, for, unlike in Europe, no tradition exists here in the training of discanti and alti. I chose the children, nevertheless, because the presence of women in the Mass, no matter how perfect they might be, would be a more serious mistake for the sense and spirit of this music than the imperfection of a chorus of children." On his 1960 recording, Stravinsky used adult voices, but the women of the Gregg Smith Singers and the soloists Adrienne Albert and Annette Baxter come remarkably close to sounding like boys, and very good ones.

Stravinsky is now a permanent Venetian, having taken up residence, so to speak, in the Orthodox enclosure of the cemetery on the island of San Michele on 15 April 1971, nine days after his death in New York. That choice was of course his own, and the most urgent single reason for it was his desire to be buried near Sergei Diaghilev, who died in Venice in 1929, and for whom Stravinsky composed *The Firebird, Petrushka, The Rite of Spring, The Nightingale, Renard, The Wedding, Pulcinella, Mavra,* and *Oedipus Rex.*[1] For Diaghilev, a man of whom one might almost say that he invented Igor Stravinsky, Venice was a magical place, and the words VENISE, INPSIRATRICE ETERNELLE DE NOS APAISEMENTS (Venice, Eternal Inspiration of the Things That Bring Us Peace) are carved on his tombstone.

But beyond that, Stravinsky had an abiding love for Venice ever since his first time there, in 1925, when he played his Piano Sonata at the International Society for Contemporary Music Festival. Paul Griffiths suggests in his book on Stravinsky that Venice may have become a kind of substitute for the composer's beloved Saint Petersburg, another city of canals. At any rate, Stravinsky visited Venice many times. Sometimes he was there as a performer, as for example in 1934, when he conducted his Capriccio with his son Soulima as soloist and met Alban Berg in the green room afterward; in 1952, for the first performances of *The Rake's Progress* at La Fenice, the theater where *Rigoletto* and *La traviata* had been introduced about a hundred years before; and for the first performances of his three commissions from the Biennale: *Canticum Sacrum* in 1956; in 1958, *Threni,* the grandest of his late sacred works and whose first notes he had composed the year before on the piano in the bar of the Hotel Bauer-Grünwald; and, in 1960, the *Monumentum pro Gesualdo.* From the middle 1950s until 1962, Venice, whose art and architecture Stravinsky came to know and to love more and more, was also a favorite spot for holidays and breaks on concert tours.

It can seem hard to believe that only four years lie between the premieres of *The Rake's Progress* and *Canticum Sacrum,* so drastically different are their musical languages. When Stravinsky began work on the Mozartian *Rake's Progress* in the winter of 1947–1948, one certain fact about the music world was that Arnold Schoenberg and Igor Stravinsky, both displaced into suburbs of Los Angeles, represented irreconcilable outlooks with respect to musical composition: the occupants of the White House and the Kremlin were hardly more different in their views on how to run the world. Yet just a few years later, here is Stravinsky exploring compositional techniques that belonged to The Other. What had happened?

---

[1] *Apollo,* although composed on commission from the Elizabeth Sprague Coolidge Foundation in Washington, D.C., was first staged by Diaghilev's Ballets Russes.

One thing is that the young conductor Robert Craft had come into Stravinsky's life, bringing, along with devotion to Stravinsky, his own extraordinary resources of inquisitiveness and erudition. These included a profound knowledge of the music of Schoenberg and his two principal students, Anton Webern and Alban Berg. Another factor is that Schoenberg, Stravinsky's senior by eight years, died in the summer of 1951, an event that seemed to give Stravinsky permission to explore the ways Schoenberg's discoveries might be useful or interesting for himself.

Schoenberg and Stravinsky are light-years apart in their artistic temperaments, Stravinsky having no affinity at all for Schoenberg's Expressionist agonies and no interest in emulating them. But Schoenberg's way of choosing notes and putting them together, invented by him in the early 1920s—that was something else again. Basing these choices on a particular ordering of the twelve notes allows for a broad range of expressive and stylistic possibilities: Schoenberg, Webern, and Berg were also remarkably divergent artistic temperaments and their works are remarkably different from one another's. And as Stravinsky began his explorations in such pieces as the Septet (1953), *Three Shakespeare Songs* (1954), and *In Memoriam Dylan Thomas* (1954), he found highly Stravinskian ways of applying whatever tickled him about Schoenberg's discoveries, using those ways to do what he had always done: write music that, whatever its stylistic surface, proclaims loudly and unmistakably IGOR STRAVINSKY WAS HERE. The voice we hear in the *Canticum Sacrum* is Stravinsky's and only Stravinsky's.

The texts are drawn from the Bible, presumably by Stravinsky himself—at least, I know of no rival claims. Several observers have suggested that Stravinsky chose a five-movement design as an aural analogy to the five domes of Saint Mark's Cathedral, where the work would have its first performance. The composers—the Gabrielis, Andrea and Giovanni, were the most celebrated of them—who worked at Saint Mark's during its musical glory years around 1600 took advantage of the possibilities for antiphonal effects offered by the interior design of the cathedral, with its opposing choir galleries, and Stravinsky, who visited Saint Mark's in 1955 specifically for the purpose of checking out its acoustical properties, enjoys those possibilities as well.

Stravinsky precedes the five "real" movements with a brief *Dedicatio* for the tenor and baritone soloists and three trombones, measures in which he actually sets to music the formal dedication to the city and its patron saint. Renaissance composers and some of the earlier Baroque ones liked occasionally to set the titles of sacred works to music, to announce what it is we are about to hear: for example, the beautiful Passion settings by Heinrich Schütz (they are the greatest before Bach) begin with such an announcement, and so do many settings—Thomas Tallis's, for instance, and Couperin's—of the Lamentations of Jeremiah sung during the Tenebrae services of Holy Week. Here, in these nine introductory bars, florid in line, austere in sonority, Stravinsky harks back to that tradition.

The subject of the first full movement, *Euntes in mundum*, is Jesus' exhortation to the Apostles to go out into the world and preach. This is grandly sonorous music for the full forces. Right away, the staccato repeated notes of trumpets with trombone and bassoons provide the Stravinsky signature. In this movement we also meet a sound to be found nowhere else in Stravinsky's music, that of the organ, which is used for punctuation as part of the orchestral *tutti*, but which, its bass line lightly doubled by bassoons, has two solemn solo interludes.

After the hieratic grandeur of *Euntes in mundum* comes a more intimate music, its text drawn from the Song of Songs. *Surge, aquilo* is a tenor solo in Stravinsky's most ecstatically florid vocal style, and with an amazing kaleidoscopic accompaniment for flute, English horn, harp, and three basses. This movement is Stravinsky's leap into full-blown, twelve-note serialism, but what is most immediately striking is the ardent lyricism of the tenor's love song. Probably the most celebrated piece written for Saint Mark's is the glorious collection by Claudio Monteverdi known as the *Vespers of 1610*: aside from general ideas of contrast and range of types of music, it also gave Stravinsky a model for the virtuoso vocal writing of *Surge, aquilo*.

The third movement is the *Canticum*'s biggest: the Stravinsky scholar Eric Walter White calls it "a miniature cantata within a cantata." (Of the five domes of Saint Mark's, it is the central one that is the biggest.) The comprehensive title of this movement is *Ad tres virtutes hortationes* (Exhortation to the Three Virtues), and its three sections, each the length of one of the other, independent movements, are headed *Caritas* (Love), *Spes* (Hope), and *Fides* (Faith). The opening organ music, which returns for the start of each section and also at the end, ties this cantata within the cantata together. We can think of this section of the *Canticum* as the counterpart to the Credo in a Mass. When Stravinsky composed a Mass between 1944 and 1948, its Credo was its biggest movement: "There is much to believe," he said. For this *Tres virtutes* movement, Stravinsky has invented a rich vocabulary of canons and other types of contrapuntal texture, and in the span of six or seven minutes he offers a wonderfully wide variety of musical sounds.

The fourth movement, *Brevis motus cantilenae*, presents a brief scene from the Gospel according to Saint Mark, that of Jesus healing the deaf and dumb. The main voice is that of the baritone soloist, and he is backed up by the chorus.

The final movement, *Illi autem profecti*, picks up the theme—verbal and musical—of the first section. There the Apostles were exhorted to go into the world and preach; here we learn that they have done so. The music of this movement is the same as that of the first, only in mirror image, as it were—in reverse order.

Requiem Canticles

Stravinsky composed the *Requiem Canticles* in 1965–1966 on commission from Stanley Seeger in memory of his mother, and the work is accordingly dedicated "to the memory of Helen Buchanan Seeger." The first performance was given on 8 October 1966 at Princeton University (Mr. Seeger was a member of the class of 1952) by the Ithaca College Choir, Gregg Smith, conductor; the New York Concert Symphony; contralto Elaine Bonazzi; and bass Donald Gramm, all under the direction of Robert Craft. On 17 April 1968, Stravinsky began writing an extra instrumental prelude for a performance of the *Requiem Canticles* to be given at a memorial concert for Dr. Martin Luther King Jr., murdered two weeks earlier, but he abandoned the project when it became clear he would not be able to finish the movement in time for the concert on 2 May.

Contralto and bass soloists; mixed chorus. Three flutes (third doubling piccolo), alto flute, two bassoons, four horns, two trumpets, three trombones, timpani (two players), xylophone, vibraphone, bells, harp, piano, celesta, and strings.

This is the last major work Stravinsky completed; the literally last one was a musical love letter to his wife, the little song *The Owl and the Pussicat* (to use the composer's own spelling on the sketches for that micromini-masterpiece). He was eighty-four when he completed the *Requiem Canticles* and, as Vera Stravinsky said to Robert Craft when she specified that this was the music she wanted performed at her husband's memorial service, "*he* and *we* knew he was writing it for himself." From Craft we learn as well that Stravinsky was also writing for friends who died while he was working on it: the composer Edgard Varèse (6 November 1965), the sculptor Alberto Giacometti (11 January 1966), and the novelist Evelyn Waugh (10 April 1966). Stravinsky clipped the obituaries—from the

London *Times* for Varèse and Waugh, from *Time* for Giacometti—and pasted them into his sketchbook, also drawing a cross on the Giacometti clipping.[1]

In the audience at the premiere was the intensely music-loving physicist J. Robert Oppenheimer. Craft noted that he "led the standing ovation at the beginning of the concert as well as defied an injunction in the program not to applaud at the end of the Requiem." At Oppenheimer's request, a recording of the work was played at a memorial gathering for himself, also at Princeton, only four months later.

An old friend and collaborator of Stravinsky's who was deeply moved by the *Requiem Canticles* was George Balanchine, who immediately began to imagine choreography for them, with arm and hand movements only, saying: "Every measure Eagerfeodorovitch ever wrote is good for dancing." In the event, though, it was Jerome Robbins who gave the *Canticles* a spare and powerful dance setting at the New York City Ballet's great Stravinsky Festival in 1972. Lincoln Kirstein wrote: "[It] was an austere abstraction of ritual lamentation, impersonally eccentric, but in an elevated range of invention in negative accents of inversion and fluttering deformation. It was a metaphor of the aberration or alienation from ordinary behavior which grief unlocks." And this was, of course, the music sung and played at Stravinsky's own funeral in Venice in 1971.

Stravinsky observed about the *Requiem Canticles* that "most listeners seemed to find it the easiest to take home of my last-period—or last-ditch-period—music, and though I know of no universal decision as to whether it is to be thought of as compressed or merely brief, I think the opus may be safely called the first mini- or pocket-*Requiem*."

He drew his text from the Roman Catholic Mass for the Dead, using just parts of the Introit and the Sequence ("Dies irae"), and the whole of the "Libera me." The nine movements are very short, the longest being the orchestral Interlude, which runs about three minutes, and the Postlude, also for instruments alone, which takes about two and a half. Stravinsky said that this "instrumental bias" was one of the first ideas he had for the piece: "My working title was actually *Sinfonia da Requiem*, and I did not use it only because I have already borrowed so much from Mr. Britten in the matter of titles and subjects."[2] Stravinsky continues: "The idea of the

---

[1]Photographs of pages from the *Requiem Canticles* sketchbook, including the clippings, as well as pictures taken at a rehearsal for the first performance and at the performance itself, can be found in *Bravo Stravinsky*, with photographs by Arnold Newman and text by Robert Craft (World Publishing, 1967).

[2]In this faintly (and not uncharacteristically) snide remark, Stravinsky refers to the fact that his 1952 Cantata uses the *Lyke-Wake Dirge* Britten had set in his Serenade for Tenor, Horn, and Strings, and that his *Flood* had been preceded by Britten's *Noye's Fludde*.

triangular instrumental frame—string prelude, wind-instrument interlude, percussion postlude—came quickly after, and I then began to compose the Interlude, which is the formal lament."

The staff lines, which Stravinsky drew with a rastrum he had used since *Petrushka*, are wobbly in the *Requiem Canticles* sketchbook, but the notes on those lines and the thought behind them are as firm as ever. He has also pulled off the miracle of writing in a Schoenberg- and Webern-influenced musical language he had made his own only late in his long life, but with every wonderful note proclaiming STRAVINSKY!

Against a background of chugging sixteenth notes, solo strings project short melodic phrases. "Exaudi" introduces the chorus, first heard alone, then accompanied by spiky music in which the harp is especially prominent, the whole being concluded by solemn measures for the strings. In the "Dies irae," the words of the chorus, some of them spoken, are surrounded by orchestral explosions, electrifying in their energy. The "Tuba mirum" begins with fanfares, just as in Berlioz and Verdi and Britten, but these involve only two trumpets—Stravinsky's joyous *Fanfare for a New Theater* comes to mind—except insofar as one might say that the bass solo is written in fanfare style as well.

Next comes the lamenting interlude with its literally mordant Stravinsky accentuations (those short notes that bite off the ends of phrases!), and this leads directly into the "Rex tremendae," sonorously scored for the chorus, with lively commentary from the brass. The contralto brings poignant weeping figures to the "Lacrimosa." In the "Libera me," which is accompanied only by the horn quartet, Stravinsky divides the chorus so that a solo quartet sings the words on repeated chords—a bow to Verdi—while the rest of the chorus quietly speaks them (another overlap with Britten).

For the Postlude I turn to Robert Craft's description: "the chord of Death, followed by silence, the tolling of bells, and again silence, all thrice repeated, then the three final chords of Death alone." To which he adds: "No wonder everything he composed after this was meant both to preserve it as his last work and to prevent it from becoming so too soon."

Michael Tippett (signature)

Michael Tippett

Michael Kemp Tippett, knighted by Queen Elizabeth II in 1966, was born in London on 2 January 1905 and died there on 8 January 1998.

A *Child of Our Time*, Oratorio for Soli, Chorus, and Orchestra

Tippett began *A Child of Our Time* on 4 September 1939, the day after England entered the war, and completed the score in 1942. The first performance was given at the Adelphi Theatre, London, on 19 March 1944. Walter Goehr conducted the London Region Civil Defence Choir, the Morley College Choir, and the London Philharmonic, and the soloists were Joan Cross, Margaret McArthur, Peter Pears, and Roderick Lloyd.

Mixed chorus; soprano, alto, tenor, and bass soloists. Two flutes, two oboes and English horn, two clarinets, two bassoons and contrabassoon, four horns, three trumpets, three trombones, timpani, cymbals, and strings.

If you had walked the streets in the center of any German city in mid-November 1938, you would have seen shop windows—those of

mom-and-pop storefronts and grand department emporia alike—
boarded up where the glass had been shattered, with JUDE! or some anti-
Semitic slogan scrawled on the plywood. It was in reference to that carpet
of shards that the Nazis sardonically called the night of 9 November 1938
Kristallnacht, the night of broken glass (literally, night of crystal).[1] Had
you walked further, you might have come across the ruins of a burned-
down synagogue, perhaps still smoking. Passing a Jewish cemetery, you
would have seen toppled gravestones.

I saw and heard and smelled all that as a ten-year-old Jewish boy
in Breslau, Germany (now Wrocław, Poland); in fact, that city's principal
Reform synagogue, a large, red-brick pseudo-Romanesque edifice with
Moorish touches, was at the end of the one-block Eichbornstrasse where
I was born. I left for England in May 1939, moving from there to America
four and a half years later; in 1944 someone was both kind and imaginative enough to send me an illustrated story from *Picture Post*, a less-glossy
English counterpart of what *Life* was in those days, about preparations for
the first performance of *A Child of Our Time*.

Looking at the photos and reading the brief article—or maybe there
were only photo captions—I was stunned. "Oratorio" called up images
of weighty figures in full-bottomed white wigs writing about things that
might well be interesting but which were certainly remote. I think I had
only recently become aware that people were still composing music at all,
and it had never occurred to me that someone might write about events
that had taken place not just in my short life but right on my short block.
It was an amazing awakening for me, this discovery that music was not
just a historical treasure but a living organism. Over and over, I looked at
those pictures, probably quite ordinary ones of musicians in rehearsal,
and read whatever words there were about Tippett and his music, and
of course yearned to hear the piece. It was probably fifteen years or so before I had a chance to do so—that would have been when John Pritchard's
recording came out in 1959—but I always feel as though I have possessed
A Child of Our Time—and it has fiercely possessed me—all my life.

What had happened to bring the horror of Kristallnacht about? In
1938, around seventeen thousand Polish Jews were living in Germany,
and most of them, or their parents, had been there since the beginning of
the century. In October of that year they suddenly found themselves in
a terrible vise when the German government decided to expel them, and
the Polish government, which could hardly be described as philo-Semitic,

---

[1]Several years ago there was discussion in Germany about naming 9 November as a national hol-
iday in commemoration of the opening of the Berlin Wall in 1989, but 3 October, the date in
1990 when East and West Germany became one, was chosen instead.

refused to take them in, even though they were Polish nationals with Polish passports. Among these unfortunate people, forced out of their homes and sent to a detention camp at the Polish border, were Zindel Grynszpan and his family, who had kept a small general store in Hanover since 1911. The Grynszpans' seventeen-year-old son, Herschel, was living with an uncle and aunt in Paris. His emigration had been messy, and, having first lived illegally with another uncle in Belgium, he was now illegal in France, without proper papers.

Enraged about his family's deportation, on 7 November Herschel went to the German embassy in Paris to protest. The highest official he was able to see was the Third Secretary, a young man by the name of Ernst vom Rath, whom he shot and who died two days later. Vom Rath's death was a gift to the Nazis in Germany, providing a perfect excuse for Joseph Goebbels, the Propaganda Minister, to organize massive demonstrations all across Germany—presented of course as "spontaneous." Looting and arson were part of these manifestations, and the police and fire departments were under orders to do nothing except safeguard "Aryan" property. Insurance claims by Jews were rendered invalid. Most Jewish adult men were arrested. Almost all returned to their homes a few days later, heads shaved. "Concentration camp" and such names as Dachau, Buchenwald, and Sachsenhausen had suddenly entered everyday vocabulary, at least for Jews. In addition, enormous fines were levied against the Jews, both as punishment for vom Rath's murder and for cleanup costs. Kristallnacht was a turning point in Hitler's war on Germany's Jewish population—a ferocious tightening of the screws and the first step on the road to the "Final Solution."[2]

Kristallnacht drew enormous attention internationally: for a week it was on the front pages of newspapers throughout the world. President Roosevelt recalled the American ambassador in Berlin in protest. One who was deeply affected by the story was the thirty-three-year-old Michael Tippett, possessed of an acute social and political conscience and, as a homosexual in the intensely homophobic atmosphere of 1930s England, sharply sensitized to the treatment of powerless minorities.

---

[2]Herschel Grynszpan's story and that of vom Rath's death are full of obscurities. After the shooting, Hitler sent his personal physician and another doctor from Munich to Paris, and some historians have suggested that the purpose was to make sure that vom Rath would die and thus become a martyr, a victim of a conspiracy by "International Jewry" against the Reich. Furthermore, vom Rath was homosexual and as such did not fit the profile of a National Socialist hero to be buried with full military honors; that was another reason for the German government to be happy to be rid of him. Later, Grynszpan implied that the shooting had to do with some personal issue between himself and vom Rath. Grynszpan was never tried in a German court, probably because of the Nazis' desire not to have the sexual question aired. He was briefly in the concentration camp at Sachsenhausen and was known to be in Berlin in 1942; then his trail vanishes.

Tippett would become a composer who mattered, but he was a slow starter. Like Haydn, Wagner, and Elgar, he is one of those whose name would be known only to specialists had he died as young as Purcell or Mozart or Schubert did. He always knew he wanted to be a composer, but the schools he attended offered no training in music, and so preparation for his future profession began only when, at eighteen, he entered the Royal College of Music in London. At twenty-five he realized he still lacked the technique that would allow him to articulate what he heard in his imagination, and so, in effect beginning again, he embarked on a strict course of lessons with the renowned theorist and pedagogue R. O. Morris. Eventually, Tippett destroyed everything he had written up to the age of thirty.

In those early years, Tippett was busy as a conductor, teacher, and political activist. Like a lot of young idealists in the 1930s he had joined the Communist Party, but was quickly disillusioned. He was a conscientious objector, so intransigent as to be unwilling even to accept a non-combatant assignment in the forces, and for a time after the beginning of World War II he served a sentence at the evocatively named Wormwood Scrubs prison.

Tippett was long overshadowed by his friend Benjamin Britten. (A scene poignant to imagine: Tippett, His Majesty's prisoner, turning pages for Britten, who had come with Peter Pears, his partner in life and art, to give a concert at Wormwood Scrubs.) Later, Tippett moved from strength to strength as Britten, in frail health, came to be less of a public figure and was composing less. In those years, some of the younger British composers used the more idiosyncratic, difficult, and undervalued Tippett as a stick with which to beat the more brilliant and successful Britten— much to Tippett's distress.[3] As Tippett moved into his sixties, honors began to come his way. Unlike Britten, Yehudi Menuhin, and the composer of *Jesus Christ Superstar*, he was never admitted into the peerage, but there was a knighthood, the Companion of Honour, the Order of Merit, and countless honorary doctorates. Tippett accepted this recognition gladly, but always less for himself than as a vindication for pacifists and homosexuals.

Michael Tippett lived his long life passionately, and his fury at injustice—wherever found and in whatever form—knew no bounds. He was also gentle, loving, and full of humor, and he had the strength of the gentle, the loving, and the humorous. He was fortunate to remain

---

[3]Tippett enjoyed pointing out that there is a tiny bit of Britten in *A Child of Our Time*: reading the score, Britten suggested a passage in one of the spirituals that punctuate the work would sound better if the tenors were put up an octave, and Tippett happily adopted his friend's suggestion.

productive far into old age, and to become ever more exploratory as an artist. Whether translating Bach Passions into a twentieth-century context, which is certainly one way of characterizing *A Child of Our Time*; revisiting ageless myths as in his operas *The Midsummer Marriage, King Priam*, and *The Knot Garden*; exploring dream states, as in the *Fantasia on a Theme of Corelli* and the Fourth Symphony; or inventing "just music," as in the Second Symphony and the Triple Concerto, Tippett all his life had an unshakable belief in music's power to address the most central concerns of the human condition.

At the end of 1938, the time of Kristallnacht, Tippett was an obscure figure, scarcely known even within the profession. He had spent time in Germany, was well-versed in German literature and culture, and felt deep distress at what was happening in the country that had produced Bach, Beethoven, and Brahms, Lessing, Goethe, and Schiller. Writing a political protest drama had been in his mind for some time. He had in fact drafted an opera on the 1916 Sinn Fein Easter uprising in Dublin but had abandoned that project. The horror of Kristallnacht fiercely focused Tippett's energies. He quickly saw that he wanted to cast his response to it in the form of an oratorio rather than an opera, and he began to draft a text. Not confident of his skill in that department, he asked T. S. Eliot, who was something of a literary mentor and even spiritual father to him at the time, to write the libretto, but after seeing Tippett's draft, the poet advised him to continue on his own. (Given Eliot's anti-Semitism, he was a strange choice and would have made an awkward partner.) Tippett went ahead, thus setting a pattern he would follow throughout his career as author of his own opera librettos.

Seeking a compositional model for his oratorio, Tippett turned to Handel's *Messiah*, which he had studied and conducted in 1929.[4] What he discerned in *Messiah* was a design whose three parts deal respectively "with prophecies and things general . . . with history . . . and with metaphysical comments." This is how he designed *A Child of Our Time* as well. In Tippett's words: "Part 1 deals with the general state of oppression in our time; Part 2 presents the particular story of a young man's attempt to seek justice by violence and the catastrophic consequences; while Part 3 considers the moral to be drawn, if any." As you listen to

---

[4]That might well have been the first twentieth-century performance of *Messiah* in what is now the accepted manner, that is, with small chorus and orchestra, and with lithe tempos and sharp articulation. It must have seemed eccentric and perverse at the time. Tippett had no pretensions to being a scholar, but he felt intuitively that the then-standard approach, with huge forces, slow tempos, and everything reorchestrated in nineteenth-century browns, was at odds with everything he saw in the score.

A Child of Our Time, you will recognize the familiar oratorio paraphernalia of recitatives, arias, ensembles, and choruses.

The solution to Tippett's search for a title presented itself when he read a review of the powerful last novel by the anti-Nazi Austrian writer Ödön von Horváth, who had been killed by a falling chestnut tree in the Champs-Élysées earlier that year.[5] Its title was *Ein Kind unserer Zeit* (*A Child of Our Time*). When Tippett went on to read the book itself, he found its story to reveal haunting similarities to Herschel Grynszpan's dark history.

One more big problem remained to be solved. Tippett wanted a counterpart to Bach's use of congregational hymns in his Passion settings. In those Passions, the chorales are musical anchors that, in their familiarity to Bach's audience and in the openness of their words and tunes, provide a powerful contrast to the more artful language, both verbal and musical, of the arias and choruses. This problem perplexed Tippett for a long time. He even thought of using Bach chorales himself, but aside from wishing to avoid their sectarian implications, he was aware that they could not resonate with a mid-twentieth-century concert audience as directly as for a Lutheran congregation in Leipzig in the 1720s. Jewish tunes would get a still-more limited response.

Then one day, listening to the radio, Tippett heard someone sing *Steal Away*, and, as he told the story in his autobiography, *Those Twentieth-Century Blues*: "At the phrase 'The trumpet sounds within-a my soul' I was blessed with an intuition: that I was being moved by this phrase far beyond its obvious context. I sent to America for a book of . . . spirituals, and when it came I saw that there was one for every key situation in the oratorio." *Let My People Go*, which is the third of the five spirituals in *A Child of Our Time*—headed "A Spiritual of Anger" in the score— explicitly posits a parallel between the situation of black slaves in North America and that of the Jews in Egypt, and even beyond that specific connection, Tippett felt that the spirituals "[symbolized] the agony of modern Jews in Hitler's Europe." Wishing to universalize the story, Tippett uses no proper names: Grynszpan, vom Rath, Paris, Hitler, etc., do not occur in the work.

All his life, Tippett believed in the power of quotation and allusion, and in the possibility of unexpected connections. His music is shot through with foreign voices naturalized: the spirituals in *A Child of Our*

---

[5]Von Horváth, one of the twentieth century's most original playwrights, described himself as a "typically old-Austrian mix—Hungarian, Croatian, Czech, German—only when it comes to Semitic I can't oblige." He was born in 1901 in Fiume, a city with an Italian name, then under Hungarian rule within the Austro-Hungarian Empire, and which is now Rijeka, Croatia, and he wrote in German.

Time are "found objects," and similarly in other works, the blues, Goethe's *Wilhelm Meister*, Schubert's *Die liebe Farbe* (in an orchestration of surpassing beauty in *The Knot Garden*), the ecstatic syllables of glossolalia, the Beethoven Ninth, Wagner, Monteverdi, Martin Luther King's "I Have a Dream" speech, Hermann Broch's great novel *The Sleepwalkers*, the sounds of a spaceship and of human breathing, and bits of his own music ghost across Tippett's landscapes.

Carl Jung is a powerful presence in *A Child of Our Time*, as he was in so much of Tippett's thinking. The words with which the tenor, who fairly consistently represents the Herschel Grynszpan figure, leads off in the oratorio's finale are a key to this side of Tippett's perception: "I would know my shadow and my light, / so shall I at last be whole." Consider also the account—as in the Bach Passions, an interlocking of reporting and commentary—of his catastrophic action:

> *Narrator:* He goes to authority,
>   He is met with hostility.
> *Alto:* His other self rises in him, demonic and destructive.
> *Narrator:* He shoots the official—
> *Alto:* But he shoots only his dark brother—

As a frame for his oratorio, Tippett uses the age-old metaphor of the year's seasons. He begins with haunting words: "The world turns on its dark side. / It is winter." Part II commences: "A star rises in mid-winter. / Behold the man! The scapegoat! / The child of our time." That the language of the Bible informs *A Child of Our Time* is as clear here as it is in the spirituals. But toward the end, "Winter cold means inner warmth, the secret nursery of the seed." And finally, "The moving waters renew the earth. / It is spring."

Trumpets summon our attention, but their *fortissimo* diminishes quickly and gives way to a lament by the strings. Slowly, human voices rise, and the winter landscape fills the space before us.[6] Solo voices assemble what Tippett calls "The Argument," in music that becomes ever more agitated. Then, in a bass recitative as formulaic as any in Handel, the narrative begins. The oppressed cry their fear, and in their chorus, *When Shall the Usurer's City Cease?*, we hear the fluid rhythms that remind us of Tippett's intimate knowledge of English madrigals. Tenor and soprano sing their arias of anguish—*I Have No Money for My Bread* and *How Can I Cherish My Man in Such Days*—until the soprano's last note makes a bridge into

---

[6]The cries of "It is winter" directly quote that beautiful saga of winter and spring, Stravinsky's *Perséphone*, but I do not know whether this is deliberate allusion or unconscious recollection.

Steal Away, beautifully set with descants by the two soloists. That concludes Part I.

Part II begins with an introductory chorus, grand and impassioned, complex in harmony and rhythm: *A Star Arises in Midwinter*. The telling of the story is resumed in a sequence of brief recitatives and concentrated choruses, culminating in the spiritual *Nobody Knows the Trouble I See*. Then back to the story—the shooting and the revenge. This, too, is capped by a spiritual, the one Tippett calls the Spiritual of Anger, *Go Down, Moses*, sung against agitated syncopations in the orchestra. Contemplative soliloquies by the Boy and the Mother carry Part II to its close, the spiritual *O, By and By, I'm Going to Lay Down My Heavy Load*, the chorus topped by the solo soprano's ecstatic descant.

Part III introduces a new sense of pace, a breadth Tippett has not given us before and which we hear in the magnificent introductory chorus, *The Cold Deepens*, and in the agitated alto solo that follows, *The Soul of Man Is Impassioned Like a Woman*. Grander still—and here is the climax of *A Child of Our Time*, musically and emotionally—is the contemplative *scena* that culminates in understanding and resolution: "I would know my shadow and my light, / So shall I at last be whole." The four soloists continue the ensemble wordlessly, on "ah": pure music has taken over. From this emerges the last of the spirituals, *Deep River*. A single *pianissimo* "Lord" ends the journey.

A Child of Our Time was slow to make its way at first, but, second only to Britten's *War Requiem*, it became the most performed large-scale choral work of the World War II/postwar years. Tippett himself conducted nearly a hundred performances on four continents and in many languages. Twenty years after he completed the score, there was a rounding-off that touched him deeply: at a performance in Israel that year, 1962, in the audience was an elderly man—Zindel Grynszpan, father of Herschel.

Ralph Vaughan Williams

Ralph Vaughan Williams was born at Down Ampney, Gloucestershire, England, on 12 October 1872 and died in London on 26 August 1958. In *R. V. W.—A Biography of Ralph Vaughan Williams*, Ursula Vaughan Williams, the composer's widow, writes about his name: "Ralph's grandfather, Sir Edward Vaughan Williams, seems to have been the first . . . to use the double-barreled but unhyphenated name. . . . Though occasionally—at school or in the army—Ralph was called Williams it is not correct. Ralph's name was pronounced Rafe: any other pronunciation used to infuriate him."

A *Sea Symphony*, on words by Walt Whitman, for Soprano and Baritone Soli, Chorus, and Orchestra

Vaughan Williams tells us that "the first sketches for this work (namely, parts of the Scherzo and slow movement) were made in 1903, and it was gradually worked out during the next seven years." Most of the concentrated writing was done in 1908–1909. While in gestation, *A Sea Symphony* had several other titles, the first of them *Songs of the Sea*, already used by Vaughan Williams's teacher Sir Charles Villiers Stanford, and another being *The Ocean Symphony*. It was first performed at the Leeds Festival under the direction of the composer on his thirty-eighth birthday, 12 October 1910. The orchestra and chorus were those of the Leeds Festival, and the soloists were Cicely Gleeson-White and Campbell McInnes. Stanford, in his last year as the Festival's principal conductor, led the rest of the program, which consisted of Strauss's *Don Juan* and Rachmaninoff playing his own Piano Concerto No. 2. Among the violinists in the orchestra that year was the composer Frank Bridge. Several details of the *Sea Symphony* were revised in 1918. In the 1918 score, Vaughan Williams indicates that each movement may be performed on its own, though I cannot imagine that this would be effective except for the Scherzo. The dedication is to R. L. W., the composer's cousin and close friend, Ralph Wedgwood.

Soprano and baritone solos; mixed chorus (in the last movement occasionally reduced to a semi-chorus of sixteen voices). Two flutes and piccolo, two oboes (one *ad libitum*) and English horn, two clarinets (one *ad libitum*) with E-flat clarinet and bass clarinet (*ad libitum*), two bassoons and contrabassoon (*ad libitum*), four horns, three trumpets, three trombones, tuba, timpani, triangle, snare drum, bass drum, cymbals, two harps (one *ad libitum*), organ (*ad libitum*), and strings. Vaughan Williams also provided a version for a smaller orchestra with just eight woodwinds, appending a note that "the following instruments may be added with corresponding advantage in the following order of importance: organ, bass clarinet, third flute, third oboe, contrabassoon, second harp, and E-flat clarinet."

In his twenties, Vaughan Williams's favorite poets, particularly for setting to music, were Tennyson, Robert Louis Stevenson, Christina and Dante Gabriel Rossetti, and the Dorset dialect writer William Barnes. In Ursula Vaughan Williams's biography we learn that as her husband entered his next decade,

> another, and very different, kind of writer was beginning to fill his mind. Walt Whitman's *Leaves of Grass*, in several editions, from a huge volume to a selection small enough for a pocket, was his constant companion. It was full of fresh thoughts, and the idea of a big choral work about the sea—the sea itself and the sea of time, infinity, and mankind—was beginning to take shape in many small notebooks.

It was Vaughan Williams's Cambridge contemporary Bertrand Russell who made him aware of Whitman, and together with John Bunyan and

William Blake, Whitman would be, throughout the composer's long life, one of his spiritual and literary lodestars.[1]

Whitman's tidal waves of verse have drawn many composers of the most varied stamp. It is at first surprising that the earliest Whitman settings are not by Americans, but it is also understandable: the (mostly) New Englanders composing around the turn into the twentieth century would not have found Whitman's unruly periods attractive, while Charles Ives, certainly not averse to the unruly and irregular, was too much in a perpetual panic about sensuality and sex, particularly the kind Whitman preferred.[2]

At any rate, the first significant composer to set Whitman was Stanford, an Irishman, who composed his *Elegiac Ode* in 1884 and would later be Vaughan Williams's principal teacher at the Royal College of Music. Harry Burleigh, Dvořák's student and friend, remembered now for his arrangements of spirituals, included some Whitman settings among his many songs, but the important Whitman pieces at the beginning of the twentieth century came from England: Frederick Delius's *Sea Drift* (1904), Vaughan Williams's *Toward the Unknown Region* (1907) and *Sea Symphony*, and the *Dirge for Two Veterans* by his friend Gustav [von] Holst (1914), a text Vaughan Williams himself set around the same time and later included in his cantata *Dona nobis pacem* (1936).

The period from 1903, when he started to carry *Leaves of Grass* around, until 1910, the year he introduced *A Sea Symphony* at Leeds, was one of tremendous growth and expansion of activity for Vaughan Williams. He began to teach, was asked to write the entries on fugue and conducting for *Grove's Dictionary of Music and Musicians* (both retained as late as the fifth edition of 1954), and commenced his activity as a collector of folk songs. On the other hand, although a couple of his songs had been published and his *Bucolic Suite* had been nicely received when Dan Godfrey conducted it at Bournemouth in 1902, he had not yet made a name for himself as a composer.

---

[1]Vaughan Williams's biographer Michael Kennedy once asked him who he thought to be the greatest man in his lifetime. After remarking that the question was "very difficult to answer," he went on to reply: "I don't think Churchill, somehow, but a few names taken at random would include Brahms, Walt Whitman and General Booth . . . and of course there is also Sibelius."

[2]We do, however, have one Ives song that at least alludes to Whitman. This is an angry and powerful piece titled *Nov. 2, 1920*, whose subject is Ives's indignation at the election of Warren G. Harding as president of the United States, a choice, as he saw it, based on rejection of the idea of the League of Nations. The text is Ives's own, and it concludes with an apostrophe to the stricken Woodrow Wilson: "Oh Captain, my Captain! a heritage we've thrown away; / But we'll find it again, my Captain."

In 1904 Vaughan Williams embarked on what would turn out to be one of his most distinguished achievements, the assembling and editing of *The English Hymnal*, completed in 1906, to which he contributed four new tunes as well as arrangements and harmonizations of at least seventy others. In 1904 he also wrote the first pieces to find a place in the repertoire: *In the Fen Country* and the *Songs of Travel* on Stevenson texts. The year 1905 was mainly devoted to the *Hymnal*, but he found time to become the heart and brain of a festival that still continues at Leith Hill in Surrey. The following year brought the three *Norfolk Rhapsodies*, and the one after that his first Whitman essay, *Toward the Unknown Region*. Stanford arranged for that relatively short "song for chorus and orchestra" to be presented at Leeds with Vaughan Williams himself conducting, and its success, plus once again Stanford's direct influence—he had been chief conductor at the Festival since 1901—laid the groundwork for the acceptance of the not-at-all-short *Sea Symphony*. In the winter of 1907–1908, Vaughan Williams took the bold and productive step of going to Paris to study with Ravel. More than forty years later, Vaughan Williams wrote: "My French fever soon subsided but left my musical metabolism, on the whole, healthier." By the time of the premiere of *A Sea Symphony*, he had composed his first string quartet, the song cycle *On Wenlock Edge* to texts from A. E. Housman's *Shropshire Lad*, and music for a Cambridge University production of Aristophanes' *Wasps*.

Of greatest significance was the completion of one of the most original as well as most beautiful works of that musically-so-heady period just before the war, the *Fantasia on a Theme by Thomas Tallis*, introduced at the Three Choirs Festival at Gloucester Cathedral just five weeks before that first ecstatic choral shout of "Behold, the sea itself" nearly knocked Dr. Vaughan Williams off his podium. The Tallis Fantasia is as different as possible from *A Sea Symphony*: it takes one quarter of the time in performance and it is scored for string orchestra only.[3] Yet at the same time the two works are deeply akin. Both are essays in transcendence and in the visionary—the one quiet, private (even though meant to be heard in a cathedral), and wordless, the other a huge public address fueled by some of the most sonorously rhetorical poetry in the English language.

[3]To be sure, this is no ordinary string orchestra. With its division into two orchestras (large and small, with *divisi* in each), plus solo quartet, the Tallis Fantasia has the richest and most complex scoring of any work for string orchestra composed up to that time. Incidentally, it has now acquired a sea connection in that it was used in the sound track of the film *Master and Commander*. I am grateful to Anne Montague for drawing my attention to this.

* * *

What a beginning it is, the one that Vaughan Williams invented for his *Sea Symphony*! A fanfare for trumpets and horns. Then the chorus alone, *fortissimo*: "Behold." And then, with timpani and organ pedals, the chorus proclaiming "the sea itself," the orchestra, blazingly alive with wide-ranging arpeggios and harp glissandi, joining on the next beat.[4] (Even the double basses on their low D are enjoined to be *brillante*.) All this on just two harmonies: B-flat minor for the fanfare and "Behold"; D major, the key of celebration, for the next three words. The compass for the B-flat-minor chord is narrow and without a deep bass, the D-major chord stands five and a half octaves tall. The anonymous reviewer in the *Times* wrote that "the opening two chords produced an almost visual effect upon the hearers as though a curtain were drawn back and the expanse of the sea revealed."

In a program note for the first performance in London, Vaughan Williams identified that powerful chord sequence as one of the "two main musical themes which run through the four movements." The other is the melodic phrase that follows almost immediately at the words "and on its limitless heaving breast, the ships." The note continues: "The plan of the work is symphonic rather than narrative or dramatic, and this may be held to justify the frequent repetition of important words and phrases which occur in the poem. The words as well as the music are treated symphonically. It is also noticeable that the orchestra has an equal share with the chorus and soloists in carrying out the musical ideas." I should add that the text Vaughan Williams assembled is big—107 lines of rolling verse.

The first movement is headed *A Song for All Seas, All Ships*, and the words come in part from a poem by the same name and in part (the beginning) from *Song of the Exposition*. The text is indeed a rhapsody to all seas, and even more to all ships and those who sail, "picked sparingly without noise by thee old ocean." Nor are those forgotten who go down with their ships, "doing their duty." The baritone enters, not with what Whitman calls "a rude brief recitative," but with a broad, proudly striding declamatory passage celebrating the ships, the waves "spreading and spreading far as the eye can reach," and "the sailors of all nations." Here and later, Vaughan Williams responds to the rhythmic challenges of Whitman's expansive and unpredictable periods with a combination of energy, sensibility, and confidence equaled only by Roger Sessions in *When Lilacs Last in the Dooryard Bloom'd*.

---

[4]It was Donald Tovey, composer, conductor, pianist, and program note writer par excellence, who suggested delaying the orchestra's D-major chord by one beat so that "sea" would be clearly heard.

The soprano entrance, "Flaunt out, O Sea, your separate flags of nations!", is bold and dramatic. Two of Whitman's lines—"But do you reserve especially for yourself and for the soul of man one flag above all the rest, / A spiritual woven signal for all nations, emblem of man elate above death"—are especially important, as the calm and sure music for soprano and chorus, beautifully seconded by the shimmering orchestra, makes clear. Important, because here is unmistakable notice that Vaughan Williams means to give us more than a gloriously colorful pageant: the human soul is the central subject of *A Sea Symphony*.

This is in effect the development of the first movement, and "Token of all brave captains," a thrilling phrase taking off from high A—and the more thrilling for being given with no accompaniment—is its high point. With "a pennant universal," the baritone initiates a recapitulation, which brings the climax of the whole movement, "one flag above all the rest," with, for the first time, all singers and players heard together. The quiet close is for voices alone, the soprano soaring above all the rest.

The second movement, *On the Beach at Night, Alone,* is a text Whitman had titled *Clef Poem.* This is the symphony's slow movement, and its opening chords, *pianissimo,* quite differently voiced and transposed up a whole tone, are the "motto" chords that begin the symphony. The speaker, contemplating the sky, thinks "a thought of the clef of the universes" and understands that a "vast similitude" forever spans "all distances . . . all souls, all living bodies . . . all lives and deaths." The baritone is the musical leader, but intimating that here are thoughts too deep for words, Vaughan Williams puts his trust in the orchestra as nowhere else in the work. The broad postlude is as lovely and affecting a passage as ever he wrote.

From the inwardness of *On the Beach at Night, Alone,* Vaughan Williams makes a huge leap into *The Waves* from a poem titled *After the Sea-Ship.* This is an exuberant bravura scherzo for chorus and orchestra, and a movement that puts philosophical and visionary contemplation aside for a few minutes. It is a genre piece, exciting (and very difficult) to sing and arrestingly pictorial in its evocation of the ocean's surfaces and moods. The end is a special delight. The last word is "following," and Vaughan Williams sets it as a *fortissimo* shout that hangs out beyond the orchestra's final chord. That, as the composer happily admitted, is a shameless crib from Beethoven, who does just that with the word "Gloria" in his *Missa solemnis.*[5] For timid conductors, Vaughan Williams

---

[5]Vaughan Williams writes interestingly about cribbing in two of the essays, "A Musical Autobiography" and "What Have We Learned from Elgar?", in his collection *National Music and Other Essays* (Oxford University Press, 1972). Vaughan Williams also points out his debts to Elgar: "I am astonished . . . to find on looking back on my earlier works how much I cribbed from him, probably when I thought I was being most original."

provided an alternative close with the orchestra hammering out two quick chords at the end of the chorus's last word. I have never heard it, nor can I imagine anyone wanting to use it.

The finale, *The Explorers*, is by far the symphony's biggest movement—about as long as the first two combined. It needs to be big, for it is a destination, the place where the promises of those first movements are kept. Vaughan Williams took the text from *Passage to India*, a strange and little-known book in which Whitman seems to seek to reconcile Eastern mysticism with the imperatives of the industrialized Western world.

Here, sailing represents the soul's hunger to explore, to "launch out on trackless seas," to "steer for the deep waters only . . . / For we are bound where mariner has not yet dared to go, / And we will risk the ship, ourselves, and all." And a word appears here that we have not met previously in this symphony: God. "Bathe me, O God, in thee," the poet prays. "Swiftly, swiftly I shrivel at the thought of God." And at the end, as the soul sets out—"O farther, farther, farther sail!"—he finds reassurance: "O daring joy, but safe! are they not all the seas of God?"

In his young years, Vaughan Williams, among whose ancestors can be found more than one churchman, was an atheist, even a rather fierce one. Later he settled into what his widow called a "comfortable agnosticism," a position that excluded going to church unless to perform or hear music. For all that, religion was a passionate concern of his: this is, after all, the man who gave more than a year of his life to editing a hymnal and whose catalogue includes the *Five Mystical Songs*, the Mass in G minor, *Sancta Civitas, Flos Campi, Benedicite, Job, Dona nobis pacem*, the opera *Pilgrim's Progress, Hodie*, and many other works steeped in religious thought and feeling. *A Sea Symphony*, although it is obviously not an expression of orthodox Christianity, belongs among these works. There are five references to God in the last movement, and four of them are set and scored in a way that, responding to Whitman's text, projects them unmistakably as high points in this movement.

In the essay he called "A Musical Autobiography," Vaughan Williams writes that as a young man he had spent "several hours at the British Museum studying the full scores of the ["Enigma"] Variations and *Gerontius*. The results are obvious in the opening pages of the finale of my Sea Symphony." These solemn measures, which desperately need a conductor with the inner calm to live in *Grave e molto adagio*, do indeed bring the Elgar of the "Enigma" Variations and of the deepest moments of *Gerontius* to mind, and it may well be true that they would not be what they are without those models; at the same time, the shape of the melody to which the chorus sings "O vast Rondure, swimming in space" unmistakably bears the Vaughan Williams DNA. As always when he cribs, what comes out is all his own.

Very soon we are far indeed from Elgar's world as the music turns modal for a darkly contemplative moment: "Wherefore unsatisfied soul? Whither O mocking life?" It is the "poet worthy that name, / The true son of God" who gives the answer: "Yet soul be sure the first intent remains." The music brightens again into a tonal world and becomes ever more urgent. Ecstatic climax leads to profound calm: "Sailing these seas or on the hills, or waking in the night, / Thoughts, silent thoughts, of Time and Space and Death, like water flowing." Ecstasy—and something Elgarian—returns as the soprano sings one of the great melodies: "Bathe me, O God, in thee, mounting to thee." The music becomes interior and hushed—*innig*, Schumann would have said—when the baritone sings "Swiftly I shrivel at the thought of God." Vaughan Williams responds to the final thoughts as the soul is bidden to "hoist instantly the anchor" with excitement, exuberance (for a moment we hear real sea shanty music), and, at the last, with awe, mystery, and love.

A supremely eloquent epilogue is a characteristic feature of Vaughan Williams's symphonies—those in the *London* and *Pastoral Symphonies*, and the Sixth and the Ninth are most notable—and here is the first of them: "O my brave soul! O farther, farther sail!," *molto adagio* and *espressivo*. The voices and finally the strings alone recede to places beyond our hearing and knowing.[6]

Sancta Civitas, Oratorio on Texts from the Authorized Version of the Bible, Taverner's Bible, and Other Sources

Vaughan Williams composed *Sancta Civitas* between 1923 and 1925. He chose the Latin title because he felt that the English version, *The Holy City*, was too firmly associated with the nineteenth-century song by Stephen Adams. The first performance of *Sancta Civitas* was given in the Sheldonian Theatre, Oxford, on 7 May 1926. Hugh Allen conducted the Oxford Bach Choir and the Oxford Orchestral Society, and the soloists were Trefor Jones, tenor, and Arthur Cranmer, baritone. The concert was part of a celebration of the three-hundredth anniversary of the proposal that a chair of music be established at Oxford.

[6]The end has been less discussed than that of Strauss's *Also sprach Zarathustra*, but its effect is no less mysterious. At the start of the epilogue, Vaughan Williams has returned to D major, the key where the symphony began. We might expect him to bring the gigantic work to a close there, but in fact—the soul is, after all, voyaging—he abandons D in favor of C minor, the key where the finale begins. High divided violins, *pppp*, reiterate a chord of C minor, while the cellos and basses respond, not with the keynote C, but with a destabilizing, still-questioning G.

Tenor and baritone solo; four-part mixed chorus, semi-chorus (about twenty voices, seated behind the full chorus), distant chorus (preferably boys, and out of sight). Three flutes, two oboes and English horn, two clarinets, two bassoons and contrabassoon, four horns, three trumpets, three trombones, tuba, snare drum, bass drum cymbals, piano, harp, organ, and strings. There is also a distant trumpet, to be placed with the distant chorus.

Between *A Sea Symphony* and *Sancta Civitas* lies what older people in England still call the Great War. Many new scores came from Vaughan Williams's study, too, including the *Five Mystical Songs*, the *London* and *Pastoral Symphonies, A Lark Ascending, Hugh the Drover*, and *Flos Campi*, but the huge thing, the thing that overshadowed and overwhelmed all else, was the war and its aftermath. And Ralph Vaughan Williams had been there, literally. He volunteered for the Royal Army Medical Corps just days after hostilities began in August 1914 and served as a "waggon orderly," that is, as part of an ambulance crew, in France, Greece, and Serbia. Later he was sent back to England to officer training school and in the summer of 1918 was appointed Director of Music to the British Expeditionary Force, meaning the army in France.[1]

He had witnessed plenty of suffering while in the R.A.M.C., but it was more than his own military service that made the war so crucial a watershed in his life. Those years had changed the world. The political consequences all over Europe were vast, and they are well known. As England would learn again in 1945, the cost of victory could be devastating. Casualties on the Allied side came to 4.5 million, more than 900,000 of these being British Empire forces (not counting another 270,000 missing). Almost everyone in England had suffered a loss or knew someone who had. In Vaughan Williams's immediate world those who did not return from France included Charles Fisher, the brother of his first wife, Adeline; the conductor F. B. Ellis; the organist, conductor, and critic W. Denis Browne; and the composer George Butterworth. Adeline Vaughan Williams never got over her brother's death, and Ralph mourned his immensely gifted young friend Butterworth all his life.

Many of Vaughan Williams's works in the 1920s have a reflective and elegiac quality. He did not like to talk about such things and was averse to wearing his heart on his sleeve, but it is impossible not to associate the atmosphere of *The Lark Ascending*, the *Pastoral Symphony*, the

[1]In France, Vaughan Williams was in sympathetic touch with his quondam teacher, Maurice Ravel, who, in defiance of his tiny and delicate physique and after failed attempts to join the French Air Force, managed to enlist and become a truck driver in the 13th Artillery Regiment of the French Army. He named his truck Adélaïde.

Mass in G Minor, *Flos Campi*, *Sancta Civitas*, *Benedicite*, *Job*, and later, *Dona nobis pacem*, with the experience of the Great War. Some of this music always makes me think of Arkel's words at the close of Debussy's *Pelléas et Mélisande*: "Mais la tristesse, Golaud, mais la tristesse de tout ce que l'on voit [But the sadness, Golaud, but the sadness of everything one sees]." But in Vaughan Williams, sadness is joined by great strength and a sense of the possibility, somehow, of deep peace.

More than ten years after Vaughan Williams's death, Maynard Solomon would stress in his Beethoven biography the necessity of remaining aware

> of the transcendent realms of play, beauty, and kinship that are portrayed in the great affirmative works of our culture[:] if we lose the reconciling dream of the Ninth Symphony, there may remain no counterpoise against the engulfing terrors of civilization, nothing to set against Auschwitz and Vietnam as a paradigm of humanity's potentialities.

That is the spirit in which Vaughan Williams, five years after the Armistice, set about evoking Saint John's vision of a Holy City, of a new heaven and a new earth.[2] Nothing he ever undertook meant more to him, and in 1953 he wrote to his young friend and future biographer, Michael Kennedy: "Sancta is, on the whole, the one of my choral works that I like best."

Someone else who was drawn to the same subject was Edward Elgar.[3] Vaughan Williams and Elgar had great respect for each other, but their temperamental differences always made their relationship a bit uneasy. Elgar heard a performance of *Sancta Civitas* in 1930 and, Vaughan Williams recalled, "gave it generous praise." Elgar went on to say: "I once thought of setting those words, but I shall never do that now, and I am glad I didn't because you have done it for me." Vaughan Williams's feeling was, "This made me sorry that I had ever attempted to make a setting myself."[4] An actually existing English work with which there is overlap is the colorful and exuberant *Belshazzar's Feast* by William Walton, a composer untroubled by the meditative and mystical traits that were so central to Vaughan Williams's being. It is interesting to contrast

[2]The book of Revelation was long attributed to the Apostle John; current scholarship, however, tells us that the author, known as Saint John the Divine, was an entirely different man.
[3]Yet another in the twentieth century was the Austrian composer Franz Schmidt, whom it inspired to write *The Book with Seven Seals*, a great work whose emphasis is completely different from that in *Sancta Civitas*.
[4]Vaughan Williams's regard for Elgar extended to occasional cribbing from his older contemporary. See his essays, "A Musical Autobiography" and "What Have We Learned from Elgar?", in *National Music and Other Essays* (Oxford University Press, 1972).

the anguished wail on the word "slain" in *Sancta Civitas* with Walton's single and gleeful hammer-blow.

On the page facing the opening page of the *Sancta Civitas* score there is a paragraph in Greek, untranslated, but identified as coming from Plato, the *Phaedo.*[5] Socrates, found guilty of "impiety" and awaiting death by hemlock, speaks about the journey the soul must take before it can enter Elysium. Here is the passage in the translation by F. J. Church, which is the one Vaughan Williams owned, read, and annotated:

> A man of sense will not insist that things are exactly as I have described them. But I think he will believe that something of the kind is true of the soul and her habitations, seeing that she is shown to be immortal, and that it is worth while to stake everything on this belief. The venture is a fair one and he must charm his doubts with spells like these.

In his excellent Vaughan Williams biography, James Day cites a comment by Byron Adams on this passage:

> By employing this excerpt, the composer clearly sets aside a Christian interpretation of the biblical text that follows, while pointing towards a reason for its selection. While the inscription from Plato is meant to distance the composer from the literal meaning of the biblical passages he has chosen, it also serves to guide performers and listeners of *Sancta Civitas* towards his symbolic intent.

And Ursula Vaughan Williams in her biography reminds us of a crucial paragraph in a 1920 article of the composer's, "The Letter and the Spirit," remarking that "in it he summed up what he believed, both then and for the rest of his life":

> We may take it that the object of all art is to obtain a partial revelation of that which is beyond human senses and human faculties—of that in fact which is spiritual? And that the means we employ to induce this revelation are those very senses and faculties themselves? The human, visible, audible, and intelligible media which artists (of all kinds) use are symbols not of other visible and audible things but of what lies beyond sense and knowledge.

"Cheerful agnostic" though he was (Ursula's phrase), Vaughan Williams knew his Bible thoroughly. He did a superb job of assembling a text for *Sancta Civitas*, drawing primarily on Revelation 18, 19, 21, and

---

[5]I have no idea why Vaughan Williams erected this language barrier.

22, allowing himself many elisions and reorderings. He went to the earlier Taverner translation when it offered more powerful diction, for example, "two-edged sword" as against the "sharp sword" in the Authorized Version.[6] "Other sources" refers to the "Holy, Holy, Holy" just before the end of *Sancta Civitas*, which is the Sanctus of the Ordinary of the Mass. Yet another source, an indirect one but vital, is the work of John Bunyan. Vaughan Williams's thoughts dwelled on Bunyan all his life, and in 1949 he completed the first version of an opera based on *The Pilgrim's Progress*, which incorporates a much earlier work, *The Shepherds of the Delectable Mountains*. His deep knowledge of such books as *The Pilgrim's Progress* and *The Holy City, or The New Jerusalem* entered into his composition of *Sancta Civitas*.

Next to the first tempo direction, *Lento,* and its metronome mark of 76 for the quarter-note, Vaughan Williams writes: "The tempo marks are approximate. The pace must be free and elastic throughout." Getting this right is crucial, and the 1968 recording by Sir David Willcocks is exemplary. As other performances have demonstrated, stiff tempos and lack of attention to the niceties of how the speeds of different sections relate to each other produce a dismal stuck-in-the-mud effect. Wagner famously remarked that the three most important things to get right in a performance are tempo, tempo, and tempo. Few works are as sensitive—indeed, vulnerable—in this as *Sancta Civitas.*[7]

Darkly the orchestra sets the scene, with brooding basses and, above them, flutes in dissonant counterpoint. The baritone steps forth in the person of John to quietly recount his vision. Within the first minute or two, Vaughan Williams acquaints us with the sonorous dimensions of his score: the music begins quietly, but the solo baritone, chorus, semichorus, and distant choir (with its always arresting distant trumpet) all play their part. The words "For the Lord God omnipotent reigneth" release the first *fortissimo.* We witness the marriage of the Lamb of God and then the appearance of the white horse whose rider bears the names Faithful and True, and who will go forth to war against "the Kings of the Earth and their armies." James Day reminds us how much Vaughan

---

[6]Taverner's Bible is an English version of the Old and New Testaments, edited by Richard Taverner and published in 1539. It is essentially a revised version of the Matthew Bible of 1537, but benefiting both from Taverner's excellence as a Greek scholar and his superb ear for the English language.
[7]Without mentioning any names, James Day remarks that, given how much *Sancta Civitas* was "at least in part influenced by [the composer's] experiences of Armageddon in 1914–1918 . . . it is hardly strange that some of the work's most convincing interpreters have gone through the experience of the battlefield themselves." That would include Willcocks, who earned the Military Cross in World War II.

Williams loved what he called the battle chorus, Satan being the enemy, in Bach's Cantata No. 80, *Ein' feste Burg* (*A Mighty Fortress*), and here he gives us a powerful battle chorus of his own, sturdy, weighty, and in a surprising 5/4 meter.

The great central section of *Sancta Civitas* is the lament for the fallen, once-prosperous, and beautiful city of Babylon. "Babylon" is code for Rome, the city from which so much early anti-Christian persecution emanated, but who knows what "Babylon" Vaughan Williams was thinking of in his heart? What is sure is that the mourning for what is lost, for what "in one hour was made desolate," yields the deepest and darkest music he invented before the epilogue finale of the Symphony No. 6 more than twenty years later.

As the repetition of the words "is fallen" die away, a solo violin, rising slowly and *pianississimo*, is heard through the darkness. Also, the harmony has made at least a tentative approach to a brighter E major. Now the chorus, also *ppp*, proclaims words of wonder: "And I saw a new heaven and a new earth. . . . And the city had no need of the sun, neither of the moon, to lighten her, for the glory of God did lighten her." Out of a silence, the distant choir is heard singing the Sanctus (in English). The other singers join in, and the music rides to a great crest on "Glory be to thee, O Lord most high." We hear again the brooding cellos and basses that, half an hour before, had begun the music. And now comes *the* miracle in this great work, a new voice, a solo tenor, saved for this moment, and singing just sixteen words: "Behold, I come quickly, I am the bright and the morning star. Surely I come quickly." Barely above the threshold of audibility the choir, *ppp* and *parlando*, responds: "Amen. Even so, come, Lord." And with last recollections of the opening music, the vision of *Sancta Civitas* fades beyond our hearing.[8]

---

[8]It is a bold and of course supremely uneconomical move, this magical introduction of the tenor for fifteen seconds of singing. And of course he must be marvelous, as the twenty-four-year-old Welsh tenor Trefor Jones surely was at the first performance; so was Steuart Wilson, who sang at the London premiere and who had so delighted Vaughan Williams with his singing of the Housman cycle *On Wenlock Edge* while still a student.

Giuseppe Verdi

Giuseppe Fortunino Francesco Verdi was born at Roncole, near Busseto, then in the department of Taro of the French Empire, on 9 or 10 October 1813 (he was baptized on the eleventh) and died in Milan on 27 January 1901.

Requiem

The theme of the "Lacrimosa" first appears in 1866 in the duet "Qui me tendra ce mort" in *Don Carlos,* and is thus the earliest part of the Requiem. The "Libera me" was written in different form in 1869 as part of a composite Requiem for Rossini. In April 1873, Verdi decided to expand this into a full Requiem of his own. He completed the "Requiem aeternam" and "Dies irae" in March 1874, using music from the earlier "Libera me." On 9 April 1874 he sent the Sanctus, Agnus Dei, "Lux aeterna," and the revised "Libera me" to his publisher, and he was done with the Offertorio on 15 April, thus completing the score. Verdi himself conducted the first performance, which took place at Saint Mark's, Milan, on 22 May 1874. Chorus and orchestra were specially assembled for the occasion, and the soloists were Teresa Stolz, Maria Waldmann, Giuseppe Capponi, and Ormondo Maini. By February 1875, Verdi had written a new "Liber scriptus," and the Requiem was first heard in its new and final version in the Royal Albert Hall, London, on 15 May 1875. Again Verdi conducted and Stolz and Waldmann sang, but this time the tenor and bass soloists were Angelo Masini and Paolo Medini.

Soprano, contralto, tenor, and bass soloists; mixed chorus. Two flutes and piccolo, two oboes, two clarinets, four bassoons, four horns, four trumpets (plus four "distant and invisible trumpets" in the "Tuba mirum"), three trombones, ophicleide (possibly replaced by cimbasso in Verdi's own Italian performances and generally replaced by bass tuba today), timpani, bass drum, and strings.[1]

One of the smartest and sharpest-tongued figures in nineteenth-century music, the pianist and conductor Hans von Bülow, was in Milan the day of the premiere of Verdi's Requiem. He was able to sneak a look at the score, and on that basis he sent a report to a German newspaper. He was not present at "the show," he wrote, at the unveiling of this "opera in ecclesiastical vestments. . . . Our quick and illicit preview of this newest runoff from *Trovatore* and *Traviata* has done away with any desire to attend these festivities." Eighteen years later, when he had actually heard the Requiem—and after his friend Brahms had declared that von Bülow had "made an ass of himself" over this matter—he wrote to Verdi, recanting his "great journalistic *imbecility.*" Verdi, privately opining that "De Bülow" was "definitely crazy," accepted the extravagantly worded apology with grace, adding a characteristically wry "Who knows? Maybe you were right the first time."

Before the Requiem, Verdi had composed very little music that was not opera—about a dozen and a half songs, most of them going back to his twenties; the *Hymn of the Nations,* a potboiler for a world's fair in London in 1862 (but exciting when Toscanini conducted it for an Office of War Information film in World War II); and an elegant string quartet,

[1]The contralto has become an exceedingly rare voice type, but Verdi imagined the part with that color, and specifically the voice of Maria Waldmann, in mind. "Waldmann," he wrote, "can do all the high A's and B-flats she wants, but she will always be a contralto."

The ophicleide, which has a starring role impersonating Bottom as Ass in Mendelssohn's *Midsummer Night's Dream* music, is a keyed bass bugle. *The New Grove Dictionary of Musical Instruments* says sternly and correctly that "its characteristic [full and resonant] tone is not always well replaced" by the tuba. The cimbasso, which was the lowest brass instrument in Verdi's orchestra through *Aida* in 1871, is a bass or contrabass valve trombone, and in his excellent book on the Requiem in the Cambridge Music Handbooks, David Rosen writes that "while a tenor tuba (or euphonium) might best imitate the sound of an ophicleide, Verdi probably would have preferred the homogeneity of sound provided by a bass trombone."

written while waiting, during the convalescence of Teresa Stolz, for resumption of rehearsals of a new *Aida* production in Naples. The Requiem was another matter. Neither an album leaf, nor something knocked off for an ephemeral occasion in a foreign country, nor a private celebration of craft, it was a public address by Verdi to his own people on an occasion of national mourning. The poet, novelist, and patriot Alessandro Manzoni, an Italian hero, had died in Milan on 22 May 1873, and Verdi volunteered a Requiem Mass, to be sung on the first anniversary of Manzoni's passing.

The genesis of Verdi's Requiem is curious and touching as well as more complicated than the last sentence suggests. The story begins with the death of Rossini in Paris in November 1868. Verdi, deeply affected, proposed that the city of Bologna, where Rossini had grown up, studied, produced his first opera, and served as honorary president of the Liceo Musicale, should sponsor a composite Requiem Mass to which thirteen Italian composers would each contribute one movement. The Requiem was written, but various jealousies diffused the energy behind the product, and the director of the Bologna Opera refused to make his orchestra and chorus available for something that would bring no income. The performance never took place, and the bundle of manuscripts was retired to the archives of the publishing house of Ricordi in Milan.[2]

To this *stufato* of highly miscellaneous ingredients and very mixed quality, Verdi had contributed the final section, the "Libera me." He was angry about what had happened, but he got on with his life, specifically with *Aida*, for the grand new opera house in Cairo. Chatting with Giulio Ricordi, his publisher, in January 1871, Verdi claimed to remember nothing about his "Libera me," a remark Ricordi passed along to Alberto Mazzucato, a composer, violinist, and critic who had served on the Rossini commemoration committee. "Let me tell you then," Mazzucato wrote to Verdi, "let me, who has at this very moment, moved and astonished, finished reading [your "Libera me"]. You, my dear Maestro, have written the most beautiful, the most magnificent, the most colossally poetic page one can imagine. Nothing more perfect has been done so far, nothing beyond it can ever be done." Coming to Verdi's original "Libera me" now with his final version in our ears, we will be well aware that it

---

[2]With one exception, the composers other than Verdi are now obscure. The exception is Antonio Bazzini, whose name violinists and violin buffs will recognize as that of the author of a bravura encore piece, the *Dance of the Goblins*. His contribution to the Requiem is the beginning of the "Dies irae," which we would probably regard as a strong piece if we did not know Verdi's setting. Four of the composers other than Verdi had their contributions performed either in their original or in an expanded form at various times, and the Requiem for Rossini finally got a complete performance on 11 September 1988, when Helmuth Rilling conducted it in Stuttgart.

has not all the strength and invention his music would achieve five years later; at the same time, we can perfectly understand Mazzucato's excitement.

Mazzucato had started something. With *Aida* finished at the end of the summer of 1871, Verdi was ready to think about writing a Requiem. When Rossini died, Verdi had called him "one of the glories of Italy. When the one other glory that is like unto it exists no longer," he had gone on to ask, "what will remain to us?" That one other was Manzoni.

Poets and composers are no longer national heroes, but in the nineteenth century that was still possible.[3] Cavour was dead, Garibaldi and Mazzini were long past their great days, and when he died in 1873, Manzoni was the most revered figure in Italian public life. His reputation had been established by the poems he had written between 1812 and 1822, and Goethe declared his ode *Il cinque maggio* to be the finest of all Europe's literary responses to the death of Napoleon. (The former emperor died on 5 May 1821.) Manzoni's most famous work is *I promessi sposi* (*The Betrothed*), and to call it one of the ten or so greatest novels written in the nineteenth century is not to put forward an exaggerated claim. Successive editions between 1827 and 1840 reflect a steady change from an artificial eighteenth-century literary style to modern Italian based on Tuscan speech, so that, aside from its merits as a novel, *I promessi sposi* became, as Verdi's biographer George Martin put it, "a primer and dictionary . . . in effect [creating] a serviceable, modern language for an emerging nation."

A more essential part of the reverence accorded Manzoni had nothing to do with literature. The poet had long been an ardent, eloquent supporter of Italian independence and unification, and in 1861 he had been elected as one of the first senators of the newly founded kingdom of Italy. Verdi, who was also elected to the Italian parliament in 1861, had likewise been committed to the Risorgimento for many years. His music had served the cause, certain passages from *Nabucco* and *I Lombardi alla prima crociata* regularly provoking political demonstrations, and even his name was co-opted when someone discovered that it was an acronym for "Vittorio Emanuele, re d'Italia." (You would not be safe from the Austrian police if you went around painting graffiti about the Piedmontese king who was the rallying point of the unification movement, but no one could object to "Viva Verdi!") The musicologist Philip Gossett, noting that Verdi's picture was on the Italian counterpart to the dollar bill until the lira was supplanted by the euro, has written that to his countrymen Verdi is "more

---

[3]By remarkable exception, the career of the Czech playwright Václav Havel took an astonishing turn at the end of the 1980s.

than a great musician and a great man. . . . [He] is a legend, a symbol of Italian art, a hero of the Risorgimento, [and the events of his] boyhood are as familiar to Italian schoolchildren as those of George Washington to American." In short, Verdi has become a kind of latter-day Manzoni.

Verdi loved Manzoni the artist, whose work so beautifully embodied his own ideal of "inventing truth"; he loved the man who bore a lifetime of private sorrows with serenity and strength; he loved the committed public figure. Deeply grieved by the death of "our Great Man," Verdi told Ricordi that he intended to stay away from the funeral but would soon visit the grave "alone and unseen." Perhaps, he added, he would "after further reflection and after taking stock of my strength, suggest a way of honoring his memory." He made his pilgrimage, and it was on that evening that he wrote to Ricordi with his offer to compose a Requiem for Manzoni. In fact, as the American Verdi scholar David Rosen has established, Verdi had already retrieved his "Libera me" from the archives and been at work on the Requiem for more than a month, but he always preferred to be secretive about his projects and he delighted in leaving false trails. He himself would conduct the first performance and assume the cost of copying the parts. Might the city of Milan cover the other expenses and, if Ricordi thought this made sense, would he speak to the mayor about it? No doubt stimulated in part by the desire to be seen as doing the right thing where Bologna had fallen on its face so miserably in the matter of the Rossini Requiem, the municipality assented at once.

Nothing in Verdi's career ever proceeded more urgently than the composition of the Requiem. He had read many of Manzoni's newspaper obituaries, he told Countess Clara Maffei, "but not one speaks the way it should. Many words, but none of them deeply felt." Uppermost now in his mind was the need to make a worthy monument to the man who represented "the purest, the holiest, the loftiest of our glories," the man he refers to in his letters as "nostro Grande" and "nostro Santo." "Nostro Santo"—our Saint, our Holy One—a surprising and moving phrase from the pen of so resolute a nonbeliever.

At its first performance, the Requiem was given as part of a service, the parish priest celebrating a so-called dry Mass, that is, one without an actual offering of bread and wine, and the movements of Verdi's work were separated—or connected—by passages of plainchant sung by the church choir.[4] (The chant was not Gregorian, but Ambrosian, the more ornate Milanese kind.) Except for this one occasion, Verdi had no

---

[4]Verdi had chosen San Marco, a thirteenth-century building with a Baroque interior and a brand-new 1873 façade, because it had the best acoustics of any church in Milan. Ricordi, who helped Verdi with the search for a suitable venue, assured the composer he would like the priest, whom he described as "intelligent, humorous, very liberal, and unfortunately very religious."

thought of a Requiem for liturgical use. What he offered his—and Manzoni's—public was a concert piece, and it was as a concert piece that the Requiem was accepted and understood the moment it moved across the street to La Scala and from there to the halls and theaters of Paris, London, Vienna, Berlin, and New York. Audiences understood the secular nature of this religious music. They applauded at every opportunity, even between the joined sections of the "Dies irae," and at the early performances many movements were encored, most often the whole of the Offertorio, the brilliant Sanctus, and the Agnus Dei. Verdi, who was as ironically amused by his acclaim as a composer of sacred music as he had been fervent in the writing of the Requiem, wrote to a friend that now, whenever he heard the word "opera," he crossed himself.

Introitus. The opening of the Requiem does in fact sound "religious," and not even von Bülow could have been scandalized by the first page. Yet drama is present here. Like all Requiem Masses, Verdi's opens with the sentence "Requiem aeternam dona eis, Domine; et lux perpetua luceat eis" (Grant them eternal rest, O Lord, and let everlasting light shine upon them). "Requiem aeternam" is ritual—these are words of an invisible crowd. With the plea of "dona eis, Domine," individual human creatures become visible as four solo soprano voices detach themselves. Their prayer is like a sigh, and it is set against the still-more-intense entreaties of the violins. It is also the strings who carry the burden of "et lux perpetua." The voices retreat once more, to step forward with greater force, but also in the most severe impersonality, for "Te decet hymnus."

Next comes the prayer for mercy—"Kyrie eleison, Christe eleison"— and now single voices, assertive and full of character, are heard for the first time. Tenor, bass, soprano, and contralto—they present themselves formally, one by one, and not without a touch of competitiveness. Even in the earliest stages of planning a work, Verdi liked to think about who would be singing it. As soon as he admitted that he really was going to go ahead and write a Requiem, he moved to secure the soprano Teresa Stolz, his first Aida after the Cairo premiere, Elisabeth in the Italian premiere of *Don Carlos*, and Leonora in the first performance of the revised *Forza del destino*. He also engaged Maria Waldmann, his favorite Amneris. Getting the right men proved harder, and the quartet that Verdi took to Paris, London, and Vienna in 1874–1875, with Angelo Masini, the Radames of the first Paris *Aida*, and Paolo Medini, the first Ramfis, was more satisfactory than the original one. The soloists, however much they may remind us of Aida and Elisabeth, Amneris and Eboli, Radames and Don Carlos, Ramfis and King Philipp, of course have no specific impersonations to deliver; nonetheless, Verdi's correspondence makes clear that he was looking for singers with voices and taste, and beyond that, with the power and imagination to project character and situation. It is a glorious moment, this presentation of the four praying and singing men and women in the Kyrie; moreover, when these first few bars have passed, we have a pretty good idea of what sort of evening we are in for. The chorus joins the soloists, and the music ends quietly, with some magical and at the same time simple turns of harmony.

"*Dies irae.*" It takes all available forces to set the scene for what comes next, the contemplation of the Day of Wrath, the "Dies irae." Thomas of Celano was the thirteenth-century author of the vivid text. Great opera composers are great scene painters. Don't bother to go to Egypt to find out what the banks of the Nile are like on a summer night; just listen to Act III of *Aida*. The tremendous noise at the start of the "Dies irae" fixes the scale for the fresco. The trilling flutes, the skidding clarinets and bassoons, the percussive accents of drums and winds and plucked strings, the half-whispering of the chorus—all people the landscape with a crowd that gradually falls silent in terror. Near and far, the Last Trump is announced.

Now, with the scene set, individual men and women speak their hopes and fears and pleas at the moment of judgment. Haltingly, the bass sings of the astonishment of death and nature when creation defies science and experience, to rise again at the summons of the Judge ("Mors stupebit et natura")—and how right Verdi was in pointing out how hard those few notes are to sing. The contralto sternly describes the great book in which all things are contained ("Liber scriptus proferetur"). This dramatic *scena* was an afterthought, this text having originally been set as a choral fugue. Verdi's change of mind, eight months after the premiere, has traditionally been interpreted as a gesture of friendship and gratitude to Maria Waldmann. This sentiment no doubt played its part, but Verdi had an urgent musical motivation, too. David Rosen points out that the "Liber scriptus" fugue "vitiates the effect" of the immediately following reprise of the "Dies irae" "by anticipating its key, its use of chorus, and nearly its tempo, and it was for this reason, rather than any defect in the fugue *per se*, that Verdi replaced it."

At the height of perplexed terror, the tenor and both women cling to one another for support ("Quid sum miser tunc dicturus?"). Their questions disintegrate into silence. Then the basses of the chorus hail the King of Awesome Majesty ("Rex tremendae majestatis"), the tenors timidly repeating the words of their invocation, and from this grow pleas, both piteous and fervent, for salvation ("Salva me, fons pietatis").

The most touching—because the most personal—portion of the "Dies irae" is the prayer addressed directly to Jesus: "Recall that I am the cause of your journey. . . . Let it not have been in vain" ("Recordare, Jesu pie"). Verdi sets it as a tender duet for his beloved Stolz and Waldmann, and for a single wondrous and unforgettable moment, at the poignant appeal to "Juste judex," the just judge, their two voices join to become one.[5] Then the tenor, fearing his prayer to be unworthy, speaks with utmost pathos ("Ingemisco tamquam reus"). This is the Requiem's most overtly operatic moment. Tenors are the authors and the victims of their passions; basses are fathers, kings, priests, sternly noble figures. This bass, even in all his humility, can firmly face the vision of the acrid flames in which the accursed are consumed ("Confutatis maledictis"). All voices unite in the summation that the Day will be one of tears ("Lacrymosa dies illa")—racking, breathless tears wept by the women soloists and the orchestra.

Offertorio. The chorus is silent. The music begins with a great upward sweep by the cellos. For a long time we hear only the three lower solo voices: Verdi is saving the soprano for a special moment. That moment is the turn from dark to bright, from the bottomless pit, from the lion's mouth, from Tartarus, to the appearance of Saint Michael, the standard-bearer who will lead the faithful into the holy light—"Sed signifer sanctus Michael repraesentet eas in lucem sanctam." As Verdi leaves the voices poised on a C-major chord on "ne cadant in obscurum," the soprano joins them, singing the word "sed" (but). For a second or two, her E hangs in the air alone; then ethereal violins, two muted solo instruments in the lead, reinterpret that note as part of the dominant of A major, a bright segment of the harmonic spectrum we have not visited since the first movement. It is but a momentary glimpse of transcendence, for almost at once the soprano slips down to E-flat and so returns us to the proper harmonic center—A-flat major—of the Offertorio. That single word "sed": it is one of the most miraculous moments in all of Verdi.

Next, following tradition, Verdi sets the "Quam olim Abrahae" as a fugue, or at least a fugato, a fugal beginning. The "Hostias," set in the brightness of C major, brings another moment of mystic luminescence. Verdi, who expects all his soloists to manage a real trill, instructs the tenor, who leads off, that the music must be *calmo* and *dolcissimo*, and the ornamental sixteenth-notes are to be slow and spacious.

Sanctus. Introduced by trumpeting and singing herald angels, this is at once an exultation and a virtuoso fugue.

Agnus Dei. This begins like plainsong, with thirteen measures for solo soprano and contralto, in octaves, unaccompanied, and famously feared for the difficulty of getting it in tune. The melody has a remarkable shape, natural and strange at the same time: a first part of seven bars (four

[5]Beyond being treasured as an artist, Stolz may also have been Verdi's lover for some years.

plus three) and a subtly compressed second part of six bars (three and a half plus two and a half). What follows is a set of five variations, the odd-numbered ones drawing in the chorus, and the last of them spinning itself out as a brief and contemplative coda.

"*Lux aeterna.*" This is a trio for the contralto, tenor, and bass soloists. Against a softly glowing background of violins divided in six parts, the alto sings the entire text while the bass, in solemn declamation, reminds us of "Requiem aeternam." At the evocation of the blessed dead lodged "with thy Saints for ever" ("cum Sanctis tuis in aeternam") woodwinds and high violins set up an angel-wing flutter familiar from many a death scene in Verdi's operas.

"*Libera me.*" Before, in the Offertorio, when Verdi wrote a trio for three lower voices, it was to set in special relief the entrance of the highest voice on "sed signifier sanctus Michael." In the "Lux aeterna," Verdi does it to give the soprano a rest before the "Libera me," for that taxing moment is hers alone, a plan already present in the original Requiem for Rossini. Here Verdi had an interesting challenge in 1868 in that the "Libera me" brings back words from earlier parts of the text. For a composer writing a whole Requiem, that is no problem: you recapitulate the earlier music along with the earlier words. But Verdi could not have quoted—or certainly would not have wanted to—music by Buzzolla and Bazzini in his "Libera me," although he does allude very subtly to their settings. In the Requiem for Manzoni, the challenge was different—and magnificently met. This time he had to extrapolate backward, as it were, the settings of "Requiem aeternam" and "Dies irae" from the music he had already written for those words when they reappear in the "Libera me." One would never guess or imagine that the earlier movements quote the later, not the other way around!

In accents of terror—and the agitation in the orchestra reminds us in every bar why we should feel terror—the soprano declaims the text. The chorus, murmuring, echoes her words. The "Dies irae" returns and so, in a wonderful new scoring, does the opening music of the entire work, "Requiem aeternam." The music disappears into silence, or at least into *pppp*. A harsh tremolo on what was, centuries ago, known as the devil's interval—the half-octave or tritone, here G to D-flat—recalls us to the world of terror. The soprano repeats her anguished plea for deliverance. This time the chorus joins her in a powerful fugue whose vigorous dominant-and-tonic punctuations at the entrance of each voice must have scandalized counterpoint professors all over Europe. The soprano's re-entrance is superb, the theme now in notes that are double their original length and presented, *espressivo* against a *dolcissimo* backdrop, at a striking harmonic slant. The music rises to a white-hot climax, the soprano bestriding all with her high C, and then sinks to a moving close: quiet but intensely scored chords of C major, through which first the soprano, still "tremens factus," then the chorus, reiterate their prayer: "Libera me."

Verdi's Requiem, even though distinct from opera—and Verdi did want a less dramatic style of singing here, and less rubato—is nourished by opera, unimaginable without opera, and ultimately unperformable by conductors and singers who do not understand and adore opera. Verdi spent most of his life in an often-frustrating search for good texts. What he was looking for he summed up in a few words when he wrote to one of his librettists: "[I want] a beautiful subject, *original*, interesting, with fine situations, and impassioned—passions above all!" Consider the words of the Requiem, formed from centuries of ritualistic response to the human drama of death—certain and often witnessed, and, by many, fervently hoped for and believed in as the necessary opening of the door to eternal bliss. It is fatuous to say, as some have done, that the Requiem is Verdi's best opera, but still, none of his poets ever approached his ideal more nearly than the authors, most of them nameless to us, who contributed to the Roman Mass for the Dead.

William Walton (signature)

William Walton

William Turner Walton, knighted by King George VI in
1951, was born in Oldham, Lancashire, England, on 29
March 1902 and died at Foro d'Ischia, Italy, on 8 March
1983.

Belshazzar's Feast, Cantata for Mixed Choir, Baritone Solo, and Orchestra

In August 1929, Walton, Constant Lambert, and Victor Hely-
Hutchinson were each commissioned by the BBC, then rapidly expanding its musical presence, to compose a work for "small chorus,
small orchestra not exceeding fifteen, and soloist." At the suggestion of
his friend Osbert Sitwell, Walton took Belshazzar as his subject and
asked Sitwell to prepare the libretto for him. Drawing on the book of
Daniel, Psalms 81 and 137, Revelation, and Isaiah, Sitwell did so in December 1929, and Walton, staying with Sitwell at Amalfi, began work on
the music in January 1930. From May to December he suffered a severe
case of writer's block—"perched" on the word *gold*, he said, "unable to
move either to right or left or up or down"—but was at last able to complete the score in the spring of 1931.[1] By this time it had long been

---

[1]According to Susana Walton, the composer's widow, in her memoir, *Behind the Façade* (Oxford
University Press, 1988), it was "the writing on the wall" that caused Walton so much trouble.
Sacheverell Sitwell, in the stable of whose house Walton was working, noted with amusement

CHORAL MASTERWORKS: A LISTENER'S GUIDE

evident that *Belshazzar's Feast* was not going to be a work for *small* orchestra and chorus; accordingly, arrangements with the BBC were canceled and plans made for the first performance to be given at the 1931 Leeds Festival. Sir Thomas Beecham, the festival director, assigned the work to Malcolm Sargent, who conducted the premiere at the Leeds Town Hall on 8 October 1931, with the Leeds Festival Choir, the London Symphony, and Dennis Noble as soloist. In 1948, Walton revised the orchestration extensively, making a few small compositional changes at the same time; this version was also introduced by Sargent—by then Sir Malcolm—in London, again with Noble as soloist. Some further alterations of details followed in 1957. The score is dedicated to Lord Berners, a fellow composer and an early supporter of Walton's who paid him 156 pounds in lieu of the forfeited commission fee from the BBC.

Baritone solo; mixed chorus. Two flutes and piccolo, two oboes, clarinet, E-flat clarinet (doubling clarinet), bass clarinet (doubling clarinet), alto saxophone, two bassoons and contrabassoon, four horns, three trumpets, three trombones, tuba, timpani, snare drum, tenor drum, triangle, tambourine, castanets, cymbals, bass drum, tam-tam, xylophone, glockenspiel, wood block, slapstick, anvil, two harps, piano (*ad lib.*), organ, and strings. Beecham did not like *Belshazzar's Feast* and, as Walton told the story, "declared in his best seigneurial manner, 'As you'll never hear the thing again, my boy, why not throw in a couple of brass bands?' So thrown in they were, and there they remain." They are optional, but consist of three trumpets, three trombones, and tuba each.

The BBC may have set things off by tendering its commission to Walton, but rivalry was the real spur. In December 1929, Walton heard the brilliant, witty, sweet, and unjustly forgotten *Rio Grande* by the even-younger and no-less-ambitious Constant Lambert, thought it "much better than anything I have ever written," an opinion to which he clung for the rest of his life, and felt needled into competing. That and the BBC commission went together perfectly.

Walton's discomfort on seeing a joke in the *Daily Express* to the effect that what the mysterious hand wrote was not "MENE MENE TEKEL UPHARSIN" but "AIMÉE AIMÉE SEMPLE MCPHERSON," referring to the American evangelist then much in the news, and who, "to make sure her congregation could be 'weighed and not found wanting' . . . ordered them to peg their donations to a clothes line strung across the hall. Sachie thought that, though William did not appreciate the joke, nevertheless the incident had inspired him to finish the work and not be himself 'found wanting.'"

Because the work was to be broadcast, it was put to Walton that the subject should be one everybody was familiar with. Osbert Sitwell, whose protégé Walton had been in his rocky undergraduate years at Oxford, suggested Belshazzar. Walton was not up on his Bible studies and got Belshazzar, who saw the handwriting on the wall, mixed up with his father Nebuchadnezzar, who went mad and ate grass. But it all ended happily. Sitwell drew a superb, strongly shaped libretto from the Bible, and Walton, with his flair for drama, English prosody, firestorm orchestration, and—let us not hedge—scores of *Salome* and a few other useful items to hand, produced what was instantly recognized as a milestone in modern choral literature. Listening to *Belshazzar's Feast*, you remember that Walton would become one of the best composers of film scores— *Escape Me Never, Major Barbara*, Olivier's Shakespeare films, and part of *The Battle of Britain*, to name a few. He was fabulous with the broad brush (but not only), and *Belshazzar's Feast* brings the crowd to its feet.

Walton was twenty-seven when he began work on his oratorio, and he was already an experienced and successful composer as well as obviously a brilliant one. At twenty-one, he had put his name on the map with a string quartet that was selected as one of three works to represent England at the first festival of the International Society for Contemporary Music at Salzburg. (It has not survived in the repertory, Walton himself becoming one of its chief detractors.) Still more significant was the first public hearing that same year of a more personal statement, *Façade*, the recitation, with dazzlingly apt chamber-musical accompaniment, of poems crackling and nostalgic by Edith Sitwell, elder sister of Osbert and Sacheverell. Especially important among the works that Walton composed between *Façade* and *Belshazzar's Feast* is the Viola Concerto (1929), still the finest example of the genre.

Walton had his first music lessons from his father, a singing-teacher, choirmaster, and organist. At ten he entered Christ Church Cathedral School at Oxford and was sufficiently precocious to matriculate as an undergraduate at sixteen. Having three times failed to pass the necessary examinations for the B.A., he left without a degree, but not before he had read many scores and formed some crucial friendships, particularly among literary people such as Ronald Firbank and the three Sitwells. Not to be forgotten are Lord Berners; Thomas Strong, dean of Christ Church and later bishop of Oxford; and the writer Siegfried Sassoon, who banded together to guarantee Walton a stipend that would obviate the need for a job. In his autobiography, Sir Osbert Sitwell remarks with pride that he, Edith, Sacheverell, and their friends were able to shield Walton from the academic training provided at the Royal Academy and the Royal College of Music in London, instead keeping him "in touch with the vital works of the age, with the music, for example, of Stravinsky."[2] As for Oxford, as Walton's first biographer, Frank Howes, put it, that "connexion was ratified many years later by the conferment of an honorary D.Mus. in 1942 and an honorary studentship at Christ Church."

Belshazzar's Feast was a challenge for Walton. He had done nothing on so large a canvas before; also, except for some juvenilia, most of it unpublished and unperformed, he had written hardly any music to be sung. (Osbert Sitwell found notably beautiful a setting of Shakespeare's *Tell Me Where Is Fancy Bred* that Walton had done at sixteen.) But even aside from his enormous talent, Walton had much going for him: a focused and vivid libretto in, for the most part, the powerful language of the King James Version, his boyhood experience with great choral music at Christ Church Cathedral, and a strong English choral tradition to lean on. Walton's *Belshazzar* music is sometimes a bit spikier than Elgar's or Vaughan Williams's or that of such composers as Sir George Dyson or Herbert Howells ever came to be; it is chiefly what I have called Walton's firestorm orchestration that distracts us from hearing that the worlds of *The Dream of Gerontius* and *Sancta Civitas* are not *that* far away. Walton became more overtly Elgarian in some of his later works, and his marches *Crown Imperial* for the coronation of George VI and *Orb and Sceptre* for that of

---

[2]The Sitwells, a commanding and demanding presence on the literary scene in Britain in the middle of the twentieth century but now rather receded from view, need a moment's attention. The three siblings—Dame Edith (1887–1964), Sir Osbert (1892–1969), and Sir Sacheverell (1897–1988)—were formidably gifted as writers and as self-promoters, particularly Edith and Osbert. All wrote poetry, but Edith is the one who is a truly significant poet. Osbert's most remarkable literary achievement is his autobiography in four volumes, one of the great works in that genre. Both he and Sacheverell were evocative travel writers, and Sacheverell also ventured effectively into writing about art and music. In their youth, they were vigorous supporters of the modern in all the arts. Walton had strong personal and professional connections with all three. Sacheverell was the one who discovered Walton at Oxford, declared him a genius, brought him into the fold, and elected him a fourth sibling, and most of *Belshazzar's Feast* was written in the stables of Sacheverell's Northamptonshire house. There was an uncanny Sitwell look about Walton, too—the resemblance to Sacheverell is especially striking—and there were those who assumed he was a love child of Sir George Sitwell, the famous trio's father. For example, the painter Pavel Tchelichev, the great love of Edith's life (but never lover), remarked to her on the tact and delicacy with which the family handled this supposed relationship. Walton set none of Sacheverell's words, but Constant Lambert's *Rio Grande*, the work that stands behind *Belshazzar's Feast*, is on one of his poems. Lambert (1905–1951) was an immensely talented composer, conductor, and writer whose life was destroyed by his tragic alcoholism. Walton dedicated *Façade* to him and thought him the best of all the reciters of that work. You can hear why when you listen to the recording Lambert made in 1929 with Edith Sitwell, also reciting, and with the composer conducting. Lambert even composed eleven measures of *Façade*. The character of Hugh Moreland in Anthony Powell's *Dance to the Music of Time* is modeled on him. And to put him in another context, he was the father of Kit Lambert, who discovered and managed the Who.

Elizabeth II are, if not so refined in workmanship as their models, worthy successors to the *Pomp and Circumstance* series.

The Leeds Festival Choir did find Walton's meter changes difficult in 1931, but they came to enjoy the work, and the first performance was a triumph. Walton himself, who was to become a superb conductor of *Belshazzar's Feast*, as his two recordings attest, was not entirely happy, mainly because Malcolm Sargent's tempos seemed much too slow to him.[3] The Three Choirs Festival, that great temple of sacred choral music in England, refused *Belshazzar's Feast* until 1957. Walton's biographer Michael Kennedy suggests that the review of the first performance in the London *Times*—"Stark Judaism from first to last. . . . It culminates in ecstatic gloating over the fallen enemy, the utter negation of Christianity"— was influential there.

Trombones summon our attention, and immediately the chorus, *a cappella*, begins with an ominous prophecy of Isaiah: "Howl ye, howl ye, therefore: For the day of the Lord is at hand." There follows a setting, first gravely beautiful, then wildly impassioned, of the opening verses of Psalm 137: "By the waters of Babylon, there we sat down, yea, we wept." So moved was the pianist Harriet Cohen by this music that she told Walton he must surely have "Jewish blood."

Walton sets all of the text with keen responsiveness to its dramatic and pictorial possibilities. Some of the outstanding moments: the unaccompanied baritone solo, "Babylon Was a Great City," so effective after the orchestral turmoil of the preceding chorus, "O Daughter of Babylon, Who Art to Be Destroyed"; the fine detail of making the word "music" in the description of the king's feast *a cappella*; the inventive and charming—if that is a permissible word in this context—catalogue of gold, silver, iron, wood, stone, and brass; another unaccompanied passage for the baritone as he tells of the writing on the wall (a straight rip-off, that, from the suspenseful minutes when Salome waits for the executioner to behead John the Baptist, but no less gripping for it); the stunning setting, which I shall not describe, of the word "slain"; the splendid swing of the triumphal jeer that so upset the *Times*, "Babylon the Great is fallen."

Michael Kennedy cites Walton's friend the pianist Angus Morrison as authority for the story that Sitwell's libretto originally had a nonbiblical postscript in the form of a nursery rhyme:

[3] Walton's greatest discontent with Sargent (known to English orchestras as Flash Harry) came in 1954 and 1963 in connection with the Covent Garden productions of his opera *Troilus and Cressida*, the conductor having failed to learn the score properly.

How many miles to Babylon?
Threescore miles and ten.
Can I get there by candlelight?
Yes, and back again.

This is indeed very like the ironic and pessimistic Sitwell, who ends his autobiography with the words, "It is difficult to know the end of the world when you reach it." Morrison remarks that this "might have been possible for Mahler to bring off but not Walton." (Or, perhaps, Shostakovich.) Walton was an artist who always had a clear sense of what he could and could not do and, as Kennedy says, "He scuppered this literary conceit . . . and ended the work as he had intended, with a pagan shout of triumph." The final grand stroke of having the organ come roaring in partway through the last of the barrage of closing chords was a product of the 1957 revision.

[signature: Charles Wuorinen]

Charles Wuorinen

Charles Wuorinen was born on 9 June 1938 in New York City, where he still lives. *Genesis*, completed on 1 December 1989, was commissioned by the Honolulu Symphony, the Minnesota Orchestra, and the San Francisco Symphony through a grant from Meet the Composer. On 26 September 1991, Herbert Blomstedt conducted the San Francisco Symphony Chorus and Orchestra in the first performance. Wuorinen dedicated *Genesis* to John Duffy, founder of Meet the Composer, "in personal affection and in admiration of his many good works on behalf of new music."

Genesis

Four-part mixed chorus (with occasional *divisi*). Three flutes and piccolo (piccolo doubling third flute), three oboes, two clarinets and bass clarinet (bass clarinet doubling third clarinet), two bassoons and contrabassoon, four horns, three trumpets, three trombones, tuba, glockenspiel, vibraphone, marimba, xylophone, tam-tam, four tom-toms, bass drum, timpani, harp, piano, and strings.

Herbert Blomstedt was the inspirer and godfather of *Genesis* as well as its first conductor. In one of Blomstedt's conversations with Wuorinen during the four years (1985–1989) that Wuorinen was the San Francisco Symphony's composer-in-residence and he its music director, Blomstedt said: "Wouldn't it be nice if somebody wrote a new *Genesis*?" or words to that effect. Also, having conducted several of Wuorinen's instrumental works, Blomstedt was curious as to what effect the challenge of writing for chorus might have on the composer's musical language. From these exchanges came the impetus for Wuorinen to add his *Genesis* to the list of compositions on the subject by Haydn, Schoenberg, Milhaud, and others.[1]

Preparing a program note for the first performance of *Genesis*, I visited the composer at his New York town house, a place filled with books, scores, prints, and a Grotrian grand piano, and where nose and eye are quickly informed that this is a place where good food is valued and provided. Wuorinen's voice and delivery are measured, the vocabulary rich and precisely aimed, and opinions on many subjects—that day they covered his composing colleagues, the merits of a 1980 Château Palmer as compared to those of its 1982 counterpart, the Second Vatican Council, and the fluoridation of New York City water—are strongly held and strongly expressed. Information flows freely on matters from Chinese syntax to the latest in rotisserie devices.

Wuorinen laid out a full score of *Genesis*, a Latin Bible, and a copy of what in the preface of his score he refers to as "the now lamentably disused *Liber usualis*," a combination of the principal liturgical Latin books formerly used by the Catholic Church—the Missal, the Breviary, the *Graduale*, and the *Antiphonale*. To establish the date on which he completed *Genesis*, Wuorinen consulted a notebook, maintained with characteristic precision, in which he records information about work completed and work in progress, commission fees, performances, and so forth.

Virtually the first decision Wuorinen made about *Genesis* was to write a nonnarrative, nonprogrammatic work. What, along those lines, can usefully be added to Haydn? Interested as he is in both theology and science, he did not want to pass up the opportunity to try a more contemplative and imaginative approach.

Wuorinen cites the work of Stanley Jaki, a Jesuit physicist, theologian, and historian of science, who has made the point that it is wrong to say that Greek thought engendered Western science: rather, the real impulse issues from the Judeo-Christian tradition. The account in the first chapters of the book of Genesis, Wuorinen maintains, is of a reasoned, orderly creation of the world, an account of a process accessible to reason. The insistent refrain of "and God saw that it was good" attests to this. There is no hierarchical bar to keep humankind from

---

[1]Arnold Schoenberg contributed a beautiful Prelude to *Genesis*, a composite work by seven composers and organized by Nathaniel Shilkret, an interesting marginal figure in American musical life in the first half of the twentieth century. He composed the second section of *Genesis*, titled Creation. Darius Milhaud wrote the fourth movement, whose subject is Cain and Abel, but he is better remembered for his jazz-flavored 1923 dance score, *La Création du monde*.

understanding the nature of the world; incentive exists, therefore, for scientific investigation.

The process of creation, Wuorinen remarks, is usually regarded as violent. To illustrate, he pulls out a late-sixteenth-century Roman missal with a woodcut of, as he says, "God rushing around creating everything." But, he points out, the biblical account makes no distinction between word and event: "The formula, over and again, is: 'And God said . . . and it was so.' What is stressed is '*Dixitque Deus . . . Dixit quoque Deus . . . Dixit autem Deus . . . Dixit etiam Deus.*'" With the exception of its fourth section—and of that more in a moment—*Genesis* is a nonexplosive, nonviolent work.

The actual words of God, the words that follow the various forms of *Dixit Deus*, are always sung by the women of the chorus. This, Wuorinen emphasizes, is *not* a feminist statement. What he has wished to convey by this unexpected, untraditional choice of register is a sense of "otherness" or "not-us-ness," the distinction between God and humanity. As for his decision to assign God's words to multiple voices, Wuorinen is quick to acknowledge the model of Stravinsky's *The Flood*, where the words of God are given to two basses.

Genesis is in five parts. The first, third, and fifth are vocal and are designated as movements; the second and fourth are instrumental interludes. The first movement, *Invocation*, begins literally with an invocation, a great cry of "Kyrie"—Lord. Catholics old enough to remember the world before Vatican II and, of course, music lovers who know their Masses from Machaut to Stravinsky are conditioned to expect "Kyrie" to continue as "Kyrie eleison" (Lord, have mercy upon us), but here the text reads "Kyrie orbis factor" (Lord, maker of the heavens).[2] And "Kyrie orbis factor" is followed by "Stelliferi conditor orbis" (Author of the star-filled heavens) which in turn leads to "Artifex terrae marisque et siderum" (Sculptor of earth, sea, and stars).

What Wuorinen has done here is to make a text by lining up the titles of all the Gregorian chant Masses that refer to the Creation—seven in all. Rather than a linear discourse or narrative, they form a series of celebratory starbursts. Finally, remembering that the first of his titles began with "Kyrie," Wuorinen ends with a great choral cry of "ELEISON." The two words are the brackets that hold the *Invocation* in place.

And the music? Wuorinen is one of the High Modernists of late-twentieth-century music, a maximalist through and through, composing music dense with notes, with event, with cross-reference and allusion. He has never thought that there must be something wrong with music that

---

[2]*Orbis*, which denotes a circle or a disk or anything round, usually refers to the heavens when it appears in a sacred context; however, it is also sometimes found as *orbis terrae*, meaning the earth.

reaches listeners at first encounter (that attitude is mostly a myth created by populist composers and critics), but he has always believed in challenging both performers and listeners to do more and better than they thought they could. His own preference is for music that reveals its riches gradually rather than all at once, and that rewards attention and effort. But the 1980s brought what Wuorinen himself has called a clarification of musical language and style. As he put it at about the time of *Genesis*: "My harmonic language is now more clearly in what I call 'pitch centricity'—I don't want to use the word 'tonality' because it's dangerous and usually misleading—and my use of rhythm is more periodic, more regular, more intimately related to the background pulse . . . which is a long, complicated, and rather pompous way of saying that the beat is clearer."

In *Genesis*, Wuorinen quotes not only the words of those Gregorian Masses but their melodies as well. For example, the Gregorian *Kyrie orbis factor* begins like this:

Ex. 1

and the opening of *Genesis* goes this way:

Ex. 2

After the initial *fortissimo* cry, the chorus basses lead off with a variant of the Gregorian melody's continuation.

Ex. 3

Invocation is a grand tutti framed between the choral exclamations of "Kyrie" and "ELEISON." Each section within the *Invocation* is sharply characterized. For example, both "Kyrie orbis factor" and "Stelliferi conditor orbis" offer the contrast between a chordal beginning and a polyphonic continuation, but each has its own distinctive orchestral texture. The latter includes a measure of repeated woodwind chords that refers to the "beyond the stars" passage in Beethoven's Ninth Symphony. Elsewhere, Wuorinen devises effective contrasts between chordal and polyphonic textures and between lines of greater and lesser smoothness. The pacing is also skillfully varied.

The first orchestral interlude is called *Meditation*. The tempo is easygoing and the direction to the performers is *piacevole*, which means both "pleasant" and "pleasing," also carrying overtones of "friendly." Here, too, the melodic lines are informed by Gregorian chant. Most of the orchestra is used at some point or other in the *Meditation*, but the effect overall is chamber-musical and the dynamics hardly rise above *mezzo forte*. The frequent meter changes—3/2–7/8–3/4–7/8–5/8–6/8–7/8 just in the first seven measures—look alarming to the score-reader's eye, but the effect for the ear is gently fluid, not jagged.

For the middle section of *Genesis*, which he calls *Creation History*, Wuorinen turns to the Creation account in the first two chapter of the book of Genesis. Bringing back the chorus, he is mindful and captivatingly expressive of atmosphere. Waves of percussion and muttering low strings suggest the state of pre-Creation earth, "without form and void." A wonderful ascent and tumble, soft, in just a few instruments, accompanies God's command, "Fiat lux"—Let there be light. There is no mistaking day and night. This *Creation History* is joyously busy music, which ends quietly as God rests on the seventh day.

The second orchestral interlude is titled *Cosmology*. Here is Wuorinen's one bow in the direction of the violent Creation tradition. This is, in fact, a "big bang" Creation. The imaginative music starts with a tremendous crash, followed by receding and diminishing waves of energy.

After this comes the *Doxology*, the expression of praise of God's glory: "Alleluia" is the shortest example, "Glory be to the Father, and to the Son, and to the Holy Spirit" a longer and familiar one. "Alleluia" is in fact the first word the chorus sings, and it does so to the same music that began the *Invocation*. Again, Wuorinen draws on various canticles in the *Liber usualis* for his texts, all of which are about making. Like the *Invocation*, the *Doxology* is richly varied in color, texture, and dynamics, and it—and with it the *Genesis* cantata—ends in a blaze of celebration: "Cantate Domino canticum novum quia mirabilia fecit Dominus, Alleluia!" (Sing unto the Lord a new song, for the Lord has done marvelous things. Hallelujah!).